D0026626

POLITICAL ECONOMY AND CONTEMPORARY CAPITALISM

POLITICAL ECONOMY AND CONTEMPORARY CAPITALISM

RADICAL PERSPECTIVES ON ECONOMIC THEORY AND POLICY

RON BAIMAN
HEATHER BOUSHEY
DAWN SAUNDERS
EDITORS

M.E. Sharpe
Armonk, New York
London, England

Library of Congress Cataloging-in-Publication Data

Political economy and contemporary capitalism : radical perspectives on economic theory and policy / Ron Baiman, Heather Boushey, and Dawn Saunders, editors.
p. cm.
Includes bibliographical references and index.
ISBN 0-7656-0529-5 (hc. : alk. paper)
1. Economics. 2. Capitalism. I. Baiman, Ron, 1951– II. Boushey, Heather, 1970– III. Saunders, Dawn, 1955–

HB71.P654 2000
330-dc21 99-047226

Printed in the United States of America

The paper used in this publication meets the minimum requirements of American National Standard for Information Sciences Permanence of Paper for Printed Library Materials, ANSI Z 39.48-1984.

BM (c) 10 9 8 7 6 5 4 3 2 1

Contents

List of Figures, Tables, and Boxes

Figures

Tables

Boxes

Preface

Ron Baiman, Heather Boushey, and Dawn Saunders

In the spring of 1997, the Steering Committee of the Union for Radical Political Economics decided that the time had come to publish a new reader of work in radical political economics. The prospective audience for this book is classroom instructors, students, and lay readers. The chapters are written for "advanced undergraduates" who have taken some introductory courses in economics or economic issues. The book is also appropriate for courses in political economy, intermediate microeconomics or macroeconomics, or more advanced undergraduate theory and topics courses in economics. The chapters are accessible for those who are not versed in the "jargon" of economics. Authors have been asked to ensure that any educated reader could understand and learn from their chapter. Thanks to all those who contributed! We appreciate your joining us in this effort to offer intermediate students in economics a broad exposure to what is possible in theory and policy analysis in political economy. We are proud to have worked on *Political Economy and Contemporary Capitalism: Radical perspectives on Economic Theory and Policy.*

Acknowledgments

The editors would like to thank all of the authors who contributed to this volume. We greatly appreciate all their hard work and their patience with us. We would also like to thank Sean Culhane, Esther Clark, and Eileen Maass for their interest in URPE and in this project.

All of the proceeds of this book go to the Union for Radical Political Economics.

URPE holds an annual Summer Conference; organizes sessions at the national economics conference, the Allied Social Science Meetings; and publishes a quarterly journal, *The Review* of *Radical Political Economics*, and a quarterly newsletter. To join URPE, or to find out more about our activities, visit our website at www.urpe.org or call 203-777-4605.

POLITICAL ECONOMY AND CONTEMPORARY CAPITALISM

1

Introduction

Political Economy Today, Political Economy Tomorrow

Dawn Saunders

Where We've Been and Where We Are

This is the third in a series of readers compiled by members of the Union for Radical Political Economics (URPE), representing three sucessive decades of political economic thought. In the introduction to *Macroeconomics from a Left Perspective*, Book I of *The Imperiled Economy* (1987), Cigdem Kurdas remarks on the predictive quality of the essays in the 1978 predecessor, *U.S. Capitalism in Crisis*, in looking ahead to the economic uncertainty and instability of the 1980s. In introducing Book II, *Through the Safety Net* (1988), David Gordon highlights the turn of 1980s policy debates toward the fashion now known as *neoliberalism.* Today, we consider again our current economic condition and our prospects for the future, as perceived by the creative and decidedly unorthodox minds of URPE members.

Economists *always* live in interesting times, but surely it doesn't get much more intriguing than now. As we stand in the twilight of what was once called "the American century," we are confounded by an American economy that refuses to slow down. We are more connected to the rest of the world than ever before, yet economists marvel as the sheer weight of stock market–driven American consumerism seems to anchor an economy on the brink of the chaos and stagnation infecting much of the world. Some see a hope that this anchor can keep the others from falling further, perhaps even pulling them up to safety.

But hope for whom? Should expansion be driven by a consumerism fueled by a massively regressive redistribution of wealth, and sustainable only by continued and erratic speculative frenzy? Few economists believe this trend is sustainable. Should we worry that the most successful consumer markets are "high-end" ones, such as high-priced homes and sport utility vehicles? Should we wonder that only in these past two years, thanks to the "tight" labor market that continues to worry Wall Street and the Federal Reserve, has income in the bottom 40 percent of income groups begun to recover from the long slide in real earnings that began in the 1970s? If these gains occur *only* during periods of "unsustainable boom," what's next for workers and families in the United States.?

Left political economy, as David Gordon explained in *The Imperiled Economy*, looks to the nature of capitalism itself as the source of the periodic swings and crises that both enrich or bankrupt the rich and powerful, and that open doors or slam them shut on everyday folks. And beyond the wilder swings of fortune are the ongoing trends that expand or contract the hopes and prospects of ordinary people. Inherent in capitalism, and the institutional structures that develop to support it, are "rules" that restrict equitable access to the productive potential of market economies. Democratic governments periodically seek to revise the rules according to the most vocal concerns of their constituencies. But political voice is itself subject to market forces, and those who cannot compete for access lose their voice over time: thus the decline in real earnings and the rise in inequality, thus the transformation of the welfare system, thus the decline in unionism, thus the potential transformation of Social Security. This latest development is perhaps the most telling sign of the current hegemony of neoliberalism, that our one almost universal support system, our last legacy of the New Deal, may yet be transformed into a wholly or partially privatized system. There again, the *marketing of policy* is demonstrated.

And Where We're Going: The Next Generation

URPE could not have lasted thirty years, certainly a period hostile to unorthodox economic thinking, if it was not able to continue to engage new thinking and new thinkers. Our journal, the *Review of Radical Political Economics*, encourages original academic scholarship, as does URPE sponsorship of presentations and panels at major economic conferences. Both of these outlets have been especially important to young scholars in the field. Our own annual summer conference offers a less formal meeting of minds, and is particularly accessible to undergraduates as well as graduate students, and also to nonacademics: many of our panels and workshops center on activism as well as academics. This book is an invitation to *all* readers to explore alternative ways to see economic reality. We hope we have achieved a collection that is accessible to *any* open mind. It is our conviction that a wider dessimation of alternative points of view will further the prospects for the democratic realization of a more equitable society, both domestically and globally.

Young readers, including those of you in college, may only dimly remember the recession of 1991–1992 and the lingering high rates through 1995. Economic restructuring transferred permanent jobs into consultancies or temporary employment in the name of "flexibility" and "competitiveness." You have heard that your own employment will be characterized by frequent job and even occupational changes. Aware that decent incomes depend on education, students today leave college with higher average debt loads than any time in history, as they and their families are asked to carry an increasing share of the costs of preparing for their future economic contributions to society.

But with all this uncertainty, many of my students are dazzled by Wall Street wealth (some experiencing it personally). They hear of a "virtuous cycle" of low inflation, low unemployment, and (finally) rising levels of productivity growth that, combined with low interest rates (thanks, they're told, to the neoliberals' elimination of the federal budget deficit) promises the end of the business cycle as we knew it. Aspiring young entrepreneurs hear that capital is cheap and easy to get: riches seem within one's grasp. *Why*, then, should they be interested in the undersides of the market economy exposed in these articles?

Because most of them *care* about the incongruity between great wealth for some and dimming prospects for others, and many wonder about the relevance of the economic abstractions of their introductory classes to the real world. Economics develops and applies analytical methods learned throughout one's education; even in its most abstract, neoclassical variant, it is good brain exercise. But critical reasoning skills are also challenged and stretched by exposure to those aspects of economic reality that do not fit neatly onto supply and demand curves or Keynesian cross diagrams. In the messy economic reality living people face, simple answers must give way to explorations, analysis, and critical discussion.

In these pages, readers will discover that political economists are asking questions that need to be asked, looking under the rug, behind the numbers, around the corners. You will find that this is not a homogenous group of thinkers and writers: many of our colleagues call themselves *heterodox* economists, emphasizing not only the differences in perspective that separate themselves from "orthodox" or mainstream economic perspectives, but also acknowledging the wide range of approaches to the real economy that fit under the broad tent of alternative economic theory. Many will disagree with each other on important points almost as much as they differ from the mainstream. All share a commitment to *how much it matters* to approach the study of our economy from a perspective that does not privilege the privileged.

The Plan of the Book

As editors, we chose to break with the precedent set in *The Imperiled Economy* of dividing the subject matter up between micro and macro divisions. This arbitrary division is rooted in the particular history of the discipline of economics, especially the period marked by the development and rising influence of Keynesian theory. But surely Keynes did not mean to bifurcate economics. Neither did the classical economists, including Marx, see economic reality this way, although they discussed topics that we would consider microeconomic (wage determination, for example) as well as macroeconomic (economic growth). But without a preconceived division between macro and micro, Marx was able to examine the relationship between wage determination and economic growth (what he called *accumulation*).

Even the concept of *the economy* is an arbitrary abstraction: it represents only certain aspects of social reality, composed largely of what radical economists refer to as *social relations* in the production and distribution of the means of material support. It is also the history of our discipline that we have separated out specific relations, such as buying and selling, working and owning, borrowing and lending, from all the other things people do *with* and *for* and *to* each other. There is a long tradition in radical economics of highlighting the social relations of production and the material basis of class divisions as being a major contributor to understanding the economic and social reality of power and subordination, and there are articles here that represent that point of view. But others would argue that in isolating its range of study away from other kinds of social relations (such as race, gender, family, and sexuality), as well as creating artificial boundaries between the various relations traditionally described as economic, the discipline of economics has limited its ability to make sense of the real world. This view is also well represented in this volume.

The sections below contain articles useful in illustrating "macro" as well as "micro" topics as they are traditionally understood, as well as articles that defy classification on those grounds. While the sections are divided into broad topical categories, we admit some of the articles could have as easily been placed in one section as another.

Section I. Conceptual Approaches to Political Economy

Are economists social *scientists* or *social* scientists? We open with Bruce Pietrykowski's reminder that the subject matter of all economic inquiry is social reality. Yet economists differ in the perspectives they bring to their study of that reality, and in the degree to which they recognize that social complexity may not be fully captured in a paradigm borrowed from the physical sciences. Mathieu Carlson suggests that left political economists can be similarly distinguished in terms of their reliance on a paradigm based on *class* categories: he suggests that "orthodox" Marxists share with neoclassical economists a reliance on a deductive method of reasoning, one based on the central role of the extraction of *surplus value* rather than neoclassical assumptions of rational individualism. Ellen Mutari describes the development of a feminist tradition that has found class alone to be insufficient in describing the real world, as it left out both gender as an organizing category and patriarchy as a system of social organization and source of power and privilege.

William Dugger and Howard Sherman return us to the tradition in political economy in which class is a starting point in social analysis. Dugger presents an institutionalist view of class, as being dependent on the differing relations of society's members to key elements of power and change: income, work, wealth, and technology. Sherman argues that change is rooted in class conflict, in which technology also plays a central role, through the mismatch that periodically develops between slowly changing social relations and rapidly changing technology.

Julie Matthaei addresses the dilemma of *what to do* with a modern, multifaceted form of political economy: how do the "hyphenated progressives" (Marxist-feminst-antiracist-antihomophobic-ecological) go about "growing a liberated economy"? The dilemma of finding unity in diversity requires, she suggests, a new discourse, and a willingness to embrace real-world attempts at establishing antihierarchical institutions.

Section II. Capitalism's Dynamic Path: Accumulation and the Rate of Profit

Opening this section, Fred Moseley examines the limited success of efforts of U.S. capital to recover from the stagnation of profit rates in the 1970s and 1980s. Moseley argues that strategies increasing the proportion of unproductive to productive capital partially counteracted capital's success in increasing the rate of surplus value. Following another Marxian tradition, Jonathan Goldstein describes U.S. economic history as being alternately affected by the shifting balance of power between labor and capital, resulting in alternate routes to economic crises ("profit-squeeze" or "underconsumption"). Recent global trends in income distribution, financial disruptions, and macroeconomic policies, he suggests, points toward the potential of a truly global underconsumption crisis. Ismael Hossein-Zadeh sees U.S. economic history through a Marxist long-wave perspective. He argues against "end of history" and "breakdown" views of capitalism, and attempts to elucidate the effects of class struggle and other social forces on the long-term development of capitalism.

Alternatively, Edward Nell explains U.S. economic history (and the long-run dynamic of aggregate demand) by reference to the changing institutional structures accompanying the transition from nineteenth-century craft-based production to corporatized mass production. What new dynamics, he wonders, might we encounter as a result of the institutional innovations wrought by the dawn of the information age?

Section III. How We Live: Employment, Labor, and Income Distribution

So, *can* Marx, Kalecki, Friedman, and Wall Street all be wrong? Meaning, *is* there something to this non-accelerating-inflation-rate of unemployment (NAIRU) business? No and yes, respectively, suggests Robert Pollin: both Marx and Kalecki understood unemployment was "functional to the operation of capitalist economies," just as neoclassicals, in their own way, understand that "unemployment rates are an outgrowth of class struggle over the distribution of income and political power." Heather Boushey considers, as did Marx, that the "reserve army" of the unemployed may have different ranks, or different categories of workers with different functions in the labor market. In examining the relationship between racial and gender differences in unemployment in specific markets, she finds evidence that employment inequality—differential access to jobs—affects wage inequality in insidious ways.

Examining the trend toward increased income inequality, Chris Tilly concludes that commonly discussed factors such as globalization and technology cannot explain why the United States has become so much *more* unequal than other industrial countries experiencing the same trends; needed, he says, is an understanding of the institutional changes promoting profits before people, especially excluding many families of color and single-parent families from our supposed prosperity. This last group, as Tilly and Randy Albelda explain, are subject to the "triple whammy" of low earnings, reliance on a single paycheck, and the need to care for children given those two constraints. Again, the U.S. stands out among the world's wealthier countries as being the *least* able (or willing?) to meet the needs of this group.

The effort to improve labor market outcomes through union organization has fallen on hard times. The forces noted by Pollin and Tilly are important here, but George DeMartino argues that unions must face the challenges of the new economy by rejecting past "business union" strategies centered on membership, and consider a *social* model of progressive solidarity that will address all workers'—all citizens'—sense of social justice as well as economic needs.

Section IV. Examining Money: Finance and Inflation

Which came first, money or credit? According to post-Keynesian economist Louis-Philippe Rochon, in the *real* world of *real* production, money is created, via credit, through the interaction of actual institutions, firms and banks, in historic time. This process, Rochon argues, cannot be adequately described by the neoclassical story of near-instantaneous supply responses to central bank decisions.

In addressing what he calls "hidden inflation," Jim Devine argues that commonly used measures of economic well-being, such as real GDP, are inadequate if they rely on a measure of inflation that fails to incorporate the full social costs of modern life, such as inequality and environmental damage. Such indicators reveal that our cost of living has actually been *rising* for many years, resolving the "puzzle" of "falling" inflation occuring alongside "falling" unemployment.

For Elmer Chase, "Inflation is a result of the class struggle over income shares," and monetary and fiscal policy are the regressive weapons of this battle. Chase suggests a new look at incomes policies, the inflation-control measures first proposed in the 1970s, improved over their predecessors by incorporating nonwage-based causes of inflation, providing a progressive alternative to NAIRU via a "negotiated settlement" between capital and labor.

Carole Biewener closes the section with suggestions for transcending the generally regressive reputation of financial institutions. Finance is a means to an end: we can, she suggests, create or expand financial institutions as a means toward a more humane set of economic values as well as economic ends.

Section V. The Global Political Economy

What do students need to know about trade and finance? Matias Vernengo suggests they go beyond the insights of Hume and Ricardo on price–specie flows and comparative advantage, and examine the work of Kaldor and the role of export demand and balance of payments in economic growth. Such an approach exposes the limitations of free-trade theory and policy, and demonstrates the need for financial regulation and other interventionist forms of trade policy.

Abelardo Marina and Fred Moseley use the Marxian concept of relative surplus value to contrast two periods in Mexican economic development, the first characterized by declining rate of surplus value (and *rising* real wages), and the second characterized by a rising rate of surplus value (and *falling* real wages). But, while the rate of profit (not surprisingly) fell during the first period, it did *not* recover in the second, an apparent anomaly that can be explained by the increasing costs of capital in a period of rapid currency devaluation.

According to Cyrus Bina and Chuck Davis, an analysis of capital as a social relation reveals that technological change today does *more* than increase the rate of surplus value: the effect of technology on capital mobility brings a new order of magnitude to the ability of capital to pit workers against each other on a global scale. David Ruccio considers the irony in the worldwide fascination with an "American" neoliberal model that has *not* brought shared prosperity to the citizens of the United States, and that has displaced an Asian model that was quite functional to capital in that region for a time. He suggests that a class analysis identifying and promoting the shared interests of average people (who, to date, have been left behind even in formerly "successful" developing countries) can be helpful in forumulating equitable routes to development.

The remaining chapters in this section examine the effects of neoliberalism on specific economies. For David Kotz, the lessons to be derived from the transition to market economies in China and Russia are clear: confounding the neoliberal "experts," the state-directed approach of China *worked* in developing competitive market segments and promoting economic growth, while the "shock treatment" of radical privatization in Russia simply *did not* work. In abandoning functional (if imperfect) institutions for untried and uncontrolled market processes, Russia experienced an avoidable economic disaster.

We have three approaches to the recent (and at this writing, continuing) Asian crisis. Ilene Grabel critiques attempts to explain away the crisis as due to peculiar situations and historical developments in each affected country, rather than to the increasing speculative risks and declining policy autonomy characterizing *each* country under neoliberal "reforms." Stephanie Seguino argues that a reliance on export-led growth in the context of liberalized capital markets generates volatility in market outcomes and leads to global economic stagnation, limiting the livelihood especially of those with the least power, including women. Martin Hart-Landsberg and Paul Burkett find that even many left-leaning analysts fail to recognize that it is the *market* under global capitalism that exposes the world to such disruptions: well-meaning reforms to control some of the disruptions of capital mobility, they maintain, will not address the demands of popular movements worldwide for an equitable share of world economic output and growth.

Section VI. Exploring Policy Questions: Theory and Applications

Anwar Shaikh and E. Ahmet Tonak open this section with extensions on their well-known research on the "social wage," a measure of total output distributed to workers, incorporating public programs and taxes. The authors find that the social wage is *not* positive and continues to hover around zero throughout the Clinton period, the result of continuing regressive state involvement in the economy. Alternatively, Max Sawicky asks us to reconsider the progressive's knee-jerk reaction to taxes normally thought of as regressive. What counts, he suggests, is the overall distributive effect of the budget as a whole. A value-added tax might offer advantages to capital that could offset hostility toward a more progressive budget, and thus be a better deal for average people.

According to Ron Baiman, deregulation of natural monopolies (such as electric power companies) is based on assumptions that presume near-competitive efficiency results, a "second-best" solution available under oligopolistic conditions. Baiman shows that such "Ramsey pricing" creates welfare losses exacerbated by the harsher sting of those losses to the people who can least afford them.

The next three chapters address alternative policy approaches to dealing with income inequality. Deborah Figart and Heidi Hartmann examine the ups and downs (1970s through 1990s) of the pay equity movement, which strives for equitable pay on the basis of a job's inherent qualities (or "worth"). It is time, they suggest, to renew the call for pay equity, in combination with other efforts to provide livable incomes to all families. Robert Cherry and Gertrude Schaffner Goldberg explain that one such policy, the earned income tax credit, fails to reach many people that need such help, and masks inequities in many people's access to jobs that can support families. They argue for a broader approach to work-based income support, such as an adequate minimum wage and effective public works programs. Kimberly Christensen says that welfare "reform" has failed to address the limitations of work as a way out of poverty for low-skilled women and their families, and has applied dangerously punitive measures that ultimately might depress market wages, expose children to greater degrees of poverty, hamper efforts to shelter women from domestic abuse, and disproportionately harm poor communities.

The final two articles are of immediate concern to all U.S. workers, at all income levels. Jerome Joffe addresses recent and ongoing changes in the market for health care provision. The clashing interests of various components ("fractions") of capital, such as employers, insurers, and health care providers, has resulted in masses of contradictory pressures that do not bode well for consumers and workers. Teresa Ghilarducci exposes the myths surrounding Social Security's funding problems, and the distributional implications of a move toward a privatized system. It is not *market* forces, she argues, but a well-financed political campaign that is eroding our one nearly universal program.

And Where Will We Be in 2009?

A humbling question, given the poor track record of economists in the last two years in predicting the end of the current expansion. But it is surely safe to assume we will have at least one cyclical downturn in this next decade, perhaps generated by disruptions in financial markets, or as continued drag from foreign stagnation reduces prospects for profitable investment. Our expansion is currently dependent on consumer confidence, which could be disrupted either by stock market problems or an end to the recent gains in real wage growth. Our reduced state sector and our abolished fiscal deficit will reduce the cushion we've enjoyed in past recessions; our transformed welfare system, now a block grant system and thus devoid of its former role as automatic stabilizer, will place severe stress on state budgets and cause great harm to people in need. In other words, the next recession *could* be unusually deep, unusually harsh, and unusually regressive in its effects.

But in a mainstream world, this would be a short-run phenomenon (however long lasting), presumably recreating the conditions for renewed expansion at virtually zero inflation. Given that the people who make policy on our behalf are generally relatively sheltered from the effects of recessions, a recession alone would not prompt a movement toward *long-term*, *structural*, *institutional* changes in the policy regime many of the authors in this book argue for, and that might move us toward a *shared* prosperity, both domestically and globally. We hope that our efforts to engage our readers in alternative economic perspectives will play some role in shaking things up a bit, in calling for an accountability based on the *real* economy and *real* people's lives.

References

Cherry, Robert, et al. 1978. "U.S. Captialism in Crisis, Union for Radical Political Economy." In *The Imperiled Economy*. NewYork: Union for Radical Political Economics.

———. 1987. "Macroeconomics from a Left Perspective." In *The Imperiled Economy*. New York: Union for Radical Political Economics.

———. 1988. "Macroeconomics from a Left Perspective." In *The Imperiled Economy*. New York: Union for Radical Political Economics.

Section I

Conceptual Approaches to Political Economy

2

A Primer in Political Economy

Bruce Pietrykowski

Economics and the Scientific Method—An Introduction

As a topic unto itself, methodology is given very little attention in courses taken by most undergraduate economics majors. Yet methodological concerns influence the very debates and disagreements that help to shape economic theory, practice, and policy. Conflicting economic paradigms[1]—ways of making sense of the economic world—are often best understood by locating the methodological suppositions that guide practitioners in the field. So, if you are able to identify methodological differences you are better equipped to understand the plurality of perspectives advanced in economic debates. This chapter offers an introduction to economic methodology with special attention given to the variety of economic methods informing the practice of radical political economy.

Many economists—both mainstream and heterodox—look to the natural sciences for a model that best describes the methods employed in economic analysis. The affinity between economics and the natural sciences, especially physics, can be seen, for example, in the use of the term "equilibrium" and in the application of calculus to describe human behavior that maximizes utility or profit and minimizes costs. The model of physics is premised upon the goal of separating reality from appearance by using measurement and precise mathematical calculations to lay bare the laws of motion of the physical world. The process requires a dispassionate attitude on the part of the scientist. Hence the association between science and objectivity.

> Economists try to address their subject with a scientist's objectivity. They approach the study of the economy in much the same way as a physicist approaches the study of matter and a biologist approaches the study of life: They devise theories, collect data, and then analyze these data in an attempt to verify or refute their theories. (Mankiw 1998, 18)

To elaborate further, the search in the natural sciences for universal principles of action (such as gravitation) or laws of nature (conservation of energy) is represented in economics as a search for universal principles governing human action. Thus, in neoclassical economics a theory of rational action is used to explain the behavior of all individuals. In Marxian economics a theory of class conflict is used to explain movements in wages and profits or a theory of capitalist economic crisis is predicated on the lawlike tendency of the rate of profit to fall. Economic theories are constructed based on these essential laws or governing characteristics of human or group behavior. Empirical economics then draws upon these theories to advance hypotheses about the nature of reality. The process of model-building, data collection, testing, and interpretation of results is part of the process of creating scientific knowledge in economics.

From this perspective, therefore, economists are regarded by many within the profession as simply social *scientists*. There is much debate about whether, in fact, economic knowledge develops in this way (Blaug 1980). For example, are economic theories ever unequivocally refuted or do theories rise and then fall out of favor as conditions change, only to return later clothed in fresh rhetorical garb? This is the stuff of methodological debate in economic policy and the history of economic thought.

The image that we conjure up when describing the scientific method employed by biologists and physicists suggests individuals in lab coats taking precise measurements and performing rigorous tests in order to ascertain some essential truths by observing the true properties of the physical world. This is the world of economic practice described as *positive economics*. The authors of a leading textbook used in economic principles courses equate positive economics with the search for facts. About positive economics, they write: "It tries to establish scientific statements about economic behavior. Positive economics deals with what the economy actually is like" (McConnell and Brue 1999, 10).

Let us look at scientific practice more closely. In contrast with the image suggested in textbook definitions of positive economics, the everyday practice of laboratory science reveals a far different world in which judgment and interpretation is constantly used to make distinctions and classifications that deviate from their textbook representations (Knorr-Cetina 1981). The "hard" sciences are themselves inherently interpretive endeavors. Normative considerations and value judgments are utilized in the very process of making sense and imputing meaning to scientific experiments. This interpretive dimension, when applied to our understanding of "economic science," can be seen in debates between rival schools of thought about the best way to measure profits. Are profits a return to the capitalist for taking risk, or are profits derived from the material process of production in which labor, not capital, acts as the creative force? The seemingly simple and straightforward task of measuring profit in order to determine the long-run trend of profitability, for example, depends a great deal on the interpretive framework you bring with you.

Similarly, debates arise as to the appropriate unit of measurement to use—for instance individual data, firm-level data, occupational data—when undertaking empirical investigations. A perspective such as neoclassical economics, rooted as it is in methodological individualism, may well favor data collected at the level of the individual. On the other hand, if institutional structures are thought to define the scope of individual action (as in the "social structures of accumulation" approach), then data that reflect organizational and institutional structures (firms, occupations) may best complement the theoretical framework employed. This is not to say that the type of data one uses always provides a clear signal about one's theoretical perspective. Rather, I wish to suggest that even so mundane a task as data collection is itself imbued with methodological considerations. Try as you might to avoid them, methodological issues abound in the practice of economics.

Economics and Social Scientific Methods

Looked at from another perspective, economics is characterized as a *social* science. It is then the subject matter of economics that truly differentiates it from that of the natural sciences.[2] Economists posit theories, collect data, and test hypotheses on a range of subjects that make up the social world. Subjects like the price level, money supply, unemployment rate, profit rate, surplus value, and cost of job loss make up the world of economists.

But these subjects are social and cultural features of our world. Money is not a natural phenomenon. Indeed, different objects may act as money in different cultures and in different time periods. Similarly, the unemployment rate and the cost of job loss only really make sense in an economy marked by persistent unemployment in social systems characterized by individual labor. So, economists confront a world created by people, a world of cultural institutions; a world of rational action, perhaps, but of passions and emotion as well. Some variants of radical political economy hew closely to the scientific method through which an objective analysis can reveal essential truths about the structure of the economic system. Nevertheless, there is an underlying commitment in Marxian economic thought to the notion that ideas and methods of investigation themselves reflect the specific economic and social conditions under which they are produced. This ideological critique of scientific method allows us to better understand how economic method both comprises and is comprised by the social world under analysis.

Radical Economics and the Scientific Method

In order to investigate the methods employed by economists working within the tradition of radical political economy, let us consider a famous passage by Karl Marx and examine in detail the methodological insight provided by this foremost radical political economist.

> Men make their own history, but they do not make it just as they please; they do not make it under circumstances chosen by themselves, but under circumstances directly found, given and transmitted from the past. (Marx 1963, 15)

The above quotation from Marx suggests a way of understanding human action in the world. As such it provides us with a way of seeing the world. By unpacking this quotation I hope to explain what a radical political economy methodological approach is and why it is so very important in understanding economic theories and economic policy—including the theories and policies that are presented as facts and opinions in the daily news.

Men make their own history . . .

This phrase tell us something about how Marx thought about "agency"—the impact of individual action on the world. Human beings have the capacity to conjure up goals and achieve those goals through action. The goals themselves are not instinctual but, rather, are conditioned by our own experiences. This is one of the key methodological insights of Marx, namely, that human beings have the ability to control and alter their external world, both their natural and social world. Marx was not alone in embracing these ideas. They form the very bedrock of the seventeenth-, eighteenth-, and nineteenth-century scientific and political movements comprising the Enlightenment. The Enlightenment period—the very foundation of modern political and economic theory and policy—was an enormously powerful confluence of economic, political, scientific, and social thought that challenged the old regime of kings, aristocrats, religion, and the fatalistic belief that individual action could not alter the divine plans of God and kings (the embodiments of God on earth). Prior to the Enlightenment, laws were thought to be divinely ordained. Therefore science was undertaken in concert with, and assessed by the standards derived from, biblical writings. The Enlightenment offered up an alternative paradigm in which human beings (exclusively men, to be more precise) were responsible to determine their own destiny. Marx was fully part of this movement.

> Men make their own history *but they do not make it just as they please . . .*

For economists, the subject of constraints or limits on one's plans, actions, and desires lurks not far from the surface. With Marx it is no different. There exist limits to human action. But what are those limits? Well, some of the limits are natural (land and other natural resources are limited in supply, for example). This fact of life certainly influenced some of Marx's predecessors, like Thomas Malthus. It also plays a role in economic theories today. For example, debates within and between environmental and ecological economists often center upon the degree to which our reliance on nonrenewable resources threatens the prospects for continued economic growth. The very notion of economic growth—namely that growth is a good thing—is an Enlightenment idea. The notion that more (of all commodities) is better and that we can develop a "technological fix" that will allow us to avoid environmental and economic catastrophe owes its persuasive power to the Enlightenment ideal of progress and human ingenuity. Acknowledging that there are limits allows economists to talk about the costs and benefits of sustained growth. This then leads to policy proscriptions to promote either zero growth, managed growth, or untrammeled growth, for instance.

> Men make their own history, but they do not make it just as they please; *they do not make it under circumstances chosen by themselves, but under circumstances directly found, given and transmitted from the past.*

Here Marx introduces the notion that individuals make free choices. The concept of freedom of choice is a hallmark of the traditional neoclassical economic method. The appeal to rugged individualism—that we can be anything we want as long as we put our minds to it and persevere—is a familiar and perhaps even comforting idea. Yet, barriers to advancement and achievement are often unrelated to individual effort, ability, or motivation. The advantages afforded the well-off to maintain their position and expand their wealth clearly contrasts with the opportunity of poor people and those without independent access to the means of production to get ahead in a capitalist economy. Many times all the effort, skill, determination, and motivation in the world do not produce the results we desire no matter how much we strive to accomplish it. There are structures of constraint that act as barriers. The barriers are higher and more numerous for some individuals and groups than for others. For example, race and gender act as visible symbols that signal a difference that may threaten the status quo of the privileged. Therefore people's race and gender structure the opportunities afforded to them and the resources available to them (see Folbre 1994).

Furthermore, using Marx's words above, the past acts as a constraining, directive force on human action and potential. The past—*history*—is made real or *materialized* through institutions, rituals, customs, and technology.[3] For example, rather than looking only at current technology as if it appeared spontaneously, a historical materialist method, a Marxian method if you will, suggests that we instead look back to the period in which the previous technological structures were themselves undergoing change. For example, twentieth-century technology developed within a particular social structure that privileges individual autonomy and independence, often at the expense of community solidarity or environmental quality. Take the automobile, for example. Is the automobile the only form of transportation? Is it necessarily the most efficient? Is it the most environmentally friendly? Does it promote social isolation or social cohesion? Yet the automobile is clearly a dominant form of transportation in the advanced sectors of the capitalist world economy today.

The dominant economic approach—the rational action and methodological individualism of neoclassical economics—makes use of the individual as the primary unit of analysis. Collectives of individuals are suspect. For example, a group of workers banding together to protest dangerous working conditions and low wages is depicted as a source of monopoly power creating an imbalance in a competitive labor market. On the other hand, a radical or Marxian political economy method would see collective action as a rational response to an existing imbalance in the workplace and labor market. By focusing on groups of individuals and their "class interest" this economic method allows us to understand broad social movements and also enables us to understand the commonality of interests shared by members of the same class, the different interests promoted by members of competing classes, and perhaps even the way in which individual interests conform to or deviate from their supposed class interest. By adding class as a category of analysis we can broaden our understanding of the way the economy works.

Let us return yet again to the quote by Marx. "Men make their own history . . ." Clearly a product of his times, Marx inhabited a nineteenth-century world in which women were treated as little more than servants or pieces of property. A feminist methodological approach argues that one's gender has profound impacts on the way one experiences the economy. This is a relatively recent, and significant, methodological contribution. In addition to gender, race also plays a distinct role in shaping the ways in which we experience economic phenomena and economic life. Finally, the very idea that natural science is the proper model for economic practice is a rhetorical argument that seeks to equate economics with the privileged status of the natural sciences. That the metaphors we use to make economic arguments are themselves open to study and critique is yet another recent methodological contribution that helps to inform radical political economy.

New Methods and Approaches to Radical Political Economic Analysis

The fuller integration of race and gender into radical political economy has helped to introduce new methodological approaches in economics. From feminist philosophy and social theory we come to understand that gender and racial categories can be seen as social constructs. Developments in literary studies help us to better understand the way in which language is used in economic theory and the way in which a rhetoric of economic analysis is created and reproduced in academic journals and textbooks. Currently, the method of radical political economics is really made up of several methods: the Marxian political economic method; institutionalist and post-Keynesian methods; the radical feminist methodological perspective; and postmodern approaches to race, class, and gender. The latter two approaches are relatively new. They are also controversial, in part, because they challenge both the mainstream and more established versions of radical political economy.

For example, those who desire to employ scientific methods that will secure an objective assessment of reality employ an especially narrow definition of the term "objectivity." The result may well be that the very quest for objectivity is thwarted because the scientist's personal situation or standpoint is not adequately taken into account as a bit of additional information. As opposed to this narrow view, feminist scholar Sandra Harding

(1996) argues for including as "data" the social and cultural beliefs and background that the researcher brings with him or her. Gender bias enters into scientific research when gender is ignored as a factor bearing on the scientific tasks of theory-formation, experimentation, and interpretation of results. For example, the fact that most economists are male may help to explain the rather limited economic literature on caring labor and household decision making—aspects of economic life traditionally identified with women's roles and sphere of influence.[4]

In addition, the challenge posed by these new contributions to economic methodology centers, in part, on a critique of the goal that many older economic methods share, namely the search for the "truth." These more recent approaches criticize the notion that there is some ultimate truth and argue instead that such methods represent a particular class, race, and gender viewpoint. There is not a single truth. Truth is contested and is itself the subject of conflict. When we speak of truth we are simply deploying language in such a way as to gain power for ourselves and for our perspective. This is a quite an unsettling concept. It opposes those who argue that there is a single correct scientific method that will bring clarity and reveal the real or essential appearance of reality. This view is variously captured by those arguing that attention be paid to the "rhetoric of economics," those who favor "methodological pluralism," and those economists who favor the antiessentialism of "postmodern philosophy and social theory."[5]

Indeed, the argument from postmodernists is that reality itself is socially and culturally constructed. The question then arises: then how do we know what we know? Yet this question itself suggests that there is a single, unitary individual that is the subject of knowledge, the creator of knowledge. The subject-centered approach to knowledge is questioned by postmodern theorists. They argue that knowledge is produced and reproduced through discourse. Furthermore, the creation of knowledge is itself an act of creating and using power. For example, consider the relatively benign task of collecting data on unemployment. The Bureau of Labor Statistics (BLS) undertakes a data collection process whereby individual household members are queried about their work status. The process of collecting data and creating categories automatically requires an integrated set of decisions that determine who is to be considered unemployed. The definition of the category, the decision to leave others out, creates a discourse of unemployment. Much of labor economics and macroeconomics is predicated on this discourse. The categories constructed have material consequences for part-time workers who are classified as fully employed or for workers who have given up looking for work—"discouraged workers." The seemingly innocuous and scientific process of collecting data creates and reproduces a body of knowledge. Power is associated with the ability to be conversant with the definition of unemployment, to address programs aimed at reducing unemployment and the like. Those who fall outside of the defined categories are subject to a system of power and their powerlessness is more than a rhetorical construct. Postmodernists are not saying that data collection and categorization is meaningless and should be abandoned. Rather, postmodern critics of the "scientific economic method" argue that such seemingly mundane tasks as data collection are rich with meaning. They are so meaningful, in fact, that we need to attend to their implications and to the system of power that such tasks help to create.

Conclusion

A concise survey of economic methodology is a daunting task. By necessity much was left out.

There is considerable passionate debate over methodological issues in economics. This primer should serve as a basis from which to explore issues in further detail. Lawrence Boland argues, "Methodology lives but it is not easy to see anymore because it is embodied in the accepted hidden research agenda" (1987, 456). Because it is often embodied in basic assumptions and cloaked in tradition, attention to method is important in order to remind yourself that while the dominant metaphor in economics equates economics with the natural sciences, there are alternative viewpoints. Indeed, there is much work to do in radical political economy. You may wish to pursue empirical economic research in order to develop the expertise and skill in econometric analysis that allows you the opportunity to enter into conversations about such pressing issues as welfare reform, minimum wage and living wage campaigns, and sustainable ecological development. You may wish to participate in the development of an economic theory that challenges the mainstream over issues such as the efficacy of market clearing wages and prices, the optimal social welfare outcomes of deregulation, or the determinants of investment and capital accumulation. Or you may be interested in subverting the discourse of scientific method by helping to redraw the boundaries between economics, philosophy, and social theory in order to provide a richer account of economic relations of power and resistance. For radical political economy, each of these tasks is informed by an understanding of methodology. Paying attention to economic method is vital because it helps to give voice to economic practices and insights too often silenced by the mainstream.

Notes

1. See Thomas Kuhn's classic work, *The Structure of Scientific Revolutions* (Chicago: University of Chicago Press, 1970), for a detailed historical account of the way scientific paradigms are established and superseded.

2. According to Philip Mirowski (1988), an especially interesting and troublesome aspect involved in neoclassical economists' use of the methods and models of physics is that the basis for modern, twentieth-century economics lies in nineteenth-century physics. Although twentieth-century physics developed to embrace, for example, a theory of relativity, twentieth-century neoclassical economists uses the foundational principles and descriptive metaphors of nineteenth-century physics.

3. In contemporary radical political economy the "social structure of accumulation" approach is especially oriented to taking into account the institutional framework within which capitalist economic development takes place (Kotz, McDonough, and Reich 1994).

4. See Randy Albelda (1997) for an examination of the history of economics as a gendered occupation and its resistance to feminist insights and contributions. Also see Ferber and Nelson (1993), Folbre (1994), and Nelson (1996).

5. See McCloskey (1986), Resnick and Wolff (1987), Samuels (1990), Milberg and Pietrykowski (1994), and Callari, Cullenberg, and Biewener (1995).

References

Albelda, Randy. 1997. *Economics and Feminism: Disturbances in the Field*. New York: Twayne.

Blaug, Mark. 1980. *The Methodology of Economics: Or How Economists Explain*. Cambridge: Cambridge University Press.

Boland, Lawrence. 1987. "Methodology." In *The New Palgrave Dictionary of Economics*. Volume 3, ed. John Eatwell, Murray Milgate, and Peter Newman, pp. 455-458. London: Macmillan.

Callari, Antonio, Stephen Cullenberg, and Carole Biewener. 1995. *Marxism in the Postmodern Age*. New York: Guilford.

Ferber, Marianne A., and Julie A. Nelson. 1993. *Beyond Economic Man: Feminist Theory and Economics*. Chicago: University of Chicago Press.

Folbre, Nancy. 1994. *Who Pays for the Kids? Gender and the Structure of Constraint*. London: Routledge.

Harding, Sandra. 1996. "Rethinking Standpoint Epistemology: What Is 'Strong Objectivity'?" In *Feminism and Science*, ed. Evelyn Fox Keller and Helen Longino. Oxford: Oxford University Press.

Knorr-Cetina, Karin D. 1981. *The Manufacture of Knowledge: An Essay on the Constructivist and Contextual Nature of Science*. Oxford: Pergamon Press.

Kotz, David M., Terrence McDonough, and Michael Reich. 1994. *Social Structures of Accumulation: The Political Economy of Growth and Crisis*. Cambridge: Cambridge University Press.

McCloskey, D. 1986. *The Rhetoric of Economics*. Madison: University of Wisconsin Press.

McConnell, Campbell R., and Stanley L. Brue. 1999. *Macroeconomics: Principles, Problems, and Policies*. 14th ed. New York: Irwin/McGraw-Hill.

Mankiw, N. Gregory. 1998. *Principles of Economics*. Fort Worth, TX: Dryden Press.

Marx, Karl. 1963. *The Eighteenth Brumaire of Louis Bonaparte*. New York: International Publishers.

Milberg, William, and Bruce Pietrykowski. 1994. "Objectivism, Relativism and the Importance of Rhetoric for Marxist Economics." *Review of Radical Political Economics* 26, no. 1: 85-109.

Mirowski, Philip. 1988. *Against Mechanism: Protecting Economics from Science*. Totowa, NJ: Rowman & Littlefield.

Nelson, Julie A. 1996. *Feminism, Objectivity and Economics*. London: Routledge.

Resnick, Stephen A., and Richard D. Wolff. 1987. *Knowledge and Class: A Marxian Critique of Political Economy*. Chicago: University of Chicago Press.

Samuels, Warren. 1990. *Economics as Discourse: An Analysis of the Language of Economics*. Boston: Kluwer Academic.

3

The Methodology of Radical Political Economics

Mathieu Carlson

This chapter contrasts the underlying methodologies, or basic principles of reasoning, of three economic theories: the dominant mainstream approach, neoclassical theory, and two nonmainstream "Marxist" alternatives—orthodox Marxian theory and what I will call radical economics. This will leave aside other important approaches, such as Keynesian and post-Keynesian economics; still, it is hoped that this exercise will help clarify the economics discipline as a whole and the place of "left" or nonmainstream approaches within the discipline.

"Radical" economics is generally understood to include a wide range of "left" approaches to economics. But here I shall confine the term to a brand of analysis that developed initially in the United States in the late 1960s and is associated with names such as Stephen Marglin, Samuel Bowles, David Gordon, Herbert Gintis, Heidi Hartmann, Andrew Glyn, and numerous others. This approach differs from most economic analysis in being inductive rather than deductive in character. Although radical economics arose within the Marxian tradition and typically goes under the name of Marxism, it generally departs from basic elements of Marx's analysis, notably Marxian value theory and its implications. Orthodox Marxian theory, on the other hand, more closely follows the letter of Marx's analysis.[1] Within nonmainstream economics I take these two cases partly to indicate the diversity of views within "Marxism," but more importantly to illustrate my thesis, which is that radical economics developed in part as an attempt to break with the deductive method characteristic of most economic theorizing, both neoclassical and Marxian. It should be noted that although many individual economists can be associated with one or the other of the two "Marxian" approaches, these categories primarily characterize modes of analysis rather than groups of people.

Methodology in Economics

Broadly, scientific reasoning can be either deductive or inductive. That is, one may reason logically from idealized premises to necessary conclusions (deductive), or infer general laws or principles on the basis of observed events (inductive). Economic theories, whether "left" or mainstream, are usually deductive, tending to proceed from ideal assumptions to logical conclusions—perhaps a reflection of the inherent difficulties of empirical work in economics. Controlled experimentation is not possible in economics, and good data, owing to the extreme complexity of economic phenomena, are difficult to obtain.

More generally, empirical scientific work faces the "problem of induction": the fact, as David Hume observed, that no necessary causal connection can be inferred from the regular conjunction of two or more observed events. To overcome this problem and account for scientific knowledge, various theories of science have been proposed. The most popular of these is "falsificationism," the view that a theory is "scientific" only if it is in principle falsifiable—that is, if there exist events that which, were they to occur, would compel adherents of a theory to abandon it. Falsificationism, however, faces the obvious problem of determining when a theory has been falsified. Moreover, observations that would refute a theory are themselves theory-laden, bringing into question the positivist separation between facts (observed events) and theories.

The impossibility of clearly distinguishing fact from theory leads to the very different conception of science of Thomas Kuhn (1970), who analyzes science in terms of "paradigms." Scientific "progress" in this view is not cumulative, with comparisons between facts and theories leading inevitably to the emergence of modern orthodoxy in a field, but highly discontinuous, with different theories embodying different and sometimes incommensurable conceptual foundations. A more extreme response to the difficulties of falsificationism is that of economist D. McCloskey (1985), who argues that since no strict separation between fact and theory is possible, economic arguments reduce to rhetoric—merely attempts to persuade the reader of one's position. In this view, empirical evidence is not a means of demonstrating the truth of a theory but is in effect a rhetorical ploy used to persuade readers of one's position.

McCloskey's argument is a denial that there are any facts of any matter. Nevertheless, McCloskey's view differs from the others mentioned only by degree. It lies at one extreme of a continuum of views, with Karl Popper (the originator of falsification) at the other extreme, and theorists such as Imre Lakatos (1970), Thomas Kuhn (1970), and Paul Feyerabend (1975) at points in between. The Popperian view is most plausible in application to the physical sciences. The McCloskeyan view may apply to "softer" fields such as literature or philosophy. Economics embodies elements of both the "hard" and "soft" sciences, suggesting that perhaps a middle ground between Popper and McCloskey ought to be struck. As social scientists we generally accept (contrary to McCloskey) the notion of a reality that is the object of economics to elucidate. But the difficulties with empirical work in economics make accessing this reality more difficult than in "harder" fields. Thus, while falsificationism may work well in physics and chemistry, it applies less well to economics, which therefore has tended to develop deductively—by way of idealized assumptions embodied in models used to deduce the logical implications of the assumptions. The result is a body of analytical results that (a) are highly dependent on the basic assumptions of a theory and thus on its basic conceptual foundations, and (b) are difficult to falsify, being well immunized from empirical considerations by ceteris paribus ("all other things equal") clauses, the latter a necessary instrument of deductive reasoning.

The difficulties of falsification in economics have encouraged the development of economics as a deductive discipline, giving rise not to a cohesive body of established results but to a set of disparate theories or paradigms that are not easily tested empirically. This chapter is an attempt to characterize several different theories or paradigms—neoclassical theory, orthodox Marxian theory, and radical economics—in the starkest possible terms, with a view to clarifying the basic principles of reasoning or methodologies that underlie each of them. As we shall see, a deductive approach is embodied to different degrees by both mainstream neoclassical theory and orthodox

Marxian theory. Radical economics, I suggest, is in part an attempt to overcome the difficulties of the deductive method by moving to a more inductive approach—a project not without costs, but also with important insights.

Neoclassical Theory

Neoclassical theory begins with individuals, assumed to have complete and transitive preference mappings, who maximize utility subject to the constraints of technology and their endowments. Each additional unit of a commodity provides the consumer with additional "utility" in increments that are assumed to diminish as more units of the commodity are purchased. Thus marginal utility falls to the level of the commodity's price, at which point the consumer ceases purchasing since nothing more can be gained from purchasing additional units. Linking the given price with the quantity demanded at that price, one point on the consumer's demand curve is obtained. By varying the price and "asking" the consumer again to purchase units of the good until marginal utility equals the price, we obtain additional points on the consumer's demand curve. Ultimately we can derive the individual's demand curve—a downward-sloping curve in price-quantity space. By summing the demand curves of all individuals in the given product market, a market demand curve is constructed.

In similar fashion, an entrepreneur or firm supplies additional units of a commodity up to the point where the increasing marginal cost of supplying the commodity is equal to the marginal revenue (the price) obtained from selling the product. By varying the commodity's price and linking each price with the corresponding quantity supplied, an upward-sloping individual supply curve is derived. An upward-sloping market supply curve is then constructed by summing the supplies of producers in the product market.

The equilibrium price of a commodity is determined by the intersection of the independently constituted market demand and market supply curves. A commodity's equilibrium price is thus market-clearing and acts as a center of gravitation for actual prices. This is the core of neoclassical theory—determination of long-run equilibrium prices by the forces of supply and demand. This result is not an empirical generalization based on the observed influence of supply and demand on prices, but arises from the specific analysis of consumer and entrepreneurial behavior (based on the idealized assumptions about such behavior) described above.

Neoclassical theory thus appears to be an account of how, given more or less plausible assumptions about human behavior, spontaneous human bargaining processes lead to the establishment of equilibrium exchange ratios for commodities and thus to the formation of markets in an environment devoid of preexisting social institutions. Indeed it is institutions (such as governments, labor unions, cartels, etc.) that give rise to market imperfections whose remedy, the theory typically implies, is their elimination or at least their withdrawal from market activity. The theory's rather crude characterization of human behavior has a peculiar status. On the one hand, marginal utility considerations are the animate force that guide individuals toward or away from given commodities. Lacking the utility concept, exchange ratios could not form and the theory would have no coherent story to tell. On the other hand, individuals in the theory behave purely mechanically, following behavioral rules dictated by mathematical requirements. Thus, although the theory is ostensibly about how economic activity arises spontaneously from natural human behavior, the theory does not (and cannot) contain a serious account of human behavior. Irving Fisher (1926, vi–vii) was quite right in recognizing that psychological considerations are strictly irrelevant to neoclassical theory.

The implausibility of the theory's basic assumptions has led some economists (e.g., Friedman 1953) to argue that a theory's validity depends not on the plausibility of its assumptions but on the success of its predictions. While regarding the plausibility of basic assumptions as strictly irrelevant to a theory's validity is questionable (especially in this case, since surely so deductive a theory cannot be that much better than its assumptions), the theory's predictive success is also highly questionable. Apart from generic (or qualitative) predictions, significant quantitative predictions that would show the theory to be a useful guide to the real world are rare at best.

If a theory seems unsatisfactory both in terms of its basic assumptions and its predictions, questions about its legitimacy naturally arise. The story of neoclassical theory then appears not to be the positivist falsificationist one in which a theory survives because of its ability to explain facts. Neoclassical theory appears to be more in the nature of a Kuhnian paradigm that for various reasons—perhaps partly ideological appeal and partly the apparent richness of the theory's analytical results—maintains its hold on the economics profession.

Nonmainstream Approaches

Orthodox Marxian Theory

An essential characteristic of class societies, Marx reasoned, is the *exploitation of labor*—the extraction of surplus labor beyond what is required to meet workers' subsistence needs. It is the ability of the dominant class to extract surplus labor through its control of the means of production that enables it to maintain its dominant position. Although exploitation of labor is essential to class societies in general (whether slave, feudal, or capitalist), it takes different forms under different modes of production. In analyzing specifically *capitalist* exploitation, Marx takes the crucial step of applying *value categories* to this process. Marx's labor theory of value (like that of his classical predecessors) stems from the principle that commodities have value only by virtue of the human labor expended in transferring materials from their natural state to the social realm of prices and commodities. For Marx, this means that the value of a commodity is the sum of direct and indirect "abstract socially-necessary labor time," where "indirect" refers to labor expended in the production of means of production and now transferred to other commodities through depreciation. Since the value of a commodity is the total labor time socially necessary to produce it, the value of labor power is the labor time socially necessary to reproduce labor power, that is, the labor time required to produce the commodities needed for the worker to subsist and continue to offer his or her labor services.

Since exploitation is defined as the extraction of surplus labor beyond what is required for workers' subsistence needs, we now can more specifically define capitalist exploitation as the extraction of *value* in excess of the value of labor power. It is then apparent that under the capitalist mode of production, exploitation is the source of profitability—which is what drives capitalist production. Suppose that the total product consists of two portions: that required to replace used-up means of production (depreciation) and that required to satisfy workers' consumption needs. If the product is exhausted by these two portions, then the value of the product will not exceed the value of labor power directly and indirectly embodied in the product. There would therefore be no exploitation (in the Marxian sense), but also no surplus, no profits, and indeed no production, since capitalists will not invest unless production is profitable. Thus exploitation of labor is essential to capitalist production.

Marx's method in *Capital* (1977, 1978, 1981), as is well known, is to move by successive approximation from the ideal or abstract world of labor values and surplus value of Book 1 to the concrete reality of prices and profits of Book 3. Justification of this method requires (1) justification of the value framework of Book 1, and (2) a method of transformation of Book 1's value framework (labor values and surplus value) into the price framework (prices and profits) of Book 3. The latter problem—the "transformation problem"—has been resolved by numerous authors (though not by Marx). The real controversy of Marxian economics concerns the former problem—how to justify Marx's value framework of Book 1 and the notion that it forms the "core" or "essence" of the price system of Book 3. For it is from this premise that Marx's "laws of motion" derive.[2]

Justification of Marx's value framework concerns Marx's characterization of the process that renders concrete private labors "abstract" or social and thus commensurable in value terms. Marxists generally agree that abstract labor reflects a real social process, a valuation process in which the individuals of capitalist society *actually* collectively engage. Thus the premise of Marxian economics, that value is abstract socially necessary labor time, has the status not of an idealization but of an "abstraction," something that is objectively true and observable when appropriate use of the "power of abstraction" is made in application to capitalist society. Marxists (e.g., Lenin 1961, 320; Mandel 1978, 13–23) have tended to characterize this method as neither inductive nor deductive but as a unity of the two methods: inductive in its initial isolation of the concrete historical reality of capitalism (isolating first the commodity and then "observing" through abstraction the reality of capitalist exploitation and the value categories inherent in it), and deductive in its reasoning back to the concrete in the movement from Book 1 of *Capital* to Book 3.

Thus many orthodox Marxists would deny that their theory is deductive on the grounds that the value categories and capitalist exploitation are not idealized assumptions (like the behavioral assumptions of neoclassical theory) but "abstractions" from a palpable reality. But this distinction between idealization and abstraction is one lost on many non-Marxists (and radical economists discussed below may well be in this category) and is indeed the conceptual leap that many non-Marxists are unwilling to make. Thus, while orthodox Marxists may believe that the Marxian method supersedes the inductive-deductive opposition—and so is immune from criticisms of either approach considered separately—a legitimate case can be made that the method is in fact deductive and as such suffers from the difficulties associated with deductive economic theorizing, that is, that theoretical results are difficult to establish or falsify empirically.

Radical Economics

Radical economists accept Marx's historical materialist premise that exploitation is a basic feature of class societies, but reject the notion that social power arises fundamentally from only one source (the class structure). They argue instead that power is "irreducibly heterogenous" and wielded by different groups over other groups through a "multiplicity of distinct structures of dominance and subordinacy" (Bowles and Gintis 1987, 32) where the latter, in addition to the capitalist economy, include the state and the patriarchal family. Thus bosses exploit workers in the economic sphere, but also certain racial/ethnic groups oppress others in the political sphere, and men subjugate women in the patriarchal family. All of these are forms of domination with no one form somehow "primary" and the others subsidiary.

But if radical economists reject the primacy of exploitation, they must also reject Marx's value categories and the logic of capitalist production (the "laws of motion") inherent therein. For if the dominant logic structuring society is simply competition among different groups for *power*, with exploitation being merely one manifestation of this, then it would be arbitrary to attribute (as above) the reproduction of the entire system of social relations to the exploitation of labor (where exploitation is the source of surplus value and thus profits, which are what motivate capitalists to invest, allowing the system to reproduce). Indeed, the system of social relations is open-ended in radical economics, since there is no limit to the "multiplicity of distinct structures of dominance and subordinacy" that may form. "Exploitation" therefore loses its technical Marxian definition and now refers simply to capitalists' exercise of power over workers when workers are on company premises.

How do radical economists arrive at their rejection of the primacy of capitalist exploitation? The orthodox Marxian position arises from Marx and Engels's famous deduction that since "men must be in a position to live in order to be able to 'make history,'. . . the production of material life itself" is "a fundamental condition of all history" that "in any interpretation of history one has first of all to observe . . . in all its significance and all its implications" (Marx and Engels 1968, 39). Thus Marx and Engels make a particular assumption about the *character* of the motivations that underlie human actions—that actions with significant social force (undertaken not by individuals but by classes, the main economic actors) are motivated by subsistence imperatives. The mode of production is thus the key to explaining the organization of society, with market phenomena, including exchange ratios, under capitalism merely a function of the social imperative of reproducing the existing class relations of production. Radical theorists, by contrast, make no a priori assumptions about the character of human motivations. Michael Mann (1986, 6), for example, maintains that motivational issues are "not strictly relevant to the issue of primacy." Adopting the more general expression "human beings pursuing their goals," he regards "human goals" as a constant into which he will "inquire no further because it has no further social force." Primacy is given instead to established "social facts," that is, empirically observable modes of behavior, whether economic, political, familial, and so on, each with its own logic, where it is unnecessary to consider how these modes of behavior fit into, or are conditioned by, the dominant mode of production. Motivations are of course an aspect of these modes of behavior, but their character is not assumed a priori from the dominant mode of production since they may have little relation to it. Hence there is no basis for application of Marx's value categories to capitalist "exploitation" (which again under the radical approach lacks the technical Marxian definition), and the implications of Marx's value theory—the laws of motion—that describe the long-term course of capitalism are lost (or at least not rigorously deduced from value theory).

A good example of the difference is crisis theory. In orthodox Marxian theory capitalists seek to raise productivity and lower unit costs of production by increasing the amount of fixed capital in their production processes. The effect of this is to raise the "organic composition of capital" and over the long term (on value-theoretic grounds) lower the general rate of profit (see Shaikh 1991a). Reduced profitability then leads to periodic crises of accumulation.

In radical economics, crises also arise from reduced profitability. But lacking Marx's value framework, in one dominant branch of radical crisis theory—the wage squeeze theory—reduced profitability arises not from increased mechanization of production but from gains of labor at the expense of capital. Crises under this approach are not a necessary aspect of capitalism but depend on the relative balance between productivity gains (which increase profitability and stave off crises) and growth of real wages. An implication of this is that if worker demands are kept within certain bounds by political means, crises can be avoided. In contrast, in the orthodox Marxian approach the rate of profit falls independently of the battle over relative product shares; hence crises are endemic to capitalism and not controllable through political means (see Shaikh 1991b).

Underlying the radical approach is the assumption that workers and capitalists (like gender and racial/ethnic groups) are simply groups that compete against each other for power. Since capitalist exploitation is not structurally tied to the mode of production, workers in principle may gain the upper hand and "exploit" capitalists—an impossibility under the orthodox Marxian approach where capitalists have a dominant position over workers by structural necessity.

Conclusion

Inherent difficulties with empirical work in economics have encouraged the development of economics as a highly deductive discipline—serving both to make analytical results in economics highly dependent on the basic assumptions of a theory and to "immunize" economic theories from empirical considerations through ceteris paribus clauses. This applies both to neoclassical theory and orthodox Marxian theory, both of which are difficult to evaluate through simple comparisons between theories and "facts."

Radical economics is in part an attempt within the Marxian historical materialist tradition to overcome this dilemma by taking a more inductive approach—by starting from established "social facts" (i.e., instances of the exercise of power by one group over another under the rules of some institutional arrangement) and making inferences (nondemonstrably) from them. This move is by no means unproblematic. By releasing "historical materialist" analysis from its "mooring" in the mode of production, radical economics may be deemed ad hoc. Why not add on more "structures of dominance" ad infinitum? And the logical implications of Marx's value framework (such as the falling rate of profit argument and the growth of the "reserve army" of labor) used to study the long-term course of capitalist society are certainly lost (or at least not logically deduced).

The cost of abandoning the Marxian logic is thus lost analytical rigor and, potentially, the loss of analytical results that accurately describe the long-term course of capitalism. Many, however, would argue that the benefit is increased relevance to real world events. One major achievement of the radical literature, for example, is the notion of segmented labor markets—that labor markets under capitalism are segmented into racial, ethnic, and gender groups, with some groups of workers exploiting others (Gordon, Edwards, and Reich 1982)—a result at odds with the orthodox Marxian framework. And radical feminist writers (e.g., Hartmann 1981) have shown convincingly that while capitalism may have accommodated and even perpetuated gender discrimination, one cannot deduce from this that the elimination of capitalism will serve to eliminate such discrimination.

Adjudicating the methodological dispute between orthodox Marxism and radical economics is well beyond the scope of this chapter. Unquestionably, however, the radical rejection of the primacy of economic exploitation has led to much relevant work that otherwise might not have been done.

Notes

1. Recent work in this tradition includes Weeks (1981), Laibman (1991), Botwinick (1993), and Shaikh and Tonak (1994).

2. The "laws of motion" that describe the long-term course of capitalism are the central analytical results of *Capital*. In brief, they include the notion of a secularly growing "reserve army" of labor (i.e., growing unemployment), the "absolute immiseration" of the working class, a tendency for small and medium-sized firms to disappear (the "concentration of capital"), and a tendency for the rate of profit to fall.

References

Botwinick, Howard. 1993. *Persistent Inequalities: Wage Disparity Under Capitalist Competition*. Princeton: Princeton University Press.

Bowles, Samuel, and Herbert Gintis. 1987. *Democracy and Capitalism: Property, Community, and the Contradictions of Modern Social Thought.* New York: Basic Books.

Feyerabend, P.K. 1975. *Against Method: Outline of an Anarchistic Theory of Knowledge.* London: NLB.

Fisher, Irving. 1926. *Mathematical Investigations in the Theory of Value and Prices*. New Haven: Yale University Press.

Friedman, Milton. 1953. "The Methodology of Positive Economics." In *Essays in Positive Economics*, pp. 3–41. Chicago: University of Chicago Press.

Gordon, David M., Richard C. Edwards, and Michael Reich. 1982. *Segmented Work, Divided Workers: The Historical Transformation of Labor in the United States.* UK: Cambridge University Press.

Hartmann, Heidi. 1981. "The Unhappy Marriage of Marxism and Feminism: Towards a More Progressive Union." *Capital and Class*, 1979. Reprinted in *The Unhappy Marriage of Marxism and Feminism*, ed. L. Sargent., 1–41. London: Pluto Press.

Kuhn, Thomas S. 1970. *The Structure of Scientific Revolutions*. 2d ed. Chicago: University of Chicago Press.

Laibman, David. 1991. *Value, Technological Change, and Crisis: Explorations in Marxist Economic Theory*. Armonk, NY: M.E. Sharpe.

Lakatos, Imre. 1970. "Falsification and the Methodology of Scientific Research Programmes." In *Criticism and the Growth of Knowledge*, ed. I. Lakatos and A. Musgrave, 96–196. UK: Cambridge University Press.

Lenin, V.I. 1961. *Collected Works*. Volume 38. Moscow: Foreign Language Publishing House.

McCloskey, D. 1985. "The Rhetoric of Economics." *Journal of Economic Literature*, 21.

Mandel, Ernest. 1978. *Late Capitalism*. London: Verso.

Mann, Michael. 1986. *The Sources of Social Power.* Volume I. UK: Cambridge University Press.

Marx, Karl. 1977. *Capital*, vol. 1, translated by Ben Fowkes. New York: Vintage.

______. 1978. *Capital*, vol. 2, translated by David Fernbach. New York: Vintage.

______. 1981. *Capital*, vol. 3, translated by David Fernbach. New York: Vintage.

Shaikh, Anwar. 1991a. "Falling Rate of Profit." In *A Dictionary of Marxist Thought*, ed. Tom I. Bottomore.

Marx, Karl, and Friedrich Engels. [1846]. 1968 *The German Ideology*, ed. S. Ryazanskaya. Moscow: Progress Publishers.

Oxford, UK: Blackwell.

———. 1991b. "Crisis Theories." In *A Dictionary of Marxist Thought*, ed. by Tom I. Bottomore. Oxford, UK: Blackwell.

Shaikh, Anwar, and E. Ahmet Tonak. 1994. *Measuring the Wealth of Nations*. Cambridge, UK: Cambridge University Press.

Weeks, John. 1981. *Capital and Exploitation*. Princeton: Princeton University Press.

4

Feminist Political Economy

A Primer

Ellen Mutari

Introduction

Feminist economists and other heterodox economists have much to teach each other. Sharing a critical perspective toward mainstream theoretical constructs, both treat economics as a social practice with concrete historical origins rather than as immutable laws of nature awaiting the scientist's gaze. Most political economists would share the sentiment offered by two feminist economists that "If we instead recognize that the discipline we call economics has been developed by particular human actors, it is hard to see how it could fail to be critically influenced by . . . the social, cultural, economic, and political milieu in which it has been created" (Ferber and Nelson 1993, 1). Several feminist economists have taken strong positions regarding the affinity between feminism and particular schools of heterodoxy such as Marxism, radical institutionalism, or social economics (see, for example, Waller and Jennings 1990; Emami 1993; Whalen and Whalen 1994; Matthaei 1996). However, there is no unified perspective on the relationship between feminist economics and other heterodox schools of economic thought.

In feminist economics, the emphasis of much of recent scholarship is on deconstructing androcentric bias within the discipline's theories, conceptual categories, and methodologies (see Ferber and Nelson 1993; Kuiper and Sap 1995). While distancing themselves from neoclassical theory, these scholars remain in dialogue with it—a dialogue long ago abandoned by many political economists. Therefore, many political economists tend to mistake this engagement for agreement, dismissing feminist economics as a reformist exercise. I would argue that this greatly underestimates the importance of the project of feminist economics. Similarly, some neoclassically trained feminist economists assume that they have little to learn from other critical approaches. This is also a mistake.

Caught in the middle are those who define themselves as feminist political economists. This group of scholars has been engaged in a critique of prevailing economic ideologies and institutions for several decades. Feminist political economists not only recognize the critical stance they share with other political economists, they also assert that feminist analyses provide unique contributions to economic and social theory. Feminist theory has contributed to the development of three key analytical constructs: the concepts of *social reproduction*, *patriarchy*, and *gender*. This primer reviews the development of each of these three concepts in recent decades and highlights their significance for contemporary research agendas.

Social Reproduction

In the United States, contemporary feminist political economy emerged with the second wave of feminism out of the civil rights and antiwar struggles of the 1960s. Feminists, along with others influenced by this grassroots New Left politics, grappled with their relationship with the intellectual tradition that seemed to provide important insights into the process of social change: Marxism. At a time when the line between academic and political discourse was blurred, political economists were among those most involved in these discussions.

Early feminist political economists took a term that was already part of Marxist discourse—social reproduction—and developed it as an analytical category. The production process is at the heart of traditional Marxist theory, especially the labor theory of value. Feminist political economists argue that social reproduction, defined as the daily and intergenerational renewal of human resources, is also integral to the economy. This is most evident in what has been termed "the domestic labor debate." A series of articles published between 1974 and 1982 poses the question of whether Marx's labor theory of value could be applied to reproductive labor in the home (see Seccombe 1974; Gardiner 1975; Fee 1976; Himmelweit and Mohun 1977; Molyneux 1979; Folbre 1982). The debate was framed by the question of whether domestic labor creates surplus value and, if so, for whom.

Some of this early feminist work on social reproduction tended to accept as given a particular model of gender relations, specifically the male breadwinner and the female full-time homemaker (for an exception, see Benería 1979). The historical development of capitalism led to the separation of production from reproduction. Production takes place outside the home and involves the making of commodities available for exchange. Reproduction is generally, but not exclusively, work performed by women within private households—unpaid if by family members or paid if by domestic workers. During the nineteenth century, this division of labor was termed the "doctrine of separate spheres": production was viewed as male, reproduction as female.

Far from being an essential element of nature or capitalism, Jane Humphries and Jill Rubery (1984) believe that the breadwinner/homemaker dichotomy was a deliberate working-class strategy to minimize family members' involvement in wage labor. Their theory emphasizes the "relative autonomy" of social reproduction, building on the methodological approach of French Marxist Louis Althusser. They dispute the argument central to the domestic labor debate that family structure is functional for capitalism (see also Humphries 1977). In contrast, Humphries and Rubery assert that capitalism depends upon expanding wage labor—including women's. The strength of this analysis is its focus on the historical process of defining family structure. (For critiques of this approach, see Sen 1980; Beechey 1988.)

A lasting contribution of feminist analyses of social reproduction is the systematic recognition of the economic contribution of domestic labor in regenerating labor power as a productive input. The household remains a place of economic activity, despite the separation of production from reproduction with the expansion of market relations. This insight continues to guide Marxist-feminist scholarship (see, for example, Davis 1997). It also underlies the concern of contemporary feminist economists with the value of unpaid household labor in national income accounts (Waring 1989; Benería 1992; Folbre and Wagman 1993; Ironmonger 1996).

Over the course of the twentieth century, more

and more activities involving social reproduction were commodified. This has gone hand in hand with the increased labor force participation and attachment of women, especially married white women with children, in most industrialized countries. In the United States, much of this paid reproductive labor is performed by women of color. Once a "privatized" employment relationship between individual women employers and their domestics, paid reproductive labor has shifted its location into the burgeoning service economy (Glenn 1992).

Contemporary feminist political economists continue to analyze the organization of social reproduction, posing questions about this commodification process. Many are skeptical about the ability of markets to optimally provision these activities, especially caring labor (see Folbre 1994, 1995; Himmelweit 1995). Nancy Folbre suggests that the organization of social reproduction is a crucial, unsettled problem that we need to face:

> Who pays for the kids? This is the short version of a larger question: How are the costs of caring for ourselves, our children, and other dependents distributed among members of our society? These are the costs of social reproduction, and they differ from the costs of production. . . .(Folbre 1994, 1)

Patriarchy

The concept of patriarchy allows feminists to give a name to the organization of social reproduction and to emphasize the structural aspects of male domination. In contrast to much of the domestic labor debate, patriarchy theory focuses on men's power and privileges. In an article that was passed around feminist reading groups between 1975 and 1977, initially published in *Capital and Class* in 1979, and reprinted as part of a dialogue among feminist theorists in 1981, Heidi Hartmann proposes an oft-cited definition of patriarchy:

> We can usefully define patriarchy as a set of social relations between men, which have a material base, and which, though hierarchical, establish or create interdependence and solidarity among men that enable them to dominate women. (Hartmann 1981, 14)

Even though men of different classes, races, and ethnic groups have different places in the social hierarchy, they all benefit from being men.

Patriarchy, as a system, interacts with the economic system of capitalism but is not subsumed by it. Similarly, Hartmann advances a systematic analysis of relations between women and men that utilizes materialist methodology rather than specific class-based categories. The material basis of patriarchy is men's control over women's labor power. Women are excluded from access to essential productive resources in each mode of production. Under capitalism, for instance, women are restricted from jobs that pay living wages. Further, within heterosexual households, men benefit from women's unpaid domestic labor.

The image of two materially based systems was the basis for the development of socialist feminism, also known as dual systems theory during the 1980s. Like Humphries (1977), socialist feminists argue that capitalism accommodates to the social relations in the household. But socialist feminists emphasize the unequal distribution of power within the household, and therefore the lack of unified working-class interests.

However, there were fundamental problems with early formulations of socialist feminism. By focusing on the interaction of capitalism and patriarchy, racial domination tends to be treated as a secondary issue (Joseph 1981). Critics charge that the theory generalizes from the experiences of white women in industrialized countries. For example, the emphasis on married women's unpaid domestic roles ignores the extensive labor force participation of both married and single black women (Glenn 1985). Women of color also affirm the importance of families as a source of strength in a racist society (Zinn 1987).

Not only does the male breadwinner model of family life exclude the concrete experiences of women of color, it has appeared less and less representative of white family structure. In the late 1980s, the shift of manufacturing to newly industrialized countries, the expansion of the service and information sectors, global market integration, and the demise of Keynesian welfare states in the West became fodder for new directions in political economy in general, and feminist political economy in particular. The concept of patriarchy became increasingly weighted down by all of this diversity and historical change. It seemed more and more difficult for one system, no matter how broadly defined, to incorporate all of the variations in women and men's experiences.

Yet, numerous feminists continue to use the concept of patriarchy to emphasize structural aspects of women's oppression (see, for example, Folbre 1994). British sociologist Cynthia Cockburn suggests that the concept of patriarchy should not be discarded:

> Patriarchy was real and it was durable. What feminism proposes is that we should understand female subordination as *systemic*. That is, it is not casual but structured, not local but extensive, not transitory but stable, with a tendency to self-reproduction. (Cockburn 1991, 6)

Even when not explicitly utilizing the term patriarchy, the concept is implicit in discussions of power relations within the household. Most notably, feminist political economists are developing bargaining models to explore the dynamics of household decision making about labor supply, consumption, and the division of unpaid labor (see, for example, McCrate 1987; Heath and Ciscel 1988; Seiz 1991). Differential bargaining power within the household exists because women in heterosexual partnerships generally face higher costs if the relationship is terminated. These costs are determined by one's access to resources in the market sphere. Thus, what bargaining power theorists have done is elucidate a linkage between the two core elements of patriarchy: women's secondary status in the labor market and the resultant unequal division of domestic labor.

Gender

Unlike the concepts of social reproduction and patriarchy, feminist political economists have not been at the forefront of generating gender theory. Anthropologist Gayle Rubin (1975) is credited with first elaborating a distinction between biological sex and gender as a social construct. Gender as an analytical category has been theorized primarily by anthropologists, historians, and other feminists in the humanities. Yet, as discussed below, feminist political economists have applied gender theory to new and important analyses of economic processes and outcomes.

Feminists use the term gender to signify society's ideas about differences between men and women. That is, society attaches various meanings and interpretations to a biological category, "sex," formulating designations of masculinity and femininity, "gender." Male and female are socially constructed as opposites, and a hierarchy is established between them.

Peoples' understanding of what constitutes gender varies historically, cross-culturally, or even within a given society. Because gender interacts with class, race/ethnicity, and sexuality—constructs that are also socially, not biologically, determined—more than one mode of gender relations may coexist. For example, the hegemonic ideal of the full-time homemaker/mother for white, middle-class, married women in the early twentieth century is distinct from married black women's expected labor force participation. This diversity of gender relations has enabled gender theorists to overcome some of the limitations imposed by the universal, ahistorical concept of patriarchy.

There has been an affinity between gender theory and the development of postmodern social theory. In particular, feminist theorists have analyzed gender ideology as a form of social discourse (see, for example, Benhabib and Cornell 1987; Nicholson 1990). Discourse analysis, pioneered by French theorists such as Jacques Derrida and Michel Foucault, focuses on how subjectivity (or consciousness) is shaped by language. Therefore, postmodern scholars have turned their attention to understanding the production of knowledge.

The dominant strain of academic feminism in the late 1980s and early 1990s has concerned itself with articulating the gendered assumptions embedded in the major "scientific" theories, including Marxism. Like Hartmann, postmodern feminists challenge the gender-neutrality of core Marxist categories such as "production" and "class" (Benhabib and Cornell 1987; Barrett 1988). However, they critique socialist feminists for treating "social reproduction" as a separate sphere or "patriarchy" as a separate system; dual systems theory left the Marxist analysis of capitalist production virtually unexamined. Instead, the postmodern feminist approaches argue that economic concepts and structures are themselves gendered.

Inspired by these intellectual currents in the humanities, much of the new wave of feminist economists has treated neoclassical theory as their subject, reexamining the gendered assumptions and principles underlying mainstream models of "economic man." For example, economic models assume a "separative self," that is, individuals whose utility (happiness) is independently achieved. Although assumed as a universal scientific principle, this form of individualism reflects social constructions of "male" rather than "female" behavior and motivations: society does not expect a mother's happiness to be independent of her child's. Thus, feminist economists use gender as an analytical tool for exposing the scientific pretenses of neoclassical economics.

Feminist political economists have, for the most part, embraced the use of the term *gender*, and with it the belief that culture and ideology are constitutive of human history rather than mere "superstructure" (see, for example, Amott and Matthaei 1996). Yet they have remained fundamentally concerned with how gender relations are institutionalized. Gender influences and is influenced by economic institutions, structures, and practices. As development theorist Naila Kabeer suggests:

> Gender is seen to be an aspect of *all* organizational relations and behavior, more distinct and explicit in some institutional locations than others, but always interacting to shape the identities, practices and life-chances of different groups of women and men in quite specific ways. (Kabeer 1994, 61)

Feminist political economists are studying the institutionalization of gender relations in the spheres of both social reproduction and production (see Mutari, Boushey, and Fraher 1997). Folbre (1994) conceptualizes gender, race, class, nation, sexuality, and age as interlocking "structures of collective constraint" rather than as autonomous systems.

Conclusion

We have seen that feminists have been working to transform the study of political economy for decades. Three key analytical categories have illuminated this endeavor. Feminist theories of social reproduction, patriarchy, and gender constitute an important contribution to recent work in political economy. The result has been a better understanding of the totality of economic processes.

Bibliography

Amott, Teresa, and Julie Matthaei.1996. *Race, Gender, and Work: A Multi-cultural Economic History of Women in the United States*. Rev. ed. Boston: South End Press.

Barrett, Michele. 1988. *Women's Oppression Today: The Marxist/Feminist Encounter*. London: Verso.

Beechey, Veronica.1988. "Rethinking the Definition of Work: Gender and Work." In *Feminization of the Labor Force: Paradoxes and Promises*, ed. Jane Jenson, Elisabeth Hagen, and Ceallaigh Reddy, 45–62. New York: Oxford University Press.

Benería, Lourdes.1979. "Reproduction, Production and the Sexual Division of Labor." *Cambridge Journal of Economics* 3 (September): 203–225.

———. 1992. "Accounting for Women's Work: The Progress of Two Decades." *World Development* 20, no. 11: 1547–1560.

Benhabib, Seyla, and Drucilla Cornell, eds. 1987. *Feminism as Critique*. Minneapolis: University of Minnesota Press.

Cockburn, Cynthia. 1991. *In the Way of Women: Men's Resistance to Sex Equality in Organizations*. Ithaca: ILR Press.

Davis, Ann. 1997. "Class, Gender, and Culture: A Discussion of Marxism, Feminism, and Postmodernism." In *Gender and Political Economy: Incorporating Diversity into Theory and Policy*, ed. Ellen Mutari, Heather Boushey, and William Fraher, 92–111. Armonk, NY: M.E. Sharpe.

Emami, Zohreh. 1993. "Challenges Facing Social Economics in the Twenty-First Century: A Feminist Perspective." *Review of Social Economy* 52, no. 4 (Winter): 416–425.

Fee, Terry. 1976. "Domestic Labor: An Analysis of Housework and its Relationship to the Production Process." *Review of Radical Political Economics* 8, no. 1 (Spring): 1–8.

Ferber, Marianne A., and Julie A. Nelson, eds. 1993. *Beyond Economic Man: Feminist Theory and Economics*. Chicago: University of Chicago Press.

Folbre, Nancy. 1982. "Exploitation Comes Home: A Critique of the Marxian Theory of Family Labour." *Cambridge Journal of Economics* 6, no. 4 (December): 317–329.

———. 1994. *Who Pays for the Kids? Gender and the Structures of Constraint*. London: Routledge.

———. 1995. "'Holding Hands at Midnight': The Paradox of Caring Labor." *Feminist Economics* 1, no. 1 (Spring): 73–92.

Folbre, Nancy, and Barnet Wagman. 1993. "Counting Housework: Revised Estimates of Real Product in the United States, 1800–1860." *Journal of Economic History* 53, no. 2 (June): 275–288.

Frader, Laura L. 1998. "Bringing Political Economy Back In: Gender, Race, and Class in Labor History." *Social Science History* 22, no. 1 (Spring): 7–18.

Gardiner, Jean. 1975. "Women's Domestic Labour." *New Left Review*, no. 89: 47–58.

Glenn, Evelyn Nakano. 1985. "Racial Ethnic Women's Labor: The Intersection of Race, Gender, and Class Oppression." *Review of Radical Political Economics* 17, no. 3 (Fall): 86–108.

———. 1992. "From Servitude to Service Work: Historical Continuities in the Racial Division of Paid Reproductive Labor." *Signs* 18, no. 1 (Autumn): 1–43.

Hartmann, Heidi I. 1981. "The Unhappy Marriage of Marxism and Feminism: Towards a More Progressive Union." In *Women and Revolution: A Discussion of the Unhappy Marriage of Marxism and Feminism*, ed. Lydia Sargent, 1–41. Boston: South End Press.

Heath, Julia A., and David H. Ciscel. 1988. "Patriarchy, Family Structure and the Exploitation of Women's Labor." *Journal of Economic Issues* 22, no. 3 (September): 781–794.

Himmelweit, Susan. 1995. "The Discovery of 'Unpaid Work': The Social Consequences of the Expansion of 'Work.'" *Feminist Economics* 1, no. 2 (Summer): 1–19.

Himmelweit, Susan, and Simon Mohun. 1977. "Domestic Labour and Capital." *Cambridge Journal of Economics* 1, no. 1 (March): 15–31.

Humphries, Jane. 1977. "The Working Class Family, Women's Liberation, and Class Struggle: The Case of Nineteenth-Century British History." *Review of Radical Political Economics* 9, no. 3 (Fall): 25–41.

Humphries, Jane, and Jill Rubery. 1984. "The Reconstruction of the Supply Side of the Labour Market: The Relative Autonomy of Social Reproduction." *Cambridge Journal of Economics* 8, no. 4 (December): 331–346.

Ironmonger, D. 1996. "Counting Outputs, Capital Inputs and Caring Labor: Estimating Gross Household Product." *Feminist Economics* 2, no. 3 (Fall): 37–64.

Joseph, Gloria. 1981. "The Incompatible Menage a Trois: Marxism, Feminism, and Racism." In *Women and Revolution: A Discussion of the Unhappy Marriage of Marxism and Feminism*, ed. Lydia Sargent, 91–107. Boston: South End Press.

Kabeer, Naila. 1994. *Reversed Realities: Gender Hierarchies in Development Thought.* London: Verso.

Kuiper, Edith, and Jolande Sap, eds. 1995. *Out of the Margin: Feminist Perspectives on Economics*. London: Routledge.

McCrate, Elaine. 1987. "Trade, Merger, and Employment: Economic Theory on Marriage." *Review of Radical Political Economics* 19, no. 1 (Spring): 73–89.

Matthaei, Julie. 1996. "Why Feminist, Marxist, and Anti-Racist Economists Should be Feminist-Marxist-Anti-Racist Economists." *Feminist Economics* 2, no. 1 (Spring): 22–42.

Molyneux, Maxine. 1979. "Beyond the Domestic Labour Debate." *New Left Review*, no. 116: 3–27.

Mutari, Ellen, Heather Boushey, and William Fraher IV. 1997. *Gender and Political Economy: Incorporating Diversity into Theory and Policy*. Armonk, NY: M.E. Sharpe.

Nelson, Julie A. 1996. *Feminism, Objectivity and Economics*. London: Routledge.

Nicholson, Linda J., ed. 1990. *Feminism/Postmodernism*. New York: Routledge.

Rubin, Gayle. 1975. "The Traffic in Women: Notes on the 'Political Economy' of Sex." In *Toward an Anthropology of Women*, ed. Rayna Reitner, 157–210. New York: Monthly Review Press.

Seccombe, Wally. 1974. "The Housewife and Her Labour Under Capitalism." *New Left Review* no. 83: 3–27.

Seiz, Janet A. 1991. "The Bargaining Approach and Feminist Methodology." *Review of Radical Political Economics* 23, no. 1/2 (Spring/Summer): 22–29.

Sen, Gita. 1980. "The Sexual Division of Labor and the Working-Class Family: Towards a Conceptual Synthesis of Class Relations and the Subordination of Women." *Review of Radical Political Economics* 12, no. 2 (Summer): 76–86.

Waller, William, and Ann Jennings. 1990. "On the Possibility of a Feminist Economics." *Journal of Economic Issues* 24, no. 2 (June): 613–622.

Waring, Marilyn. 1989. *If Women Counted: A New Feminist Economics*. London: Macmillan.

Whalen, Charles, and Linda Whalen. 1994. "Institutionalism: A Useful Foundation for Feminist Economics?" In *The Economic Status of Women Under Capitalism: Institutional Economics and Feminist Theory*, ed. Janice Peterson and Doug Brown, 19–34. Aldershot: Edward Elgar.

Zinn, Maxine Baca. 1987. "Structural Transformation and Minority Families." In *Women, Households, and the Economy*, ed. Lourdes Benería and Catharine R. Stimpson, 155–171. New Brunswick: Rutgers University Press.

5

Class and Evolution

An Institutionalist View

William M. Dugger

Institutionalism deals with the evolution of institutions (Dugger 1988, 1989a). So in institutionalism the concept of class means more than a statistical interval such as all families with incomes in, say, the $50,000 to $75,000 range of a table. The number or proportion of families receiving an income within a particular range can rise or fall without evolution taking place. Such rises and falls are important, but usually represent mere mechanical movement—mere rises and falls in the positions of families within a stable institutional structure, not evolution of that structure. So to understand institutional change, class must be thought of as a social relation, not as a statistical interval (Dugger 1996).

What Is Class?

E.P. Thompson's definition of class is quite apropos.

> Class happens when some men, as a result of common experiences (inherited or shared), feel and articulate the identity of their interests as between themselves, and as against other men whose interests are different from (and usually opposed to) theirs. The class experience is largely determined by the productive relations into which men are born—or enter involuntarily. (Thompson 1966, 9)

In institutionalism, class is understood in terms of four different social relationships: (1) relationship to income, (2) relationship to work, (3) relationship to wealth, (4) Relationship to technology (see also Dugger and Sherman 1994, 1997).

1. Relationship to Income

When a person is able to establish a differentially advantageous relationship to a particular source of income through whatever keeps the money going to them rather than someone else, he or she establishes a vested interest. Vested interest involves a protected, strategic position in the commercial flow of traffic. It is a product of power (Tool and Samuels 1989). Those who benefit from or are harmed by the same kind of vested interests share a class interest as a group and may engage as a group in class conflict. So, vested interest, a relationship to income, is one of the elements of class. Frequently a vested interest involves a property right or contract right (Commons 1968; Dugger 1980).

2. Relationship to Work

Following Veblen (1975), the upper class is the leisure class. The leisure class is a class because of its particular relationship to work. Members of this class receive income but do not have to work for it and they flaunt their exemption in front of everyone. Their conspicuous leisure and their conspicuous consumption are all symbols of their privileged relationship to work. Others, who are beneath them in class position, have to work for their money. Members of the leisure class are superior in class position and do not have to work. So, relationship to work is another element of class. In terms of class attributes, if you are exempt from paid labor, you are a dominant creature of power and prestige. If you have to work to obtain income, you are a subservient creature of weakness and contempt. Of course, nuances in this exist. Rich CEO types, such as Bill Gates, who work but are paid wildly high amounts of money, are exceptions.

3. Relationship to Wealth

To be in the leisure class, you must own enough wealth to exempt you from having to manage it or work it. The growing absentee ownership of wealth is crucial. Most important in this regard has been the rise of collective structures—institutions—that enable the owners of wealth to enjoy the benefits of wealth ownership without the burdens of wealth management (Fusfeld 1972). The operating corporation and the conglomerate, the holding company and the mutual fund have all facilitated the concentration of ownership in a class of people who are absent from its management (Berle and Means 1968). This relationship to wealth in the form of absentee ownership is another important element of class. It helps institutionalize the exemption from work for members of the leisure class.

Absentee ownership of wealth through operating corporations, conglomerates, holding companies, mutual funds, and trusts have given rise to the "manager." Numerous layers of managers in both large and small business bureaucracies now have a new kind of relationship to wealth (Dugger 1989b). They do not own it and enjoy its usufruct as an absentee. So they are not, strictly speaking, leisure class. They do not work with it in actually making a product or performing a service. So they are not, strictly speaking, working class either. Instead, they manage the working class as it uses the wealth of the leisure class in the making of goods and performing of services. Managers are a kept class. Like all kept classes, emulation determines their outlook: they look down with vicious contempt and they look up with fawning adulation. Seldom do they pursue their own interests in conflict with the leisure class, but instead are usually socially conditioned to be content to be kept in the good graces and good pay of that class. At the higher levels of management, individuals often own large blocks of stock, so to that extent they have the same institutional relationship as the leisure class itself, with the crucial difference being that their managerial position, even much of their ownership, is due to their relation to work.

In special circumstances, however, managers may come to form a true class and pursue their class interests against the interests of other classes. John Kenneth Galbraith, a close student of Thorstein Veblen, argued that in the 1950s and 1960s special circumstances in the United States gave rise to what he called the technostructure—a true managerial class (Galbraith 1967). The special circumstances of the 1950s and 1960s involved the wide separation of ownership from control of the corporation, with ownership losing some of its power over management (control). As long as management earned sufficient profits to keep the diffused, absentee stockowners content, management was the more powerful of the two. This created a kind of gap between ownership and management. But the gap was soon closed by the creation of a "market" for corporate control. In the 1970s and 1980s corporate ownership (the leisure class stockowners) had regained their more powerful position relative to management (Dugger 1992).

4. Relationship to Technology

Engineers and workers, Veblen argued, are interested in technology. Absentee owners, the leisure class, are more interested in making money than in applying technology. Members of the leisure class do not have to relate directly to work through technology. Members of the working class do. This relation to technology or lack thereof also differentiates the working class from the leisure class (Veblen 1965). And, note that the class formulation of institutionalists is consistent in this regard with respect to work and technology. On one hand you work and relate to technology. This positions you in the working class. On the other hand, you do not work and do not relate to technology. This positions you in the leisure class (see also Galbraith 1992).

How Many Classes Are There?

In one sense very many classes exist. In this sense, the nature and position of each class is determined by the myriad of relationships to income, work, wealth, and technology. Coal miners, schoolteachers, pensioners, corporate managers, and many other such groups would each be a class because they share particular relationships, either to income, work, wealth, and/or technology. In this sense, classes are quite fragmented sets of people sharing very specific interests. Shifting coalitions and loose alliances continually form and break up among these classes as special interest group politics pull them this way and that. The winners and losers change places, but the system does not necessarily undergo evolutionary change.

In another sense, however, just two classes exist—the leisure class and the underlying population or working class. In this sense, classes are not fragmented sets, but more unified and larger sets of collectivities. Members of the leisure class have acquired a vested interest in the continued receipt of income without working for it. Most have acquired this vested interest through absentee ownership of securities issued by traditional corporations, conglomerates, holding companies, and mutual funds. Members of the underlying population, on the other hand, have not acquired such vested interests in income and do not enjoy such exemption from work. Instead, they have to earn their bread through the sweat of their brow. If members of the working class are unaware of or confused about their class position, they are in the amorphous position of being in the underlying population (see also Hunt 1979).

Since the leisure class does not work, part of the work done by the underlying population or working class must go to support the leisure class. The class relationship, then, is exploitative. But only if members of the underlying population come to fully understand their subordinate position and the interests they share with their fellows, only then would they come to act like a working class instead of just an underlying population. If the underlying population coalesces into a working class, class conflict between the working class and the leisure class may begin to move the whole system into evolutionary change. This, however, seldom happens (but see Strobel and Peterson 1997).

Numerous and powerful enabling myths make the underlying population's true situation unclear to its members and enable the leisure class to continue its dominant position vis-à-vis the underlying population (see Arnold 1937). Enabling myths are the stuff of classism, racism, sexism, and jingoism. Enabling myths falsely convince the underlying population that their lack of income, wealth, and social influence is not due to the leisure class, but is instead due to low-class lazy people or people of another color getting an unfair share or due to women or foreigners doing the same. Enabling myths create scapegoats and protect leisure class interest against popular discontent. Enabling myths make it difficult for members of the working class to conceptualize distinct class interests in the first place. Instead of thinking in terms of the leisure class versus the working class, enabling myths encourage thinking in terms of industrious people versus lazy welfare cheats, humble white folks versus arrogant black ones, hardy men versus frail women, and true Americans versus shifty foreigners (Dugger 1996, 1998).

Class Dominance

Enabling myth is important to the maintenance of class dominance. In particular, enabling myth keeps the members of the underlying population from realizing their shared interests. So, the underlying population does not coalesce into a working class that opposes the leisure class. This enables the leisure class to continue its dominance.

Also of great importance in maintaining class dominance is emulation. Emulation exerts a profoundly conservative influence on the class structure. Veblen's book on the leisure class provides a theory of social conservation, an explanation of why revolution is a fairly rare occurrence (1975). That explanation emphasizes the power of emulation. Instead of a working class opposing the leisure class in class conflict, as a general rule, the underlying population emulates the leisure class in conspicuous consumption. Because of emulation, the underlying population does not want to revolt against its masters. It wants to be like them. Emulation keeps the underlying population thinking in terms of younger sex, older whiskey, and faster horses; not in terms of liberty, equality, and fraternity (see also Stanfield 1995).

Emulation exerts its most powerful effect on the managerial strata of corporate capitalism. It drives managers to strive harder and harder to rise in pay scale and in status. Emulation is the motive force behind the fabled rat race in which the runners all push themselves to run faster and faster in order to get ahead. Since all the runners are going faster, however, nobody really gets ahead. Instead, everybody must run faster just to keep from losing his or her place. Managers try harder and harder to please those above them in pay scale and prestige. They compete against their friends on the same pay scale and prestige level by trying to create invidious distinctions—putting others down while raising themselves up. Caught up in the rat race, managers find it very hard to recognize their shared interests with other managers and so managers seldom come together as a class to struggle against the leisure class. They want to join the leisure class, not overthrow it. Although they may have the knowledge needed to change the system, they lack the desire (see Dugger 1989b).

Novelty and Change

If technology never changed, members of the leisure class could continue receiving their income and enjoying it without having to manage it. The underlying population would remain befuddled by enabling myth and besotted by emulation. Individual fortunes might rise and fall, the number of observations falling within different statistical intervals of family income might rise and fall as well. Nevertheless, in the absence of technological change, such change would not be evolution. Institutional structures would remain essentially the same.

But changing technology introduces novelty. New ways of producing or distributing old products or new products themselves cause changes in institutional structure. Structural change is also induced by new ways of performing services or by new services. New sets of skills are required and new authority relations between workers and managers emerge. As new technology continues being implemented, new sources of income emerge to enlarge some flows of commercial traffic and to shrink others. New relations to wealth begin to emerge. Joseph Schumpeter coined the phrase "creative destruction" to describe the changes that take place (Schumpeter 1961). Some vested interests are destroyed; others are created. The whole institutional system may begin to evolve as old vested interests become threatened and collapse and as new ones open up and become entrenched. New occupations rise as new tool-skill combinations are created by new technology. Old occupations fall. Perhaps, whole classes rise and fall with the new technology.

New values, beliefs, and meanings will begin to emerge in the culture as people experience new ways of doing things and new things to do, as some people find new ways of getting incomes and other people find their old ways of getting incomes no longer work, and as people try to justify, deny, or attack the new relationships. These new values, beliefs, and meanings make the old enabling myths less and less effective in hiding shared class interests and in confusing the underlying population. Of course, professors, artists, pundits, writers, and such are busy creating new enabling myths. But, nonetheless, technology opens up a kind of window of opportunity—the opportunity to see things clearly for a while at least, until new enabling myths obscure the truth once again.

The introduction of the technology of the automobile caused change not only in industrial production and class relations but also in sexual morality, gender relations, family structure, community living patterns, and much else. So, new technology is the wild card in social evolution's deck.

It is new technology and the creative destruction it causes that can initiate or facilitate institutional change. Such change stretches far beyond the workplace itself. The automobile destroyed old occupations and businesses and created new ones. New industries came under enormous pressure to organize, and bitter resistance to such organization also arose. But even more, the automobile speeded up urbanization and urban sprawl. It changed family relations as it opened up new opportunities for young people to break away from family supervision. It changed community relations as cities sprawled and highways spread everywhere. It changed taxes and expenditures of states, counties, and municipalities. It raised up Texas oil tycoons and the politicians that oil money put in office. It pulled down other tycoons and the politicians they had put in office.

Evolution in major classes involves far more than changes in the number of families with incomes falling within certain statistical intervals. It involves changes in basic institutional structure and technology (see also Tool 1979; Peterson 1994).

Bibliography

Arnold, Thurman. 1937. *The Folklore of Capitalism.* New Haven: Yale University Press.

Ayres, Clarence E. 1978. *The Theory of Economic Progress.* 3rd ed. Kalamazoo: New Issues Press of Western Michigan University.

Berle, Adolf A., and Gardiner C. Means. 1968. *The Modern Corporation and Private Property.* Rev. ed. New York: Harcourt, Brace & World.

Commons, John R. 1968. *Legal Foundations of Capitalism.* Madison: University of Wisconsin Press.

Dugger, William M. 1980. "Property Rights, Law, and John R. Commons." *Review of Social Economy* 38 (April): 41–53.

———. 1988. "Radical Institutionalism: Basic Concepts." *Review of Radical Political Economics* 20 (Spring): 1–20.

———, ed. 1989a. *Radical Institutionalism.* Westport, CT: Greenwood Press.

———. 1989b. *Corporate Hegemony.* Westport, CT: Greenwood Press.

———. 1992. "The Great Retrenchment and the New Industrial State," *Review of Social Economy* 50 (Winter): 453–71.

———, ed. 1996. *Inequality: Radical Institutionalist Views on Race, Gender, Class, and Nation.* Westport, CT: Greenwood Press.

———. 1998. "Against Inequality." *Journal of Economic Issues* 32 (June): 1–17.

Dugger, William M., and Howard J. Sherman. 1994. "Marxism and Institutionalism Compared." *Journal of Economic Issues* 28 (March): 101–127.

———. 1997. "Institutionalist and Marxist Theories of Evolution." *Journal of Economic Issues* 31 (December): 991–1009.

Fusfeld, Daniel R. 1972. "The Rise of the Corporate State in America." *Journal of Economic Issues* 6 (March): 1–22.

———. 1977. "The Development of Economic Institutions." *Journal of Economic Issues* 11 (December): 743–84.

Galbraith, John Kenneth. 1967. *The New Industrial State.* Boston: Houghton Mifflin.

———. 1970. "Economics as a System of Belief." *American Economic Review* 60 (May): 469–478.

———. 1973. "Power and the Useful Economist." *American Economic Review* 63 (March): 1–11.

———. 1992. *The Culture of Contentment.* Boston: Houghton Mifflin.

Hunt, E.K. 1979. "The Importance of Thorstein Veblen for Contemporary Marxism." *Journal of Economic Issues* 13 (March): 113–140.

Peterson, Wallace C. 1994. *Silent Depression.* New York: W.W. Norton.

Schumpeter, Joseph A. 1961. *The Theory of Economic Development.* Oxford: Oxford University Press.

Stanfield, James Ronald. 1995. *Economics, Power and Culture.* New York: St. Martin's Press.

Strobel, Frederick R., and Wallace C. Peterson. 1997. "Class Conflict, American Style: Distract and Conquer." *Journal of Economic Issues* 31 (June): 433–443.

Thompson, E.P. 1966. *The Making of the English Working Class.* New York: Vintage Books.

Tool, Marc R. 1979. *The Discretionary Economy.* Santa Monica: Goodyear.

Tool, Marc R., and Warren J. Samuels, eds. 1989. *State, Society, and Corporate Power*, 2d ed. New Brunswick: Transaction.

Veblen, Thorstein. 1964. *Absentee Ownership and Business Enterprise in Recent Times.* New York: Augustus M. Kelley.

———. 1965. *The Engineers and the Price System.* New York: Augustus M. Kelley.

———. 1975. *The Theory of the Leisure Class.* New York: Augustus M. Kelley.

6

Class and Evolution

A Marxian View

Howard J. Sherman

Social scientists using an individualist approach—plus almost all popular references to class—define class in terms of the attributes of an individual. How much wealth does the individual own? What is the individual's income? What is the individual's status and prestige?

Marx always insists that class is a relationship, not an individual attribute. Marx asks, Which group works and which group profits? Which group exploits other groups, and which group is exploited by other groups? What is the relationship between the worker and the capitalist in the productive process? Capitalists are defined as a group of people who own the means of production and appropriate profit from workers. Workers are defined as people who own little or none of the means of production and work for capitalists to earn their income.

In the individualist view, there is a smooth spectrum from individuals in the lower, lower class to those in the upper, upper class, defined by such things as less money or more money, less status or more status. But in the Marxian view, in which classes are defined by their relation to others, there is a discontinuity: capitalists do not simply have a little more money than workers do; they own capital and exploit workers. Thus, in the individualist view there is no room for conflict between classes—because they are composed of individuals who succeed or not only as individuals, while in the Marxian view classes may have opposing interests.

Only in abstract models do we find pure classes, such that every individual exactly meets the definition. In reality, some workers own tiny amounts of stock, while some capitalists also do managerial work. Therefore, members of classes must be defined by the source of most of their income, not all of their income.

Marx's enemies always assume that he thinks there are only two classes in every society—a ruling, exploiting class and a ruled, exploited class. Although Marx used a simple two-class model in some parts of volume 1 of *Capital*, where many classes were an unnecessary complication to his argument, Marx was perfectly clear that this was a simplification of reality: "The actual composition of society . . . by no means consists of only two classes, workers and industrial capitalists" (Marx 1967, 493).

Is there a middle class? This is a very controversial issue within Marxism. There are obviously

For a more extensive analysis of the issues in this chapter, see Sherman 1995.

many people with incomes in the middle of the spectrum, but that does not fit the Marxian definition of a class. More seriously, there are strata of the working class, such as managerial workers and professional workers, who are like other workers in some respects, but unlike other workers in other respects. The capitalist firm pays managerial and professional workers for their work in the same way that other workers get paid. But they are different in that they have far more independence, they often issue commands to other workers, and they get many types of benefits that ordinary workers do not get. So their relationships are complex and often ambiguous—and they might be called a new middle class.

For a complete understanding of the middle class in the United States, Marxist class analysis encourages the formidable task of tracing it historically in all of its changes. Thus, at one time the middle class consisted of independent farmers and small craftspeople. Now the bulk of it can probably be described as lower-level managers and professionals. (See Sherman 1995, ch. 6, for the Marxian literature on class.)

Levels of Class Conflict

Most Marxists, using the class relations approach, argue that it is wrong to speak as if one only had to pay attention to the economic level of class conflict (Wright 1985, ch. 1; Wolff and Resnick 1986). Most Marxists have focused on three different levels of class conflict (Sherman 1995, ch. 6). First, there has always been a Marxist literature, often in great depth, on the economics level of strife in production (Marx 1967). Thus, there is an enormous theoretical literature on exactly how workers are exploited by capitalists in the production process (Sweezy 1942; Sherman 1995, ch. 7). In addition, there have been numerous descriptions of the history of trade unions in the United States, the analysis of particular strikes, and the analysis of the overall pattern of strikes in relation to economic circumstances (Foner 1947, 1955, 1964, 1965).

Second, Marxists have analyzed class conflict at the political level (Miliband 1991). There has been controversy over how much the political level reflects the economic level and how much it is autonomous. There has also been a lengthy controversy over whether the ruling class rules directly through representatives in every branch of government (plus all those who agree with them through ideology or bribes) versus the structural notion that even progressive lawmakers (and unions) are forced to support corporations in many ways in order to protect jobs within the system. (See Miliband 1973, 1991, and Bowles and Gintis 1986, for a description of the literature.)

Third, there is class conflict at the level of ideology. For example, there are conservatives who claim that all inequality is due to differences in intelligence. This argument implies that the working class is stupider than the capitalist class and therefore deserves less income. This is a prime example of false ideology.

Marxists have long argued over the exact importance of ideological class conflict. Some Communist parties spent most of their resources on ideological class conflict, but denied its importance by saying that socialism is the inevitable result of purely economic factors. Other Marxists have concentrated on nothing but the development of class ideology, with little or no attention to the political-economic circumstances. Most contemporary Marxists would agree on the importance of all three levels of class conflict, though their own research might focus mostly on just one level.

There is nothing in contemporary Marxism that says that class conflict is the only conflict or even that it is always the most important. Class relations and class conflict are considered the best beginning point to understand the structure of any class-divided society. Without understanding the social and economic process of a society, one cannot understand race, gender, or nationality within it. Having found and examined class conflicts, however, the critical method of Marxism insists that one must then also study racial, gender, and nationality conflicts. The Marxian relational method sees all of society as a set of unified relationships. (See Sherman 1995, ch. 3, for an extensive discussion of the literature on this point.) Since society is a unified organism, one must examine how race, gender, and nationality conflicts are affected by class conflict, but one must also examine how class conflict is affected by race, gender, and nationality conflicts. Only a unified picture of these interpenetrating conflicts can give us an undistorted analysis.

Class conflict frequently prevents progress, when the ruling class finds that reform is not to its liking. In the United States, a clear example of this is found in looking at how economic interests fought over the issue of health care in the media and political arena. How U.S. health care reflects U. S. class interests has been detailed in a book by Dr. Vicente Navarro (Navarro 1993). Navarro finds that the United States spends the highest proportion of gross national product of any country in the world on health care, 14 percent in his data (Navarro 1993, 15). Yet the United States does not provide good health care to its citizens, since 17 percent of the population have no health care benefits (1993, 15). If someone was really sick for a long time, the cost of long-run health care was over $27,000 a year, while the median income was only $30,000 (1993, 16). The problem is that most people have very little power, while those with power have very little interest in extending health care to everyone. The people without health care are poorly paid workers and the unemployed with little economic power and little political power. The control by the wealthy is exercised in many ways, including financing candidates and parties, lobbying, controlling the media, considerable control of education, and so forth. Those same wealthy individuals and corporations that exercise political power over health care legislation also receive immense profits from health care, and wealthy individuals hold 70 percent of the directorships on health care institutions (Navarro 1993, 28).

How Classes Are Reproduced

The average person born into the working class never has much savings. Therefore, he or she can never become a capitalist with significant ownership of corporate stock. So the average worker must remain a worker because he/she has no opportunity to become a capitalist. The average capitalist inherits a significant amount of ownership of capital. Moreover, the average capitalist family can afford to help its children get a good education. Therefore, with significant initial capital and good training, the child of capitalists can remain a capitalist by getting an average profit on capital plus an average managerial salary.

Variety and Change in Class Structure

When a class structure has reproduced itself for centuries, when the ruling class has created an ideology that has been dominant for centuries, when certain institutions have upheld the status quo for centuries, why would all of this ever change? What usually happens is that the march of technology—be it infinitely slow or very rapid—eventually undermines and changes the old class structure, producing new classes that eventually change the institutions of society.

Why does technological change occur? Technological change is not God given nor is it external to a society. There have been many societies in which, because of the socioeconomic structure, stagnation has been the rule for centuries. Technological change was extremely slow in feudal Europe. Yet there was enough change that it eventually led to the emergence of new classes and to revolutionary changes in society.

Marx himself, and many Marxian historians since him, have spelled out how this change occurred. (See, for example, the debate on the Brenner hypothesis in Ashton and Philpin 1985.) Here, only the main issues can be listed. For one thing, better agricultural technology, introduced over a long period of time, led to agricultural surpluses. The surpluses were sold for other needed items. A class of merchants grew up to facilitate these early market exchanges. Slowly, marketplaces were created, which became villages, then small towns, and then cities. Within the villages lived craftspeople as well as merchants. They produced many necessary goods and exchanged them for the agricultural surplus. Feudal estates had consisted of lords and serfs; now there were also merchants and craftspeople who did not fit so easily within the feudal model and whose interests were often opposed to those of the feudal lords. Eventually, in a lengthy process, feudalism was replaced by capitalism.

Under capitalism, technology advanced rapidly at certain times and places. But the rapid improvement of technology undermines existing institutions and class relationships. For example, computers have changed the workplace, changed the relations of bosses and workers, changed the course of various industries, and changed which industries are dominant. As another example, in the mid-nineteenth century most people in the United States were still small farmers self-employed. As a result of technological change, by the mid-twentieth century most people were workers, employed by capitalist industrial and service firms. The result has been a complete change in class relations and relative class power.

The change in the United States from an agricultural to an industrial nation was evident by the time of the Civil War. At that time, the ascension of Northern industry to a greater economic power than Southern slave plantations was apparent. This change was reflected in the politics of the time and then in the Civil War and the eventual eradication of the slave-owning class. It might be said that a change in technology—the industrial revolution in the United States—eventually caused a change in class relations, via the Civil War.

What Does Class Conflict Have to Do with Evolution?

Marx says that the history of all preceding societies is the history of class struggle. Yet Marx also says that revolutionary change comes about when the forces of production are held back by the relations of production. So is evolution caused by the class struggle or is it caused by the tension or lag between forces and relations?

In Marx's mind, there is no logical contradiction here, but a sequence. First, it is a necessary condition of major historical evolutionary changes that there be a tension or lag between frozen class relations of production and the potential for improvement in the productive forces. Marx defines the relations of production to be the relationships of classes in the economy. Marx defines the forces of production to be land (and resources), labor, capital, and technology—of which technology is the factor that sometimes changes in a dramatic fashion.

Marx sees a lag between the rapid advance of technology and the glacial pace of change in basic institutions and class relations. This lag or tension may show up as stagnation, depression, or many other types of economic crisis. Such an economic crisis may (but does not necessarily) lead to intensification of class conflict. An intensified class conflict may (but does not necessarily) lead to social evolution—in the shape of reform or revolution. The lag between revolutionary changes in the productive forces and frozen laws of private property has been evident in the computer era. We keep having revolutions in the information technology available, but each revolution causes a crisis because it causes situations not previously foreseen by the legal system of capitalist states. One example of this process is the problem of introducing high-resolution television in the United States, which has been tossed around politically for some time. The new technology cannot be used over the present television stations, but ownership of television stations is an incredible source of wealth and power. Since the government owns the franchises to new channels, the public should be paid large sums of money by private capitalists for the privilege of using the new channels. After long negotiations, the problem was resolved in favor of the special interests by giving the new channels for free to the owners of the present channels. Thus, crises within the capitalist system caused by new technology are generally solved by benefiting the capitalist class (or some part thereof) and harming the working class as workers, consumers, or taxpayers.

A classic example of the lag between the productive forces and the class relations was the Great Depression. In the neoclassical view, there is no involuntary unemployment and the system only declines because of outside shocks. But post-Keynesians, institutionalists, and Marxists are all agreed that it is the institutions of capitalism that give rise to depressions and recessions. The institutionalist Wesley Mitchell showed how each stage of the capitalist business cycle derives from the dynamics of the previous stage (Mitchell 1941, 1989). John Maynard Keynes (1936) and Karl Marx both showed that aggregate demand may be well below aggregate supply, causing a depression, as a result of the internal dynamics of capitalism. (See detailed discussion and citations in Sherman 1967.)

Why is there a deficiency of aggregate demand? Marx explains aggregate demand in terms of class income, workers wages versus capitalist profit. The ratio of consumption out of profits is far lower than consumption out of wages because capitalists have far higher incomes and can use much of them to save and perhaps to invest. Thus the structure of class relationships and the power of opposing classes will determine aggregate demand. In every capitalist expansion, as productivity rises, the additional surplus automatically goes to the capitalist under the rules of private property. Workers are always playing catch-up by negotiation or strikes. Thus the ratio of wages to profits declines in every expansion, causing aggregate demand to be limited. This is one cause of economic crises. Such a condition did exist in the late 1920s and was a major cause of the Great Depression. One may conclude that the Great Depression was caused by the class relations of capitalism holding back the forces of production, causing unemployment and lower and lower capacity utilization.

This condition gave rise to intensified class conflict. Capitalists tried to speed up production to keep profits high. Workers went out on strike for livable wages. Workers organized in new, more militant labor unions. Millions of workers went to the polls to elect a very liberal Congress, with large increases in the Socialist and Communist votes. This high level of class conflict eventually led to major reforms in the United States (such as unemployment compensation and Social Security), but it resulted in fascism in Germany. So reforms as well as revolutions are caused by the lag between the productive forces and class relations. Existing class relations are defended to the last drop of blood by those who benefit from them (such as the slave owners in the U.S. Civil War). Those who are harmed by the existing class relations may fight to change them if the situation becomes unacceptable (such as the Northern industrialists in the U.S. Civil War). Such a situation leads to evolution, which may be reforms (the New Deal), revolutionary change (the Civil War), or retrogression (fascist Germany).

We may generalize the process as follows: (1) certain class relations may become obstacles to further technological advance; (2) this leads in complex ways to class conflict between those who defend the old system and those who might benefit from a new system; (3) after various struggles caused by the impasse of the old system, a new system may arise with higher productivity (though retrogression is also possible).

Of course, it is also possible that external enemies may simply destroy that particular civilization. Instead of change to a more productive economy, the existing one may be destroyed without any substitute. (This happened to some degree with the devastation caused by the Mongols during their period of expansion.) Either evolution of technology—or stagnation preventing technological improvement—must eventually lead to class conflicts, but unfortunately this conflict is not guaranteed to result in technological or institutional progress, it is only guaranteed to cause change.

This chapter has attempted to show that class is a powerful weapon if it is defined in a nonindividualist and historical way. Looking at class as a relationship between exploiting and exploited groups, it was shown how this relationship is usually reproduced year after year. It was also shown, however, that new technology under capitalism may cause major frictions between classes. These frictions may lead to institutional change. Thus, past evolution has been the result of class conflict, and future institutional evolution is possible. So the theory shows the possibility of the end of capitalism and a better, democratic socialist society, but there is no guarantee of such a result, only a possibility.

Bibliography

Ashton, T. H., and C. H. E. Philpin, eds. 1985. *The Brenner Debate: Class Structure and Economic Development in Pre-Industrial Europe*. New York: Cambridge University Press.

Bowles, Samuel, and Herbert Gintis. 1986. *Democracy and Capitalism.* New York: Basic Books.

Foner, Phillip S. 1947, 1955, 1964, 1965. *History of the Labor Movement in the United States.* Volumes 1–4. New York: International.

Keynes, John Maynard. 1936. *The General Theory of Employment, Interest, and Money.* New York: Harcourt Brace.

Marx, Karl. 1967. [1867]. *Capital.* Volume 1. New York: International.

Miliband, Ralph. 1973. "Poulantzas and the Capitalist State," *New Left Review* 82: 83–92.

———. 1991. *Divided Societies: Class Struggle in Contemporary Capitalism.* New York: Oxford University Press.

Mitchell, Wesley Clair. 1941, 1989. *Business Cycles and Their Causes.* Philadelphia: Porcupine Press.

Navarro, Vicente. 1993. *Dangerous to Your Health.* New York: Monthly Review Press.

Sherman, Howard J. 1967. "Marx and the Business Cycle," *Science and Society* 31 (Fall): 484–504.

———. 1987. *Foundations of Radical Political Economy.* Armonk, NY: M.E. Sharpe.

———. 1995. *Reinventing Marxism.* Baltimore: Johns Hopkins University Press.

Sweezy, Paul. 1942, 1958. *The Theory of Capitalist Development.* New York: Monthly Review Press.

Wolff, Richard, and Stephen Resnick. 1986. "Power, Property, and Class," *Socialist Review* 16, no. 86 (March-April): 97–124.

Wright, Eric Olin. 1985. *Classes.* New York: Verso.

7

Beyond Racist Capitalist Patriarchal Economics

Growing a Liberated Economy

Julie Matthaei

While radical economists have had an excellent critique of capitalism for years, the revolution that we have advocated toward a postcapitalist socialist feminist antiracist economy seems to be slipping further and further out of reach. In this chapter, I will examine some problems with current progressive organizing, as informed and inspired by radical political economic analysis. Then I will suggest an alternative, radical view of our economy and its problems. Finally, I will discuss current developments that could provide the basis for an emergent, liberatory economy.

Problems with Single- and Multi-Issue Radical Analysis and Organizing

Most if not all "radical economists" have used Marx's economic analysis, particularly his analysis of class, exploitation, and accumulation in capitalism, as their starting point. Marx's theoretical framework is full of insights, and provides a far superior starting point for economic analysis than does neoclassical theory (Matthaei 1996). However, it ignores other forms of oppression endemic to capitalism—sexism, racism, and heterosexism—as well as capitalism's destructive and life-endangering relationship to the environment. In particular, Marx's analysis of class is problematic because it ignores the fact that workplaces are places in which gender and racial-ethnic oppression also operate, both between capitalists and workers, and among workers struggling to survive and better themselves (Amott and Matthaei 1996).

The past thirty-plus years of progressive economic analysis—as well as the emergence of vibrant feminist, antiracist, lesbian and gay, and ecological movements—have helped enrich and expand the Marxist framework. A "radical economic" analysis has been developed that takes into account race, class, gender, environmental destruction, and even sexuality. This complicated analysis of racist capitalist patriarchy is a great analytical achievement.

However, the development of multipronged progressive analysis has not ushered in a new, stron-

This chapter is based on a paper I wrote with Teresa Amott, "Global Capitalism, Difference, and Women's Liberation: Towards a Liberated Economy." It was presented in April 1997 at the Southeast Women's Studies Association Meetings in Athens, Georgia.

ger wave of radical organizing. Why this is the case is *the* important question for progressive activists as the third millennium approaches. Obviously, there is the ideological and political power of the mainstream establishment. But there are also weaknesses in radical theorizing and organizing that bear examining.

One obvious problem with multidimensional, multi-issue analysis—especially analysis of race, class, gender, and sexuality—is that, in highlighting differences and unequal relationships among people, it tends to lead to political fragmentation and infighting. This fact led Marxists in the early seventies to criticize the emergence of Marxist-feminist theory and organizing out of the fear that, by setting women against men, it would split the movement for socialism and weaken it. "Wait until after the Revolution," Marxist men told aspiring Marxist-feminists. However, their suggested solution for political fragmentation—ignoring racism and sexism—is not the answer either (Matthaei 1996). Experience has shown that single-issue organizing results in worker movements that are sexist and racist, women's movements that are classist and racist, antiracist movements that are sexist and classist, and so forth. Not only are such movements often reactionary in their results, they also alienate potential members who are not of the majority group.

The answer that hyphenated progressives (Marxist-feminist-antiracist-antihomophobic-ecological) have always given to this dilemma is that progressives need to encourage people to fight not only against their own oppression(s), but against all forms of oppression. This is true not only because one needs the support of others who are different to be able to organize effectively for social change (i.e., in order to build effective coalitions), but also because one cannot be a true progressive if one does not actively oppose all forms of oppression. However, in reality, it is difficult to create movements that live out these principles. In a society where our survival is often threatened, the pull of self-interest often draws us away from solidarity with the struggles of others. And it is also difficult to transcend the racist, sexist, classist, homophobic conditioning that has enveloped us since birth, as well as the well-founded mistrust we have of those from privileged groups.

The concrete difficulty of sustaining truly multi-issue organizing among workers, feminists, antiracists, and lesbians/gays has led to the predominance, within these movements, of single-issue "identity politics." For this reason, while these movements have achieved major victories, they have been essentially reformist vis-à-vis capitalism's basic economic institutions. So, for example, the "liberation" of Blacks or women is equated with the absence of discrimination in the labor market and evidenced by the advancement of women and/or Blacks up the corporate managerial hierarchy. Meanwhile, in spite of its new emphasis on organizing women and people of color, the labor movement continues to fall into the trap of protecting one group of workers at the expense of others—be they "scabs" or foreign workers—rather than challenging the private ownership of capital and existence of a reserve army of the unemployed.

The Need for a New Discourse of Liberation

What can be done? The solution to this puzzle is to shift the discourse of liberation. The radical analysis of multiple oppressions, while insightful, incorporates problematic aspects of our racist capitalist patriarchal homophobic economy. Most important, it posits social life as a competition between different groups, and views the solution to the past domination of one group by the other as the organizing of the oppressed group against the oppressor. While this is a meaningful view of liberation on a very abstract level, when applied concretely it tends to collapse into a reformist, quantitative critique of income and wealth inequality that leaves basic economic institutions untouched. "The problem" gets defined as the lower incomes and earnings, and higher poverty rates, of workers, women, and people of color. "The solution" then becomes the redistribution of jobs and income (or even of unpaid work) across races, genders, or classes, to be achieved through organizing to influence the state. The goal becomes the improvement of the oppressed group's average position in the economy, through the advancement of more of its members up the hierarchy of income and wealth.

Solidarity or no solidarity, in an economy that structures work hierarchically, generates a reserve army, and does not pay housework, the gains of the "oppressed" do come directly at the expense of those who were privileged, in the form of a lost monopoly on higher paid jobs, higher unemployment risk, and so on. If one accepts the basic economic rules, as these movements have, the economy is essentially a zero-sum game—what I win, you lose. The system and its basic institutions stay the same as we fight each other for a bigger piece of the pie: women versus men; whites versus Blacks versus Puerto Ricans versus Chicanos; gays versus straights. The union movement, always viewed as somehow more "politically correct" by the left, is equally problematic, since one group of striking workers' gains are as likely to be at the expense of another group of less privileged workers as at the expense of capitalists. Essentially, then, we could see this stage of political organizing as an intensification of the competition between workers that has characterized our capitalist economy since its inception. In a sense, women and people of color are fighting for acceptance as "equal competitors" in the labor market or for a bigger chunk of a shrinking welfare pie; and workers are fighting for jobs and higher wages at the expense of other workers, not just of capitalists.

So one can see how easily "radical" discourse collapses into an argument for getting more within the system, and can hence be co-opted. That vulnerability to co-optation is tied to a tendency to view groups of people rather than institutions as the enemy—as well as to a tendency to view oppression and liberation in quantitative rather than qualitative terms. This tendency is endemic in society, and in the writings of economists, including Marx, who specifically focused on economic exploitation (the quantitative process of the extraction of surplus value) rather than on alienation (the worker's qualitative experience of powerlessness and separation from other workers and from his or her product).

What about Marxist and radical economists' advocacy for revolution, for replacing capitalism with socialism? The socialist project has never garnered strong support among workers in the United States, or in most other developed countries—not to mention women and people of color. As pointed out by many analysts, this is partly because white male Western workers have been privileged, both vis-à-vis the rest of the world, and vis-à-vis the women and people of color in their own countries. These privileges have led them to support racist capitalist patriarchy rather than to oppose it. Moreover, socialist movements have never directly and consistently addressed the concerns that have been raised by the broad-based activist movements of the second half of this century—feminism, antiracism, gay liberation, and the ecology movement (Laclau and Mouffe 1985).

The problem with Marxist theory is that it has not yet been radical enough. It provided a critique of capitalism that ignored other key problems in that system. Its notion of progressive politics as struggle against the oppressive group has been adopted by antiracist and feminist movements, but it has taken on the bourgeois form of a struggle for more pay. Current market socialist models generated in the West redistribute profits, or even offer workers ownership of their firms (Nove 1983; Roemer 1994). But this leaves unaddressed other oppressive aspects of the economy, particularly its core components of hierarchy and competition, its focus on material fulfillment, and its devaluation of housework, not to mention sexism and racism. The participatory economic model of Michael Albert and Robin Hahnel (1991) goes further in its creation of a participatory, cooperative economy, but does not mention masculinity or violence, nor provide a solution for the child-care issue or a feasible path to get from here to there.

The shift in discourse necessary at this historical moment is to move from the critique of racial, gender, or class inequality to a critique of hierarchy, competition, and violence per se. Class alone is not the problem: hierarchy, competition, and violence as the core of social practices and institutions—be they war-making, capital accumulation, breadwinning, consumerism, or the devaluation of child-rearing—are. One must critique the ideology of racist capitalist patriarchy: the whole notion, taken for granted in our society and in mainstream economics, that people are naturally self-interested, competitive, and warlike, and hence only productive when tamed by the "invisible hand of the market." This view of "human nature" leads us to accept hierarchy, competition, violence, and the subordination of the feminine and of "nature" and of other groups of people as inevitable. The reality is that the well-being of the individual is integrally dependent upon the well-being of other human beings; on being part of a healthy, loving community of individuals; and on a healthy ecology of interdependent relationships between different life forms. And it has become increasingly clear that basing our economy and society on narrow notions of self-seeking as the pursuit of profits or economic advancement is destructive to this well-being, not just for women and racial and sexual minorities.

When one enters into this new discourse, not of "us against them," but of "us against hierarchy, competition, and violence," other systematic problems appear, problems that can generate broad-based movements across the dividing lines of race, class, gender, and sexuality. Alienation and the lack of democracy in the workplace are endured by almost all who are employed, even at high managerial levels. The degradation of the environment, and the resulting threat to physical, mental, and spiritual health and perhaps to life itself, is certainly a shared problem, even if its effects are suffered unequally depending on one's race, class, or gender. Certainly other problems endemic to our economy bear pointing out: pervasive economic insecurity (due to the threat of job loss or disability); high levels of violence and physical insecurity; the breakdown of community and family ties (and the resultant sense of social isolation and alienation); feelings of deprivation in the midst of plenty (due to advertising and "consumerism"); and a sense of spiritual emptiness, of a lack of meaning in one's life. While radical analysts have addressed these concerns in the past, they have been downplayed in a radical discourse focused on division and opposition between social groups.

The Emergent Liberated Economy

When one shifts the radical discourse in this way, a myriad of radical initiatives come into focus that are in the process of constructing countercultures, new ways of living and working that involve a new system of values (Brandt 1995). These countercultures have been emergent in the United States for almost forty years and involve, at their essences, a variety of emergent alternative, liberatory economic values and practices. They include: (1) the structuring of institutions based on mutuality and egalitarian cooperation, rather than hierarchy, competition, and violence; (2) an awareness of one's connectedness to others, including the importance of healthy, mutually supportive relationships with the members of one's family and community, and with other species; (3) a focus on the soul and on spiritual fulfillment rather than on money, power over others, and consumption as the goal in life; (4) the use of therapy to retrieve one's emotions and "true self" (Miller 1981) and of new methods of child-rearing and education that preserve the feelings and self of the child, and that teach children to cooperate, "use their words" instead of violence, and accept difference without turning it into hierarchy. Individual goals in the larger world of work are shifting from the pursuit of money and power in the service of corporations to finding ways to contribute, through one's energies and creativities, to the sustenance of life in all its forms, and to the evolution of our economy and society.

A key aspect of the shift away from capitalism and toward a liberated economy is the disengagement from capitalist culture's obsession with material consumption, with things (and with having more than others), in favor of life-centered, liberatory values. This shift is beginning in the United States in the form of the "downshifting" and "voluntary simplicity" movements (Elgin 1993; Schor 1991 and 1998). These movements reject the notion—key to capitalism and to mainstream economic analysis—that people can find true fulfillment through the ever-greater individual consumption of goods and services, that is, that the consumption of commodities can provide our lives with meaning. They also reflect the belief that the affluent individuals and nations must reduce their consumption of the world's resources to more proportionate levels (Mies and Shiva 1993, ch. 17), and that resources must be used, first and foremost, to ensure that the basic needs of all people are met. The more people can disengage from capitalist consumerism and instead simplify their consumption, the more they are freed from dependence on corporations as a source of income and the more time they will have to spend in constructive and meaningful social activities (Dominguez and Robin 1992). This rejection of consumerism is part and parcel of the evolving ecology movement—for it allows for an economy based on a relationship of coexistence and communion with nature, rather than on the consumption and destruction of it (Daly 1980).

As people begin to shift their values from materialistic, consumption-centered ones to socially responsible, liberatory ones, these values are beginning to be infused back into economic institutions, particularly into the realms of production and employment, currently monopolized by capitalist firms bent on the pursuit of profit. This infusion is occurring in three areas, which I will discuss in turn: cooperative firms, consumer movements, and investment movements.

Since the rise of capitalism, progressives have experimented with a form of the firm that was free of worker exploitation—the cooperative. The basic rules of the world capitalist economy—private property and exchange—allow for the construction of these progressive firms alongside capitalist ones. Cooperatives are owned by their workers, who elect or hire managers to help coordinate their activities. The workers then accrue whatever profits are earned. The most successful current group of cooperatives at present is probably the Mondragón complex in the Basque region of Spain, which is made up of an interconnected economy of over one hundred industrial cooperatives, as well as numerous associated "second-degree" cooperatives, including schools, day-care centers, supermarkets, hospitals, and so on (Morrison 1991). A number of successful cooperatives exist in the United States today (Krimerman and Lindenfeld 1992; Brandt 1995, ch. 11).[1]

Because workers run these cooperatives themselves, they are able to shape production around goals other than growth and profits, such as decent wages, safe working conditions, secure employment, worker training, and minimization of hierarchies among workers. At Mondragón, for example, cooperatives established a maximum three-to-one ratio between the highest and lowest earning workers. However, the ability of worker-run cooperatives to take on goals other than profit maximization and growth is limited by the fact that they compete for consumers in markets against capitalist-run firms. Thus, for example, worker cooperatives' commitment to job security disadvantages them vis-à-vis capitalist firms in periods of economic downturn, when the latter can cut costs by laying off or firing workers.

The growth of cooperatives is being aided by the burgeoning movement for socially responsible consumption. Consumer movements have worked to humanize capitalism since the end of the nineteenth century (Matthaei 1982, ch. 8). Such movements help consumers use their combined purchasing power to pressure firms to better fill their needs. In the emergent, liberatory economy, a variety of movements organize their members to support, through targeted consumption, those firms that serve the movement's goals—such as recycling, fair treatment of workers, empowerment of women workers, protection of the environment, nonabuse of animals. Members are also encouraged to boycott those firms whose products or practices they find problematic. Because these movements organize consumers to choose products on criteria other than simply the competitiveness of the price, they in turn motivate firms to organize their production around goals other than simple cost minimization/profit maximization. Thus consumers, powerless as individuals against capitalist firms, are able, in groups, to put into practice their concerns for liberatory economic principles. The bigger the group, the more the power—the consumer sovereignty that mainstream economics makes so much of can actually be exercised! The power of this movement is already evident in the growing number of firms, both traditional and alternative, that advertise their products as "green" or environmentally friendly.

Co-Op America, for example, is an organization that sees itself as a "crucial link between active consumers and an economy based on cooperation, a concern for the environment, and social justice." It provides its members with the *National Green Pages*, listing "Green Businesses" — including "worker-owned companies" and environmentally friendly "producers of energy-efficient and non-toxic products."[2]

Such consumer groups can be expected to grow in strength as we enter the third millennium, organizing consumers into a powerful feminist, antiracist, ecological, procooperative force that can both pressure traditional firms to be more socially responsible, and support the development of truly liberatory firms. Such firms would have egalitarian and cooperative work structures that counter gender, racial-ethnic, and class inequality—either by creating diverse workplaces without traditional hierarchies, or by bringing together marginalized workers in empowering partnerships. They would offer paid maternity/paternity leaves, shorter workweeks with full benefits, and flexible hours and work location arrangements. They would offer products (films, books, computer games, clothes) that are feminist, pacifist, ecological, and multicultural in content. Their products would be durable, and easy to maintain and repair (reducing housework and waste). They would be willing to give some of their revenues to the creation of an alternative social safety net, and to work to extend this safety net throughout the world. We can imagine that more and more retail stores will begin to crop up that specialize in delivering the products of such firms to progressive consumers.

A key issue in growing such a liberated economy is the need for investable funds. The capitalist world economy is full of workers who are either unemployed, underemployed, or unhappy with their jobs who would be more than willing to join liberated worker cooperatives if offered the chance. But new firms require funds to begin and expand operations. Sources of such funds are already present in the contemporary movement for "socially responsible investing"—a movement organizing people and institutions to invest their savings, their wealth, their pension funds in firms that behave in a more socially responsible manner than the traditional capitalist firm (Hutton, D'Antonio, and Johnsen 1998). There are already a number of banks and mutual funds that specialize in socially responsible investing.[3] Such financial institutions need to grow and develop commercial banks at which progressives can place their checking and saving accounts. Then such institutions can provide the seed money that workers can use to start up liberatory firms, harnessing the power of progressives' savings toward the development of a liberated economy. These financial institutions can also join other emerging institutions to provide technical assistance such as market studies and training to workers seeking to join new cooperatives.

Lest this appear to be a complete pipe dream, the Mondragón complex in Spain was able to take off because it started a people's bank to which most of the community switched their bank accounts, and then used these funds to finance their first cooperative. At present, the Mondragón complex includes a technical cooperative whose job it is to help start new cooperatives—from finding a marketable product, to designing the plant, to hiring and training the workers. With this technical support, not one of the cooperatives they have launched has ever failed (Morrison 1991). Communities all over the world can follow in the footsteps of Mondragón and harness progressives' funds toward the provision of jobs in this way, creating a way to grow, not through exploitation and accumulation, but by drawing consumers and workers and investors to a higher form of economic life.

The task now for progressives of all kinds is to put forth and advocate for a coherent set of alternative, liberatory values, and to challenge ourselves and others to work to live up to them in our economic lives. At the same time, we must work to make visible the emergent, liberatory economy, and to strengthen and link its consumer, worker, and investor institutions to one another, across the various constituency and issue groups, and across countries. In this way, progressives can help to evolve the global economy to a higher stage in which the human potential to cooperate creatively across differences and to live in security and harmony with one another and nature can be realized.

Notes

1. See *GEO Grassroots Economic Organizing Newsletter* (RR1, Box 124A, Stillwater, PA 17878) for ongoing discussion of the developing cooperative movement worldwide.

2. Quotes are from an undated letter to Co-op members. Co-Op America can be reached at 1612 K Street NW, Suite 600, Washington, DC 20006; (202) 872–5307.

3. Visit Co-op America's Web site at www.socialinvest.org for information on various socially responsible investments.

References

Albert, Michael, and Robin Hahnel. 1991. *Looking Forward: Participatory Economics for the Twenty First Century*. Boston: South End Press.

Amott, Teresa, and Julie Matthaei. 1996. *Race, Gender and Work: A Multicultural History of Women in the United States*. Rev. ed. Boston: South End Press.

Brandt, Barbara. 1995. *Whole Life Economics: Revaluing Daily Life*. Philadelphia: New Society.

Daly, Herman. 1980. "Introduction to Steady State Economics." In *Economics, Ecology, and Ethics: Essays Toward a Steady-State Economy*, ed. Daly. San Francisco: W.H. Freeman.

Dominguez, Joe, and Vicki Robin. 1992. *Your Money or Your Life: Transforming Your Relationship with Money and Achieving Financial Independence*. New York: Penguin Books.

Elgin, Duane. 1993. *Voluntary Simplicity: Toward a Way of Life That Is Outwardly Simple, Inwardly Rich*. New York: Quill.

Hutton, Bruce, Louis D'Antonio, and Tommi Johnsen. 1998. "Socially Responsible Investing: Growing Issues and New Opportunities." *Business and Society* 37, no. 3: 281–292.

Krimerman, Len, and Frank Lindenfeld, eds. 1992. *When Workers Decide: Workplace Democracy Takes Root in North America*. Philadelphia: New Society.

Laclau, Ernesto, and Chantal Mouffe. 1985. *Hegemony and Socialist Strategy*. London: Verso.

Matthaei, Julie. 1982. *An Economic History of Women in America: Women's Work, the Sexual Division of Labor, and the Development of Capitalism*. New York: Schocken Books.

———. 1996. "Why Feminist, Marxist and Anti-Racist Economists Should be Feminist-Marxist-Anti-Racist Economists." *Feminist Economics* 2, no. 1 (22–42).

Mies, Maria, and Vandana Shiva. 1993. *Ecofeminism*. London: Zed Books.

Miller, Alice. 1981. *The Drama of the Gifted Child*. New York: Basic Books.

Morrison, Roy. 1991. *We Build the Road as We Travel*. Philadelphia: New Society.

Nove, Alec. 1983. *The Economics of Feasible Socialism*. Boston: G. Allen & Unwin.

Roemer, John. 1994. *A Future for Socialism*. Cambridge: Harvard University Press.

Schor, Juliet. 1991. *The Overworked American: The Unexpected Decline of Leisure*. New York: Basic Books.

———. 1998. *The Overspent American: Upscaling, Downshifting, and the New Consumer*. New York: Basic Books.

Section II

Capitalism's Dynamic Path

Accumulation and the Rate of Profit

8

The Rate of Profit and Stagnation in the U.S. Economy

Fred Moseley

According to Marxian theory, the performance of capitalist economies depends above all else on the rate of profit. When the rate of profit is high, capitalism is relatively prosperous: business investment is high, unemployment is relatively low, and the living standards of workers generally rises. However, when the rate of profit is low, prosperity turns into stagnation and depression: investment is low or nonexistent, unemployment is high, and living standards decline. Marx of course argued that there is an inherent tendency for the rate of profit to eventually decline during periods of prosperity and expansion, thus turning periods of prosperity into periods of depression. In other words, recurring crises and depressions are inevitable in capitalist economies.

I and others have argued that the main cause of the higher unemployment and higher inflation in the U.S. economy beginning in the 1970s was a very significant decline in the rate of profit in the 1950s and 1960s (Weisskopf 1979; Wolff 1986; Shaikh and Tonak 1994; and Duménil and Lévy 1993). This theory of the recent stagflation will be briefly reviewed in the first section of this chapter, below. From this theory it follows that, if U.S. capitalism is to fully recover and return to the more prosperous conditions of the 1950s and 1960s, the rate of profit must be restored to its earlier higher levels. The main purpose of this chapter is to examine the trend in the rate of profit since the mid-1970s in order to determine whether or not there has been a significant recovery of the rate of profit, which would make a return to prosperity more likely. The estimates of the rate of profit and related variables since the mid-1970s are presented in Section 2. Finally, Section 3 will speculate about the future of capitalism based on the recent trends in the rate of profit and its determinants presented in Section 2.

1. The Decline of the Rate of Profit, 1947–1977

The rate of profit in the U.S. economy declined significantly in the 1960s and early 1970s, and many radical economists have argued that this significant decline in the rate of profit was the main cause of the economic stagflation of the last two decades. There are different measures of the rate of profit, but they all show essentially the same strong negative trend during the postwar period. According to my estimates, presented in Table 8.1,

This chapter is a condensed version of Moseley 1997.

the rate of profit declined almost 50 percent, from 22 percent in the late 1940s to 12 percent in the mid 1970s.[1]

I (and others) have argued that this significant decline in the rate of profit was the main cause of both the "twin evils" of higher unemployment and higher inflation, and hence also of the declining living standards of recent decades (see Moseley 1992, ch. 4). As in periods of depression of the past, the decline in the rate of profit resulted in a decline in business investment and higher unemployment. One new factor in the postwar period is that many governments in the 1970s responded to the higher unemployment by adopting Keynesian expansionary policies (more government spending, lower interest rates, etc.) in an attempt to reduce unemployment. However, these government attempts to reduce unemployment generally resulted in higher rates of inflation, as capitalist enterprises responded to the government stimulation of demand by raising their prices at a faster rate in order to reverse the decline in their rate of profit. In the 1980s, financial capitalists revolted against these higher rates of inflation and have generally forced governments to adopt restrictive policies (less government spending, higher interest rates). The result was less inflation, but also sharply higher unemployment and sharply reduced living standards. Therefore, government policies have affected the particular combination of unemployment and inflation that has occurred, but the fundamental cause of both of these "twin evils" has been the decline in the rate of profit.

The most widely held theory of the decline of the rate of profit in the postwar U.S. economy is generally referred to as the "wage-push profit squeeze" theory (e.g., Weisskopf 1979). According to this theory, the decline of the rate of profit was caused by an increase of wages that resulted from the workers' struggles of the late 1960s and early 1970s. It is argued that the lower rates of unemployment of this period increased the bargaining power of workers and enabled them to gain higher wages at the expense of capitalists' profits. Thus, according to this view, the current crisis of capitalism is mainly the result of the power and militancy of workers, which increased wages and reduced the rate of profit.

I have presented an alternative explanation of the decline of the rate of profit in the postwar U.S. economy, which emphasizes Marx's distinction between productive labor and unproductive labor and, to a lesser extent, an increase in the composition of capital (see Moseley 1992, ch. 2–4). Shaikh and Tonak (1994, 122–124) have presented a similar explanation of the decline in the rate of profit, although they emphasize the increase in the composition of capital more than the increase of unproductive labor. I will argue below that this alternative explanation is more consistent than the "profit squeeze" theory with the trend in the rate of profit since the 1970s. I will first very briefly review Marx's distinction between productive labor and unproductive labor and then briefly present this alternative Marxian theory of the decline in the rate of profit.

Within Marx's labor theory of value, some labor within capitalist enterprises performs functions, that by themselves, according to Marx, do not result in the production of additional value and surplus-value. These unproductive functions are entirely necessary within capitalist economies, but nonetheless, according to Marx's theory, do not result in additional value or surplus-value.

There are two main types of unproductive functions in capitalist economies, and therefore two main types of unproductive labor that perform these unproductive functions.[2] *Circulation* functions are related to the exchange of commodities and money, including such functions as buying and selling, accounting, check processing, advertising, debt–credit relations, insurance, legal counsel, and securities exchange. The function of circulation labor is the transformation of a given amount of value from commodities to money, or vice versa; no additional value is created in this change in the form of a given amount of value. Marx argued that the circulation labor that performs these circulation functions does not produce value and surplus-value because exchange is essentially the exchange of equivalent values. *Supervisory* functions are related to the control of the labor of production workers, including such functions as management, direct supervision, record-keeping, and so forth. Marx argued that supervisory labor does not add to the value of commodities because this labor is not technically necessary for production, but is instead necessary because of the antagonistic relation between capitalists and workers over the intensity of labor of workers.[3]

Capitalist enterprises must of course pay unproductive labor to carry out these necessary functions, even though, according to Marx's theory, these functions do not produce value and surplus-value. Therefore, the costs of this unproductive labor cannot be recovered out of value that it produces. Instead, these unproductive costs can only be recovered out of the surplus-value produced by productive labor employed in capitalist production. If these unproductive costs increase faster than the surplus-value produced by productive labor, then there will be proportionally less profit left over for capitalists. As we shall see below, according to this Marxian theory, the negative effect of rising costs of unproductive labor was the main cause of the decline in the rate of profit in the postwar U.S. economy.

The rate of profit being analyzed here is by definition equal to the ratio of the amount of profit (P) to the total stock of capital invested (K). According to Marx's theory, profit, the numerator in the rate of profit, is the difference between the annual flow of surplus-value (S) and the annual flow of unproductive costs (U_f) (almost entirely the wages of unproductive labor, but also includes a small part—about 5 percent—of the costs of materials and the depreciation costs of buildings, machinery, etc., used in unproductive functions):

$$P = S - U_f \tag{1}$$

Similarly, according to Marx's theory, the stock of capital, the denominator in the rate of profit, is divided into two components: constant capital (C), the capital invested in means of production, and the stock of capital invested in unproductive functions (U_s):[5]

$$K = C + U_s \tag{2}$$

Combining equations (1) and (2), we obtain the following Marxian equation for the conventional rate of profit:

$$RP = \frac{P}{K} = \frac{S - U_f}{C + U_s} \tag{3}$$

Finally, we divide all terms on the right-hand side of equation (3) by the annual flow of variable capital (V), the capital invested in labor-power, which is the source of surplus-value according to Marx's theory, and we obtain:

$$RP = \frac{S/V - U_f/V}{C/V + U_s/V} = \frac{RS + UF}{CC + US} \tag{4}$$

From equation (4) we can see that, according to this Marxian theory, the rate of profit varies directly with the rate of surplus-value (RS) (the ratio of surplus-value to variable capital) and varies inversely with the composition of capital (CC) (the ratio of constant capital to variable capital) and the two ratios of unproductive capital to variable capital (UF and US).[4]

Estimates of the rate of profit and its Marxian

determinants for the U.S. economy from 1947 to 1977 are shown in Table 8.1. We can see from these estimates that over this period the rate of surplus-value increased 17 percent and the composition of capital increased 41 percent. We can also see that the two ratios of unproductive capital to productive capital had even more striking trends: the ratio UF increased 74 percent (from 0.54 to 0.94) and the ratio US increased 117 percent (from a small initial magnitude). Thus, according to the Marxian theory presented here, the proximate causes of the decline in the rate of profit were the significant increases in the composition of capital and in the two ratios of unproductive capital to variable capital.

In Moseley 1992, Table 4.2 and pages 111–112, I estimated the individual contributions of each of these proximate determinants to the total decline in the rate of profit by decomposing the total decline into components that could then be used to analyze the effects of changing each of these four determinants of the rate of profit, one at a time. According to these estimates, the ratio UF was the proximate determinant that contributed the most to the decline of the rate of profit, accounting for approximately two-thirds of the total decline. By the end of this period, the annual costs of unproductive labor (U_f) was over half (approximately 55 percent) of the total surplus-value produced by productive labor. The composition of capital accounted for most of the rest of the total decline.

These conclusions raise the obvious further question: what were the underlying causes of the very significant increases in the two ratios of unproductive capital to productive capital, especially the ratio UF? It turns out that the increase in the ratio UF was due almost entirely to a roughly proportional increase in the ratio of unproductive labor to productive labor; the relative average wages of unproductive labor and productive labor remained more or less constant during this period. The ratio of unproductive labor to productive labor increased 83 percent, from 0.35 in 1947 to 0.64 in 1977 (see Moseley 1992, Table 4.3 and pages 111–115). According to the Marxian theory presented here, this very significant increase in the ratio of unproductive labor to productive labor was the main cause of the decline of the rate of profit in the postwar U.S. economy.[6]

2. Has the Rate of Profit Increased, 1975–1994?

Since the mid-1970s, capitalist enterprises have responded to the significant decline of the rate of profit discussed above by attempting in a variety of ways to increase their rate of profit back up to its earlier higher levels. The most important of these strategies has been the attempt to reduce workers' wages in a number of ways: by direct wage cuts, by increasing prices faster than wages, and by moving their operations to low-wage areas of the world (this has been the main driving force behind the "globalization" of recent decades). The negative effect of these wage cuts on the living standards of workers is only too well known: the average real wage in the U.S. economy has declined about 20 percent over the last two decades.

The extent to which capitalist enterprises have succeeded in restoring the rate of profit is shown in Table 8.2. According to these estimates, the rate of profit has increased somewhat over the last two decades, from around 0.12 in the mid-1970s to around 0.16 in the mid-1990s. However, the surprising result is that only about 40 percent of the earlier decline (a decline of 0.10 from 0.22 to 0.12) has been recovered. Hence, the rate of profit remains 25 to 30 percent below its earlier peaks.[7]

We can also see from Table 8.2 the reasons why the increase in the rate of profit has been so lim-

Table 8.1

The Rate of Profit and Its Marxian Determinants, 1947–1977

	RS	CC	UF	US	RP
1947	1.40	3.58	0.54	0.30	0.22
1948	1.35	3.60	0.53	0.30	0.21
1949	1.50	3.83	0.59	0.32	0.22
1950	1.42	3.94	0.58	0.32	0.20
1951	1.44	3.78	0.56	0.31	0.22
1952	1.41	3.69	0.57	0.31	0.21
1953	1.35	3.56	0.58	0.30	0.20
1954	1.46	3.84	0.64	0.33	0.20
1955	1.51	3.85	0.65	0.34	0.21
1956	1.44	3.96	0.67	0.36	0.18
1957	1.50	4.08	0.70	0.38	0.18
1958	1.59	4.33	0.75	0.42	0.18
1959	1.61	4.14	0.75	0.41	0.19
1960	1.62	4.11	0.78	0.42	0.19
1961	1.68	4.18	0.81	0.45	0.19
1962	1.71	4.07	0.81	0.45	0.20
1963	1.71	3.99	0.80	0.46	0.21
1964	1.73	3.92	0.81	0.47	0.21
1965	1.73	3.92	0.80	0.48	0.21
1966	1.72	3.91	0.81	0.50	0.21
1967	1.72	4.03	0.84	0.52	0.19
1968	1.69	4.02	0.84	0.53	0.19
1969	1.62	4.07	0.85	0.54	0.17
1970	1.61	4.29	0.89	0.58	0.15
1971	1.71	4.50	0.93	0.62	0.15
1972	1.67	4.37	0.89	0.61	0.16
1973	1.59	4.39	0.87	0.61	0.14
1974	1.55	5.13	0.92	0.69	0.11
1975	1.71	5.39	0.98	0.69	0.12
1976	1.66	5.15	0.95	0.66	0.12
1977	1.63	5.03	0.94	0.66	0.12

Sources: See Moseley (1992, Appendix B) for a complete description. See also Moseley (1997, Appendix) for a brief description.

RS: Rate of surplus-value.

CC: Composition of capital.

UF: Ratio of the flow of unproductive capital to variable capital.

US: Ratio of the stock of unproductive capital to variable capital.

RP: Rate of profit.

Table 8.2

The Rate of Profit and Its Marxian Determinants, 1975–1994

	RS	CC	UF	US	RP
1975	1.71	5.39	0.98	0.69	0.12
1976	1.66	5.15	0.95	0.66	0.12
1977	1.63	5.03	0.94	0.66	0.12
1978	1.70	5.26	0.98	0.70	0.12
1979	1.64	5.32	1.00	0.67	0.11
1980	1.70	5.66	1.06	0.72	0.10
1981	1.81	5.76	1.09	0.74	0.11
1982	1.89	5.92	1.16	0.78	0.11
1983	1.93	5.76	1.20	0.80	0.11
1984	2.08	5.58	1.22	0.73	0.14
1985	2.15	5.47	1.26	0.79	0.14
1986	2.23	5.50	1.32	0.80	0.15
1987	2.22	5.48	1.33	0.79	0.14
1988	2.25	5.25	1.39	0.80	0.14
1989	2.28	5.03	1.41	0.81	0.15
1990	2.31	4.86	1.39	0.82	0.16
1991	2.27	4.89	1.45	0.83	0.14
1992	2.28	4.80	1.45	0.82	0.15
1993	2.29	4.71	1.46	0.83	0.15
1994	2.33	4.61	1.46	0.83	0.16

Sources: See Moseley (1992, Appendix B) for a complete description. See also Moseley (1997, Appendix) for a brief description.

ited, in spite of the declining wages of this period. The higher rates of unemployment and lower wages resulted, as expected, in a significant increase in the rate of surplus-value (a 36 percent increase from 1.71 to 2.33). In addition, the composition of capital declined somewhat (15 percent, from 5.39 to 4.61), especially since the late 1980s, due to the decline of oil prices, a slower rate of technical change, and perhaps to an increase of bankruptcies and the resulting devaluation of capital. However, the positive effect of the increase of the rate of surplus-value and the decline of the composition of capital was offset to a large extent by continued increases in the ratio UF (a 49 percent increase, from 0.98 in 1975 to 1.46 in 1994), and to a lesser extent in the ratio US (a 20 percent increase, from 0.69 in 1975 to 0.83 in 1994). Therefore, the main underlying cause of the limited increase in the rate of profit is the same as the main cause of the previous decline in the rate of profit: a continued increase in the costs of unproductive labor. The total cost of unproductive labor is now 62 percent of the total surplus-value produced by productive labor.

The main cause of the increase in the ratio UF in this more recent period was again a continued increase in the ratio of unproductive labor to productive labor, which increased 22 percent from 0.64 in 1975 to 0.78 in 1994, although the rate of increase of this ratio was somewhat slower, approximately 1 percent per year compared to the almost 2 percent a year in the early postwar period.

In addition, there was another cause of the increase in the ratio UF in this more recent period—an increase in the average wages of unproductive relative to the average wages of productive wages, which increased 23 percent from 1.45 in 1975 to 1.78 in 1994 in contrast to the earlier period, in which this ratio remained more or less constant. Therefore, the relative increase of the costs of unproductive labor since the mid-1970s was due not only to a continued relative increase of the number of unproductive workers, but also to a new increase in the relative wages of these unproductive workers.

These estimates for the last two decades support the alternative Marxian theory that I have presented of the prior decline of the rate of profit, and contradict the "profit squeeze" explanation presented by Weisskopf and others. My alternative Marxian theory can explain not only why the rate of profit declined in the early postwar period, but also why the increase of the rate of profit has been so limited in recent decades. The profit squeeze theory can explain the prior decline, but it cannot explain why two decades of higher unemployment and lower wages have not fully restored the rate of profit.

The limited increase of the rate of profit since the mid-1970s explains why slow growth and stagnation have continued in these decades: the rate of profit still has not increased sufficiently to make possible a return to a more rapid rate of expansion. These results also of course imply that a full recovery from this stagnation in the years ahead is not very likely. The future implications of these results are explored further in the final section.

3. The Future Trend in the Rate of Profit?

What is the future trend of the rate of profit likely to be, based on the above analysis of the causes of the decline of the rate of profit in the early postwar period and the limited increase in the rate of profit in recent decades? According to the Marxian theory of the rate of profit presented above, the rate of profit depends on three variables: the rate of surplus-value, the composition of capital, and the ratio of unproductive labor to productive labor. What are the likely trends of these three Marxian determinants of the rate of profit?

The rate of surplus-value is very likely to continue to increase in the years ahead. The trend of the rate of surplus-value depends on the relative rates of increase of productivity and real wages. The continuation of stagnation and high unemployment in the years ahead will continue to put downward pressure on wages, which will make it very difficult to avoid further declines in real wages; increases of real wages are even less likely. Therefore, any increases in productivity that occur will result in further increases in the rate of surplus-value.

The future trend of the composition of capital is more difficult to predict. Continued stagnation will likely be accompanied by a continuation of slow investment, which suggests that the composition of capital will not increase much, if at all, in the year ahead and may even decline somewhat.

However, the future trend of the rate of profit would seem to depend mainly on the trend of the ratio of unproductive labor to productive labor. The strong increase of this ratio throughout the postwar period was the cause both of the significant decline of the rate of profit in the early postwar period and of the limited increase of the rate of profit in recent decades. The strong increase of this ratio, although somewhat less in recent decades, would by itself seem to suggest that this ratio will continue to increase in the years ahead. The main cause of the relative increase of unproductive labor identified by my preliminary analysis (Moseley 1992, ch. 5) was the slower "productivity" growth of circulation labor compared to productive labor, which seems to be due to the inherent difficulties of mechanizing the functions of buying and selling, which must remain to a large extent person-to-person transactions. However, there is one important new factor to consider: computer technology. New computer technology is being applied to many of the unproductive functions of circulation (accounting, billing, check processing, cashiering, etc.). This new technology has reduced—and probably will continue to reduce—the need for circulation labor. However, this effect has not yet been strong enough to fully eliminate the relative increase of circulation labor.

Therefore, it appears likely that the ratio of unproductive labor to productive labor will continue to increase in the years ahead, although probably at a somewhat slower rate. This continued relative increase of unproductive labor will continue to put downward pressure on the rate of profit and will continue to offset the positive effect of further increases of the rate of surplus-value. Therefore, it seems unlikely that the rate of profit in the U.S. economy will increase significantly in the years ahead.

In summary, it seems that the best we can hope for in the years ahead is a continuation of the current stagnation and slow growth. Capitalist enterprises will continue to try to restore their rate of profit by every means possible, including cutting wages. However, they will likely continue to be only partially successful in achieving this objective. Therefore, a return to the more prosperous conditions of the early postwar period, with fuller employment and rising wages, appears to be unlikely.

Therefore, as we move into the twenty-first century, it seems very likely that capitalism will remain in a condition of stagnation and slow growth for the foreseeable future. The rate of profit is still too low to make possible a faster rate of expansion and a return to more prosperous conditions. Capitalism may be able to avoid another Great Depression for the foreseeable future, but it is extremely unlikely that capitalism will be able to provide a return to prosperity and improving living standards for the vast majority of the world's population, and will probably instead continue to produce lower living standards and increasing misery.

Whether or not these conditions of stagnation and deteriorating living standards will generate significant oppositional movements in the United States and elsewhere is a very important question that is beyond the scope of this chapter. (For a discussion of some issues, see chapter 28 by Hart-Landsburg and Burkett in this volume.) However, further consideration of this question should take into account the very strong probability that the objective social conditions will continue to deteriorate in the years ahead for the vast majority of the world's population, including in the United States.

Notes

1. My estimates are for the business sector as a whole. Estimates for the nonfinancial corporate business sector are also frequently used and these show essentially the same strong downward trend.

2. Marx also used to concept of unproductive labor to refer to labor employed outside capitalist enterprises, such as government employees and household employees. In this chapter, unproductive labor refers solely to unproductive labor within capitalist enterprises.

3. Marx's distinction between productive labor and unproductive labor is controversial and not accepted by all Marxian economists. Criticisms of this distinction are dis-

cussed in Moseley 1992 (Appendix to chapter 2), along with my responses to these criticisms.

4. Elsewhere, I have referred to this rate of profit, which is net of unproductive costs and is related to the total capital invested, as the "conventional" rate of profit, to distinguish it from the Marxian rate of profit, which is gross of unproductive costs and is related to the productive capital only (see Moseley 1992, chapters 3 and 4). Marx's theory of the "falling rate of profit" is in terms of the Marxian rate of profit, but the conventional rate of profit is a more direct determinant of the rate of capital accumulation. Profit is defined here to include all forms of property income, including interest and rent.

5. Here the simplifying assumption is made that the stocks of both variable capital and the wages of unproductive labor are equal to zero. Since capitalists pay workers only after they have worked, this assumption is not far from reality.

6. See Moseley (1992, chapter 5) for an analysis of the causes of this very significant increase in the ratio of unproductive labor to productive labor in the postwar U.S. economy.

7. The rate of profit for the nonfinancial corporate business sector has increased even less since the mid-1970s.

Bibliography

Duménil, Gérard, and Dominique Lévy. 1993. *The Economics of the Profit Rate: Competition, Crises and Historical Tendencies of Capitalism*. Brookfield, VT: Edward Elgar.

Moseley, Fred. 1992. *The Falling Rate of Profit in the Postwar United States Economy*. New York: St. Martin's Press.

———. 1997. "The Rate of Profit and the Future of Capitalism." *Review of Radical Political Economics* 29, no. 4.

Shaikh, Anwar M., and E. Ahmet Tonak. 1994. *Measuring the Wealth of Nations: The Political Economy of National Accounts*. New York: Cambridge University Press.

Weisskopf, Thomas E. 1979. "Marxian Crisis Theory and the Rate of Profit in the Postwar U.S. Economy." *Cambridge Journal of Economics* 3, no. 4.

Wolff, Edward. 1986. "The Productivity Slowdown and the Fall in the Rate of Profit, 1947–76," *Review of Radical Political Economics* 18, no. 1/2.

9

The Global Relevance of Marxian Crisis Theory

Jonathan P. Goldstein

Introduction

As we approach the dawn of the twenty-first century, 150 years after the development of Marx's crisis theory, it seems appropriate to reassess the relevance of this approach for understanding the potential crisis tendencies of global capitalism. Here, I focus only on the important long-term tendency for capitalist economies to produce a continuing succession of profit squeeze (PS) and underconsumption (UC) crises and assess the likelihood that a global UC crisis will evolve out of the institutional and policy changes that emerged in response to the well-documented PS crisis of the postwar period.

The Simple Analytics of and Relation Between PS and UC Crises

The Relationship Between Costs, Price, Profitability, the Distribution of Income, and Demand and Supply

Both PS and UC crisis mechanisms rely on the causal nexus between firm production costs, pricing decisions, and profitability in an environment characterized by intense, but changing, competition and power struggles between social classes. On the micro level, it is assumed that firms set price using a mark-up pricing rule (Lerner 1934; Goldstein 1985, 1986) where variable costs are restricted to labor costs:

$$P = \alpha(W/(Q/N)) \qquad (1)$$

where P is price, α is the markup ($\alpha > 1$), W is the money wage, Q is the quantity produced, N is the number of workers hired, and (Q/N) is output per worker (productivity). W/(Q/N) comprises unit labor costs. Thus, the firm determines the average cost per unit of output and charges a price that is a multiple of (markup over) the unit cost. The markup covers the firm's fixed costs and profit and is constrained by the level of competition facing the firm and by the balance of political and economic power between social classes—ceteris paribus, more competition leads to lower values for α as does a shift in the balance of power toward workers.

Thus markup pricing establishes the micro relationship between price, costs, and profits. More importantly, the markup determines, on the macro level, the distribution of income—holding all else constant a higher (lower) mark-up increases (decreases) profit per unit and thus increases (decreases) the profit share of total income. Multiplying both sides of equation (1) by Q and aggregating over all firms yields

The author is grateful to James R. Crotty for valuable discussions on this subject matter.

$$Y = PQ = \alpha WN, \text{ or } WN/Y = 1/\alpha,$$

where Y is gross domestic product and WN/Y is labor's share of income, which is inversely related to the markup. In a world with only workers and capitalists, both income shares sum to one. Thus, profit's share of income is $\pi/Y = (1 - 1/\alpha)$ where π is total profits. The important linkage between the markup, its determinants—class power and competition—and the distribution of income has been established. As α rises, π/Y increases and WN/Y declines.

Next, I consider the relationship between the distribution of income and aggregate demand and supply. The accumulation process can be expressed through the dependence of investment (I) on the profit rate (π_R) where the profit rate is the return to invested capital or total profits divided by the value of the capital stock (π/K). Increases in π_R lead to more investment activity as the firm's expectations of future profitability are enhanced. In an intensely competitive environment, firms must pursue all feasible profit opportunities in order to establish a reserve of funds used to defend against future competitive onslaughts. When the general π_R declines, the firm must cut back production and future investment so as not to end up with costly inventories and excess capacity that could reduce its war chest. Note that I is also an element of supply because it increases the productive capacity of the economy.

Using Weisskopf's (1979) decomposition of π_R, we can establish a linkage between π_R, the distribution of income, the mark-up, and I:

$$\pi_R = \frac{\pi}{K} = \left(\frac{\pi}{Y}\right)\left(\frac{Y}{Z}\right)\left(\frac{Z}{K}\right) \tag{2}$$

where K is the capital stock and Z is potential output at full capacity. Thus the profit rate is determined by the profit share of income, Y/Z as a measure of capacity utilization and the output-capital ratio at full capacity. Changes in the markup that alter the distribution of income (π/Y), affect π_R and thus I. Decreases in I lower both the level of demand and the growth of productivity capacity (capital stock). Thus a linkage between the distribution of income and supply has been developed.

Consumption can be characterized by an income share weighted consumption function:

$$C = A + MPC_L\left(1 - \frac{\pi}{Y}\right)Y + MPC_K\left(\frac{\pi}{Y}\right)Y \tag{3}$$

where C is consumption, MPC_L and MPC_K are the marginal propensity to consume of labor and capital respectively, $MPC_L > MPC_K$, and A is a constant. Recognizing $(1 - \pi/Y)Y$ and $(\pi/Y)Y$ respectively as total labor income and total profit income, workers spend MPC_L percent of their additional income and capitalists spend MPC_K percent of their additional income. The overall MPC for the economy is an income share weighted average of the two different MPCs. The linkage between α, the distribution of income and demand via consumption, has now been established—as α increases capitalists have a larger share of income (π/Y rises), workers have a lower income share, and because workers spend more and capitalists less on the margin, the overall MPC for the economy declines, implying that C declines.

Thus, the interconnections between prices, costs, profitability, the distribution of income, the essential components of aggregate demand, and supply have been established. The dynamics of these key variables is determined by changes in the competitive environment and shifts in the balance of power between social classes.

The Potential for Crisis

Prior to considering dynamics, the tenuous relation between aggregate demand, aggregate supply and the distribution of income is addressed. Increases (decreases) in α and the profit share of income have competing effects on aggregate demand—C decreases (increases) while I increases (decreases), at the same time that supply increases (decreases). In an environment in which adversarial class relations exist, the ensuing struggle over the distribution of income makes it difficult to achieve stable growth as demand falls (rises) when supply increases (decreases).

To discuss the dynamic evolution of this economic system, consider the dynamic variant of the mark-up pricing rule. Taking the log of both sides of equation (1) and totally differentiating yields a dynamic pricing equation:[1]

$$\dot{P} = \dot{\alpha} + \dot{W} - \left(\frac{\dot{Q}}{N}\right) \quad (4)$$

where a dot denotes the percentage change in a variable. The percentage change in P equals the sum of the percentage change in α and W minus the percentage change in productivity.

Now consider both changing competitive and class relations. If the balance of power between capital and labor shifts in favor of labor such that $\dot{W}$ rises, and the competitive environment is intense enough that $\dot{W}$ cannot be fully passed on by firms in the form of higher prices, then $\dot{P} < \dot{W}$ and $\dot{\alpha} < 0$, implying that the markup declines and the distribution of income shifts in favor of labor. As a result, aggregate demand is affected through a decline in I and an increase in C and aggregate supply declines or grows at a slower pace. If the change in C is either small or slow to occur, then a profitability crisis emerges where unemployment is expected to rise.

While it is possible that the opposite movements in C and I cancel each other out, this is rarely the case. Due to the linkage between I and supply, supply growth will wane. Also, I responds more quickly and more steeply than C, but protracted changes in the distribution of income may result in changes in C that ultimately dominate the changes in I, thus avoiding a problem.

Even under the most favorable conditions for avoiding a crisis, balanced growth may be elusive. When wage gains parallel productivity gains, $\dot{W} = (\dot{Q/N})$, the economy grows by $(\dot{Q/N})$ and α and the distribution of income remain the same, implying that both social classes' real incomes rise by $(\dot{Q/N})$. As long as $(\dot{Q/N})$ is high enough to produce desirable growth in real income, distributional strife is less likely to evolve and aggregate demand problems are possibly avoided. In this scenario, distributional conflict is minimized and the intensity of competition is less relevant because price increases are not necessary to preserve the profit share of income—$\dot{P} = 0$ when $\dot{W} = (\dot{Q/N})$, and as a result α is maintained ($\dot{\alpha} = 0$). Despite this, such periods of balanced growth may be short-lived because the level of unemployment is not determined in this scenario. Any change in the unemployment rate will tilt the balance of power between classes, resulting in a changed distribution of income and the potential for a demand–supply imbalance. This impact of unemployment on the class balance of power stresses the political aspects of full employment.

PS and UC Crisis Mechanisms

Now the PS and UC crisis mechanisms can be developed. The PS theory argues that $\dot{W}$ and $(\dot{Q/N})$ depend on labor's relative power vis-à-vis capital. If economic conditions and institutions are favorable toward labor, labor's power rises, implying that $\dot{W}$ rises and $(\dot{Q/N})$ declines.[2] If the competitive environment restricts rising unit labor costs from being passed on by $\dot{P}$, then $\dot{\alpha} < 0$ (α declines) and the distribution of income shifts in favor of workers (π/Y declines). In a global economy where inter-competition looms large, domestic increases in $\dot{W}$ and decreases in $(\dot{Q/N})$ are less likely to be fully passed on. Thus, the profit rate declines and investment falters. When any subsequent increase in C from an increase in the worker share of income is offset by the decline in I, the level of income, production, and employment in the economy decline.

A UC crisis occurs when economic conditions and institutions are hostile to labor such that either workers are unable to capture productivity gains in their wage increases ($\dot{W} < (\dot{Q/N})$), or wage increases decline or may be negative. In both situations, unit labor costs decline and firms do not pass the lower costs on to lower prices. Thus α rises ($\dot{\alpha} > 0$) and the distribution of income shifts in favor of capital. While I increases at first, a prolonged shift in the distribution of income will lead to a decline in C that ultimately renders expanded I opportunities useless as the increases in supply from the expanded capacity outruns the diminished demand growth. Here production itself is profitable, but the profits embedded in output cannot be realized due to deficient demand. As a result, capacity utilization (Y/Z) declines and π_R falls, inducing a decline in I, income, production, and employment. π_R may even increase as α rises, but the effective π_R is reduced as profits cannot be fully realized.

Counteracting tendencies for a UC crisis include activities that increase demand without increasing production. These include advertising expenditures, government expenditures, and the cultivation of foreign demand for domestic goods (exports). In addition, a restructuring of production toward luxury consumption goods, more likely to be purchased out of increased profit income, may also postpone a crisis. At the same time that these activities may avert a UC crisis, they create other potential problems. For instance, a greater dependency on foreign trade renders the domestic economy less insulated from economic crises originating in other nations.

The Likelihood of a UC Crisis

The prolonged decline in the profit share of income and the profit rate from the late 1960s until the early 1980s in most advanced capitalist nations, as a result of intensified international competition and a shift in the balance of class power toward labor, generated the impetus for a restructuring of the economic environment.

In many of the advanced capitalist economies a radical shift in macroeconomic policy took place. Keynesian high employment policies lost favor as the reduction of inflation and budget deficits became prioritized goals. This political decision concerning the Phillips Curve tradeoff—low inflation favored over high employment—was directly aimed at weakening the political and economic position of labor. Central banks became more independent, developed stronger alliances with the financial community,[3] and were able to use monetary policy to control inflation, which led to secular increases in the unemployment rate. Rising unemployment increased budget deficits, which were less likely to be tolerated by the growing power of financial authorities, and, as a result, the social safety net was dismantled in many nations. The agreements underlying European Union placed strict controls on deficits, further restricting fiscal policy and dramatically reducing democratic control over macro policy and seriously weakening the relative strength of labor. In addition, tax cuts redistributed income away from labor and to the wealthy. This resulted from an increasing reluctance to tax capital, which had become globally mobile. The resulting budget deficits were used as a further excuse to restrict employment-creating fiscal policy. In the United States, budgetary priorities shifted from activities with large job creation multipliers such as education and infrastructure, to less job-intensive spending on defense. The argument was that such belt-tightening policies were a necessary evil to revitalize the economy.

On the microeconomic level, labor's power was further eroded through restrictive interpretations and applications of labor law, outright attacks on unions and union organizing efforts—the U.S. government's handling of the PATCO strike is one example—and a massive reorganization of the labor process geared at wrestling control away from labor.

At the same time, the intensity of international competition began to rise at even faster rates, but under these new circumstances its impact was different. Labor, in its weakened state, bore the brunt of the competitive adjustment. Instead of responding in a win–win manner by attempting to increase competitive standing through productivity enhancement, capitalists responded by demanding wage and benefit concessions.

In terms of the model developed, the weaker position of labor and the intensification of competition led to reductions in $\dot{W}$ and possibly increases in $(\dot{Q/N})$, both leading to restored profitability $\dot{\alpha} > 0$ and possibly enhanced price declines ($\dot{P}$ declines). Given the long-term nature of this regime shift in competitive and class relations, one would expect to find protracted increases in the profit share of income and shifts in the distribution of income away from lower-income groups in the advanced capitalist nations.

Table 9.1 reports income share data for twenty-four countries divided geographically into seventeen non-Asian and seven Asian economies. The labor share is measured as the percentage that total earnings are of total value added in manufacturing, while changes in the distribution of income are reflected by the percentage of income attributable to the lowest two quintiles (40 percent) and the lowest four quintiles (80 percent) of the income distribution. For the non-Asian economies, the labor share data show mixed results for the period 1970–1978, with approximately half of the economies experiencing a rise and half a decline in labor's share. This occurs because the end of the period of rising labor strength is different in different countries. In some economies a transition occurs as early as 1970, while in others it does not occur until 1980. The results are different in the 1978–1991 period: available data show that labor share declines in thirteen of sixteen advanced capitalist economies.

For the most part, the limited data on the distribution of income are consistent with the trends in the share data. In eight out of thirteen of the non-Asian nations with available data, the distribution of incomes becomes less equitable. Of the nine nations whose labor share declined and for which there exist distribution of income data, six experience a deterioration in the distribution of income.

To assess the impact of this income shift on consumption, I consider in Table 9.2 trends in the consumption–income ratio (C/Y) and the capacity utilization (Y/Z) rate measured as one minus the percentage that output is of potential. In approximately one-half of the non-Asian economies experiencing a decline in labor's economic power, C/Y experiences small declines indicative of a developing UC problem. The lack of pervasive and large declines in C/Y suggest that countervailing tendencies to a UC crisis have been active. Yet a widespread and sharp tendency to lower average capacity utilization rates (Y/Z in Table 9.2) exists in the post-1980 period—a manifestation of a UC crisis, particularly when the shift to luxury good consumption is small or lags behind the decline in regular consumption.

Further countervailing tendencies are associated with the greater dependency of capitalist economies on exports (E). Table 9.2 reveals that between 1970 and 1994 all countries but one became much more dependent on exports as a source of demand growth. Finally, increased levels of private debt in the non-Asian countries have also acted to tempo-

Table 9.1

Measures of Income Distribution

	Labor Share (Manufacturing)				Distribution of Income					
Country	1970	1978	1985	1991	Year	40%	80%	Year	40%	80%
Australia	53	55	51	39	1975	15	53	1985	16	58
Austria	47	58	57	54						
Belgium	46	49	50	42	1978	22	64			
Canada	53	49	49	46	1977	15	58	1987	18	60
Denmark	56	58	51	55	1976	20	63	1981	17	61
Finland	47	45	42	52	1977	20	63	1981	18	62
France					1975	17	58	1989	19	58
Germany	46	48	47	42*	1978	20	61	1988	19	60
Ireland	49	41	42	27	1973	20	61	1993	21	59
Italy	41	40	41	42	1977	18	56	1986	19	59
Netherlands	52	57	58	48	1981	22	64	1988	21	63
New Zealand	62	66	54	56	1981	16	55			
Spain	52	44	41	41	1980	19	60	1988	21	63
Sweden	52	47	35	36	1981	21	63			
Switzerland					1978	20	62	1982	17	55
United Kingdom	52	46	46	42	1979	19	60	1988	15	56
United States	47	41	40	36	1980	17	60	1985	16	58
ASIA										
Hong Kong	NA	56	48	55	1980	16	53			
Indonesia	26	20	23	19	1976	14	51			
Japan	32	38	35	33	1969	21	59	1979	22	63
Korea	25	27	27	27	1976	17	55			
Malaysia	29	26	NA	27	1973	11	44	1989	13	56
Philippines	21	25	25	24	1970	14	46	1988	17	52
Thailand	25	25	24	28				1992	14	47

Source: World Development Report, the World Bank, various years. All figures are percentages.
*1988 data.

rarily sustain C levels in the face of a shrinking wage share.

The underlying signs of a UC crisis are present in many of the non-Asian economies analyzed. Major political and economic offensives against labor in an environment of intensified international competition have resulted in radical shifts in the balance of power and the related distribution of income toward capitalists. This in turn has weakened the systematic consumption structure that underlies the demand side of the balanced growth equation. On the supply side a more profitable environment for the accumulation of capital has been established. Despite this more profitable scenario, growth has remained lackluster due to the threat that profits generated on the supply side may fail to be realized on the demand side. While a wider reliance on debt and exports has managed

Table 9.2

Consumption, Capacity Utilization, and Exports

Country	C/Y		Y/Z				E/Y		
	1980	1992	1970–80	1980–96	1970–83	1983–96	1970	1980	1994
Australia	59	62	101.4	99.0	100.7	98.8	14	16	19
Austria	56	55	100.9	99.5	100.3	99.5	31	37	38
Belgium	63	63	101.4	99.4	101.0	98.5	52	63	69
Canada	55	60	101.0	98.2	99.9	99.0	23	28	30
Denmark	56	52	100.3	99.0	99.8	99.2	28	33	34
Finland	54	56	100.7	98.9	100.5	98.5	26	33	33
France	59	60	100.8	99.0	100.6	98.7	16	22	23
Germany	57	54	100.9	99.6	100.2	99.6	21	NA	22
Ireland	67	56	98.9	97.9	98.6	97.8	37	47	68
Italy	61	63	100.6	99.6	100.4	99.3	16	22	23
Netherlands	61	60	100.4	99.7	99.7	98.5	43	50	51
New Zealand	62	64	100.0	98.7	99.6	98.7	23	30	31
Spain	66	63	100.8	99.6	100.0	100.2	13	16	19
Sweden	51	54	100.7	100.9	100.4	101.2	24	29	33
Switzerland	64	59	99.5	99.5	99.8	98.9	33	37	36
United Kingdom	59	64	101.6	100.2	100.8	100.5	23	27	25
United States	63	67	100.5	99.4	99.6	99.8	6	10	10
ASIA									
Hong Kong	60	61							
Indonesia	57	53					13	33	25
Japan	59	57	100.0	99.6	100.0	99.4	11	14	9
Korea	64	NA					14	34	36
Malaysia	51	52							
Philippines	67	72					22	24	34
Thailand	66	65					15	24	39

Sources: C/Y and E/Y—*World Development Report,* the World Bank, various years; Y/Z —OECD.

to avert a full-fledged crisis, at the same time it generates a fragile demand structure more vulnerable to both the international transmission of crises and disturbances to an interdependent and layered debt structure.

Implications of the Asian Crisis: Fragile Demand Meets Fragile Finance

In sharp contrast, Tables 9.1 and 9.2 show that the Asian economies have avoided the path to UC problems. The majority of these nations have experienced unprecedented high growth rates, improvements in the distribution of income, and an increasing or constant share of income going to labor. Average annual growth rates in the 6 to 7 percent range accompanied by constant income shares imply that workers' real wages have been increasing by 6 to 7 percent per year. This real income growth has fueled the export booms of the non-Asian economies. While C/Y only rises in three of six available cases, this does not constitute evidence that deficient demand has been present in the region. In contrast, a declining C/Y in some economies in the region, particularly the least developed, is a sign of the rapid industrialization taking place where present consumption has been foregone in the form of investment so that future consumption may be increased.

The current economic crisis in the Asian region, which fully surfaced in October 1997, is not a UC crisis. It is the result of the anarchy of production and finance that emerges out of a fiercely contested phase of rapid growth (Crotty 1993; Crotty and Dymski 1999; Crotty and Goldstein 1992; Minsky 1986). In this situation, euphoric expectations of producers bolstered by overoptimistic expectations of creditors led to a crisis of overinvestment and expansion resulting in the disappointment of unrealistic expectations and the collapse of fragile financial structures built on those expectations. While it is beyond the scope of the chapter to analyze the causes of the Asian crisis, it is important to understand its aftermath by assessing its implications for the fragile demand structure in the non-Asian nations and its future effects on Asian demand (Crotty and Dymski 1999).

The immediate impact of the Asian crisis has been the depreciation of the Asian currencies against non-Asian currencies and the collapse of the Asian economies (declines in income and production) due to the emergence of overcapacity and the bankruptcy of both industrial and financial firms in light of debt-deflation. This crisis is readily transmitted to the non-Asian economies through international trade. The depreciation of the Asian currencies and the decline in Asian incomes that accounted for the vast majority of increased export intensity in the non-Asian countries will dramatically reduce the level of non-Asian exports and thus remove a major offsetting tendency for a UC crisis.

In addition, the fallout from the financial aspects of the Asian crisis, which involved many Western banks and the impending UC crisis in Western economies, is likely to lead to the restriction of credit in the Western nations. Thus another offsetting tendency to the UC crisis may be removed.

Finally, the proposed long-term solutions to the Asian crisis will not only exacerbate the UC problems in the Western economies, but are likely to generate the conditions for a UC crisis in the Asian nations. The result would be a truly global UC crisis. The resolution of the Asian crisis has taken the form of a power struggle between international capitalists and finance capitalists, and domestic capital and labor, with the fate of the Asian working class swaying in the balance. International bankers and industrialists, with the enlisted help of the International Monetary Fund (IMF), have attempted to insulate themselves from the fallout of the crisis at the expense of Asian capitalists and, ultimately, the Asian working class. The injection of short-term liquidity into the Asian financial system has come with a stiff price: the imposition of a macroeconomic austerity program of restrictive monetary policy, high interest rates, and the reduction of government deficits. Such a strategy is simply bad economic policy for countries in the throes of deflation and depression, but is optimal for Western economies who are insulated from the crisis. Further, Western economies stand to gain much in terms of economic power. High interest rates will temporarily halt the appreciation of Western currencies, which threatens to result in demand deficiencies and at the same time will make it difficult for Asian banks to raise capital and could potentially plunge the Asian economies into recession and more bankruptcies. International capitalists and bankers stand ready to serve as powerful merger partners to shore up failing banks and firms. In addition, the weakening of Asian labor will shift the balance of power to Asian capitalists in the postcrisis restructuring.

The long-term implications of the bailout is the imposition on the Asian economies of the same conservative macroeconomic policy agenda that resulted in sharp changes in the balance of power between domestic capitalists and workers that underlie the Western UC problems. Such programs will be readily embraced by Asian capitalists long after their short-term liquidity crisis is resolved as a result of the loss in power suffered at the hands of international capitalists and bankers and the prospects of increasing their position vis-à-vis their own labor force.

The removal of offsetting tendencies to a UC crisis in the non-Asian economies where UC problems have been festering for long periods of time and the likely evolution of UC problems in Asian economies as a result of the aftermath of the financial crisis, strongly suggest that a global UC crisis is likely to evolve in the near future.

Conclusion

The continued relevance of the Marxian approach stems from its focus on class/social relations including competitive relations. The impending economic crisis is a crisis of social relations. It is the direct result of the irrationalities of a capitalist system of production and distribution based on conflictual class relations. In such a system, crises evolve either when the capitalist class is too strong (UC crisis) or too weak (PS crisis). Yet intense competitive pressure continually strains the productive (class) relations, producing an adversarial set of industrial relations that ensures cycles of crises mechanisms through continuing shifts in the balance of power between capital and labor. Global capitalism's ratcheting up of competitive pressures further ensures that the Marxian approach will be fruitful for analyzing the contradictory nature of this latest stage of capitalist development.

Alternatively, structural economic change can alter the irrational growth path of advanced capitalist economics. In the current situation, a redistribution of power to labor and the development of economic cooperation between social classes through the establishment of economic democracy can lead to large productivity gains. As a result, intensified competition can be met by harmonious growth/productivity-enhancing policies instead of conflictual wage concessions and austerity programs that continue the undesirable shifts in power that plague the current system.

Notes

1. Taking the log of equation (1) yields: $\ln P = \ln \alpha + \ln W - \ln (Q/N)$. Totally differentiating this result produces: $1/P\, dP = 1/\alpha\, d\alpha + 1/W\, dW - 1/(Q/N)\, d(Q/N)$, where d in front of a variable represents the total change in that variable. Recognizing that dP/P is the percentage change in P or $\dot{P}$ and that each of the three other terms on the right-hand side of the above equation similarly represent the percentage change in each of those variables, then this last equation is equivalent to equation (4) in the text.

2. Productivity growth is affected by the strength of labor because productivity is influenced by social as well as technical determinants, see Naples (1986).

3. The increased mobility of financial capital forged this alliance. Central banks that do not act in the interest of financiers could be forced to alter their policies in response to short-term capital flows.

References

Crotty, James R. 1993. "Rethinking Marxian Investment Theory: Keynes–Minsky Instability, Competitive Regime Shifts and Coerced Investment." *Review of Radical Political Economics* 25(1): 1–26.

Crotty, James R., and Gary Dymski. 1999. "Can the Global Neoliberal Regime Survive Victory in Asia? The Political Economy of the Asian Crisis." *International Papers in Political Economy* 5(2): 1–47.

Crotty, James R., and Jonathan P. Goldstein. 1992. "A Marxian-Keynesian Theory of Investment Demand: Empirical Evidence." In *International Perspectives on Profitability and Accumulation*, ed. F. Moseley and E. Wolff. Aldershot, UK: Elgar.

Goldstein, Jonathan P. 1985. "The Cyclical Profit Squeeze: A Marxian Microfoundation." *Review of Radical Political Economics* 17, no. 1–2: 103–28.

———. 1986. "Markup Variability and Flexibility: Theory and Empirical Evidence." *Journal of Business* 59, no. 4: 599–621.

Lerner, Abba. 1934. "The Concept of Monopoly and the Measurement of Monopoly Power." *Review of Economic Studies* (June): 157–73.

Minsky, Hyman P. 1986. *Stabilizing an Unstable Economy. Twentieth Century Fund Report Series.* New Haven: Yale University Press.

Naples, Michele I. 1986. "The Unraveling of the Union–Capital Truce and the U.S. Industrial Productivity Crisis." *Review of Radical Political Economics* 18, no. 1–2: 110–31.

Weisskopf, Thomas E. 1979. "Marxian Crisis Theory and the Rate of Profit in the Postwar U.S. Economy." *Cambridge Journal of Economics* 3, no. 4: 341–78.

10

Long Waves of Capitalist Development and the Future of Capitalism

Ismael Hossein-Zadeh

Judgment on the future of capitalism has always been controversial. Two polar views emerge: first, the almost fetishistic view that capitalism is eternal; and second, the deterministic view that capitalism will somehow collapse of its own accord. We argue that both views are analytically wrong—as well as nonoperative for any policy determination—and that the question of the future of capitalism ultimately boils down to the balance of social forces and the outcome of class struggle.

A judgment on the future of capitalism requires an understanding of how it works. A basic property of capitalist development is that it grows in erratic and contradictory ways: as it expands it also creates conditions for contraction. It is during long periods of contraction that the system becomes vulnerable and its future uncertain. During such periods, business and government leaders dispel all pretensions of deferring economic affairs to Adam Smith's "invisible hand" and rush to the rescue of the system with all kinds of crisis-management, or restructuring, schemes. The ability to manage such crises is critical to the functioning of the capitalist system. An understanding of the theory and experience of "long waves" of capitalist development is, therefore, crucial to our discussion of the future of capitalism.

Theoretical Framework: The Marxian Profit-Rate Theory of the Long Waves

Alternating periods of boom and bust are rather well established in the history of advanced capitalist economies. Economists make a distinction between the "usual" business cycles, ranging from a few to several years, and the longer cycles of a few or several decades known as long waves or "Kondratieffs."[1]

While mainstream economists focus primarily on short-term fluctuations, heterodox economists provide a number of theories of long waves of capitalist development. Three of the most well known of these theories are: (a) innovation or technologically determined theory, associated with Nikolai Kondratieff and Joseph Schumpeter; (b) the "social structure of accumulation" (SSA) theory, expounded by David Gordon and his various co-authors; and (c) the Marxian profit-rate theory, associated largely with Leon Trotsky and Ernest Mandel.

The innovation theory maintains that long waves of expansion result from clusters of innovations in particular industries or sectors. Depressed economic conditions trigger clusters of major innovations first in a new "leading" sector that grows rapidly and then, through diffusion and linkages, drives a general economic upswing. In the early stages of the expansion there will be high rates of follow-through product and process innovation in the leading sectors, which will result in high rates of profit and accelerated growth. As the process set in motion gradually moves toward market saturation in new lines of business, and results in tight labor markets and rising wages, a slowdown in new innovations and in the rate of follow-through product and process improvements will follow. This will eventually weaken, if not put in reverse, the innovation multiplier (à la Keynes), thereby ushering in a new wave of economic stagnation.

The SSA approach places the primary emphasis on institutions: a set of institutional arrangements that "alternately stimulates and constrains the pace of capital accumulation. If constituent institutions of the SSA are stable, working smoothly and without challenge, capitalists are likely to feel secure about investing in the expansion of productive capacity." This will then foster a long-wave of upswing. "But if the SSA begins to become shaky, if class conflict or past capitalist accumulation have pressed the institutions to their limits and they begin to lose their legitimacy," then investment and accumulation will slow down, ushering in a long period of stagnation. Eventually, a new SSA is "constructed" in order to bring about a new expansion, and the process begins again (Gordon et al. 1994, 15–16).

In the Marxian profit-rate theory there is a tight relationship between the movements of the long-term average rate of profit and general, economywide long-wave developments. Indeed, "a Marxist long wave theory," as Mandel points out, "is in the last analysis a theory of long waves in the average rate of profit." According to this theory, while the transition from periods of expansion to periods of stagnation can be explained by the inner laws of the accumulation of capital (specifically, by the Marxian law of the tendency of the rate of profit to fall), the reverse is not true. That is, the turn from long periods of stagnation to those of expansion cannot be explained by "purely endogenous" factors: "exogenous" or "extraeconomic" factors are required to bring about such upward transitions. These extraeconomic factors include not only domestic policies of restructuring, but also external factors and foreign policy measures that are designed to capture new markets and enhance profitability on a global level. They are, in essence, economic, legal, political, institutional, and, at times, military instruments of class struggle that are employed by business and government leaders in pursuit of profitability (Mandel 1980, 20–22, 51–52).

The asymmetry of upturns and downturns in Mandel's theory stands in sharp contrast to the SSA theory's symmetric account of such turns according to which long waves of capitalist development are just as able to endogenously move from down- to upswings as they are from up- to downswings (Gordon 1978, 28).

How does this SSA view stand in light of experience? Not very well. It finds relevance primarily in the social structure of accumulation and the restructuring policies that were developed in response to the Great Depression of the 1930s, and in the subsequent social and economic developments leading up to the late 1970s. But this is not entirely fortuitous, as the SSA theory seems to have been both prompted by and largely based on the prewar restructuring experience, the subsequent postwar expansion, and the decline of that expansion in the 1970s. Not surprising, then, the SSA approach finds only limited relevance to the restructuring policies of other major economic crises. Both the restructuring policies in response to the crisis of the 1890s as well as those in response to the crisis of the 1970s were crafted and implemented unilaterally by the business and government leaders, rather than being mapped out by a collective or pluralistic social structure of accumulation, as claimed in the SSA theory. To the extent that this theory finds relevance to the depression of the 1930s, it is limited primarily to the U. S. case: it cannot explain why in the United States it led to FDR's New Deal coalition, while the depression in Europe and elsewhere led to fascism and war.

Mandel's theory of exogenous "extraeconomic" factors, by contrast, better explains such unpredictable outcomes of the interplay of social forces in the course of long periods of crises. For, according to this theory, the outcome of crisis-management strategies, of institutional overhauls, and of class struggles, are not "pre-determined by the process of capital accumulation and labor organization in the previous period," that is, by "the previous social structure of accumulation," as argued by the SSA theorists (Mandel 1980, 52–53). In other words, sociopolitical and institutional changes in response to long periods of crises at times develop in relatively autonomous, random, and uncontrollable ways that could then place the capitalist system at fateful crossroads, including the road to socialism and the road to war and fascism.

This perspective of long waves serves as the theoretical framework of our study as it integrally ties together the major tendencies of technical change, profit-rate, capital accumulation, and class struggle, under capitalism.

Major Crises of the U.S. Economy and the "Extraeconomic" Measures Adopted to Overcome Them

The Challenge of the First Great Depression (1873–1897)

The long economic hardship that began in the early 1870s and lasted through the late 1890s was bound to create social tension. The resulting protest reactions occurred among the working class and urban poor, as well as the farming population. While labor protests were largely sporadic, they were nonetheless threatening to capitalist interests as they were at times very radical. Militant labor responses included the Knights of Labor movement, miners' protests against their working conditions in both the northern and southern coal fields, dock workers' massive strikes in New Orleans, and the steel workers' fight against the Carnegie lockout at Homestead, Pennsylvania. The Pullman strike led to "a dramatic confrontation between Eugene Deb's American Railway Union and federal troops; roughly fourteen thousand police, militia, and troops were called upon to crush the strike, with hundreds arrested and at least thirty killed" (Bowles, Gordon, and Weisskopf 1990, 20–21).

The farmers' protest activities developed into a systematic and well-organized movement, constituting the backbone of the Populist movement and the People's Party. The National Farmers' Alliance, which grew in membership to hundreds of thousands by the early 1880s, focused on agrarian populist demands such as easy money, public control of the banks, and public ownership and control of the railroads and telegraph lines. But while the primary concerns of individual members or chapters were immediate economic demands, the Populists' overall or national concerns—as reflected in the policies of the People's Party—went beyond their own narrow economic interests; they also "demanded a graduated income tax, restraints on monopoly, education, the direct election of senators, . . . and the referendum" (McConnell 1959, 5).

The elections of 1892, which showed considerable support for People's Party candidates among the farming and laboring population, boded ill for the interests of big business and industrial giants. The pillars of U.S. capitalism felt threatened:

> Business interests rallied as if in a fire emergency. They concluded that agrarian and urban interests must be split. . . . Beginning with the congressional elections of 1894, the wealthy mobilized their support behind the Republican party. . . . They concentrated on building an electoral alliance with industrial wage earners, seeking to forestall their potential coalition with populist farmers in the West. . . . The strategy worked. While the Democrats carried the states where the People's party had scored most substantially in 1892, McKinley [the Republican candidate] won the election on the strength of his margins in the industrial states. . . . The populists lost, soon to disappear from the political arena, and a new and powerful electoral coalition guided by big business had triumphed. (Bowles, Gordon, Weisskopf 1990, 21–22)

Building on this newly gained political strength, big business moved swiftly on several fronts to implement further political and institutional changes in order to bring about economic recovery. On the labor front, they combined ruse with sheer force: on the one hand, they promised tariffs to protect "American jobs"; on the other, they called out federal troops and private militias to crush unions. Simultaneously, business and government leaders sought to end the so-called "cutthroat" competition of the nineteenth century by removing political, legal, and institutional barriers against industrial and business combinations and consolidations. This paved the way for the gigantic wave of mergers and takeovers around the turn of the century (Bowles, Gordon, and Weisskopf 1990, 22).

Another factor that helped end the long wave of economic depression was the new and growing world market for U.S. exports. Rapidly catching up with European economic and/or colonial powers, U.S. industrial giants began making headway into international markets around the turn of the century. The government actively supported the aims of businesses wishing to establish foreign ventures and compete internationally. Teddy Roosevelt's blunt statement, "I should welcome almost any war, for I think this country needs one," succinctly captures the mood of this time and the need of big business in the United States for the expansion of foreign markets (Zinn 1980, 290).

Extensive economic, political, and institutional restructuring (including suppression of the labor and trade union movements, fostering of big business and concentrated industries, and corporate welfare plans), combined with the opening of markets abroad, helped to end the protracted economic crisis that began in the early 1870s, and ushered in a new long wave of economic expansion that lasted until the late 1920s.

The Challenge of the Second Great Depression (1929–1937)

The economic crash of 1929 and the ensuing long depression resulted from a complex set of factors. A discussion of those factors is beyond the scope and the focus of this study. Whatever its causes, the fact is that the depression made living conditions for the overwhelming majority of people extremely difficult.

Once again, as during the Great Depression of 1873–1897, economic distress precipitated popular unrest. Large numbers of the discontented frequently took to the streets in the early 1930s. Their desire for change swelled the ranks of socialist, communist, and other opposition parties and groups. Left activists gained influence in labor ranks, and workers' movements for unionization, illegal in many industries until 1935, spread rapidly. "The union literature was like the labor literature of a century ago—looking toward a successor to capitalism" (Terkel 1970, 309).

Labor and other grassroots support led to an unprecedented number of votes for third-party candidates in the 1932 presidential election. Third-party votes were even more impressive in congressional and local elections (Piven and Cloward 1977; Terkel 1970).

Business and government leaders clearly understood the gravity of the situation and the need for reform to fend off revolution: "F.D.R. was very significant in understanding how best to lead this sort of situation. . . . The industrialists who had some understanding recognized this right away. He could not have done what he did without the support of important elements of the wealthy class" (Terkel 1970, 268–69).

The core principle of the ensuing big business–government consensus, known as the New Deal, was that government intervention must be limited to stimulative and distributive measures. These policies would provide relief to the economically hard-pressed and reduce social tension while stimulating the economy and promising stable growth and rising profitability.

The New Deal stimulus package of government spending was further strengthened by the huge expenditures of World War II. Those expenditures not only served to expand the domestic market, they also paved the way for the U.S. dominance of world markets. A number of other "extraeconomic" factors also contributed to the postwar recovery: bureaucratic, pliant labor leadership and peaceful trade unionism; further penetration into and expansion of world markets by the U.S. transnational corporations; establishment of the Bretton Woods System and restoration of international trade and finance; increased investment in the armaments sector with state-guaranteed profits; Cold War ideology and the suppression or pacification of any possible dissent; relative decline in the price of oil and other raw materials, especially after 1950; and so on (Mandel 1980, 23–24; Kotz et al. 1994, 68–69).

Thus a combination of extensive economic and extraeconomic factors, initiated and implemented by business and government leaders, helped once again to turn a long wave of economic depression into a long wave of economic expansion. And while the crisis-resolution tactics of the 1930s were quite different from those of the 1890s, the end result was the same: rescue of the capitalist system and restoration of the political and economic power of the capitalist class.

The Challenge of the Latest Long Wave of Economic Crisis (1973–1982)

In his *Long Waves of Capitalist Development* (1980), Ernest Mandel argued that a reversal of the protracted economic crisis that had begun in the early 1970s depended on (a) "shattering defeats for the working class" in key industrialized countries; (b) "radical rather than marginal changes in . . . some key areas of the so-called third world into large markets for capitalist commodities"; and (c) "the possibility of huge expansion of markets in the postcapitalist [Soviet-bloc] countries." In short, Mandel argued that such a reversal "depended on the outcome of momentous battles between capital and labor" (113–19).

To varying degrees, almost all of these conditions for a long-term economic upturn have since materialized. To begin with, the opening of the Chinese and the formerly Soviet-bloc markets to Western products and capital is offering tremendous opportunities for global business and international capital—the current economic chaos in the so-called emerging markets notwithstanding.

Second, the Third World is much different than it was twenty or even fifteen years ago. It is considerably more open to doing business with corporations from the "North" and the "West" than it was in the past. Many of the Third World nationalist leaders who shunned Western capital and advocated policies of import substitution and economic planning have been replaced by promarket leaders eager to import foreign capital.

Third, the corporate offensive against labor since the mid-1970s proved successful in reducing labor costs for businesses. The antilabor collaboration between the business and government leaders in the United States resulted in (a) 12 to 20 percent cuts in real wages and benefits between the mid-1970s and the mid-1990s; (b) easier dismissal of union workers and hiring of contingency workers; and (c) further mobility of capital throughout the world (Schor 1991; Yates 1994).

Additional restructuring measures to reverse the economic slowdown of the 1970s included a systematic curtailment of the social "safety net" of unemployment compensation, public education and public health benefits, housing subsidies, food stamps, and the like. Deregulation of business and relaxation of antitrust laws have also been vigorously pursued. Most importantly, tax overhauls since the early 1980s in favor of the wealthy have made income distribution increasingly more lopsided.

The combined business–government efforts to revive corporate profitability have had the desired effects: labor costs in real terms fell (on average) by about 16 percent between 1975 and 1995, and the long declines of the 1970s in productivity, profitability, and investment have all been turned into long expansions. After almost a decade of aggressive policies of economic restructuring, most U.S. corporations regained their international competitive edge by the late 1980s. Evidence shows that manufacturers' gain in productivity, combined with flat or falling real wages (certainly until 1995–96), has resulted in a considerable rise in total profitability since the early 1990s.

Financed by strong profits, investment spending has also been on the rise since the early 1990s. While in the first few years of expansion most investment spending was in the form of increased capital intensity of production in existing operations, in recent years manufacturers have begun to put new capacity in place. Since 1995, overall business spending on new equipment has risen to about 8 percent of national output annually, a very high rate of capacity building. The rate of increase of business spending on computers and/or information technology during this period has been twice the rate of other capital goods. Capital spending in 1998, for example, was up a "spectacular" 17.5 percent, way above the 11 percent average annual growth rate for the 1990s. For high-tech industries capital spending was 32 percent in 1998, with a 19 percent annual average since 1991. High rates of investment since the early 1990s have raised the long-term productivity growth rate to 2 percent or more, which, while not quite as high as those of the mid-1960s, is double the rate in the 1970s and 1980s (*Business Week,* February 15, 1999, 30–31).

Impressive as this investment boom is, it does not tell us much about how long the current expansion might continue. In fact, the investment boom sends a mixed message: as it enhances productivity and economizes on labor costs, it also increases the capital–labor ratio—the organic composition of capital à la Marx—which tends to lower the rate of profit. The presence of a number of strong counteracting tendencies, however, indicates that the expansion may not come to an end any time soon. What are such counteracting factors?

To begin with, it is highly likely that the recently heightened productivity increase will continue for some time, due to the now pervasive use of information technology throughout the economy. Second, because economic growth in the United States is now driven largely by high-tech information-related technology where prices are falling, the capital–labor ratio will not grow as fast as previously when the driving forces of economic growth were steel, railroads, or automobiles. The declining price of the leading growth technology will serve as a countervailing force acting against the rising organic composition of capital, thereby propping up profits for a longer period of time. Third, drastically expanded global markets, combined with computer technology and the aggressive global economic policies of neoliberalism, mean that U.S. big business now can produce and sell anywhere, as well as source from anywhere. The heightened competitive pressure on an international level means that both prices (especially of primary products) and wages can be kept under control for a longer period than in past expansions.

Despite the presence of these strong countertendencies to the tendency of the rate of profit to fall, it is not possible to predict how long the current expansion of the U.S. economy will continue. One thing is clear, however, the combined economic and extraeconomic measures that business and government leaders employed in response to the stagnation of the 1970 have succeeded in turning that long declining cycle into a long expansive one.

Lessons and Implications for Social Change

Both in the 1890s and 1980s the reversal of long economic downturns were brought about as a result of, among other things, huge transfers of income from labor to capital. In the 1930s, in contrast, workers and other popular forces achieved employment and income security as a result of sustained pressure from "below." The contrast between these two different types of "restructuring" strategies shows how resourceful business and government leaders can be in employing all kinds of instruments of class struggle—at times, even diametrically opposed instruments—in order to restore capitalist profitability, accumulation, and expansion.

What are the implications of this for the future of capitalism? Does it mean that the reign of capitalism has thus become permanent and that we have reached "the end of history"?

Not necessarily. It simply means that the capitalist system is much more resilient than many of its radical opponents—especially proponents of the so-called theory of "automatic collapse"—imagine, and that the course of the apparently automatic alternation of periods of economic expansion and contraction is dialectically intertwined with that of social developments and class struggle. It signifies capitalism's ability to restructure the conditions for profitability and reproduction as long as the costly consequences of such restructuring policies in terms of job losses, economic insecurity, and environmental degradation are tolerated. More specifically, as long as the working class keeps producing according to the desires and designs of the capitalist system, the reign of capital will continue. No other social class or stratum, no matter how militant or numerous, has the unique or strategic position and capability to bring capitalist production to a standstill—and the capitalist system to an end. Only the working class can play such a role.

When will workers gain the necessary consciousness and determination to appropriate and utilize the existing technology for a better organization and management of the world economy in the interests of the majority of world citizens? No one can tell. One thing is certain, however: to play such a role, the working class needs new visions and new politics. The new labor politics will need to (a) go beyond trade unionism, (b) go beyond national borders, (c) build independent labor organizations, and (d) operate through coalitions and alliances with nonlabor grassroots opposition groups.

Many people would view these ideas and projections as unrealistic. What they probably mean by this is that these proposals cannot be realized under the present socioeconomic and political structure. And they are right. But, as this social structure is reorganized, many of the currently "impossible" alternatives will become possible.

There is definitely no dearth of material resources for this purpose. Certainly not in the United States and other industrialized countries. What is lacking is the political will and/or capacity to reorient society's priorities and reallocate its resources. The realizability of these proposals (and the fate of capitalism) ultimately comes down to the relationship of social forces and the balance of class struggle.

Note

1. Although long waves of capitalist development have become synonymous with Kondratieff's name, his contribution to the study of long waves was by no means prototypical or original. Earlier contributions had been made (among others) by Parvus, Kautsky, Van Geldren, and De Wolff (see, e.g., Day 1976; Kleinknecht et al. 1992; Mandel 1980).

Bibliography

Bowles, Samuel, David Gordon, and Thomas Weisskopf. 1990. *After the Wasteland*. Armonk, NY: M.E. Sharpe.

Day, Richard B. 1976. "The Theory of Long Waves: Kondratieff, Trotsky, Mandel." *New Left Review* 99: 67–82.

Goldstein, Joshua S. 1988. *Long Cycles: Prosperity and War in the Modern Age*. New Haven: Yale University Press.

Gordon, David. 1978. "Up and Down the Long Roller Coaster." In Cherry et al., *US Economy in Crisis*, 22–35, New York: Union for Radical Political Economics.

Gordon, David, Richard Edwards, and Michael Reich. 1994. "Long Waves and Stages of Capitalism." In *Social Structures of Accumulation*, ed. Kotz, McDonough, and Reich.

Kleinknecht, Alfred, Ernest Mandel, and Immanual Wallerstein, eds. 1992. *New Findings in Long Wave Research*. New York: St. Martin's Press.

Kotz, David, T. McDonough, and M. Reich. 1994. *Social Structures of Accumulation*. UK: Cambridge University Press.

McConnell, Grant. 1959. *The Decline of Agrarian Democracy*. Berkeley: University of California Press.

McDonough, Terrence. 1998. "The Economics of Marxian Stage Theory." Unpublished paper, Department of Economics, National University of Ireland–Galway.

Mandel, Ernest. 1980. *The Long Waves of Capitalist Development*. UK: Cambridge University Press.

Piven, Francis F., and Richard A. Cloward. 1977. *Poor People's Movements*. New York: Pantheon Books.

Schor, Juliet. 1991. *The Overworked American*. New York: Basic Books.

Terkel, Studs. 1970. *Hard Times: An Oral History of the Great Depression*. New York: Pantheon Books.

Yates, Michael. 1994. *Longer Hours, Fewer Jobs: Employment and Unemployment in the United States*. New York: Monthly Review Press.

Zinn, Howard. 1980. *A People's History of the United States*. New York: Harper & Row.

11

On Transformational Growth

Interview with Edward J. Nell

Edward J. Nell and Steven Pressman

Introduction

The theory of "transformational growth" starts with the historical observations discussed in this interview and expands to develop structural and behavioral theories of capitalist and precapitalist economies that build on the works of Marx, Sraffa, Marshall, and Keynes. The structural theory links Sraffian classical price and quantity equations to economic growth through the "golden rule," and to monetary circulation through the "Marxian balancing condition" (Nell 1996, 1998a, 1998b).[1] These conditions lead to a linear wage/profit tradeoff in a growing economy, which anchors a modified "circulation theory of money" (Deleplace and Nell 1996).[2] The theory then derives behavioral insights for nineteenth-century "craft economies" and twentieth-century "mass production" economies that build on Marshall and Keynes.

Transformational growth theory implies that neoclassical economics is largely based on nineteenth-century institutional patterns and that the Keynesian view is more applicable to twentieth-century mass-production economies. This wide-ranging approach has applications to everything from economic methodology and the Marxian transformation problem to class structure and the future of global capitalism.

The following is excerpted from interviews conducted by Steve Pressman, co-editor of the *Review of Political Economy*, with Edward Nell in April and June of 1993 (Nell 1998a, 287–311).

Interview[3]

Pressman: How do you see the analysis of the changing institutional structure of the business firm as leading to an explanation of long-term economic growth, and specifically an explanation for the slowdown of growth in the United States and other developed economies throughout the world?

Nell: Let me postpone the second half of that for a moment and take up the issue of the changing nature of the firm and economic growth. We were talking about the emergence of the modern corporation from the family firm, a development that took place in the late nineteenth century and early twentieth century. This transformation requires some careful scrutiny, because if we look at the

The "introduction," "conclusion," "notes," and "bibliography," sections of this chapter were written by Ron Baiman, and reviewed by Margaret Duncan and Raymond Majewski with the consent of the authors. All errors and deficiencies in these sections are the responsibility of Baiman, Duncan, and Majewski.

time series for the business cycle and for the changing structure of the economy in the nineteenth century and compare it with later periods, we find some really very striking differences. In the late nineteenth century we find a very similar pattern of statistical time series behavior in the United States, the U.K., Canada, and Germany. We find that prices generally tend downward until the period just before the First World War. We find that money wages are rather steady; they don't fluctuate much, although they do fluctuate in both directions, and over time they rise slightly. We find that manufacturing prices fluctuate both up and down; they're flexible in both directions. Manufacturing prices are not, however, as flexible on the whole as raw material prices, except in Germany where we have Bismarck's supports for agricultural prices.

Thus, we find that raw material prices are more flexible in both directions than manufacturing prices, which are more flexible in both directions than money wages, which only occasionally fall and tend to be level or slightly rising. Interestingly, we find that fluctuations in employment are restrained; the fluctuations in employment may be even smaller than during the post–Second World War period.

This sounds a little bit like Christina Romer (1986, 1989), but the point is quite different.[4] Fluctuations in output are more considerable than fluctuations in employment, but fluctuations in output are highly correlated in the short run with fluctuations in productivity. Productivity fluctuates a lot in the short run, and fluctuates more than employment. It's this that gives rise to the fluctuations in output. Now when we look at the pattern formed by taking these statistical series in relation to each other, we find that it is rather distinctive; indeed, it is quite a famous pattern. Marshall called attention to it in connection with the 1870s in England; it is the pattern associated with marginal productivity theory — real wages are inversely related to employment and output. Hicks suggested a very simple explanation for this. What happens is that changes in demand drive up prices initially, lowering the real wage, and making it worthwhile to disrupt work crews and routine by introducing additional workers.

Pressman: What about the long run? Do changes in demand drive up prices over a longer period of time?

Nell: In the nineteenth century prices fell over the long run. Rising productivity and competition forced them down. But in the short run, prices varied with demand, because output could only be varied with difficulty. Productivity could be increased in the short run by working more intensively, but this is a temporary response and it can't last. Therefore, when demand increases permanently, employment will have to be increased; but to increase employment means to add workers to a labor force that has to work together. That is to say, you have to reorganize work crews. You are not simply adding people to an assembly line, you are adding them to a group of skilled workers who have to cooperate. This requires disrupting the normal flow of work in order to reorganize. It is, therefore, expensive. Thus, a rise in prices is necessary to pay for the disruption and the reorganization of the labor process. Hence we find the inverse relationship between real wages and employment. It is a consequence, on the one hand, of demand pressures, and the other hand of the nature of the labor process—that is to say technology and the organization of labor that exists in the conditions of the family firm and in what I have called craft-based factories. Once the reorganization is complete, and production has expanded, prices may very well fall below their earlier level, or drift even lower, if economies of scale are eventually realized. Hence the long-run downward trend of prices.

Pressman: How does this relationship between demand and prices change with the introduction of the modern corporation?

Nell: The rise of the modern corporation based on mass production technology changes a number of economic relationships. First of all, continuous throughput makes it possible to greatly speed up work, and because work is carried out in a way that does not require all labor crews to work together all the time, it makes it possible to shut down and start up production, and to lay off and rehire workers in a relatively simple and not very costly manner. It makes it possible, in short, to adjust employment and output to demand. Hence, we would expect to find that the variation of productivity with output in the short run was much less after the introduction of mass production. This is not to suggest that the correlation of productivity and output in the long run would be affected by the changing nature of the firm. This is a different matter, and the connections have come to be known as Kaldor's Laws.[5] But the relationship between output and productivity in the short run is different. Quarterly data, half yearly, and yearly data show a very strong correlation in the nineteenth century where we have such data, which is only industry by industry. We would expect to find after the introduction of mass production that prices were very much less sensitive to demand, particularly manufacturing prices. We would expect prices not to fall, because when demand falls, employment and output will be reduced, so there would be no necessity to dump and force prices down, while costs will be adjusted by laying off workers. So with mass production, layoffs will develop as an institutionalized practice. When workers are laid off, there is either an implicit or an explicit promise to rehire them, generally in line with seniority. So we would expect the adjustment process here to be significantly different from the adjustment process in the nineteenth century.

Pressman: Are the two adjustment processes, in fact, different?

Nell: We do find that the time series are different. Prices in the post–Second World War period rise almost without exception, in all advanced countries. We find very few downtrends in prices. We find money wages rising; and here's an interesting phenomena, we find money wages rising faster than prices, in marked contrast to the relationship before the First World War. Productivity gains in other words accrue through the more rapid increase of money wages than of prices. In contrast, during the pre–First World War period we find money wages tending to be steady and prices falling. Productivity gains are transmitted to the economy through falling prices in the pre–First World War period. In the post–Second World War period they're transmitted by the more rapid rise of money wages, a different kind of mechanism, a point Sylos-Labini (1989, 1993) has stressed.[6]

As a result of this different mechanism, we would expect to find output and employment quite flexible in response to demand. With prices relatively stable in the short run, we would also expect to find a multiplier, and perhaps a multiplier-accelerator, process. We see this most clearly in the interwar period because in the interwar period there is no attempt to stabilize the economy through countercyclical government spending or other countercyclical measures. Hence, there were very large fluctuations. In the post–Second World War period, these fluctuations are dampened by countercyclical measures—and by the presence of a large government sector. But the countercyclical measures are only partly successful—in the post–

War period we find that employment and output are more flexible in both directions than prices, which are flexible only upwards.

Pressman: Does this help to account for the prevalence of inflation in the post–Second World War era?

Nell: In the advanced countries, moderate inflation has been a consequence of the way the price mechanism distributes the gains from rising productivity. When productivity rose, the money wages of the production workers, the workers on the lines, would rise in proportion. That is the effect of collective bargaining. But these increases disrupt relative status positions; so the wages and salaries of other kinds of workers or workers in other sectors would have to rise, too, to keep pace. If auto and steel workers earned more as their productivity rose, teachers and lawyers and doctors—to say nothing of business executives—had to maintain their relative social standing, so their earnings would have to rise more or less in step. (A similar point was made by Baumol and Bowen about the performing arts.) But this implies that costs will rise. So prices rise, and a wage–price spiral is established.

Transformational growth suggests another mechanism. Even when mass production has become dominant, some sectors and industries retain characteristics of the craft system. In particular, agriculture and primary production tend to have inflexible employment and to produce goods that, after a point, are expensive to stockpile and have to be dumped. Their prices are therefore flexible. Another industry that retained strong craft characteristics (for different reasons) is machine tools, and there again, prices tend to be demand sensitive.

In each case when demand falls, prices will tend to drift down, even, on occasion, to collapse. Conversely, when demand rises, prices in these sectors will rise. Price flexibility reflects difficulties in adjusting; hence the effect depends not only on size of the movement, but also on the speed. These price changes will be transmitted as cost increases to all the other sectors: raw materials and primary products enter production at the beginning, while machine tools affect the cost of investment, and hence influence future prices.

Prior to the First World War this flexibility would cut both directions. But not anymore. The price-flexible industries supply the dominant mass production sector, which adapts its level of output to demand. Prices rise when demand is strong, and large quantities of raw materials are needed. The price increase is therefore weighted heavily, and has a substantial impact on other sectors. When demand is weak prices will be low, but their impact will be weak, because the quantity is low. Similarly for machine tools: when demand is strong investment will be large, and the high prices will have a strong impact; but when demand is weak prices will decline; however, the impact will be small, because little investment will be undertaken. Hence price increases will always be weighted more heavily than price declines and the effect of fluctuations will be to impart an upward bias to prices.

Once we understand that moderate inflation results from the way the system works, it should be clear that most anti-inflationary policy is misguided.

Pressman: Let's try to carry this analysis up through the 1970s, 1980s, and 1990s. You talked about a change of the business enterprise from family-owned firm to a large modern corporation that operates as Galbraith describes in *The New Industrial State*. But the modern corporation itself has undergone important changes in a number of ways over the past quarter century. In the United States there has been a decline in manufacturing and a similar decline in use of mass production manufacturing processes. Likewise, the firm is no longer a national firm, but is really a global firm that is producing all over the world. How does this changing nature of the corporation affect the relationships between demand, prices, productivity, and employment?

Nell: These recent changes in the corporation are important, but hard to analyze because we are at the beginning of the process. Hegel says somewhere the owl of Minerva takes wing only at dusk. So it's easier to see the shape of the mass production economy now, at the end of its life, and as it's beginning to change into the information economy, than it is to see the real shape of the emerging economy based on information technologies and global production.

However, I think that some things are clear. One is that there is a changing cost structure and these changes are very considerable. Fixed costs are important in the mass production economy; but such fixed costs are embodied in capital equipment. In the information economy, we find a lot of invisible sunk costs. They show up in the contractual obligations of firms. These costs were incurred in the process of research and development. So there's nothing tangible like a factory or set of buildings that correspond to them. This is one change. Another change is that variable costs appear to be shrinking, very remarkably. Variable costs are quite important in mass production; it appears they're not so important in the cost structure of the global multinational corporation. The importance of information, and of managerial and technical skills (that is, the skills of highly trained Ph.D. engineers, computer specialists, software developers, and managers), is clearly very significant in the global arrangements of firms. These skills and information inputs tend to be "lumpy," to come in discrete units. The implication is that as output levels increase, such inputs will be spread over more units of output, so that unit costs will tend to fall; that is, the new information economy may exhibit increasing returns in many activities.

Moreover, the multi-division structure of the large corporation may be giving way to a more fragmented structure—that is, less hierarchical and based more on contacts and franchising than on command from above. The image is of a network, rather than a hierarchy, a spiderweb rather than a pyramid. These developments mean greater flexibility in moving capital around the globe, and also greater flexibility in moving highly skilled, high-paid managerial and entrepreneurial labor from country to country. The position of the working-class labor force, however, is much less flexible. Such labor is much less mobile, whereas in those aspects of production that can be separated and shifted about, jobs can be moved in search of the cheapest wages. The result is that the lowest wage for labor of a given productivity will tend to set the standard internationally.

A similar result holds for short-term interest rates. Financial capital can be moved faster and more easily than ever. But shifts in short-term capital threaten exchange rates. To defend exchange rates, interest must be set at the level of the highest rate, for a given level of safety. Thus wages will be driven down and interest rates will be driven up. And, of course, local government structures and even national government structures are likewise at the mercy of those who can pull up stakes and leave for better climates. Taxes and the "climate for investment" have to be adjusted to compete. As a result governments are experiencing much greater difficulty in controlling macroeconomic processes and in regulating microeconomic issues and disputes. Part of the economic malaise that we're facing at present surely comes from the inability of government to keep pace.

Pressman: Do you see this relative increase in the

ability of capital to cross national boundaries, especially in comparison with the relative immobility of laborers and governments, as contributing to the slowdown of economic growth and the slowdown in productivity growth that we have experienced recently?

Nell: Yes, if you mean national growth and national productivity. The problems of government in the face of the changing nature of capital have been quite significant. As capital's mobility has increased and as the nature of technology has changed, capital has been very anxious to remove regulations and restrictions in order to take advantage of the new possibilities. Therefore, they have put considerable political pressure on governments to remove regulations and they have tried to limit government control, government investment, government domination of economic decisions. They have weakened or undermined the instruments of government control.

Conclusion

The theory of transformation growth highlights the limitations of currently dominant branches of economics by revealing their dependence on transient historical conditions. The transformational growth approach is an attempt to both uncover essential structural aspects of market-based economic systems, and offer historically specific policy insights that relate to the core class and power structures of capitalism. In this sense, the theory of "transformational growth" is directly descended from Marx and squarely within the tradition of radical political economics.

Notes

1. The "classical equations" are input–output equations, which link profit, wages, and prices on the one hand, and growth, consumption, and output on the other. The "golden rule" stipulates that the rate of profit equals the rate of growth. The "Marxian balancing condition" states that for economic reproduction to occur, the wage goods bill of the investment sector must equal the investment goods bill of the consumption sector (Nell 1998b, ch. 7).

2. A "linear wage/profit tradeoff" implies that monetary means of payment will not change if distribution, or wage and profit levels, change. "Circulation theories of money," which have been developed primarily by French authors, emphasize the role of money as a means of circulation rather than as a financial asset (Deleplace and Nell 1996).

3. This interview was excerpted and edited from its original version by Heather Boushey and Dawn Saunders and reviewed by Margaret Duncan and Raymond Majewski with the consent of the authors. All errors and deficiencies in this section relative to the original are the responsibility of Boushey, Saunders, Duncan, and Majewski.

4. Christina Romer (1986, 1989) has questioned the validity of Simon Kuznets's national income data for studying business cycles in the U.S. economy claiming that more accurate estimates would reduce the volatility of pre–World War II data.

5. Nicholas Kaldor (1966, 1975) has argued that: (a) there exists a strong correlation between the growth of manufacturing output and the growth of GDP; (b) there is a strong positive relation between the rate of growth of productivity in manufacturing and the growth of manufacturing output; and (c) the faster the growth of manufacturing, the faster the rate of labor transfer from manufacturing to nonmanufacturing, so that overall productivity growth is strongly correlated with manufacturing output and employment growth and negatively associated with the growth of employment outside of manufacturing.

6. Paolo Sylos-Labini (1989, 1993) has argued that the growth process in the nineteenth century was characterized by the transmission of productivity growth through falling prices but that after World War II prices and wages became inflexible downward because of oligopolization and unionization of the economy.

References

Deleplace, Ghislain, and Edward J. Nell. 1996. *Money in Motion: The Post Keynesian and Circulation Approaches*. New York: St. Martin's Press.

Kaldor, Nicholas. 1966. *Causes of the Slow Rate of Economic Growth of the United Kingdom.* Cambridge: Cambridge University Press.

———. 1975. "Economic Growth and the Verdoorn Law: A Comment on Mr. Rowthorn's Article." *Economic Journal* (March).

Nell, Edward J. 1996. *Making Sense of a Changing Economy.* New York and London: Routledge.
———, ed. 1998a. *Transformational Growth and the Business Cycle.* New York and London: Routledge.
———. 1998b. *The General Theory of Transformational Growth.* New York: Cambridge University Press.
Romer, Christina. 1986. "Is the Stabilization of the Postwar Economy a Figment of the Data?" *American Economic Review* 76: 314–39.
———. 1989. "The Prewar Business Cycle Reconsidered: New Estimates of Gross National Product, 1869–1908." *Journal of Political Economy* 97, no. 1: 1–37.
Sylos-Labini, Paolo. 1989. *The Forces of Economic Growth and Decline.* Cambridge, MA: Harvard University Press.
———. 1993. *Economic Growth and Business Cycles.* Aldershot: Edward Elgar.

Section III

How We Live

Employment, Labor, and Income Distribution

12

The "Reserve Army of Labor" and the "Natural Rate of Unemployment"

Can Marx, Kalecki, Friedman, and Wall Street All Be Wrong?

Robert Pollin

I was extremely honored when the URPE Steering Committee invited me to give the first annual David Gordon Memorial Lecture at the URPE Summer Conference. In fact, in preparing for the lecture, I began jotting down some of the reasons why I felt honored. I quickly realized that I could spend my whole allotted time going through that list. But, exercising self-restraint, I'll just mention two crucial things.

First, as long as I knew David Gordon—and by this I literally mean from the first day I met David as a student in his 1975 New School class on Workers' Control until our last conversations—I knew him as a committed URPE worker. I want to emphasize my choice of words. David really did *work* for URPE. He did lots of work, including lots of the grubby work that is the foundation of any shoestring left organization. Almost all of this work he did quietly but relentlessly. He continued making contributions to URPE even after he became seriously ill.

Second, David made fundamental contributions in opening up a new research approach in political economy. It was research that made the best possible use of existing formal empirical techniques to address questions that concerned us on the left. In doing this, David—and others who have followed his approach—have been able to challenge orthodox pretensions on their own terms.

His research was also policy oriented in that it recognized with open eyes the world where it is right now. David correspondingly thought a lot about how to move the world from where it is today to where we want it to be: how to get from here to there. Part of the reason David thought in this way was due to his long-term active involvement in the U.S. labor movement, even at a time when many on the left felt uncomfortable being connected with mainstream labor institutions. David took this approach without wavering even one inch from his commitment to democratic socialist ideals. His approach seems especially pre-

This chapter was originally presented as the David Gordon Memorial Lecture at the 1997 Summer Conference of the Union for Radical Political Economics. It was previously published in the summer 1998 *Review of Radical Political Economics* 30, no. 3, 1–13, and is reprinted here with permission of the Union for Radical Political Economics. I am grateful for the stimulating comments of many participants at the initial presentation of this paper at the 1997 URPE Summer Conference, including John Miller, Tom Palley, and Jerry Epstein.

scient today—two years after his death—as the U.S. labor movement is undergoing such an exciting revival.

Given David's research concerns and political commitments, it was inevitable that he would spend much time reflecting on the subject of my lecture—the "Reserve Army of Labor" and the "Natural Rate of Unemployment." In 1987–88, David published two important papers explicitly on the natural rate and its offspring, the NAIRU, or nonaccelerating inflation rate of unemployment. But using different terminology, almost all of David's work on social structures of accumulation was about the same issues that occupy discussions about the reserve army and the natural rate—that is, how labor markets really work; the role of unions and other institutional forces in the economy; and the connections between an economy's macro performance and how that performance affects the well-being of ordinary people. I want to draw out some of those connections later. But I first want to recount a bit of the last conversation I had with David, while he was in the hospital, waiting for his heart transplant operation.

Believe it or not, we spent much of the time talking about the natural rate and NAIRU. We had both reached the conclusion that these were the single most powerful ideas in mainstream macroeconomics. We also agreed that these ideas were wrong, but we were not entirely clear on all the specific ways they were wrong. David said then that he really wanted to concentrate on this as soon as he got out of the hospital.

Since my last conversation with David, I have tried to become more clear in my thinking on this issue. I still believe that the natural rate and NAIRU are obviously wrong in some important ways and seriously misleading in others. But I also think that the natural rate/NAIRU are not wrong in other important ways, as I will try to explain. Moreover, I will argue that it is dangerous politically to dismiss entirely the ideas associated with the natural rate and NAIRU even though they are wrong in significant ways. I say this because I believe dismissing the natural rate and NAIRU because of the ways they are wrong can invite complacency in evaluating the very real and serious obstacles to sustaining full employment in capitalist economies. Let me try to flesh out some of these points.

The "Natural Rate": The Power to Do Harm

There are aspects of the contemporary idea of a natural rate or NAIRU about which someone on the left can justifiably feel hostile or at least suspicious. For starters, the idea originates with Milton Friedman (1968)[1] —as David Gordon said, "a person rarely noted for his irrepressible sympathies for the downtrodden and jobless," (1987, 225). But Friedman primarily just repackaged and gave a new name to an argument that had deep roots within classical economics and the so-called "classical dichotomy." The classical dichotomy asserts that endowments, tastes, and technology alone determine employment, incomes, and productivity and that government-controlled monetary forces alone determine fluctuations in the price level.

The way employment and incomes specifically are determined by endowments, tastes, and technology is that, in a competitive labor market environment, businesses will be forced to pay workers a wage equal to their marginal product. Wages can rise from this competitive equilibrium level, but only when productivity increases through technical change. At a given level of technology, workers can either accept a job at the equilibrium wage, or they can choose leisure over labor and become *voluntarily* unemployed. In Friedman's terminology then, the "natural rate" of *involuntary* unemployment is thus effectively zero (after allowing for frictional joblessness) as long as all workers earn their equilibrium wage. The natural rate of unemployment will become positive only when workers refuse to accept the equilibrium wage, or when nonmarket forces, such as labor unions, prevent the wage from falling to its full employment equilibrium point.

We know that packaging is crucial to selling a product. Friedman's restatement of the classical labor market model gave new life to an idea that was predominant among mainstream economists before Keynes: that unemployment is really the fault of workers themselves and their putative representatives, the labor unions. But building from Friedman, the natural rate concept really takes flight in some of the wild claims of Robert Lucas and other "new classical" economists. These claims include the idea that markets always clear instantaneously, so that—contrary even to Friedman's position—government policies to increase aggregate demand cannot have a positive impact on employment or real incomes even in the short run. New classicals have also argued that workers somehow massively chose leisure over labor during the Great Depression.

But more important than having just inspired such academic tall tales, the natural rate idea has also had pernicious effects in the area of real-world policy formation, through giving the stamp of scientific respectability to all sorts of attacks on working people. Such attacks include Thatcherism and Reaganism in the 1980s as well as the ongoing resistance in financial markets to any tendencies suggesting that workers' living standards might be improving. How many times in recent years have we heard about Wall Street becoming exercised over falling unemployment or prospects of wage increases, and responding exuberantly when, quarter after quarter, real wages fail to rise? Of course, the natural rate theory is not the cause, but only one expression of anti–working class politics. But it certainly has done a stellar job reinforcing antiworker perspectives that already exist. It is therefore easy to feel legitimate hostility toward anything connected with the natural rate.

Unemployment as an Instrument of Class Struggle

But before letting this justified hostility overtake us, we need to confront the ideas of Marx and Kalecki on a parallel concept—that is, on the reserve army of unemployed. In his justly famous chapter 25 of Volume I of *Capital* (1967), "The General Law of Capitalist Accumulation," Marx makes clear his view that unemployment is functional to capitalism. That is, when a capitalist economy is growing rapidly enough so that the reserve army of unemployed is depleted, then workers will utilize their increased bargaining power to raise wages and shift the distribution of income in their favor. Profits are correspondingly squeezed. As a result, capitalists' animal spirits are dampened and they reduce investment spending. This then leads to a fall in job creation, higher unemployment, and a replenishment of the reserve army. In other words, the reserve army of unemployed is the instrument capitalists use to prevent significant wage increases and thereby maintain profitability.

Kalecki makes parallel though distinct arguments in his also justly famous essay, "The Political Aspects of Full Employment," (1971). Kalecki is writing in 1943, immediately after the depression had ended and the Keynesian revolution—to which Kalecki was himself a major contributor—was gathering its head of steam. Combining his understanding of Marx with his perspective on the Keynesian revolution, Kalecki advanced three important points:

1. We now have sufficient understanding of the economics of aggregate demand such that we can devise workable policies to sustain a capitalist economy at full employment.

2. Contrary to Marx, full employment can be beneficial to the level of profits if not the rate of profit, because the economy will be operating at its highest possible rate of capacity utilization. Capitalists may well get a smaller share of the pie at full employment, but will nevertheless benefit from the full-employment economy because the size of the pie is growing far more rapidly than would be possible with significant positive rates of unemployment.
3. Even though capitalists can benefit from full employment, they still will not support it because full employment will threaten their control over the workplace, the pace and direction of economic activity, and even political institutions.

Relative to Marx, Kalecki thus focuses more on the broader social and political problems capitalists face due to full employment rather than prospects for a full-employment profit squeeze. From this perspective, Kalecki then also reasoned that full employment *was* sustainable under capitalism if these challenges to capitalists' social and political hegemony could be contained. This is why he held that fascist social and political institutions could well provide one "solution" to capitalism's unemployment problem: workers would have jobs, but they would never be permitted to exercise the political and economic power that would otherwise accrue to them in a full-employment economy.

Despite these differences with Marx, Kalecki does nevertheless clearly embrace the central thrust of the Marxian position: that some significant level of unemployment is functional to the operation of capitalist economies. But I want to push this notion of a common thread further. In my view, Marx and Kalecki also share a common conclusion with natural rate proponents, in that they would all agree that positive unemployment rates are the outgrowth of class struggle over the distribution of income and political power. Of course, Friedman and the new classicals reach this conclusion via analytic and political perspectives that are diametrically opposite to those of Marx and Kalecki. To put it in a nutshell, mass unemployment results in the Friedmanite/new classical view when workers demand more than they deserve, while for Marx and Kalecki, capitalists use the weapon of unemployment to prevent workers from getting their just due.

Liberal Keynesians are the only real opponents of the idea that unemployment serves a function in capitalist societies. Of course, John Maynard Keynes himself held that unemployment was irrational since it meant wasting available resources. Keynes was convinced that the wise application of well-designed policies could create and sustain full employment capitalism. Contemporary liberal Keynesians—and here I include some of our best allies, such as Professor Robert Eisner—hold firm to this view. Eisner himself has done important research (1997) demonstrating fundamental errors in the empirical specification of NAIRU. Among other prominent liberal Keynesians, Eisner has also emphasized the irony that right-wing economists such as Friedman seem to have appropriated an idea that originates with Karl Marx.

A Buried Truth Amid Errors

The world would certainly be a more civilized place if, by exposing all the sloppy research, logical errors, and downright foolishness bound up with the natural rate and NAIRU, we could then also conclude that unemployment serves no function in capitalism: that, as liberal Keynesians would have it, mass unemployment is just a big mistake. But let us examine some of the most obvious and egregious errors associated with the natural rate and NAIRU, and consider where these errors actually lead.

One point on which many natural rate critics, including David Gordon, have pounced is that there is nothing really "natural" about the "natural rate." But we need not expend much energy trying to win that argument. Even Milton Friedman accepts the point. He stated this quite clearly in his initial 1967 American Economic Association Presidential Address, in which he introduced the natural rate concept:

> [B]y using the term "natural" rate of unemployment, I do not mean to suggest that it is immutable and unchangeable. On the contrary, many of the market characteristics that determine its level are man-made and policy-made. In the United States, for example, legal minimum wage rates, the Walsh-Healy and Davis-Bacon Acts, and the strength of labor unions all make the natural rate of unemployment higher than it would otherwise be. (1968, 9)

So let's be clear here. The "natural rate" term has worked well for the right as an advertising concept, and we should be adamant in opposing false advertising. Scratch this surface though, and look at what Friedman himself is really saying: that what he terms the "natural rate" is really a social phenonenon measuring the class strength of working people, as indicated through their ability to organize effective unions and establish a livable minimum wage.[2]

Critics of the natural rate and NAIRU also correctly point out, again and again, that there is no set unemployment rate at which inflation reliably accelerates, either in the United States or elsewhere. This, of course, is irrefutable. For example, in 1990, unemployment in the United States was 5.6 percent and inflation, as measured by the consumer price index, was 5.4 percent. By 1997, unemployment was down to 4.9 percent, while inflation, far from accelerating, had fallen to 2.3 percent.

But even recognizing such recent patterns, as well as the wider variety of inconsistent inflation/unemployment relationships that have prevailed over the past thirty years, this does not mean that there is *no* relationship between workers gaining in terms of employment and higher wages and inflation. In this regard, it will be useful to consider some of the main results of the winter 1997 *Journal of Economic Perspectives* symposium on NAIRU. One paper is by Robert Gordon, David's brother (1997). It summarizes the extensive econometric evidence he has assembled over the past two decades, on the basis of which he concludes that a "time-varying" NAIRU exists. For example, according to Robert Gordon, the NAIRU fell from 6.2 percent in 1990 to 5.6 percent by mid-1996.

Douglas Staiger, James Stock, and Mark Watson also summarize extensive econometric research into this question (1997). They also conclude that a NAIRU does exist, but that it is subject to wide variations. They find that, as a point estimate, NAIRU in 1997 was between 5.5 and 5.9 percent, which was a full percentage point below its level for the early 1980s. They also find that "the most striking feature of these estimates is their lack of precision." Indeed, for their current point estimate of 5.5 to 5.9 percent, the 95 percent confidence interval ranges between 4.3 and 7.3 percent. So their NAIRU estimate not only varies over time but also has the capacity to range widely at a given point in time.

The discussions by Joseph Stiglitz and Olivier Blanchard and Lawrence Katz in the same symposium offer similar empirical conclusions. I do not see any reason to dispute the general thrust of these findings. Indeed, it is difficult to dispute them *precisely because* they are so broad. But focusing exclusively on point estimates, confidence intervals, and their variation over time really misses the point. There is a fundamental question jumping out at us from these results that is almost entirely neglected in all the papers. That is, what makes the "time-varying" NAIRU vary in the first place? It is remarkable that leading economists who have devoted so much time to estimating values for NAIRU almost completely neglect this question. Nevertheless, a few hints are dropped as asides. Robert Gordon, for example, writes,

> The two especially large changes in the NAIRU . . . are the increase between the early and late 1960s and the decrease in the 1990s. The late 1960s were a time of labor militancy, relatively strong unions, a relatively high minimum wage and a marked increase in labor's share in national income. The 1990s have been a time of labor peace, relatively weak unions, a relatively low minimum wage and a slight decline in labor's income share. (1997, 30)

Gordon also cites the role of increased global competition in product and labor markets and the increase of unskilled immigrant labor as contributing to the declining NAIRU in the United States. Though again these observations are mere asides in Gordon's paper, let's still look at what he is saying: that changes in the relative power of capitalists and workers, and the related increase in the extent to which the U.S. economy has become integrated into the global economy, are the major factors that have forced the NAIRU to fall. Thus, even if by partial inadvertence, and in any case almost completely camouflaged amid a welter of econometric detail, Robert Gordon's conclusion returns the discussion of unemployment to where Marx and Kalecki wanted it to be: the analysis of class struggle and the distribution of income and power.

From Natural Rate to Egalitarian Social Structure of Accumulation

Class struggle is the specter haunting the analysis of the natural rate and NAIRU: this is the consistent message beginning with Milton Friedman in 1968 and continuing through to Robert Gordon in 1997, with most other stops in between. Once we recognize this, many other issues in the analysis of unemployment also become much clearer. Let me raise just a few.

1. While economists have long studied how workers' wage demands cause inflation as unemployment falls, it is never the case that such wage demands directly cause inflation. This is definitionally true, since inflation refers to a general rise in product prices. Workers, by definition, do not have the power to raise product prices. Capitalists raise product prices. Inflation happens as unemployment is falling when capitalists respond to workers' increasingly successful wage demands by raising product prices so that they can maintain profitability by passing on their increased costs. If workers were simply to receive a higher share of national income, it would follow that lower unemployment and higher wages need not cause inflation at all. It is therefore always and everywhere the case that capitalists, not workers, directly cause inflation when unemployment falls.

2. There is little mystery as to why, at present, the "time-varying" NAIRU has diminished to a near vanishing point, with unemployment at a twenty-five-year low while inflation remains dormant. The main explanation is the one alluded to by Robert Gordon—that workers' economic power has been eroding dramatically through the 1990s.[3] Workers have been almost completely unable to win wage increases over the course of the economic expansion that by now is seven years old. Indeed, by the end of 1997, the average wage for nonsupervisory workers was still 14 percent below the level of 1973, even though the U.S. economy was 34 percent more productive than it was in 1973. A recent econometric study by Cara S. Lown and Robert Rich (1997) of the New York Federal Reserve confirms this perspective. They found that between 1990 and 1995, the absence of wage and benefit increases itself fully explains the lack of inflationary pressures at such low levels of unemployment.

3. This experience over the past seven years, with unemployment falling but workers showing almost no income gains, demonstrates dramati-

cally the crucial point that full employment alone can never be an adequate demand of the left, even as a transitional "nonreformist" reform: it wasn't under German fascism, as Kalecki pointed out, and it isn't today. The importance of this point was conveyed vividly to me when I was working in Bolivia in 1990 as part of an economic advising team led by Professor Keith Griffin of UC Riverside. Griffin and his team were brought to Bolivia primarily to develop a program that would address the human devastation wrought by the "shock therapy" program designed by Jeffrey Sachs to end the Bolivian hyperinflation of the 1980s.

Professor Griffin asked me to examine employment policies. I began by paying a visit to the economists at the Ministry of Planning. When I requested that we discuss the country's employment problems, they explained, to my surprise, that the country *had no employment problems*. When I suggested we consider the situation of the people begging, shining shoes, or hawking batteries and Chiclets in the street just below the window where we stood, their response was that these people *were* employed. And of course they were, in that they were actively engaged in trying to scratch out a living. It was clear that I had to specify the problem at hand far more precisely. Similarly, in the United States today, we have to be much more specific as to what workers should be getting in a fair economy: jobs, of course, but also living wages, benefits, reasonable job security, and a healthy work environment.

4. In our current low unemployment economy, should workers, at long last, succeed in winning higher wages and better benefits, some inflationary pressures are likely to emerge, even though global competition has increased the difficulty of firms' successfully raising product prices. However, if inflation does not accelerate after wage increases are won, this would mean that the distribution of income is shifting in favor of workers. But the main point is this: in response to *either* inflationary pressures or a downward shift in national income, we should then expect that many, if not most, segments of the business community will welcome a Federal Reserve policy that would slow the economy and raise the unemployment rate. Put another way, it is not likely that, should wages and benefits start rising significantly, most businesses will come to their Keynesian senses and embrace the universal virtues of a full employment economy.

Does this mean that, until the hour of the big bang when the capitalist system is supplanted, capitalist control over the reserve army of labor must remain the dominant force establishing the limits of workers' strivings for jobs, security, and living wages? It will be useful to consider this question in terms of David Gordon's concept of social structures of accumulation. The challenge for the progressive movement in the United States today is to think through the features of a new social structure of accumulation through which full employment at living wages can be achieved and sustained. Of course, for this exercise to be at all useful, one must first and foremost take the full measure of how unemployment does serve capitalists' interests. But, at the same time, unless we are only interested in interpreting the world in various ways and not in changing it, this recognition should be only the beginning point, not the end, of our analysis.

Especially given the dismal trajectory of real wage decline over the past generation, workers should of course continue to push for wage increases. But it will also be crucial to advance these demands within a broader framework of proposals. One important component within a broader package would be incomes policies—that is, explicit efforts at regulating the relative growth of wages and profits. Such policies obviously represent a form of class compromise. This is intrinsically neither good nor bad. The question is the terms under which the compromise is achieved. Workers should be willing to link wage increases to productivity; after all, if the average wage had just risen at exactly the rate of productivity growth since 1973 and not a penny more, the average hourly wage today for nonsupervisory workers would be $19.07 rather than $12.24.

But linking wages to productivity then also raises the question of who controls the decisions that determine the rate of productivity growth. As David Gordon was among the most forceful in arguing, substantial productivity gains are attainable through operating a less hierarchical workplace and building strong democratic internal labor market institutions. This was the central point of David's last book, *Fat and Mean* (1996).

But productivity growth does also still result from both the public and private sector investing in capital goods. Investing in capital goods has the additional benefit that it increases aggregate demand within the domestic economy. A proworker economic policy will therefore also have to be concerned with increasing the level and composition of investment. Many specific policy measures are needed to achieve that end, including expanding public investments, the strategic allocation of pension funds, and a set of monetary and financial regulatory policies to circumscribe speculative finance and promote the productive allocation of credit. Such a package of investment policies will also serve to reduce the hypermobility of international capital flows, which has had such destructive consequences throughout the world in recent years.[4]

In proposing such a policy approach, have I forgotten the lesson that Marx and Kalecki taught us, that unemployment is functional to capitalism? Given that this lesson has become part of the standard mode of thinking among mainstream economists ranging from Milton Friedman to Robert Gordon, I would hope that I have not let it slip from view. My point nevertheless is that through changing power relationships at the workplace and the decision-making process through which investment decisions get made, labor and the left can then also achieve a more egalitarian social structure of accumulation, one in which capitalists' power to brandish the weapon of unemployment is greatly circumscribed. If the labor movement and the left neglect issues of control over investment and the workplace, we will continue to live amid a Bolivian solution to the unemployment problem, where full employment is the by-product of workers' vulnerability, not their strength.

Notes

1. To be precise, Edmund Phelps actually was the co-originator of the modern version of the natural rate theory, though Friedman has priority in the use of the term. Two important references are Carlin and Soskice (1990) and Cross (1995).

2. Actually, Marx himself comes much closer to drawing a parallel between the movements of the reserve army and the laws of nature. He writes in *Capital,* volume 1, ch. 25, "The whole form of the movement of modern industry depends, therefore, upon the constant transformation of a part of the labouring population into unemployed or half-employed hands. . . . As the heavenly bodies, once thrown into a certain definite motion, always repeat this, so it is with social production as soon as it is once thrown into this movement of alternate expansion and contraction" (1967, 633).

3. The solid class analysis offered by Robert Gordon certainly invites one to speculate—especially on the occasion of the David Gordon Memorial Lecture—whether, toward the end of David's life, Robert had allowed his younger brother to start talking sense to him.

4. Some details on designing investment and labor market policies to promote sustained full employment in the United States are presented in Pollin and Zahrt (1997).

Bibliography

Carlin, Wendy, and David Soskice. 1990. *Macroeconomics and the Wage Bargain: A Modern Approach to Employment, Inflation and the Exchange Rate*. New York: Oxford University Press.

Cross, Rod, ed. 1995. *The Natural Rate of Unemployment: Reflections on 25 Years of the Hypothesis*. Cambridge, UK: Cambridge University Press.

Eisner, Robert. 1997. "A New View of the NAIRU." In *Improving the Global Economy: Keynesianism and the Growth in Output and Employment*, ed. Paul Davidson and Jan Kregel. Brookfield, VT: Edward Elgar.

Friedman, Milton. 1968. "The Role of Monetary Policy." *American Economic Review* 68, no. 1: 1–17.

Gordon, David M. 1987. "Six-Percent Unemployment Ain't Natural: Demystifying the Idea of a Rising "Natural Rate of Unemployment." *Social Research* 54, no. 2: 223–245.

———. 1988. "The Un-Natural Rate of Unemployment: An Econometric Critique of the NAIRU Hypothesis." *American Economic Review* 78, no. 2: 117–123.

———. 1996. *Fat and Mean: The Corporate Squeeze of Working Americans and the Myth of Managerial "Downsizing."* New York: Free Press.

Gordon, Robert J. 1997. "The Time-Varying NAIRU and its Implications for Economic Policy," *Journal of Economic Perspectives* 11, no. 1: 11–32.

Kalecki, Michal. 1971. "Political Aspects of Full Employment." In *Selected Essays on the Dynamics of the Capitalist Economy*, ch. 12, 138–145. Cambridge, UK: Cambridge University Press.

Lown, Cara S., and Robert W. Rich. 1997. "Is There an Inflation Puzzle?" *Federal Reserve Bank of New York Economic Policy Review* (December): 51–69.

Marx, Karl. 1967. Capital, Volume I. New York: International.

Pollin, Robert, and Elizabeth Zahrt. 1997. "Expansionary Policy for Full Employment in the United States: Retrospective on the 1960s and Current Period Prospects." In *Employment and Economic Performance: Jobs, Inflation, and Growth*, ed. Jonathan Michie and John Grieve Smith, 36–75. New York: Oxford University Press.

Staiger, Douglas, James H. Stock, and Mark W. Watson. 1997. "The NAIRU, Unemployment and Monetary Policy." *Journal of Economic Perspectives* 11, no. 1: 33–50.

13

The Political Economy of Employment Inequality

Job Access and Pay Differentials

Heather Boushey

Over the past few years, public sentiment has turned against policies aimed at remedying discrimination in the labor market and in access to education. In 1998, the Board of Regents in California eliminated racial preferences—Affirmative Action—in admission policies, and the public, by passing Proposition 209 in California, says this is okay. The public is also no longer pushing a government role in the promotion of workplace equality as the Equal Pay Amendment, once on the forefront of the women's movement, has quietly slipped into history.

It has been argued that women and minorities no longer need "special preferences," even though there are substantial differences in unemployment and labor force participation by race and differences in the types of jobs that women and men hold. This chapter identifies differential access to employment as a form of discrimination, and examines the effect of such discrimination on pay levels available to specific groups in specific markets.

What Is Discrimination?

Discrimination in the labor market causes inequitable outcomes in terms of employment, promotions, and wages. In the United States, it is most common to speak of discrimination against minorities or women, although there is discrimination against gays and lesbians, disabled workers, older workers, and others. Discrimination in the labor market takes three forms: (1) wage inequality; (2) occupational segregation; and (3) employment inequality.

Wage inequality is when ostensibly identical workers are paid different wages. For example, there is wage inequality when two college professors with similar responsibilities, tenure, and publication records are paid different salaries. The Equal Pay Act of 1963 makes paying people different wages for the same work illegal, and, at the federal level, the Equal Employment Opportunity Commission investigates complaints of such discrimination on the job.

Occupational segregation is when workers of a certain gender and/or race are segregated into particular occupations. For example, women tend to be crowded into the secretarial, teaching, and other "caring labor" occupations. One-third of all women are employed in just ten occupations. In three of those occupations, "over 90% of persons who work in them are women, and another four have over 80% women in them" (Albelda, Drago, and Shulman 1996, 33). African American men tend to be crowded into the operators, fabricators, and laborers category, and African American women tend to be in service occupations (Albelda, Drago, and Shulman 1996, 35).

This occupational crowding entails wage penalties; in 1997, the full-time median earnings of women in female-dominated jobs (over 50 percent female) were $51 per week *less* than those of other full-time women workers. By contrast, men who worked in male-dominated jobs earned $18 per week *more* than other men. Policies such as pay equity seek to remedy the discrepancies in pay that result from occupational crowding (see Figart and Hartmann this volume).

Employment inequality is when there is unequal access to employment. Unequal access can take many forms. One example is systemic discrimination against workers who are trying to gain access to the skills and education necessary for employment. Another is "neighborhood" inequality: Holzer and Ihlanfeldt (1996) document that the spatial distribution of African American employment is related to the location of housing and the affordability and accessibility of transportation. American cities are highly segregated by race (Massey and Denton 1993) and this segregation in housing leads to differential access to employment. Finally, African Americans and other minorities often cannot even get interviews for jobs because employers believe that their "soft skills" (specifically, their skills at interacting with customers, attitude, etc.) are unacceptably low, especially for men (Moss and Tilly 1995). Through surveys of employer attitudes, Joleen Kirschenman, Philip Moss, and Chris Tilly (1996, 3) find that "employers rate black workers worse than others in terms of soft skills—specifically interaction skills and motivation—as well as hard skills; few, if any, rate them better." Further, some employers held stereotypical—and discriminatory—views of potential African American workers.

Explaining Discrimination

"So what?" some people may say to occupation crowding and employment differences; women and minorities have different skills, varying time on the job, and different responsibilities on the job than do whites and males. One could ask whether differences in employment outcomes or in occupations are really discrimination or merely reflect differences in the preferences of women and men.

Labor economists, those who study the dynamics of employment and pay, have developed a body of literature devoted to the study of discrimination in the labor market and how it affects worker's employment and pay. One strand of discrimination literature is within the neoclassical economic paradigm. These authors explain inequality in labor market outcomes by gender and race as the result of different endowments of human capital, compensating differentials, differences in worker's or employer's preferences, imperfect information, or differences in the types of jobs they do. The "residual"—that is, the wage gap left over once all these factors have been accounted for—is how they measure discrimination.

An alternative framework for viewing labor market discrimination comes from the radical political economy tradition. In this framework, institutions and social structures may lead to discrimination even if it seems irrational—or not cost-effective—on the part of individual employers.

The Neoclassical Model

Within the neoclassical perspective, discrimination is that part of the wage gap that the model cannot explain after identifying worker and job characteristics and any other factors that may affect wages and can be empirically measured. Therefore many neoclassical theorists spend time trying to "fine tune" their models to fully account for all the elements that go into wage determination.

In the standard neoclassical (or Walrasian) model of the labor market, wages are equal to an individual's marginal product of labor. This means that each individual is paid a wage equal to their contribution to production. Individuals with a greater amount of human capital, because they have more education, more job training, or have spent a longer time on the job, should have higher wages because they add more "capital" (human capital, that is) to production. The aggregate dynamics of this model are based on the equilibration of supply and demand because wages will adjust to equilibrate the supply and demand for labor. Wages will move up or down in response to excess supply or demand for labor.

In this model, differences in wages are the result of differences across workers in their human capital endowments or their preferences. Discrimination is the result of imperfect information. Gary Becker (1957), in the seminal work on this topic, argues that differences in labor market outcomes are due to differences in human capital and the "unexplained" wage gap is discrimination—although this will not persist in the long run. Recent work in the neoclassical tradition rejects the notion that discrimination explains wage gaps arguing instead that "unobserved" differences in labor quality explain these gaps (O'Neill 1990). Unobserved differences are those that economists cannot measure, but are evident to employers, such as attitudes about work or inappropriate behavior.

Employment discrimination does not enter the neoclassical model. Here, unemployment is the gap between the demand for and supply of labor. In the short run, unemployment is seen as an "inefficient outcome" due to market imperfections. In the long run, unemployment will be eliminated as either wages fall to equilibrate the supply and demand for labor or, alternatively, workers alter their labor supply or firms alter their demand for labor. The important thing to note in this model is that unemployment is not the equilibrium outcome.

Taken as a whole, the neoclassical model of the labor market is one that is beautiful in its simplicity and does not leave room for discrimination to affect either pay or the employment level in the long run. Wages are directly related to a workers' contribution to productivity and, in the aggregate, will adjust to the level of employment as necessary. The level of employment is determined by the equilibration of firms' need for workers and workers' desire to work.

The Radical Political Economy Model

An alternative model of the labor market begins from the premise that unemployment is endemic to the capitalist economy. Unemployment and discrimination are intricately linked, unlike in the neoclassical model.

Many in the radical political economy tradition argue that unemployment serves to discipline labor. Juliet Schor and Sam Bowles (1987) point to the important role that the "cost-of-job-loss" plays in the determination of wages. The cost-of-job-loss is the drop in pay a worker would experience if she lost her job and had to go out on the job market. It is an index based on the current wage, unemployment benefits, and the probability of finding new employment. Workers who live in areas where there is high unemployment will have a higher cost-of-job-loss than will workers who live in areas with low unemployment because the chances of finding a new job are lower in high unemployment regions. When unemployment is high, workers see that they will be unable to find a new job if they are fired or quit. They are therefore less likely to strike, less likely to demand higher pay, and generally more likely to put up with whatever their employer demands.

This analysis can be derived directly from Karl Marx, in chapter 25 of Volume I of *Capital*. Here,

Marx lays out an analysis of the dynamics of the labor market and how differences among workers translate into differences in pay. He argues that, in the aggregate, unemployment regulates wages. As accumulation proceeds—that is, as the economy "booms," employers continue to hire workers, and the unemployment rate is low—the labor market will become "tight" as the pool of available workers shrinks. Workers may be able to use this to their advantage and organize to increase their wages. Increases in wages may happen, but if the rate of accumulation is beyond the point of profitability, accumulation will slow. Given this antagonism between capital and labor over wages, in the long run, capital will tend to mechanize to increase productivity and lower the necessary labor power—increasing the extraction of surplus value (see Braverman 1974). The long-run effects on the supply of and demand for labor are that the rate of accumulation does not lead to greater labor demand, but, as the production process makes some workers redundant, unemployment occurs. This swells the ranks of the reserve army of labor.

The process of accumulation not only puts pressure on capitalists to cheapen labor to maintain profitability but also puts pressure on labor to work to sustain living wages and employment. As the unemployment rate rises in a local labor market, employed workers feel increased downward wage pressure from employers and the pools of unemployed workers. In a region of high unemployment, the probability that an employed worker will find a new job—if she is fired, laid off, or quits—decreases. Therefore, employed workers may be less likely to demand higher wages and less likely to quit if working conditions are unsatisfactory in a high unemployment region. Concurrently, in a high unemployment region, employers may find many suitable applicants for each job opening. The task of replacing workers becomes easier and employers have less of an incentive to pay a "wage premium" or to acquiesce to worker demands for higher wages or better working conditions. Thus, the Marxian theory of the reserve army of labor predicts that unemployment and pay are inversely related.

The theory of the reserve army of labor contains within it a second dynamic, which elucidates the relationship between unemployment and pay *inequality*. Unemployment does not occur "abstractly" but happens to individuals. In the United States, unemployment does not strike individuals randomly, but is more likely to happen to the young, the less educated, and minority workers. African Americans (men and women) experience a greater level of unemployment than do women (as a whole) relative to the aggregate population. This diverging pattern of unemployment between African Americans and whites also occurs across U.S. cities (see Figure 13.1).

Marx argued that capitalism breeds these different relationships to employment. Marx ([1887] 1986) argued that the reserve army is composed of groups of workers with different relationships to the capitalist economy. He divides the reserve army of labor into four specific types: the floating, the latent, the stagnant, and paupers. These distinctions may provide insight into the ways that the unemployment rate in the modern era affects African Americans and women. Some argue that women form the latent reserve army of labor. Marx defined the latent reserve army as those workers who are currently not participating in the labor force but whom the market will induce or force into paid employment. Power (1983) argues that capitalism's invasion of home production changed women's role in the home from primarily production to maintenance. As maintenance of the household became the focus of women's labor, rather than production of goods in the home, this reduced women's ability to contribute earned income to the family's finances. In the latter half of the twentieth century, the capitalist sphere of production

Figure 13.1 **Unemployment By Race and Gender**

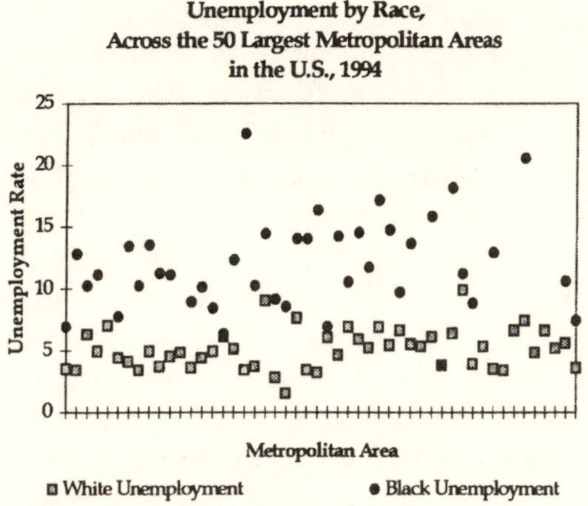

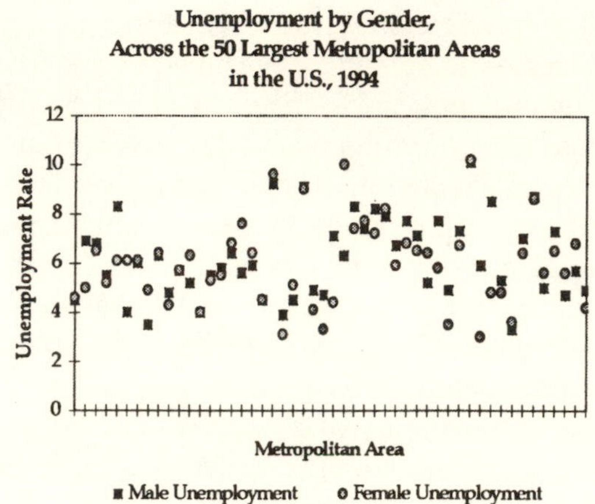

Source: Bureau of Labor Statistics.

drew women into paid employment. This experience of being "drawn in" is indicative of women's status as the latent reserve. African Americans experience a greater level of unemployment than do women, relative to the aggregate population. Their relationship to unemployment may be better described as part of the floating reserve army of labor, which Marx defines as those workers who cycle between work and nonwork on the periphery of the labor market.

These categories are useful in that they help us think about the fact that unemployment happens to actual workers; if unemployment occurs in a way that is biased toward some group, then it is on the backs of this group that the negative macroeconomic relationship between unemployment and pay occurs.

The Effects of Employment Discrimination on Pay

Although all three types of discrimination are evident in today's economy, employment discrimination may be the most important and insidious. First, employment discrimination creates the conditions for the other two to exist. The negative relationship between unemployment and pay is fundamental to the capitalist process—it is what keeps wages in check, and growth on its upward path. This is apparent every time the Federal Reserve bumps up interest rates because of a decrease in the unemployment rate. The relationship between unemployment and inequality is the result of this broad macroeconomic relationship between unemployment and pay because unemployment happens to individuals—usually individuals who have less overall economic power.

Second, employment discrimination is insidious because it means that some people never get the chance to prove themselves in the labor market. Unemployment is correlated with high crime, family dissolution, and depression. Employment discrimination is also related to reliance on public aid (welfare) as those who experience labor market discrimination are also more likely to need public assistance.

There has recently been a great deal of economic research on the "wage curve," which predicts that individuals who live in areas with relatively high unemployment will, all else being equal, have lower pay than individuals who live in low unemployment areas. Blanchflower and Oswald (1994) have documented that the wage curve is stable across time and space, with an elasticity of about –.10. This means that individuals who live in an area with an unemployment rate twice as high as another area will have wages that are 10 percent lower.

This research confirms the hypothesis that unemployment and pay are inversely related. This analysis is in the aggregate, however, and does not distinguish among types of workers. The reserve army of labor hypothesis also predicts that unemployment is used to differentiate among workers and to keep wages down—discrimination in employment is a mechanism to lower pay for some workers, thereby helping to keep wages in check for all workers.

The methodology of the wage curve can be used to test this hypothesis econometrically. To do this, I estimate wage curves for various demographic groups. The model is:

$$w_{ij} = \gamma_{ij} (U, X_{ij}) \tag{1}$$

Where w_{ij} is the wage of person i; X_{ij} is a set of measured characteristics of individual i (such as gender, age, and education) in the jth group; and U is the unemployment rate. Since women and racial-ethnic minorities experience labor market discrimination, the expectation is that their wage curve will be more elastic than that of either the aggregate population or of non-discriminated–against workers. Therefore, their pay will be more responsive to changes in unemployment.

The individual-level employment, earnings, and background data come from the Current Population Survey Outgoing Rotation Group Files for 1991 and 1996. The unemployment data come from the Bureau of Labor Statistics Web site www.bls.gov. To be included in the sample, an individual must be between 18 and 64 years old, employed in either the private or public sector, excluding those who are self-employed, and live in one of the fifty largest metropolitan areas of the United States.

I estimate a regression of the form:

$$\ln w_{ij} = \beta_0 + \beta_1 \ln U + \beta_2 X_{ij} + \beta_3 D_{reg} + \beta_4 D_{indy} + \beta_5 D_{occ} + e_{ij} \tag{2}$$

Where $\ln W_{ij}$ is the log of earnings per week or the log of the hourly wage (earnings per week over usual hours) for individual i in the jth group where the labor market is defined by the metropolitan area an individual lives in; ln *U* is the natural log of the unemployment rate for the local labor market; and X_{ij} is a vector of characteristics particular to individual i; D_{reg}, D_{indy} and D_{occ} are regional, industrial, and occupational dummies. The variables in X are dummies for gender, race, marital status, union membership, private sector employee, part-time (less than 30 hours/week), and paid hourly; variables for educational attainment (less than high school, high school graduates, some college, 4 years of college, and beyond 4 years of college); and age and its square (to measure for experience). Each specification also includes 13 dummies for industrial classification, 14 dummies for occupational grouping, and state dummies.

Tables 13.1 and 13.2 show the unemployment coefficient for the regressions for 1991 and 1996, respectively.

In 1991, a recession year in which unemployment hovered around 6.8 percent and African American unemployment was at 12.5 percent, the wage curve is far more elastic for African American workers than for white workers. Specifically, African American men have a wage curve of –.35. By 1996, well into the current economic re-

Table 13.1

Wage Curve by Demographic Group, 1991

Log of Earnings Per Week	Log of Unemploiyment Rate	Number of Observations	R^2
Total population	–0.17 (.05)*	68,673	0.61
African American	–0.33 (.10)*	8,581	0.57
Female	–0.30 (.10)*	4,793	0.57
Male	–0.35 (.12)*	3,788	0.57
White	–0.16 (.06)*	56,565	0.61
Female	–0.17* (.07)*	26,796	0.58
Male	–0.15 (.07)*	29,769	0.60

Source: Author's calculations.
Standard errors in parentheses.
*Significant at the 1% level.

Table 13.2

Wage Curve by Demographic Group, 1996

Log of Earnings Per Week	Log of Unemploiyment Rate	Number of Observations	R^2
Total population	–0.13 (.03)*	57,846	0.56
African American	–0.10 (.04)**	7,756	0.48
Female	–0.03 (.05)*	4,528	0.50
Male	–0.18 (.05)*	3,228	0.45
White	–0.15 (.03)*	49,911	0.57
Female	–0.11 (.04)*	22,497	0.55
Male	–0.18 (.04)*	24,414	0.55

Source: Author's calculations.
Standard errors in parentheses.
*Significant at the 1% level; **significant at the 5% level.

covery, the wage curve for African Americans is lower than for whites. However, on closer examination, both white and African American men have relatively high wage curves (at –.18 each) and African American women have a relatively low wage curve, with an elasticity of –.03.

These findings indicate that African American pay is more elastic with respect to unemployment in times of recession. That is, when the jobs are scarce, African American workers lose out in terms of pay. In times of high employment, African American workers are able to gain some ground, although for men, their elasticity of pay with respect to unemployment is not different than that of whites.

The use of group-specific unemployment can be employed to ask whether the unemployment of discriminated-against workers affects the pay of the total, aggregate population, or whether the unemployment of these groups only affects their pay. I estimate a regression of the form:

$$\ln w_{ij} = b_0 + b_1 \ln U_j + b_2 X_{ij} + b_3 D_{reg} + b_4 D_{indy} + b_5 D_{occ} + e_{ij} \quad (3)$$

Where U_j is the unemployment rate of the jth group. The only difference between equation (2) and equation (3) is that in equation (3), the unemployment rate is that of specific demographic groups (white, African American, female, male) regressed on the wages of all workers, rather than the aggregate unemployment rate.

The expectation is that the group-specific unemployment rate of discriminated-against workers should serve to pull down the average wages of the aggregate population. There should be a greater elasticity of aggregate average pay with respect to African American and/or female unemployment than with respect to aggregate unemployment.

Regressions are run for this model, and these results are presented in Tables 13.3 and 13.4 for 1991 and 1996, respectively. Aggregate earnings are most sensitive to the unemployment rate of whites and males in the recession year 1991. The elasticity of pay of the aggregate population with respect to white unemployment is –0.17, and the elasticity of pay of the aggregate population with respect to male unemployment is –0.13. Both of these elasticities are statistically significant. The elasticity of pay with respect to African American unemployment is only –0.04 and statistically insignificant. Thus, in the recession year of 1991, the unemployment of African American workers had no statistical effect on aggregate earnings. However, in the boom year of 1996, the coefficient on African American unemployment grew to –0.10 and is statistically significant. The coefficients on white and male unemployment are still larger than for African Americans, but the effect of African American unemployment on aggregate wages does have some statistical significance in the boom year of 1996.

These findings show that the unemployment rate of whites has the strongest effect on the earnings of the aggregate population. The unemployment rate of the groups that are hypothesized to be in the reserve army of labor does not have a strong effect on the earnings of the aggregate population in a recession. These findings also point to the conclusion that the labor market is highly segmented along the lines of race and that there are different dynamics for these labor markets.

Increases in unemployment for discriminated-against workers lowers all earnings, but to a *lesser extent* than the unemployment of non-discriminated–against groups. Thus, all else being equal, individuals who lived in large urban areas with relatively high unemployment rates for whites experienced lower pay than individuals living in large urban areas with a relatively high unemployment rate for African Americans.[1]

These findings provide empirical support for

Table 13.3

Wage Curve with Unemployment by Demographic Group, 1991

	Log of Group Unemployment Rate					
Log of earnings per week	African American	White	Female	Male	Number observed	R^2
	−0.04 (.03)				62,639	0.61
		−0.17 (.05)*			68,673	0.61
			−0.14 (.05)*		68,673	0.61
				−0.13 (.04)*	68,673	0.61

Source: Author's calculations.
Standard errors in parentheses.
*Significant at the 1% level.

Table 13.4

Wage Curve with Unemployment by Demographic Group, 1996

	Log of Group Unemployment Rate					
Log of earnings per week	African American	White	Female	Male	Number observed	R^2
	−0.10 (.01)*				52,240	0.56
		−0.15 (.02)*			57,846	0.56
			−0.13 (.03)*		57,846	0.56
				−0.11 (.03)*	68,673	0.56

Source: Author's calculations.
Standard errors in parentheses.
*Significant at the 1% level.

the argument that it is in the interest of whites and males to maintain their employment privilege because it sustains their higher earnings. When events are such that even whites lose their jobs, all groups suffer in terms of pay, but when African Americans lose their jobs, pay does not fall for other groups as much. These findings suggest a rationale for why there is very little discussion in the media or even in academia of the excruciatingly high unemployment rates for African Americans in urban areas. The high unemployment rate of African Americans does not affect the pay, or employment, of the majority, white working class.

Conclusions

Employment inequality is responsible for some pay inequities, demonstrating an important link between the two forms of labor market discrimination. Occupational segregation is also responsible for pay inequities. Employment discrimination is, however, the most insidious form that discrimination takes because it is the concrete mechanism by which the negative trade-off between unemployment and pay occurs with the burden of this trade-off falling unfairly on individuals in the labor market's most marginalized segments.

Note

1. This makes intuitive sense in that the unemployment of high earners, relative to low earners, has a more negative effect on average earnings since high earners are a large proportion of the labor market.

References

Albelda, Randy, Robert Drago, and Steven Shulman. 1996. *Unlevel Playing Fields: Understanding Wage Inequality and Discrimination*. New York: McGraw-Hill.

Becker, Gary. 1957. *The Economics of Discrimination*. Chicago: University of Chicago Press.

Blanchflower, David G., and Andrew J. Oswald. 1994. *The Wage Curve*. Cambridge: MIT Press.

Braverman, H. 1974. *Labor and Monopoly Capital*. New York: Monthly Review Press.

Holzer, Harry, and Keith R. Ihlanfeldt. 1996. "Spatial Factors and Employment of Blacks at the Firm Level." Discussion paper no. 1086–96. Madison: Institute for Research on Poverty.

Kirschenman, Joleen, Philip Moss, and Chris Tilly. 1996. "Employer Screening Methods and Racial Exclusion: Evidence from New In-Depth Interviews with Employers." New York: Russell Sage Foundation, September. http://epn.org/sage/rstikm.html.

Marx, Karl. [1887] 1986. *Capital*. Volume 1. Moscow: Progress Publishers.

Massey, Douglas, and Nancy Denton. 1993. *American Apartheid: Segregation and the Making of the Underclass*. Cambridge: Harvard University Press.

Moss, Philip, and Chris Tilly. 1995. "Raised Hurdles for Black Men: Evidence from Interviews with Employers." New York: Russell Sage Foundation, November. http://epn.org/sage/rstimo.html.

O'Neill, June. 1990. "The Role of Human Capital and Earnings Differences Between Black and White Men." *Journal of Economic Perspectives* 4, no. 4: 24–45.

Power, Marilyn. 1983. "From Home Production to Wage Labor: Women as a Reserve Army of Labor." *Review of Radical Political Ecnomy*, 15, no. 1, 71–91.

Schor, Juliet, and Samuel Bowles. 1987. "Employment Rents and the Incidence of Strikes." *Review of Economics and Statistics* (November).

14

Falling Wages, Widening Gaps

U.S. Income Distribution at the Millennium

Chris Tilly

As the Dow Jones industrial average shatters one record after another, many Americans feel left out of the celebration. Rightly so, the benefits of economic growth in the last three decades have been very unequally distributed. While stock prices and profit rates have soared, average wages and income have fallen or stagnated, and income instability has worsened. Income and wealth inequality have widened. The late 1990s boom has moderated some of these trends, but not sufficiently to undo the damage of the previous twenty-five years. These changes mark the reversal of post–World War II trends toward broader prosperity, and reductions in poverty and inequality. While globalization and technological change have contributed to these shifts, conscious business strategy has also played a crucial role.

The Growing Divergence Between Business and Worker Fortunes

Unlike in the past, a business boom no longer means prosperity for working people as well as for business. In our parents' and grandparents' time, business and worker fortunes rose and fell more or less in tandem. Of course, not all benefited equally from the rising tide: people of color and women of all racial and ethnic groups lagged behind in wages, and families with limited ability to take part in the labor market (notably, elders and single mothers of young children) depended on social welfare generosity rather than labor market dynamism. But in general, business cycle booms brought with them significant booms in wages and employment.

No more. The divergence between business and worker prosperity, which began to appear in the 1970s, became particularly apparent during the most recent economic expansion, which began in 1991. This upturn saw business activity and profits lift in spite of, and to some extent because of, stagnant wages and initially slow employment growth. Business analysts attributed the "health" of the expansion to low labor costs. "From the perspective of business," points out economist John Miller (1995, 9), "it is lagging wage growth that sustains the boom. Modest wage increases guarantee that rising labor costs will not cut into profit margins even as the economy expands."

The bottom line for business: U.S. profit rates

A longer version of this chapter, "Falling Wages, Widening Gaps: U.S. Income Distribution at the Millennium," will appear in *Housing: Foundation of a New Social Agenda,* edited by Rachel G. Bratt, Chester Hartman, and Michael E. Stone (Temple University Press, (forthcoming). It is printed here with the permission of the publisher.

are currently at their highest level in decades. U.S. corporations received a dazzling $825 billion in profits in 1998, or about one dollar in eight of total national income (U.S. Bureau of Economic Analysis 1999). The current profit rate surge does *not* mean that business is claiming a larger share of the economic pie, but rather that businesses are taking home about the same share *in spite of investing less to generate these profits.* The profit rate is the ratio of annual profits to accumulated business investment in plant and equipment—much as an interest rate is the ratio of annual interest to principal. Businesses have continued to reap profits despite much reduced additions to productive investment (though the late 1990s did see an uptick in such investment), and this has pushed the ratio upward (Baker 1995). But U.S. workers and their households are paying the price in terms of wages, income, and employment.

Businesses' failure to make productive investments helps explain the fact that wage levels have remained flat—and have even fallen somewhat. Productivity has grown slowly, especially by comparison with other industrialized countries. U.S. real output per worker (a measure of productivity) grew only about two-thirds as fast as output in Western Europe, and one-third as fast as in Japan, between 1979 and 1990 (Freeman 1994, 26). Although the business press made much of strong productivity growth in the late 1990s, overall 1990–98 growth in output per hour for all businesses plodded along at 1.4 percent per year, only slightly up from the 1.1 percent per year crawl of 1979–90 (U.S. Bureau of Labor Statistics 1999a). Thus, the per-worker "slice" of pie available to be shared between labor and management has expanded relatively little.

Figure 14.1 shows one set of consequences for U.S. workers and households. To put wages and income on the same scale, the figure uses an index of 1973 = 100, so that an average wage of 200 would mean two times the 1973 wage, whereas a wage of 50 would mean half of the 1973 wage. The average real (inflation-corrected) hourly wage, periodically beaten down over the last three decades, stood in 1998 at only 88 percent of its 1973 value—though wage growth did begin to pick up with the late 1990s economic expansion. This ended an unbroken string of real wage advances from the 1950s through 1973. Median real annual household income (the level of income that exactly half of U.S. households stand above, and the other half below) was not battered as badly, and crawled ahead a scant 3.5 percent over the same twenty-five-year period—again, ending a "golden age" of far more rapid income growth.

If wages have tumbled, why has household income held its ground over the past twenty-five years? The key is that in an attempt to overcome wage declines, households have put more members to work—especially mothers. As of 1995, 45 percent of all U.S. households deployed two or more earners (U.S. Census Bureau 1998a, Table 2). In short, U.S. households have managed to win small increases in real income only by what some observers have called a "family speed-up" (Currie, Dunn, and Fogarty 1980).

Income has also become more unstable in a variety of ways. Economywide downward mobility has become markedly more common. Among prime working age adults, about one-fifth experienced declines of 5 percent or more in real earnings over the decade of the 1970s; that proportion rose to one-third during the 1980s (Rose 1994). More frequent job changes and job losses contributed significantly to this shift in trajectory (Rose 1995). Permanent layoffs have become more common (Farber 1996). Displacement rates in 1991–93, nominally years of recovery from a mild recession, were higher than during the deep recession years of 1981–83. In turn, displacement rates for the 1980–92 period as a whole exceeded

Figure 14.1 **Losing Ground: Average Hourly Wage and Houselold Income, Adjusted for Inflation, 1959–1998** (index: 1973 value = 100)

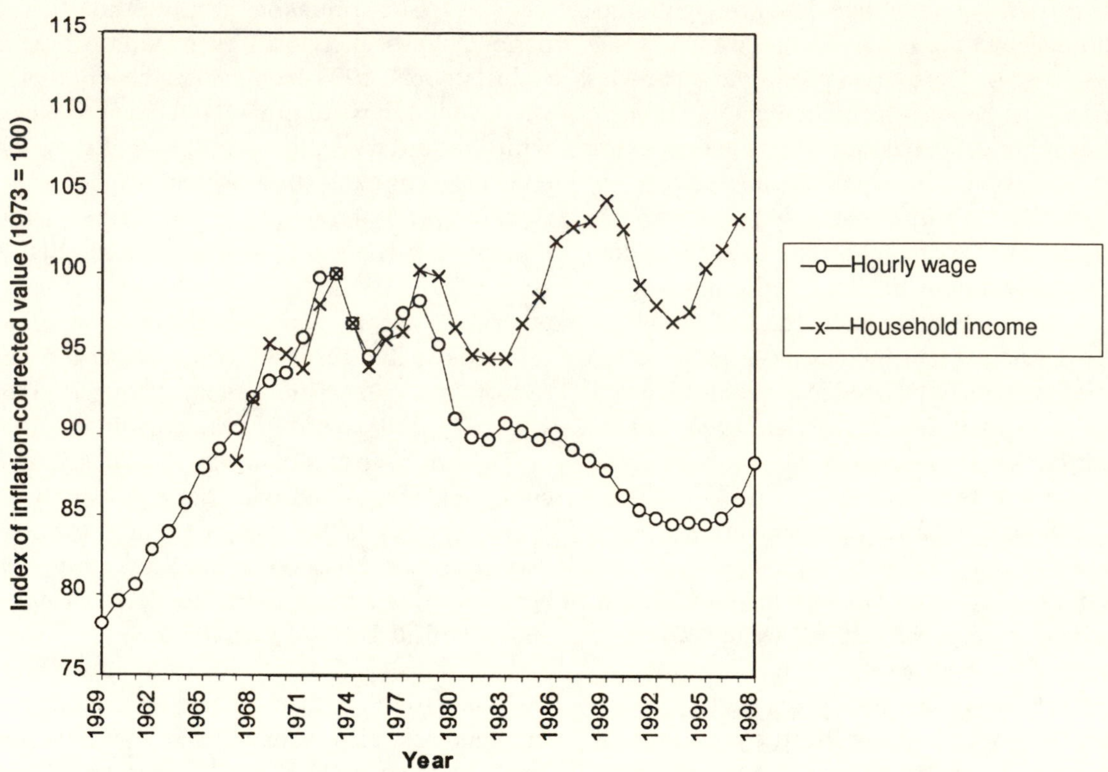

Sources: Average hourly wage is for production or nonsupervisory workers in private industry (Table B-47, U.S. Council of Economic Advisors 1998, updated frm U.S. Bureau of Labor Statistics Web site, http://stats.bls.gov). Median household income from Table B-2, U.S. Census Bureau, 1998a.

Note: To put wages and income on the same scale, the figure uses an index of 1973 = 100, so that an average wage of 200 would mean two times the 1973 wage, whereas a wage of 50 would mean half of the 1973 wage.

job loss rates during 1968–79 (Boisjoly, Duncan, and Smeeding 1994). Between these two periods, the percentage of people laid off increased by one-third, and the percentage fired doubled.

Growing Income Inequality

All of the evidence so far spells out the results of the divergence between business and worker fortunes. But there has been a second large economic shift as well, the growth of inequality among rich, middle-income, and poor. Figure 14.2 shows the shares of total income obtained by the richest 5 percent, the next-richest 15 percent, the middle 60 percent, and the lowest 20 percent of U.S. households.

In the mid-1970s the richest households began to gain, at the expense of middle-income households and to a lesser extent of the poorest. This upward shift of income accelerated during the 1980s, with the very richest cashing in and everybody else losing out. As with the U-turn in wage levels, this marked a significant reversal: during the 1950s and 1960s, income shares remained relatively stable, with a slight trend toward greater equality.

Income disparities are a very serious matter: recent research shows that inequality kills. On average, states with greater gaps between rich and poor households also have higher overall death rates, as well as higher rates of mortality from heart disease, stroke, and homicide. Public health researchers attribute these higher death rates to the "increased levels of stress and hopelessness" caused by inequality (Bass 1996).

Figure 14.2 tells the story of *income*—the amount of money received in a given year; not *wealth*—the total value of assets possessed by a household. Wealth is even more unequally distributed: in 1989, the top 5 percent of U.S. households controlled 72 percent of net financial assets, and 61 percent of total wealth (Wolff 1994). Furthermore, inequality in wealth has been widening apace. The richest 1 percent, which held 20 percent of the nation's net worth in 1976, had nearly doubled its share to 39 percent by 1989 (Wolff 1996, Figures 3-1, 3-3). Moreover, racial differences in wealth loom large. In 1988 (the most recent year researchers have examined), the median net worth of white households was more than six times as great as that of black households ($23,818 vs. $3,700; Oliver and Shapiro 1995, table 4.4).[1]

It is tempting to suppose that growing income and wealth inequality simply represents another facet of the divergence between workers and business. To some extent this is true: given the ebullient stock market of the last fifteen years, dividends and capital gains have enriched the richest. But income polarization involves more than labor–capital polarization, for two reasons. First of all, a key determinant of household income is the *composition* of that household. More adults in a household can contribute additional income (particularly earnings). For a variety of reasons, more Americans are living alone, or as single parents whose earning potential is curtailed by the time demands of child care, swelling the number of low-income households. At the same time, rising rates of paid employment by wives and mothers create more two-earner households, frequently (though by no means always!) at the upper end of the income distribution.

The other reason why widening income inequality involves more than a widening labor–capital divide is that even among the rich, most are working people. So most of the worsening of income inequality represents an increase in earnings inequality. Between 1979 and 1995, the hourly earnings of a worker at the 90th percentile (earning more than 90 percent of other workers) relative to a worker at the 10th percentile, increased by 23 percent for men and by 46 percent for women (Mishel, Bernstein, and Schmitt 1997, tables 3.7, 3.8). If fringe benefits are taken into account, inequality between the highest and lowest earners has increased even more (Passell 1998).

Reasons for the Changes in Income Distribution

The context for all of these changes is the breakdown of the post–World War II "golden age" for U.S. capital and labor. That rosy era was based on U.S. domination of global financial and goods markets. It also incorporated a "capital–labor accord" in which unions in the central mass production industries exchanged labor peace for growing wages, and a "capital–citizen accord" bartering social peace for an array of social programs such as Social Security and unemployment insurance (Gordon, Edwards, and Reich 1982). By the 1970s, all three elements of the golden age were crumbling. At a global level, the United States's industrial rivals, Europe and Japan, had rebuilt

Figure 14.2 **Trickle Up: Shares of Total U.S. Income Received by Families at Different Income Levels, Selected Years 1967–1997**

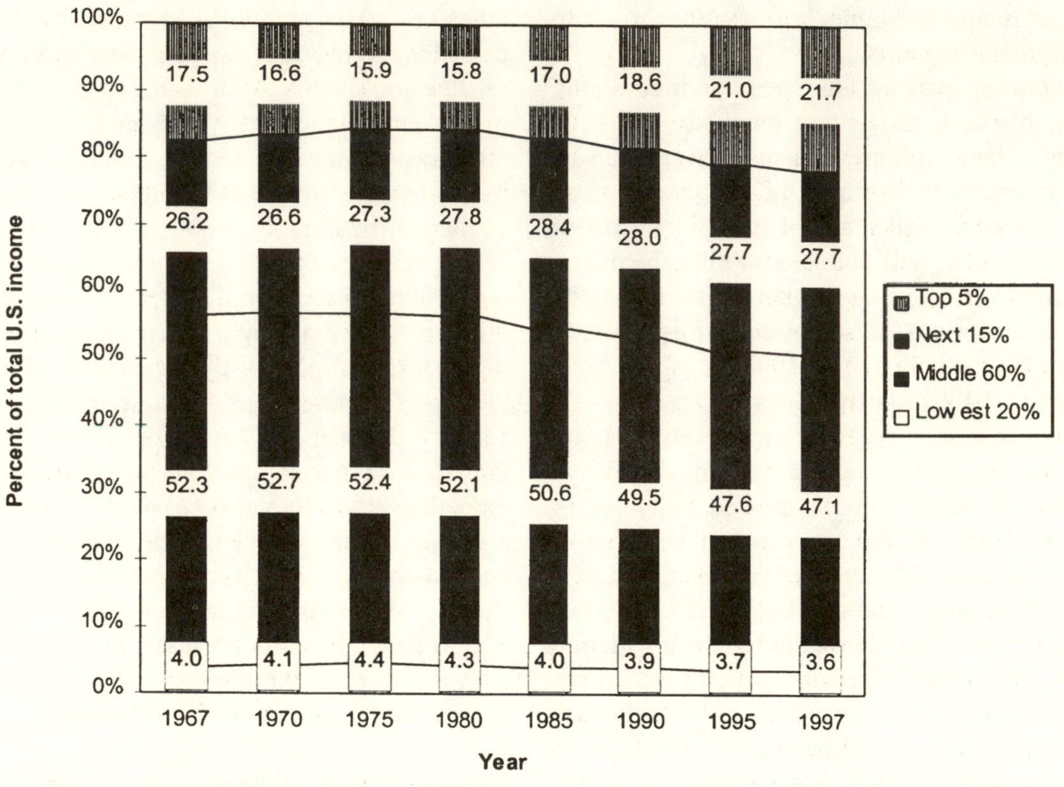

Source: U.S. Census Bureau 1998a, Table B-3.

from wartime destruction. The Third World, from Vietnam to the Organization of Petroleum Exporting Countries (OPEC), began to assert itself as well. The two domestic accords came under attack both from those who had been excluded—such as African Americans, other people of color, and women of all races—and from businesses unhappy that the concessions had been made at all. As the postwar economic order unraveled, then, three specific mechanisms reshaped the U.S. wage structure: globalization, technological change, and shifting business strategy.

U.S. corporations have globalized by outsourcing parts of the production process to Mexico, China, and dozens of other low-wage countries. At the same time, producers based in the industrialized countries of North America, Europe, and Asia are far more aggressively contesting each other's markets for a wide range of items. Both shifts remove the former protected status of many companies and workers: workers are subject to more competition from both low-wage and high-wage countries, and this competition exerts downward pressure on wages. Overall, however, these changes in the global economy are relatively small contributors to the changing structure of U.S. earnings. Despite the hubbub over globalization, the sum of U.S. imports and exports still equals only one-fifth of the nation's total domestic output; exports and imports each make up about half of this fraction (U.S. Council of Economic Advisors 1998).

Technological change has also rocked the boat. Businesses have striven to replace labor with machines, whether by mechanizing tasks completely (as with robots) or by using machines to make workers more productive (as with personal computers or supermarket scanners). Over the last thirty years, they have been disproportionately successful in eliminating lower-skill jobs, while creating more high-skill jobs, many of which involve interacting with new tools such as computers. This displaces workers at the low-skill end of the labor market and shrinks the pool of jobs they compete for, while heightening demand for high-skill workers, stretching wages further apart. As with globalization, although the technological change significantly affects income trends, its importance should not be overstated. As noted earlier, over the last three decades U.S. business investments in productive capacity (including machinery and equipment) and consequent productivity growth have actually been slow by historical and international standards. Economist Steven Allen (1996) found that technological change accounted for less than one-third of the 1980s growth in the wage gap between college and high school graduates—the piece of wage inequality that one would expect to be *most* related to changes in technique. There is little evidence of substantial shifts of U.S. labor demand toward higher skill levels after the early 1980s, despite the fact that the "microcomputer revolution" began during precisely those years (Howell, Duncan, and Harrison 1998).

Indeed, the rest of the industrialized world has experienced increased global competitiveness and new forms of technological change. But despite significant stress on their industrial relations systems, no other country has experienced the kind of collapse in job quality and surge in inequality that the United States has undergone. Explaining this difference is a third factor: U.S. businesses have for the most part responded to new competitive pressures by cutting costs rather than enhancing quality. This translates into a concerted effort to keep wages low and minimize long-term commitments to the workforce. Another corollary of this "low road" strategy is the slow productivity growth already noted, resulting from sluggish investment in both physical and human capital.

This newly dominant strategy accelerates the erosion of institutions such as unions, the minimum wage (which remains far below its 1970s level even after the 1996 increase), and job ladders within companies. But these are precisely the institutions that historically have defended worker wage levels, particularly those of workers with less individual bargaining power, and have provided avenues for upward mobility.

Two Key Dimensions of Income Changes: Race and Gender

As globalization, technological change, and the low road strategy transform the economy, not all groups in the population are equally affected by crumbling wages, sluggish income growth, and heightened economic polarization. In income terms, race and ethnicity continue to divide America. Stagnant incomes and rising income inequality have struck particularly hard at African Americans and Latinos. Figure 14.3 shows median household income by the racial or ethnic group of the household head, and Table 14.1 lists family poverty rates by race and ethnicity and family structure.

Some elements of the racial/ethnic hierarchy are immediately clear from Figure 14.3 and Table 14.1; others require further elaboration. The in-

Figure 14.3 **Persistent Gaps: Median Annual Household Income by Race and Ethnicity, 1972–1996** (in 1996 dollars)

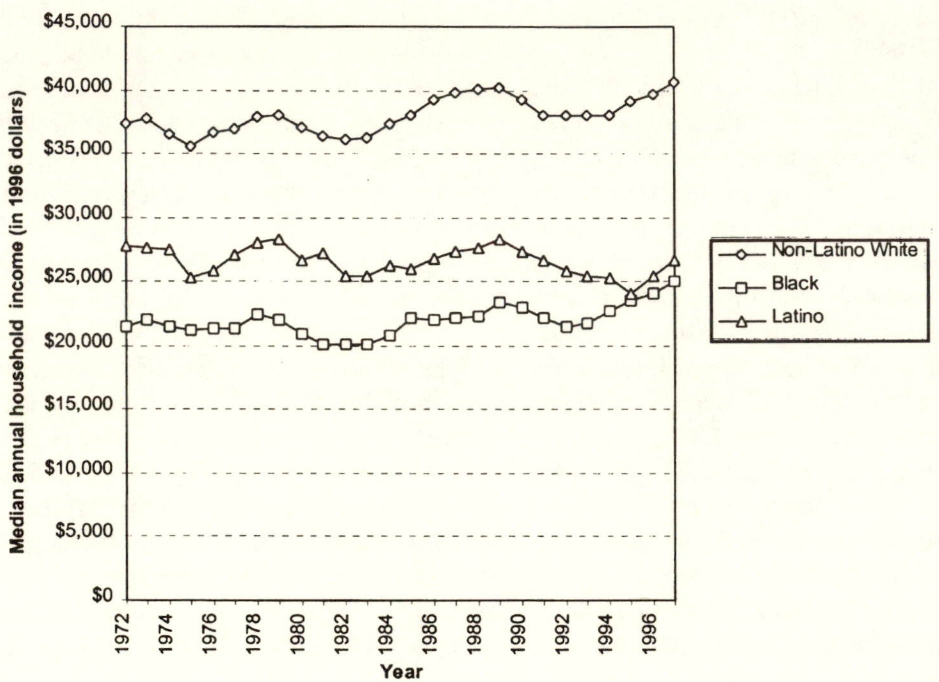

Source: Calculated by the author from U.S. Census Bureau 1998a, Table B-2.

comes of black and Latino households lag far behind those of non-Latino white households, and the last twenty-five years have not brought them appreciably closer. Other census data reveal that Asians have a higher median income than non-Latino whites (U.S. Census Bureau 1998a, ix). Native Americans, on the other hand, had the lowest income of any racial group in 1989 (Harrison and Bennett 1995, Figure 4.10, Table 4.7). Table 14.1 confirms that black and Latino poverty rates are highest. Asian and Native American poverty rates fall between those of whites and blacks (Albelda and Tilly 1997, Table 2.1).

The median incomes of Latinos and Asians are somewhat deceptive, since incomes are highly polarized *within* both populations. The Asian population, for example, includes high-income Japanese-American professionals, but also low-income recent immigrants and refugees from Southeast Asia and China. So although the median income of Asians exceeds that of whites, a greater proportion of Asians than of whites fall below the poverty line as well.

Of particular interest are the *changes* in relative incomes over time. Over the past twenty years as the epochal shifts in the economy took place, Latinos have lost ground relative to non-Latinos. Black household incomes have actually caught up slightly with white incomes, but the full picture is more troublesome. Over the same period of time,

Table 14.1

Poor, Poorer, Poorest: Percentage of Families in Poverty, by Race, Ethnicity, and Family Type, 1997

	All families	Single mother families
White	8.4	37.6
Black	23.6	46.9
Latino	24.7	54.2
Total	10.3	41.0

Source: U.S. Census Bureau 1998b, Table C-3.

Notes: Latinos can be of any race. "Single mother families" refers to "female householder, no husband present" with children aged under 18. Families (unlike the households appearing in Figures 14.1–14.3) are limited to groups of two or more people living together and related by birth, marriage, or adoption.

a thirty-year trend of black hourly wages to catch up with white wages was reversed. In terms of hourly wages, controlling for education and labor market experience, black men fell further behind white men, and black women behind white women (Bound and Dresser 1998; Bound and Freeman 1992; Corcoran 1998). And the black/white employment gap has also widened: in business cycle peak year 1973 black males were 88 percent as likely to be employed as white males, and black women 105 percent as likely as white women (that is, *more* likely than white women). Two business cycle peaks later, in 1989, these percentages had slipped to 85 percent and 95 percent, respectively (U.S. Council of Economic Advisors 1998, Table B-41). In the late 1990s economic boom, blacks did regain some ground, reaching 86.5 percent (men) and 100 percent (women) in 1998 (U.S. Bureau of Labor Statistics 1999b). Latinos also fell farther behind non-Latinos in wages, though not employment (Borjas 1994; Corcoran, Heflin, and Reyes 1998; Hinojosa-Ojeda, Carnoy, and Daley 1991; Melendez 1993).

Why? Part of the income story is one of family structure. Single-mother families have become more common among all race and class groups, but this family structure has grown most rapidly among black families. The prevalence of this family structure is in part the result of limited economic opportunities available to black men, and to higher risks of imprisonment and early death in these populations (Wilson and Neckerman 1986). But widening gaps in hourly wages and employment tell us that an important part of the problem stems from the labor market. And in fact, blacks were hit particularly hard by the three drivers of economic change: globalization, technological change, and revised business strategy. Among Latinos, one major factor in wage gaps is the influx of immigrants (many of whom earn low wages), although there is also some evidence that many of the same trends are at work as for blacks (Ortiz 1991; Melendez 1993).

In addition to race and ethnicity, gender powerfully stratifies incomes and wages. The gender gap is one area in which wage inequality is actually *falling*, not rising. Women advanced from 59 percent of men's wage level in 1975 to 74 percent in 1997—still not earnings equality, but a step in the right direction (Albelda and Tilly 1997, Figure 1.3; U.S. Census Bureau 1998a, Table 10). While a smaller gender gap in wages is a welcome development, the problem is that this change has taken place primarily *not* because women's real wages were rising, but because men's real wages were falling. With—on average—men's wages lower and women's wages little higher, two earners have become increasingly necessary to support a family. This family speed-up is not an improvement in the standard of living! And the group squeezed hardest by the continuing gender wage gap and the family speed-up is single mothers. In this context, recent waves of state and federal welfare "reform" have slashed away at a critical lifeline for single mothers, the program popularly known as welfare (see Albelda and Tilly in this volume).

Conclusion: The Downward Spiral

Recent economic trends in the United States tell a story of income stagnation, growing income insecurity, and widening income inequalities. They also form part of a self-perpetuating economic cycle. Businesses feeling competitive pressure curb wages, reducing consumer income and tightening competition still more. Businesses underinvest in knowledge and equipment upgrading, slowing productivity growth and reducing the surplus available for reinvestment.

But as troubling as this economic vicious circle may be, the *political* vicious circle is even more discouraging. The experience of sharpening income inequality, abetted by ubiquitous pro-market ideology, divides low- and moderate-income people, as they scramble to get closer to the haves and to distance themselves from the have-nots. Those running to keep up on the economic treadmill, unable to counteract the changed rules of the game, too often direct their resentment at those still worse off—immigrants, welfare recipients, Mexican workers—who are seen as competitors or undeserving beneficiaries of taxpayer-funded aid. But in the national and global market, weakening one's competitors simply hastens the process of bidding down wages and job security; undermines any notions of universal rights to housing, employment, or income; and divides the coalitions that could potentially resist the dangerous economic trends.

Stopping this downward spiral requires weaving a politics *and* economics based on solidarity rather than division. Politically and economically, the target must be policies protecting the weakest and bolstering living, housing, and work standards so that we can all rise together. Without such policies, the downward spiral of worsening economic inequality and insecurity is bound to continue.

Note

1. I have adopted the shorthand of calling households headed by black people "black" households, and so on. Given the limited degree of intermarriage among racial groups in the United States, this shorthand is relatively accurate, though becoming less so.

References

Albelda, Randy, and Chris Tilly. 1997. *Glass Ceilings and Bottomless Pits: Women's Work, Women's Poverty*. Boston: South End Press.

Allen, Steven G. 1996. "Technology and the Wage Structure." Working paper no. 5534, National Bureau of Economic Research, Cambridge, MA.

Baker, Dean. 1995. "The 'Profits–Investment' Scam." *Dollars and Sense* (September/October): 34–35.

Bass, Alison. 1996. "Income Inequality, Mortality Linked." *Boston Globe*, April 19.

Boisjoly, Johanne, Greg J. Duncan, and Timothy Smeeding. 1994. "Have Highly Skilled Workers Fallen from Grace? The Shifting Burdens of Involuntary Job Losses from 1968 to 1992." Mimeo, University of Quebec, Rimouski.

Borjas, George J. 1994. "The Economics of Immigration." *Journal of Economic Literature* 23: 1667–1717.

Bound, John, and Laura Dresser. 1998. "The Erosion of the

Relative Earnings of Young African American Women During the 1980s." In *Latinas and African American Women at Work*, ed. Irene Browne, 61–104. New York: Russell Sage Foundation.

Bound, John, and Richard Freeman. 1992. "What Went Wrong? The Erosion of Relative Earnings and Employment for Blacks." *Quarterly Journal of Economics* 107: 201–232.

Corcoran, Mary. 1998. "The Economic Progress of African American Women." In *Latinas and African American Women at Work*, ed. Irene Browne, 35–60. New York: Russell Sage Foundation.

Corcoran, Mary, Colleen M. Heflin, and Belinda I. Reyes. 1998. "The Economic Progress of Mexican and Puerto Rican Women." In *Latinas and African American Women at Work*, ed. Irene Browne, 105–138. New York: Russell Sage Foundation.

Currie, Elliott, Robert Dunn, and David Fogarty. 1980. "The New Immiseration: Stagflation, Inequality, and the Working Class." *Socialist Review* 54: 7–31.

Farber, Henry S. 1996. "The Changing Face of Job Loss in the United States, 1981–1993." Working Paper #360, Industrial Relations Section, Princeton University, Princeton, NJ.

Freeman, Richard B. 1994. "How Labor Fares in Advanced Economies." In *Working Under Different Rules*, ed. Richard B. Freeman, 1–28. New York: Russell Sage Foundation and National Bureau of Economic Research.

Gordon, David M., Richard Edwards, and Michael Reich. 1982. *Segmented Workers, Divided Work: The Historical Transformation of Labor in the United States*. Cambridge, UK: Cambridge University Press.

Harrison, Roderick J., and Claudette Bennett. 1995. "Racial and Ethnic Diversity," In *State of the Union: America in the 1990s*, Volume 2, ed. Reynolds Farley, 141–210. New York: Russell Sage.

Hinojosa-Ojeda, Raul, Martin Carnoy, and Hugh Daley. 1991. "An Even Greater 'U-turn': Latinos and the New Inequality." In *Hispanics in the Labor Force: Issues and Policies*, ed. Edwin Melendez, Clara Rodriguez, and Janis Barry Figueroa, 25–52. New York: Plenum.

Howell, David R., Margaret Duncan, and Bennett Harrison. 1998. "Low Wages in the U.S. and High Unemployment in Europe: A Critical Assessment of the Conventional Wisdom." Working paper no. 5, Center for Economic Policy Analysis, New School for Social Research, New York, NY. Revised August.

Melendez, Edwin. 1993. "Understanding Latino Poverty." *Sage Race Relations Abstracts* 18, no. 2: 3–43.

Miller, John. 1995. "Hard Times Roll On: Growth and Well-Being on Different Tracks." *Dollars & Sense* (May/June): 8–9, 38–39.

Mishel, Lawrence, Jared Bernstein, and John Schmitt. 1997. *The State of Working America, 1996–97*. Armonk, NY: M.E. Sharpe.

Oliver, Melvin L., and Thomas M. Shapiro. 1995. *Black Wealth/White Wealth: A New Perspective on Racial Inequality*. New York: Routledge.

Ortiz, Vilma. 1991. "Latinos and Industrial Change in New York and Los Angeles." In *Hispanics in the Labor Force: Issues and Policies*, ed. Edwin Melendez, Clara Rodriguez, and Janis Barry Figueroa, 119–132. New York: Plenum.

Passell, Peter. 1998. "Benefits Dwindle Along with Wages for the Unskilled." *The New York Times*, June 14.

Rose, Stephen J. 1994. *On Shaky Ground: Rising Fears about Income and Earnings*. Research Report 94–02. Washington, DC: National Commission on Employment Policy.

______. 1995. *Declining Job Security and the Professionalization of Opportunity*. Research Report 95–04. Washington, DC: National Commission on Employment Policy.

U.S. Bureau of Economic Analysis. 1999. "Selected NIPA Tables" to be published in the May 1999 *Survey of Current Business*. http://www.bea.doc.gov/bea/dn/dgpa.exe, April 30.

U.S. Bureau of Labor Statistics. 1999a. Web site, http://stats.bls.gov. Series PRS84006092 (Output per hour, all business, quarterly percentage change), accessed May 1999.

______. 1999b. *Employment and Earnings*, January.

U.S. Census Bureau. 1998a. *Money Income in the United States: 1997*. Current Population Reports, Consumer Income, P60–200. Washington, DC: U.S. Government Printing Office.

______. 1998b. *Poverty in the United States: 1997*. Current Population Reports, Consumer Income, P60–201. Washington, DC: U.S. Government Printing Office.

U.S. Council of Economic Advisors. 1998. *Economic Report of the President 1998*. Washington, DC: U.S. Government Printing Office.

Wilson, William J., and Kathryn M. Neckerman. 1986. "Poverty and Family Structure: The Widening Gap Between Evidence and Public Policy Issues." In *Fighting Poverty: What Works, What Doesn't*, ed. Sheldon Danziger and Daniel Weinberg, 232–259. Cambridge: Harvard University Press.

Wolff, Edward. 1994. "Trends in Household Wealth in the United States, 1962–83 and 1983–89." *Review of Income and Wealth* 40, no. 2: 143–74.

______. 1996. *Top Heavy: The Increasing Inequality of Wealth in America and What Can Be Done About It*. New York: The New Press.

15

Single, with Children

The Economic Plight of Single Mothers

Randy Albelda and Chris Tilly

It's not just thinking about whether or not you can afford to go to a movie, but you have to think about can the kids and I stop and get a soda if we've been out running errands. It's a big decision, 'cause we just don't have much spending money.

Single mother of two in Wisconsin, (Rank 1994, 61)

As of 1997, 41 percent of single-mother families lived in poverty, as opposed to 8 percent of other families with children (U.S. Bureau of the Census 1998, C-9). And while the people in single-mother families only account for 6 percent of the U.S., population, they account for close to 30 percent of all poor people. The high rate of poverty among single-mother families has been under intense scrutiny over the last two decades and the policies intended to alleviate that poverty—usually referred to as "welfare" in the United States—have come under attack and been radically transformed by the states and the federal government. This chapter discusses the reasons why single mothers fare so poorly, dispels some of the powerful myths used to justify harsh welfare policies, and discusses what alternative policies might look like.

The Triple Whammy

Poverty among single mothers is not new: women raising their children alone have always been poor. Four decades ago, in 1959, 60 percent of single-mother families were poor, compared to 16 percent of other families with children. Despite all the sound and fury around the issue since the early 1980s, the basic reasons why single mothers and their children are poor have not changed. We call them the "triple whammy."

The Gender Wage Gap

The first strike against single mothers is that the one working-age adult of the family is a woman, and women still only earn about two-thirds as much per hour as do men. While the vast majority of women who work could support themselves, only about half could support an entire family. The Institute for Women's Policy Research found that nationwide, 45 percent of all women would earn too little to bring a family of three up to the poverty threshold (including day care costs for one child) *even if they worked full-time, year-round* (Spalter-Roth et al. 1993).

Adapted from Randy Albelda and Chris Tilly, *Glass Ceilings and Bottomless Pits*. (Boston: South End Press, 1997) www.lbbs.org/sep/sep.htm 1–800–553–8478.

Cradles to Rock, Mouths to Feed

Having children affects families' economic well-being. Young children add to the family's needs without contributing to its earning power. Caring for them claims time, energy, and money. Child care imperatives limit many mothers to part-time work, workplaces close to home, and/or jobs that offer flexibility—usually at a cost in terms of compensation and promotion opportunities. In a recent survey of women in four cities, child care constraints prevented almost one-third of women from seeking a job, prompted one in eight to turn down a job, and caused one in ten job-holding women to quit or be fired (Moss and Tilly forthcoming). Recent research by Jane Waldfogel (1997) finds that mothers earn less than women who are not mothers, while lone mothers earn less than married mothers, after adjusting for age, experience, and educational levels.

Not Enough Hands

The simple fact is that families with more adults can earn more. Single-mother families, by definition, have one adult to both earn income and take care of children. This completes the triple whammy.

Why Aren't "They" Married?: New Choices, Old Problems

In 1997, one out of four families with children was a female-headed household, compared to one out of every ten in 1960 (U.S. Census Bureau 1998, C-9). The trend of a growing proportion of women who are single mothers—including those who were once married and those who were never married—holds for black, white, and Latino women; for middle-class as well as poor women; and in all parts of the country. In fact, the trend is growing in Europe as well—and the United States is far from the extreme case. In Denmark, for example, births out of wedlock increased from 8 percent of all births in 1960 to 45 percent in 1988! In fact, rates of out-of-wedlock births in France, Britain, Norway, and Sweden all exceeded U.S. rates (Lewis 1993). Of course, having a child out of wedlock is only one source of single motherhood; separation, divorce, and the death of a spouse are others. In the United States, only one-quarter of U.S. single parents have never been married.

Why are more women becoming single mothers? Women have more choices than they once did. Divorce has become easier, tolerance for domestic violence has decreased, and there is far more acceptance of a woman raising a child alone. Men have more choices, too, with fewer strictures against divorce or abandonment, and fewer pressures to marry the mothers of their children. Shifting patterns of labor force participation and wages have also influenced family structure. As more women become economically active in the paid labor force, their ability to be self-supporting increases, making marriage less of an economic necessity, even though earning enough to raise children as a single mother is far from easy. Men's falling wages and employment rates have also contributed to diminishing marriage rates. Men are reluctant to get married when their incomes are low—although they are not hesitant about becoming fathers.[1] Other reasons for women ending up single include high rates of incarceration and early death in the poor communities where single motherhood is most common, as well as the simple inability to find the right match.

Single Motherhood, Welfare, and Teen Motherhood: Debunking the Myths

In the current political climate, many are prepared to brand single mothers as bad mothers. But is this fair? To be sure, single mothers face a formidable set of economic obstacles, and these economic disadvantages have costs for their children. But single mothers have their reasons for being single. Denouncing single mothers as a group implies that if only they could find a man—any man—they and their children would be better off. This preposterous claim potentially leads to a very distasteful set of policy proposals, including forced marriage or the forced removal of children from single mothers, regardless of their ability to parent. Instead, we should acknowledge that poverty, not single motherhood, is the problem.

One source of confusion is that discussions often tangle single motherhood with welfare recipiency, teen pregnancy, and out-of-wedlock childbearing. But although there are overlaps, these are *not* all the same thing, nor the same group of people. Prior to the elimination of the Aid to Families with Dependent Children (AFDC) program in 1996 (the federal program was replaced by state programs funded by a federal block grant called Temporary Assistance to Needy Families, or TANF), only one-third of single mothers received AFDC. Only one AFDC household in twelve was headed by a teen mother; only one-quarter of single mothers had never been married. Out-of-wedlock births have increased among *all* women, not just among those eligible for welfare. Women of *all* income groups are less likely to marry and stay married. While the childbearing rates of single women have changed very little, single women are now a larger percentage of all women, so births to single women are a larger percentage of all births (Blank 1995). Despite a large volume of research, the myths persist, holding that teen pregnancy is an epidemic (actually, teen birth rates are declining) and that overly generous welfare benefits encourage unwed motherhood (in fact, research shows no connection).

Even divorced mothers are under attack. But the claims that divorce is bad for children do not take into account that they might have fared worse if their parents had remained together in a loveless, angry, or even violent marriage (Stacey 1994, Furstenberg and Cherlin 1991). Poverty and the public stigma that has always been attached to receiving public assistance are far more harmful to children than their mother's marital status. The most important factor accounting for the difficulties experienced by children from mother-only families, divorced or otherwise, is low income (McLanahan 1994). Just as poverty and unemployment make providing for basic needs more difficult, they put strains on marriages and family life.

Differences Among Single Mothers

While single mothers as a group face formidable economic disadvantages, single mothers are *not* all the same. Close to two-thirds of single mothers were white in 1997, and over two-thirds did *not* receive welfare during that year. Comparing welfare recipients with nonrecipients gives some clues about why those who opt for welfare have little alternative. Single mothers who receive cash assistance look very different from those who do not. They are less educated and younger—both factors leading to lower wage potential. Recipient mothers are more likely to be Latino or black, which also depresses earnings due to discrimination. They more commonly live in a large city or rural area—again, locations associated with reduced earnings.

Furthermore, welfare recipients face more constraints on their working time than do single mothers not receiving aid. Recipient mothers are much more likely to have young children—a factor that makes it difficult to do large amounts of paid labor without reliable child care. Over half of women receiving welfare have never been married. The great majority of nonrecipient single mothers were once married, giving them better prospects of collecting child support or alimony.

By comparison, married mothers are more educated, older, and more likely to be white, non-Latino, and suburban, than single mothers, especially single mothers on welfare. In short, the single mothers who resort to public assistance do so because of a whole series of limitations on their earnings opportunities.

Struggling to Survive

Public assistance to single mothers and their children has become far less generous. The inflation adjusted (in 1996 dollars) AFDC benefits for a typical family of four in a typical state plummeted from $910 in 1970 to $450 in 1996 (U.S. House of Representatives 1998, 414). Over 80 percent of the states went on to overhaul their welfare policies during the 1990s. The new state reforms are a mixed bag. In some cases they incorporate sensible changes that work in the direction of reducing poverty, such as allowing welfare recipients to keep more of the money they earn. But on the whole, such positive initiatives are being overwhelmed by an avalanche of misguided, punitive policies that welfare rolls, time-limited benefits, and workfare. The federal reform, passed in 1996, is as bad or worse. It emphasizes compelling recipients to work for pay or else lose assistance. The new law gives states full authority with virtually no accountability, eliminating any federal guarantee of assistance for those in need. And it imposes a lifetime five-year limit on welfare receipt. Overall, it signals a low point in U.S. poverty policy. Neither the federal or state approaches hold promise for significantly diminishing poverty; they amount to new ways to punish welfare recipients and bully them off the welfare rolls.

But being on welfare is punishment enough. The benefits are remarkably low. The median benefit in 1996 was $389 a month for a family of three. Women scrape through by piecing together a variety of income sources in a precarious patchwork. They scrimp and go without things that many of us would consider necessities. And an unexpected expense—for example, for a medical problem—or a delay in any income source can precipitate a household financial crisis.

States and the federal government have been largely promoting jobs—any jobs—as the route out of welfare. However, this strategy without solid supports for going to work (such as child care, health care, and transportation), is tenuous one at best. The dilemma of welfare versus paid work is most clearly seen in research done by sociologists Kathryn Edin and Laura Lein (1996). They constructed average budgets based on multiple interviews with 450 low-income single mothers in Boston, Charleston, Chicago, and San Antonio. They found that these women were subsisting on extremely low incomes: $10,700 a year among welfare mothers, and $14,900 among working single mothers—including food stamps and the Earned Income Credit, which supplements the income of very low-income families. While conservatives like to claim that welfare creates a cycle of dependency, Edin and Lein found that on average government aid (including AFDC and Supplemental Security Income grants as well as food stamps) does not even cover half of recipients' expenses. The inadequate levels of benefits force mothers to find alternative forms of income, even if some of these sources are not legal under current welfare rules. Women do so in order to clothe, house, and feed their children. And here's the rub: employment offers only a limited route out of poverty for single mothers. Compared to women on welfare, low-wage working mothers end up taking one step forward and two steps back. Edin and Lein found that the average wage-earning mother made an added $758 a month on her main job compared to the average welfare-reliant mother. But the wage-reliant mother lost $505 in government aid and took on $190 in added work-related expenses. What's more, on average, the wage-earning mothers pay $128 more per month on housing, because they have less access to housing subsidies. Bottom line, the main job leaves these mothers $65 *behind* where they would have been on welfare! It takes added earnings from a second job or overtime just to break even. Like welfare mothers, low-wage working mothers cannot meet all of their families' needs with their own wages, and continue to depend on government aid (especially food stamps), and above all on aid from family and friends. It's not surprising that while 86 percent of the AFDC recipients in this study planned to leave welfare for paid work at some point, 73 percent were deferring employment until they could lower the costs of work and improve their earning power.

Given the gender gap in wages and the rest of the "triple whammy," economic survival is a constant struggle for most single mothers. This is true for those trying to support a family on meager welfare benefits, and true as well for women trapped in the low-wage labor market. Unfortunately, the ongoing process of welfare "reform" which stresses getting a job—any job—threatens to remove much of the limited support that does exist.

An Alternative Future?

The "triple whammy"—women's lower wages, the demands of caring for children, and the limitation of having only one adult in the household—explains why single mothers and their children in the United States are so likely to be poor. But there is nothing about single motherhood that inevitably condemns lone moms to penury. Rather, it is the harsh market rules and impoverished public policies characterizing the U.S. economy that create this outcome.

A few public policy changes could dramatically alter the economic plight of single mothers. Raising the minimum wage to a living wage, making it easier for workers to organize unions (which help equalize wages in the workforce), and paid family leaves (instead of the twelve-week unpaid leave mandated by current federal law) would improve jobs for single mothers, as well as many other women and men. Pay equity policies (i.e., equal pay for work requiring comparable skills) would help as well. A recent study by the Institute for Women's Policy Research and the AFL-CIO found that if employed single mothers earned as much as comparably skilled men, their income would be boosted by 17 percent and their poverty rates would be halved—from 25.3 percent to 12.6 percent (AFL-CIO 1999). But upgrading jobs is not enough. Lifting single mothers out of poverty requires rebuilding and extending the social safety net: guaranteeing universal, affordable child care, assuring health coverage for all, and, yes, providing cash assistance for the times and situations when parents must stay home to take care of their children rather than working for pay.

While this agenda seems ambitious in the current conservative policy context in the United States, most of our international counterparts have adopted many parts of it—and it shows. U.S. public policies are less effective in lifting single-parent families out of poverty than those in Canada, France, Germany, the Netherlands, the United Kingdom, and Sweden, according to one study comparing the United States with these six countries (McFate et al. 1995). Closer to home, U.S. policies do far better at lifting elderly families than single mothers out of poverty, since Social Security benefits are considerably more generous than welfare (though continuing attacks on Social Security may undo this as well). In fact, while the federal government and the states have slashed aid for the poor, they have preserved and expanded government aid for the middle class and wealthy, including the mortgage interest tax deduction and ever-lower capital gains taxes. Why not shift some of the assistance to those most in need?

Importantly, a policy program to aid single mothers would not help them alone. By helping to level the labor market playing field and creating an income "floor," the program would benefit all low-income families and all working people, especially women. We all deserve a better society: one where women and men receive equal treatment, where employers and the government recognize family needs, and where poverty is replaced by opportunity. Taking steps to help single mothers, the poorest of all families, would be a major stride in that direction.

Note

1. Some research that suggests a link between male employment opportunities and marriage includes Wilson and Neckerman, 1986; McLanahan, Garfinkel, and Watson, 1987; and Testa, Astone, Krogh, and Neckerman, 1989.

References

AFL-CIO. 1999. *Equal Pay for Working Families: National and State Data on the Pay Gap and Its Costs.* Washington, DC. Executive Summary available at www.aflcio.org/women/exec99.htm.

Blank, Rebecca. 1995. "What Are the Trends in Nonmarital Births?" In *Looking Before We Leap: Social Science and Welfare Reform*, ed. R. Kent Weaver and William T. Dickens. Washington, DC: Brookings Institution.

Edin, Kathryn J., and Laura Lein. 1996. *Making Ends Meet: How Single Mothers Survive Welfare and Low-Wage Work.* New York: Russell Sage Foundation.

Furstenberg, Jr., Frank F., and Andrew J. Cherlin. 1991. *Divided Families. What Happens to Children When Parents Part.* Cambridge: Harvard University Press.

Lewis, Jane. 1993. "Introduction." In *Women and Social Policies in Europe: Work, Family and the State*, ed. Jane Lewis. Aldershot, England: Edward Elgar.

McFate, Katherine, Timothy Smeeding, and Lee Rainwater. 1995. "Markets and States: Poverty Trends and Transfer Effectiveness in the 1980s." In *Poverty, Inequality, and the Future of Social Policy: Western States in the New World Order*, eds. Katherine McFate, Roger Lawson, and William Julius Wilson, 29–66. New York: Russell Sage.

McLanahan, Sara. 1994. "The Consequences of Single Motherhood," *The American Prospect* no. 18 (Summer).

McLanahan, Sara, Irwin Garfinkel, and Dorothy Watson. 1987. "Family Structure, Poverty, and the Underclass." University of Wisconsin–Madison, Institute for Research on Poverty, discussion paper 823–87.

Moss, Philip, and Chris Tilly. Forthcoming. "Hiring in Urban Labor Markets: Shifting Labor Demands, Persistent Racial Differences." In *Sourcebook on Labor Markets: Evolving Structures and Processes*, ed. Ivar Berg and Arne Kalleberg. New York: Plenum.

Rank, Mark. 1994. *Living on the Edge: The Realities of Welfare in America.* New York: Columbia University Press.

Spalter-Roth, Roberta, Heidi Hartmann, and Linda Andrews. 1993. "Combining Work and Welfare." In *Sociology and the Public Agenda.* Newbury Park, CA: Sage.

Stacey, Judith. 1994. "The New Family Values Crusaders." *The Nation*, July 25/August 1, 119–21.

Testa, Mark, Nan Marie Astone, Marilyn Krogh, and Kathryn M. Neckerman. 1989. "Employment and Marriage Among Inner-City Fathers," *Annals of the American Academy of Political and Social Science* 501 (January).

U.S. Bureau of the Census. 1998. *Poverty in the United States 1997.* P-60–201. Washington, DC: U.S. Government Printing Office.

U.S. House of Representatives, Committee on Ways and Means. 1998. *Background Material and Data on Major Programs.* Washington, DC: U.S. Government Printing Office.

Waldfogel, Jane. 1997. "The Effects of Children on Women's Wages." *American Sociological Review* no. 62: 209–17.

Wilson, William J., and Kathryn M. Neckerman. 1986. "Poverty and Family Structure: The Widening Gap Between Evidence and Public Policy Issues." In *Fighting Poverty: What Works and What Doesn't*, ed. Sheldon Danziger and Daniel Weinberg. Cambridge: Harvard University Press.

16

U.S. Labor Faces an Identity Crisis

George DeMartino

Introduction

By virtually any measure, the U.S. labor movement is immersed in a protracted crisis. Over the past several decades, the percentage of U.S. workers who are union members has plummeted. At the same time, unions have suffered a dramatic loss of bargaining power, political influence, and social standing. What has gone wrong?

Union leaders most often attribute the crisis to adverse changes in the political and economic landscape. The election of successive anti-union administrations (from Reagan onward) has deprived labor of government support. Moreover, global economic integration has undermined union bargaining power by intensifying market competition, and by providing multinational corporations with the ability to relocate around the globe in search of cheaper labor. Indeed, new trade and investment pacts, like the North American Free Trade Agreement (NAFTA) and the World Trade Organization, enhance the credibility of corporate threats to relocate to avoid union campaigns for worker rights (see Bronfenbrenner 1996).

Though there is a good deal of truth in this account, it is not the whole story. Labor's difficulties began well before the election of President Reagan. The crisis also spans all sectors of the economy, not just those hit by foreign competition or capital flight. These factors have amplified the crisis to be sure, but they did not induce it.

This chapter emphasizes instead a fundamental but largely unacknowledged identity crisis facing the labor movement. By *union identity* I refer to what unions have become, and what it is that they do. When we speak of union identity, we must keep in mind that there is no single model of unionism. Instead, different union movements around the world embrace distinct visions of what a union is and what it is to do. These visions influence the way they define their goals and strategies. When these strategies fail, we should therefore investigate whether part of the problem lies in the particular identity adopted by the union in crisis.

Social Versus Business Unionism

In the United States, two models of unionism have competed for workers' allegiance over the past century. One, "social unionism," struggles for social justice throughout society. The other, a much narrower, bread-and-butter form known as "busi-

The arguments of this chapter are further developed in DeMartino 1999. This chapter is a substantially revised version of "The Future of the US Labor Movement in an Era of Global Economic Integration" in *Labour Worldwide in the Era of Globalization*, ed. Ronaldo Munck and Peter Waterman, 83–96. London: Macmillan.

ness unionism," accepts the broad contours of capitalist society, but seeks a fair deal for workers. The former model identifies unions as vehicles for broad social mobilizations against entrenched privilege and inequality; the latter sees unions as partners with business in achieving competitiveness for domestic firms while ensuring that some of the gains achieved through productivity increase flow to union members. The former advances multifaceted campaigns (in and beyond the workplace) for equality and justice; the latter manages the conflict between capital and labor in the workplace so as to secure gains for workers while minimizing industrial strife.

To the dismay of many progressives labor activists and observers, the latter model of unionism has largely eclipsed the former in the United States (cf. Moody 1988). The defeat of social unionism has occurred over the course of a century of government repression of and corporate resistance to more radical unions. But many conservative union leaders also opposed social unionism. In the view of progressive critics, these leaders forfeited the broader vision of union identity represented by social unionism because they were coopted by the state and business interests. The autocratic structure of the union movement facilitated the transition to business unionism by depriving union activists of meaningful opportunities for participation. The payoff for the advocates of business unionism was the extension of important legal protections to unions in their efforts to secure employer recognition and collective bargaining agreements (Milton 1982).

On the basis of this analysis, progressives argue that unions must be democratized to allow rank-and-file members to take back control of their own institutions. They argue that once freed from the constraints imposed by authoritarian union hierarchies, union members will devise broad economic and social agendas, forge coalitions with other progressive groups, and restore mass mobilization as the chief union weapon in pursuit of social and economic justice.

But like the view offered by union leaders, the progressive diagnosis and prescription misses something important. It fails to recognize the *class* nature of contemporary U.S. unions. As Annunziato (1990) has argued, U.S. unions today act very much like *capitalist enterprises* that sell a commodity for a fee. Like insurance companies, unions today sell a service commodity—what Annunziato calls "union representation." This capitalist aspect of unionism is reflected in the priority unions place on collective bargaining as the primary means to secure employment protections for their customers (union members). Labor contracts typically provide due process in cases of discipline, wage increases, some measure of job security (e.g., seniority protection), and so forth. Unions attempt to sell this service through organizing drives. These may be viewed as marketing campaigns during which the union must convince potential customers of their need for the service they provide.

Compared with other services commodities, union representation has several peculiar attributes. First, potential customers (unorganized workers) must commit to its purchase prior to its production. Production of the service comes in the form of initial contract negotiations, during which the union attempts to force a firm to provide the protections and benefits that the union promised during the organizing campaign. Second, production of the service requires the willing efforts—often Herculean—of those who purchase it. That is, union members must be enlisted in what is often a protracted struggle to secure a contract that provides the protections and benefits they seek. Like certain other commodities, such as handguns or abortions, union representation is one that is produced and marketed *under siege*—against the opposition of well-mobilized groups with a strong interest in preventing its existence. Corporations undertake tremendous expense and effort to disrupt union sales efforts. Third and as a consequence, the union's effort to overcome employer opposition also often requires a broad campaign to secure community support beyond those who will receive the direct benefits of union representation.

The Contradictions of Commodity Unionism

This commodity character of union representation rests on a fundamental contradiction between two requirements. The first requirement is that the sale of any commodity typically depends on its *not being generally available outside of the market for it.* After all, people will not buy a commodity when it (or some close substitute) is available for free. Like other commodity providers, then, the union must market something that customers cannot otherwise obtain. But this means that unions must be wary of government initiatives to generalize the benefits of union representation to nonunion members. And indeed, U.S. unions have historically displayed an ambivalent attitude toward universal employment protections, and have concentrated their legislative efforts on securing protections for union rights and other conditions for unions to be able to provide union representation (Aronowitz 1983).

To be marketable, then, union representation must entail a *differential:* union members must receive something not available to nonmembers. The benevolent face of this differential is that it serves as an inducement to nonunion members to join and thereby enjoy this benefit. But the differential is less benevolent when combined with exclusionary practices that define some workers (and other members of society) as ineligible for membership. The typical unwillingness of unions to organize those who work without wages (such as those who perform household labor), the self-employed, the unemployed, and workers outside of the United States leaves these groups permanently excluded from the benefits associated with the commodity that U.S. unions produce. It is not that unions are uninterested about the welfare of such groups. Rather, these groups are excluded as a natural consequence of the particular union identity that U.S. unions have adopted.

But this requirement, that the protections associated with union representation not be available outside the market for it, contradicts a second, equally important requirement. As noted above, the fact that this service is produced and marketed under siege requires that union members and other community members bear risk and contribute substantial effort (among other things) to the union campaign to ensure its success. But why would they do this? Those who buy Ford automobiles do not regularly mobilize to secure access to this commodity, and would no doubt find a request by the Ford Motor Company that they do so to be laughable. Historically, workers have undertaken such efforts *precisely because and to the degree that union representation is seen not to be a commodity, but a social movement.* People generally do not risk their incomes, careers, and even lives to ensure the production and sale of a commodity—but they do, sometimes, when some important value is at stake. Some people campaign for the right to buy and possess handguns because they see the matter as a constitutional right; others advocate for access to legal and safe abortions because they see it as vital to a woman's personal autonomy and control over her own body. Similarly, workers sometimes engage in struggles to secure union representation in the belief that so doing defends a fundamental right: the union organizing campaign reflects the aspiration for human dignity and justice. On these grounds, workers have historically fought against the state, public and private police forces, corporate power, and sometimes the clergy, community leaders, and even family members to secure union representation. And indeed, they are warranted in doing so. Union organization *is* a fundamental right; union struggles *are* potentially struggles for higher human and social values; the fight to secure union representation *can be and often is* a transformative experience.

Herein lies the contradiction. Securing the first requirement of commodity unionism (the union differential) may undermine the second (the conception of unionism as a social movement), especially if eligibility for union representation depends on restrictive criteria that exclude many who need collective organization and protection. The commodity nature of union representation may be exposed, jeopardizing the union's purchase as a social movement worthy of broad support and sacrifice. In this case, unions may come to be branded as a special interest whose claim to social movement status is self-serving and undeserved. When this happens, the broader community may not be so willing to endorse union strikes; it may come to see them as an inconvenience perpetrated by a self-serving institution rather than as a laudable campaign. Moreover, once the conception of social movement evaporates (so that union leaders become the moral equivalent of insurance executives), even union members might chafe at the idea of their leaders speaking on their behalf, or determining what terms of employment they should accept, or what they should be prepared to sacrifice for the "good of the union" (cf. Tasini 1995).

The most important manifestation of this contradiction may be that workers have come to take an *instrumental* view of union membership. Having been trained by unions themselves to see unions as providers of a commodity, they may come to evaluate union membership against just this criterion. Rather than ask how their union membership and participation contribute to a campaign for social justice, they may come to ask whether they are getting good value for their dues payments. Is the union in a position to deliver the goods (the differential) it purports to guarantee? Will the cost of striking be offset by the direct financial improvements that the strike might induce? Just as consumers of other goods might perform a private cost–benefit analysis in contemplation of a purchase, so might union members come to assess their union membership in precisely these terms.

The Impact of the Conservative Resurgence and Globalization

What light does this analysis shed on the question of the impact of the election of anti-union administrations and economic globalization on the fortunes of U.S. labor? These events have undermined the ability of U.S. unions to deliver higher wages, employment protections, and so forth. On this, there is little disagreement today. But we can now see that this inability jeopardizes the union movement precisely because of the degree to which unions have adopted the identity of commodity producer. Having "advertised" the union differential, they now find themselves victims of the very standards of assessment that they themselves devised. Workers can hardly be blamed for abstaining from union participation today on instrumental grounds when this is exactly how unions have marketed themselves for much of the postwar period. In the contemporary era, when unions are having greater difficulty producing the goods, union membership may not seem to be a particularly good buy. The prospective union member might rightly calculate that she is better off investing her savings in her company's stock option plan than she would be taking the considerable risk of organizing or joining a union in pursuit of higher wages and benefits.

In short, then, the union crisis reflects the failure of a *particular union identity*—that of capitalist producer of the commodity union representation. It is undeniable that the resurgence of conservatism and economic globalization has adversely affected the environment in which unions operate. But adversity itself is not a sufficient explanation. A union movement primarily oriented around broad, inclusive social campaigns for economic and social justice might indeed find enhanced worker commitment during tough times. But the commodity nature of unionism has ultimately come to obstruct this kind of commitment among most workers.

Possible Futures for U.S. Labor

Following from the above, we can discern two distinct futures for labor, reflecting the options of business and social unionism. The first largely takes union identity as commodity producer for granted and seeks to reestablish the conditions for the survival and success of this model in the new context of global economic integration. This is perhaps the most likely future, and it is already under way. In this case, for example, U.S. unions might be expected to respond to NAFTA by deepening their cooperation with Mexican and Canadian unions. A bold gesture in this direction would be the institution of continentwide bargaining, either within multinational corporations or across an entire industry. Less dramatically, we might expect to see increased transnational strike support, boycotts, and other acts of direct action. These kinds of initiatives are already under way (for examples, see Kidder and McGinn 1995; Hunter 1995; and Brecher and Costello 1991). This approach also entails efforts to secure the harmonization of labor protections across the continent. Harmonization might forestall what has come to be called "social dumping," or the race by corporations to seek out the lowest labor, environmental, and other standards.

These initiatives mark important steps of solidarity, and their success would bring about a welcome reversal of the shift in power from labor to capital. It might also be expected to induce greater worker protection and income equality. These are indeed laudable aims.

But we should take note that this model continues the commodity-producing nature of U.S. unionism. This feature presents formidable obstacles to those who would restore social unionism—including those who seek the formation of enduring coalitions and networks with progressives outside the labor movement (such as the women's and environmental movements). Unfortunately, the model does not resolve the fundamental identity crisis examined above. Most importantly, this model retains the imperative that the union provide services and protections to union members that are not universally available to other workers and members of society who badly need them.

An alternative approach entails a reworking of the class character of the union and, consequently, the definition of union representation. In this approach, unions would take account of the fact that people identify not just (or even primarily) as workers, but that this is but one identity that defines their full subjectivity. In their everyday lives, people are also consumers, and the nature of the goods and services to which they gain access may fundamentally affect the quality of their lives. They are also family and community members, and they may find that their ability to sustain these sets of relationships is undermined by political, economic, and social strains that they are individually powerless to confront. They are also marked by their race, ethnicity, gender, and by their relationship to the natural environment—and each of these attributes might also be a site of struggle for respect, freedom, and control. These distinct relationships and identities overlap in shaping people's aspirations and needs. Hence, their concerns range from matters of employment to the quality of life much more broadly defined; from the quality of the physical environment, to the quality of educational opportunities and health care, to the quality of government services, to the viability of the family unit, and so forth.

Armed with this recognition, a reconstituted, noncapitalist unionism might come to recognize that it has a role in constructing social movements that span sites in the community, from the workplace to the household, to the school and the hospital (cf. Tasini 1995; Waterman 1993). The union might set for itself the task of advancing universal social and economic justice, taking into account the broad range of human needs. A reconstituted union movement might therefore seek to organize people around an institution like a corporation or the state by integrating their diverse encounters with the institution; by speaking to the multiple demands they have with respect to the institution. For example, students and teachers might be organized into the same union, to address teacher compensation to be sure, but also student–teacher ratios, the quality of and access to education, and the need of adults for continuing educational services. Critically, such unions would set for themselves the task of advancing the interests and rights of all workers (both waged and nonwaged) *and* those outside the workforce. While organization of waged workers would remain an important tactic, such organization would be in service of much broader social objectives, and much wider constituencies (DeMartino 1992).

Tasini presents one possible approach for creating this inclusive unionism. He argues for the expansion of existing Labor Councils—the regional coalitions of local unions throughout the United States that direct the political campaigns of the AFL-CIO—to include "a vast array of unique and overlapping coalitions: labor, seniors, environmental, people of color, children" (Tasini 1995, 38). These new constituencies would pay dues and gain full membership rights in the councils. Concomitantly, this reform would require that unions cede absolute control of the councils and face the prospect of their engaging issues and agendas far beyond those traditionally associated with organized labor. It would require that unions pursue social justice for all rather than a union differential for members only.

Conclusion

Of the two possible futures for a more progressive U.S. labor movement, the more pragmatic approach may be the revival of traditional business unionism, expanding members' solidarity across national borders and among international firms. But this approach largely ignores the question of who is to be a union member and receive the benefits associated therewith, and more importantly, what a union is to be. In contrast, the construction of an inclusive social unionism places on the agenda a difficult but potentially rewarding debate about the kinds of unionism that will be most likely to engender campaigns for social justice, and about who shall be included in a revitalized union movement. It widens substantially the range of potential union members, while promising to deepen the attachment of members to their unions. This is a radical proposal, fraught with difficult challenges. But the depth of the contemporary union crisis—and the crises facing working people, the poor, and the powerless—may require nothing less.

References

Annunziato, Frank. 1990. "Commodity Unionism." *Rethinking Marxism* 3, no. 2 (Summer): 8–33.

Aronowitz, Stanley. 1983. *Working Class Hero: A New Strategy for Labor*. New York: Adama.

Brecher, Jeremy, and Tim Costello. 1991. *Global Village vs. Global Pillage*. Washington, DC: International

Labor Rights Education and Research Fund.
Bronfenbrenner, Kate. 1996. *Final Report: The Effects of Plant Closing or Threat of Plant Closing on the Right of Workers to Organize*, submitted to the Labor Secretariat of the North American Commission on Labor Cooperation, September 30.
DeMartino, George. 1992. "Trade-Union Isolation and the Catechism of the Left." *Rethinking Marxism* 4, no. 3 (Fall): 29–51.
———. 1999. "The Future of the US Labour Movement in an Era of Global Economic Integration." In *Labour Worldwide in the Era of Globalisation: Alternative Union Models in the New World Order*, ed. Ronaldo Munck and Peter Waterman, 83–96. London: Macmillan.
Hunter, Allen. 1995. "Globalization from Below? Promises and Perils of the New Internationalism." *Social Policy* (Summer): 6–13.
Kidder, Thalia, and Mary McGinn. 1995. "In the Wake of NAFTA: Transnational Workers Networks." *Social Policy* (Summer): 14–21.
Milton, David. 1982. *The Politics of U.S. Labor*. New York: Monthly Review.
Moody, Kim. 1988. *An Injury to All*. London: Verso.
Tasini, Jonathan. 1995. *The Edifice Complex: Rebuilding the American Labor Movement to Face the Global Economy*. New York: Labor Research Association.
Waterman, Peter. 1993. "Social Movement Unionism: A New Union Model for a New World Order?" *Review* 16, no. 3 (Summer): 245–278.

Section IV

Examining Money

Finance and Inflation

17

The Role of Credit and Commercial Banks in the Creation of Money

A Post-Keynesian Interpretation in the Circuitist Tradition

Louis-Philippe Rochon

Introduction

This chapter introduces a post-Keynesian/circuitist approach to monetary theory, defined by the role of bank credit in the circuit of production and money: money is created in the process of production and the creation of incomes, and credit is key to starting this process.

In contrast to neoclassical economics, post-Keynesian theory is grounded in history and institutions. Markets operate according to the macro environment in which they are set. While neoclassical is perhaps appropriate for given institutions and a given time period (nineteenth century), times change, and so must our theories. This was basically John Maynard Keynes's view of the world. His criticism of neoclassical theory was not based on some internal inconsistency, but rather on the fact that it was an outdated theory, no longer applicable to the "economic society in which we actually live."

This chapter presents a brief description and comparison of neoclassical and post-Keynesian/circuit economics, focusing on the nature and origin of money, and the role played by bank credit in the respective approaches. The chapter closes with an overview of the policy implications of the importance of credit (and low interest rates) to aggregate demand and economic growth.

Neoclassical and Post-Keynesian Economics: An Introduction

Students of economics are rarely told that the economics they are learning is labeled neoclassical. Most of them believe they are simply learning economics. Yet, economics is divided into several schools of thought—or approaches—which have distinct views of the real world.

Neoclassical economics sees the world as essentially tranquil, and when it is disrupted, there is a natural (invisible) tendency of returning to equilibrium. When starting from a position of long-run equilibrium, any demand or supply shock will force the economy to deviate temporarily from its equilibrium position. Eventually, however, the price mechanism will ensure the economy's gravitation toward its supply-side–determined full-employment level.

An important assumption of neoclassical models is that all goods are scarce—the essence behind a supply curve. Given this assumption, economics naturally becomes the study of the allocation of scarce resources among various possible uses. Optimization is the objective of all agents. Prices are the barometer of that scarcity.

Neoclassical economics is divided into various approaches: Keynesian, monetarist, New Keynesian, rational expectation, and more. Overall, these approaches share a foundational neoclassical theoretical structure, as demonstrated by their agreement over their respective treatment of the long and short run. In the long run, the price mechanism will eventually force the economy to gravitate toward a full-employment equilibrium position. But the approaches differ (albeit slightly) in their treatment of the short run, where the economy may not be in its full-employment position. Keynesians and New Keynesians believe it is because of sticky wages, although New Keynesians have provided substantive microeconomic rationale for price and wage stickiness. Monetarists believe it is because expectations do not adjust quickly enough. New Classical economists claim that deviations from the long-run level of employment are explained by unanticipated fiscal or monetary shocks.

Despite their seemingly different explanations of the short run, these approaches all reduce to the same view: they all rest on some imperfection in the price or other mechanisms preventing the economy from adjusting quickly. The inability of the economy to guarantee price flexibility generates unemployment in the short run. Once you remove wage stickiness and the other imperfections, you return to a (long-run) vertical aggregate supply curve.

Neoclassical macroeconomics tries to explain how the economy moves to full employment, regardless of history or institutions. The model is the same whether you are studying nineteenth-century agricultural or twentieth-century industrial economies. Hicks's IS-LM model, which is meant to capture Keynes's insights, still tries to explain the process to equilibrium in an ahistorical way, making the model neither Keynesian nor post-Keynesian.

Post-Keynesian/circuit economics is different. It starts with the assumption, implicit in Keynes, that the economy does not tend to full employment on its own. The price mechanism does not exist and hence is not operative. Even if it were, it would not be a sufficient condition to bring us back to the long-run position. Post-Keynesians and Keynes, in fact, do not wish to modify neoclassical economics by incorporating some imperfection. Rather, they wish to replace neoclassical economics with a different set of assumptions reflecting the modern and industrial nature of our economies.

The normal state of affairs for post-Keynesians is not full employment equilibrium, but rather an unemployment equilibrium. Analysis shifts away from the supply side of the equation to the demand side. If firms do not undertake investment projects, because of uncertainty, then they will not be employing workers. Decisions on whether to invest are themselves a choice. In a short-run equilibrium, there are no net forces driving the economy to full employment. Unemployment is not caused by the imperfection of wages or prices, but rather by the firms' reluctance to employ the factors of production given their expectations of the unknown future: firms do not see the level of effective demand in the future as being sufficiently high to accommodate full employment levels. This, as we will see, also has an important impact on the demand for credit and the creation of money.

The economy, as described by Franco-Italian circuit theorists (see Rochon 1999a; Rochon 1999b; Parguez and Seccareccia 1999), is seen as a sequence of irreversible events taking place in time. The economy is divided into three major groups: the central and commercial banks, firms, and households, although one could add the government and the open economy.

For post-Keynesian/circuit economists, the

study of economics is grounded in history, time, and institutions. History is important because we study modern, industrial economies, not agricultural economies of the nineteenth century. Firms are not perfectly competitive (if they ever were), but increasingly oligopolistic, especially in these times of megamergers. Institutions are important, too, and they reflect the changing times. Governments are big, but so are firms, and unions. Rather than trying to explain why the real world is not operating according to the theory, which is how neoclassical economists operate, post-Keynesians observe the real world and try to make sense of it.

The Orthodox (Neoclassical) View of Credit, Money, and Banks

Students of neoclassical economics are generally taught that the money supply is exogenous, set by the central bank through its control over the supply of reserves to the banking system.

But how does this money find its way into the real economy? What is the "transmission mechanism" of monetary policy? Orthodox economists have two complementary explanations. According to the "money view," when the central bank increases reserves (through open-market operations and the supply of bonds), commercial banks' ability to issue bank deposits (liabilities) also increases. If the supply of money increases, however, it must also be demanded. Households must choose to hold more money and fewer bonds, moving us along a given money demand curve. By increasing the demand for bonds, the central bank pushes up the price of bonds, reducing their return. The opportunity cost of holding money falls, and households freely choose to hold more money and fewer bonds.

According to the "credit view," however, the transmission mechanism is through the loans market. As the central bank's decision to supply reserves increases banks' deposits, this also allows them to extend more loans. In contrast to the money view, there are three assets in this model: money, publicly issued bonds, and bank loans. The influence is through the supply of loans for investment.

Both of these views can be well illustrated by referring to the money multiplier model where the money supply is exogenous, that is when the central bank creates money independently of the real economy and the "needs of trade." Money is scarce since it is supply-determined, and in many versions of neoclassical theory, must be rationed. The supply of money is a mere multiple of the supply of reserves. Money is imposed on the system. Many economists have reduced this "monetary" system to an exchange economy in which money is added as a simple afterthought: money is a veil. The money supply equation is the following:

$$M = mH = \left(\frac{1 + C/D}{C/D + R/D} \right) H \qquad (1)$$

where M is the money supply, H is the monetary base, D is deposits, C is currency, and R is reserves. The ratio inside the bracket, m, is called the money multiplier, and is assumed to be stable, as are C/D (the currency–deposit ratio, the tendency of the public to hold one versus the other) and R/D (the proportion of reserves over deposits, presumed set by the Federal Reserve). The causation running from right to left is stable and predictable. The role of the money multiplier is essential to the neoclassical theories of money. Given the relative stability of the multiplier, the central bank regulates the supply of money though its control of H.

Some early post-Keynesians critiqued this approach by exploring the role of financial innovations. Hyman Minsky (1957a, 1957b), for example, noted that as the rate of interest increases, and the

Figure 17.1 **The Neoclassical Money Market**

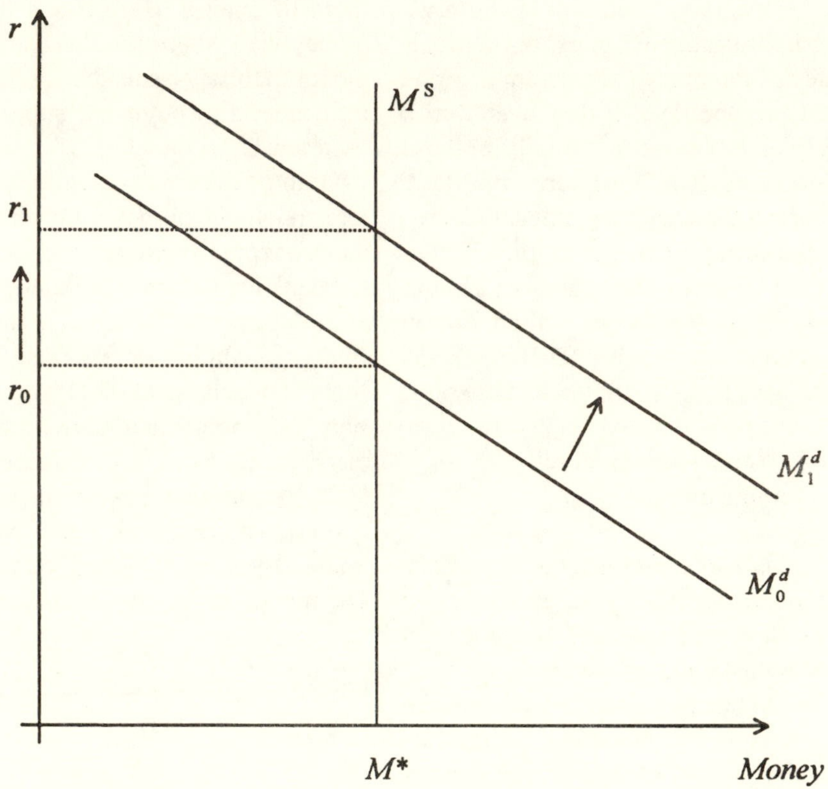

opportunity costs of holding money as opposed to other assets increase, households seek to get out of money and into other assets: they demand other assets. Similarly, banks will find ways of creating new types of deposits that earn interest, and that are more attractive to households: they supply other assets. According to Minsky (and some of his post-Keynesian followers), this amounts to a theory of endogenous money since banks are able to extend loans and thus create money beyond the direct attempts by the central bank to control the growth in the money supply. Elsewhere (see Rochon 1999a, 1999c), I have shown that this view is compatible with the loanable funds approach where Minksy's views on financial innovations become a "special" case of neoclassical economics.

But according to the neoclassical view, as in Minsky, money is essentially an asset. The decision to hold (demand) money becomes a choice between money and other assets. Money is valuable as an asset because of its perfect liquidity: money has intrinsic value.

The money supply curve, as in Figure 17.1, is usually vertical, although some will draw it positively sloped, allowing for some changes in velocity (the multiplier would change) as a result of financial innovations. Changes in the demand for money will increase the rate of interest, from r_0 to r_1. The rate of interest is an endogenous variable. The system is in equilibrium when the money rate of interest, determined by the supply and demand for money, is equal to the natural rate of interest, determined by the supply and demand for savings.

The money multiplier model applies to both orthodox approaches. We begin by using two foundational arguments common to both approaches. First, we have the saving–investment causality. For orthodox economists, increases in savings lead to increases in investment, where saving and investment are brought into equilibrium through changes in the rate of interest (the loanable funds model). Second, bank deposits (or liabilities) dictate the quantity of loans (assets) a bank can extend to its customers. But these two arguments are the same since deposits are a component of household savings. Savings are that part of income that households do not consume or place in financial markets. Hence, as households save and deposit their money into banks, banks are able to increase their supply of loans. For neoclassical economists, therefore, banks are simple financial intermediaries: they facilitate the channeling of savings from savers (households) to investors (firms).

Referring to our money multiplier equation from above, the loans market, via financial innovations, is incorporated into the multiplier. As banks innovate, they are able to reduce the reserve–deposit ratio, thereby increasing the value of the multiplier. A given amount of deposits now supports more loans, as argued by the early Minsky. The same amount of money can circulate more goods, thus explaining the increase in the velocity of money. The relationship between reserves and the money supply is no longer predictable and stable due to changes in the multiplier. It is in this case that the money supply curve is slightly upward-sloping.

On a related issue, the Quantity Theory of Money (shown below) suggests that with the money supply exogenous, inflation is "always and everywhere a monetary phenomenon":

$$MV = PY \tag{2}$$

where M is the exogenous supply of money, V is the velocity of money, P is the price level, and Y is output. In growth rates, the equation simply becomes:

$$\dot{M}+\dot{V}=\dot{P}+\dot{Y} \tag{3}$$

Given the monetarist assumption of stable velocity, this reduces to

$$\dot{M}=\dot{P} \tag{4}$$

Thus any growth in the exogenous supply of money leads to increases in the nominal value of production, but not in its real value. In the short-run, V may be taken as variable, as seen above, and we may have some deviations from the long-run position. In the long run, however, the aggregate supply curve is vertical, and money is neutral: changes in the money supply, which shifts the aggregate demand curve upward, have no impact on the real economy. Money only leads to inflation. The central bank needs to control the money supply in order to control inflation.

The early post-Keynesian criticism of the monetarist counterrevolution attacked its premise by arguing that the velocity of money was in fact unstable (Kaldor 1964, Rousseas 1960; Minsky 1957a, 1957b). As I argue elsewhere (Rochon 1999a), the early post-Keynesians largely accepted the exogeneity of the money supply but claimed that given the fluctuations in the velocity of money, the relationship is indirect and imprecise. Monetary policy is therefore not a useful tool with which to fight inflation. Yet, this is indeed an imperfectionist argument, explaining why money is not neutral in the short run.

If money is exogenously determined by the central bank's supply conditions, then it is conceivable to see money in terms of scarcity, and the rate of interest as the price of scarcity, which rations available money among those who need it most. In the credit view of the monetary transmission mechanism, decreases in reserves will decrease the supply of bank loans. For New Keynesian macroeconomists (Kasyap and Stein 1994; Bernanke and Gertler 1995), the supply of loans must be "rationed" and many firms will not have their demand met because of the scarcity of funds. Following a critique by Romer and Romer (1990), many now also recognize the opportunity for banks to circumvent central bank controls with liability management.

In this "money market," both the quantity and the price of money are determined simultaneously by the forces of supply and demand. As in any other typical market, prices (the rate of interest) and quantities (the money supply) will change with changes in market forces, that is, shifts in the demand and/or supply schedules. If the central bank decides to restrict the supply of money, then money is scarcer and its price rises. Also, the money supply is quite independent from the demand schedule, the very definition of exogeneity. The supply of money will not fluctuate with changes in demand.

The Post-Keynesian/Circuitist Alternative

Post-Keynesians have a different view of markets, banks, the real economy, and of the way that money is created. This view is shared by a great number of heterodox economists, including post-Keynesians, neo-Ricardians, and some Marxists. It is also shared by French and Italian circuit theorists, structuralists, and institutionalists. I will call this view "post-Keynesian," thereby encompassing all these various approaches, although some have called this the postclassical view. And while there are considerable debates and disagreements among the various protagonists (see Pollin 1991; Palley 1991, 1994; Rochon 1999d), they all share the view that money is primarily endogenous, since its creation depends on the needs of trade.

The post-Keynesian analysis of money begins with specific conceptions of the nature of money and the relationship between saving and investment. For neoclassical economics, money is primarily an asset, its stock determined by agents' willingness to hold on to money rather than other assets. The emphasis is placed on the functions or roles of money.

For circuit theorists, the primary emphasis is on the nature of money; the functions of money are secondary. Money is bank deposits, not a commodity. The amount of money that is created is a response to the amount of bank loans banks accept to grant. Money is a flow responding to the needs of trade. It is a result of credit and is therefore a debt, a liability.

This approach is directly linked to how money is created. Rather than the orthodox causality between savings and investment, it is investment that determines savings. Because our economies are credit-economies, banks are able to create money without the prior existence of bank deposits. This suggests that deposits do not create loans, but rather that bank loans (assets) create deposits (liabilities).

In the post-Keynesian approach, money is not seen as a stock imposed by the central bank but rather as a result of credit flows in the economy. Money is part of a circuit, and must be understood in terms of specific hierarchical relationships between the various agents, the central bank, commercial banks, entrepreneurial firms, and workers (or households). Money is first created, then circulated, and finally destroyed. Money allows goods to circulate in the economy in a continuous flow. The theory of the monetary circuit explains not only how money comes into existence, but also how production cannot be differentiated from the creation of money. Unlike neoclassical economics, in post-Keynesian theory, there can be no production without money.

The circuit begins with the central bank. In post-

Keynesian theory, it is the rate of interest that is set exogenously by the central bank, as argued by Keynes after the *General Theory* (see Rochon 1997). The central bank, in setting the rate of interest, will react to certain economic indicators, such as the rate of inflation (actual or expected), unemployment, or the value of the domestic currency.

According to this view, the rate of interest is neither set by productivity and thrift (the natural rate, see Smithin 1994), nor is it determined by the supply and demand for money (as Keynes argued in the *General Theory*).

The circuit then continues with business firms' demand for bank credit. As an economy set in historical time (where events do not occur all at once but follow one another through time), firms' costs occur before they can begin receiving revenues from the sale of their goods. To begin the production process firms must first borrow credit from banks. Banks are therefore at the heart of the production process.

Both production and investment depend on expectations and are influenced by uncertainty, but production depends on expectations of what the level of effective demand will be in the near future, while investment depends on expectations of the long run (or the growth of effective demand). Firms place bets on the future. They may be good ones, in which case firms make profits, or they may be bad ones, in which case firms may go bankrupt.

Banks are also subject to uncertainty. Banks make two types of loans: short-run loans (repaid within, say, one year) covering firms' wage bills and other short-run production costs, and long-run loans (repaid over a longer period) covering the purchase of capital goods. Micro-uncertainty surrounds the ability of the firm to repay its short-run loan, that is, on the possibility that irrespective of economic conditions, a firm will not go bankrupt. This means that firms were not able to recapture a sufficient proportion of their outlays. Macro-uncertainty concerns the future course of the business cycle and how it may impact on all firms. It is a bet also on the future course of central bank–determined interest rates.

Banks may or may not approve all the demand for bank credit, of course. They will carefully evaluate each proposal carefully and set up creditworthy criteria. As long as a firm's rating is above this minimum level required by banks, then a loan will be made. If banks become increasingly pessimistic of the future, they will not set out to necessarily restrict loans, but rather raise the minimum required creditworthiness criteria. Most likely, there will be a number of firms who will no longer be seen as creditworthy. In this case, the economy may suffer.

This view stands in stark contrast with the neoclassical approach, in which a credit crunch arises because the central bank has reduced the supply of reserves. For circuit theorists, a credit crunch arises because of the pessimism of commercial banks (see Rochon 1999d). It may be the result of the central bank's decision to raise the rate of interest, and the policy's subsequent impact on the firm's ability to repay its existing loan.

The graphical representation of this approach is to draw the credit supply curve as horizontal in interest rate/credit space, as in Figure 17.2, although the use of a supply curve remains problematic (Rochon 1999a). Note that we are no longer speaking of a "money" supply curve, but of a credit supply curve. As indicated above, the credit demand schedule drawn below should be referred to as the "creditworthy demand for credit." Banks will meet all the creditworthy demand for bank loans.

In this approach, the existence of money is due to the payment of wages and the purchase of capital goods out of credit extended to the firms by banks. Once created, money is simply circulated. And as workers draw down their own accounts to consume goods, they give a portion of their

Figure 17.2 **The Post-Keynesian Credit Market**

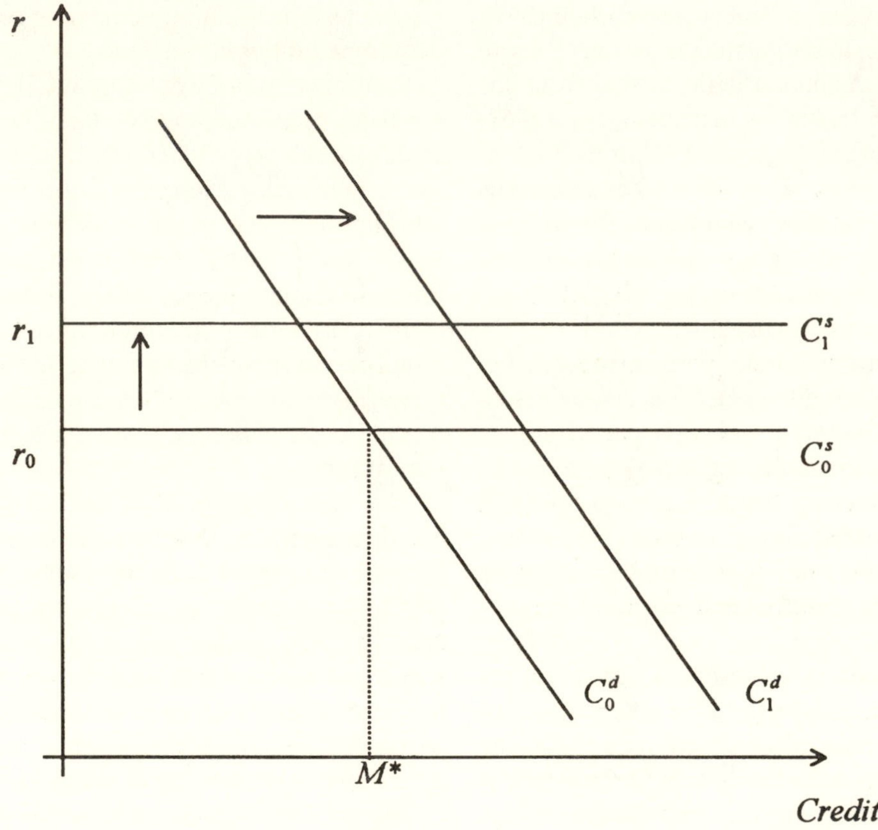

income back to firms. Firms therefore succeed in capturing back a portion of their outlays through the sale of goods. This is called the "reflux principle."

Households will also save a portion of their income in bank accounts (representing a leakage in the circuit back to firms) and purchase some financial assets. Households therefore express their preference for liquidity, influenced by uncertainty about the future, on how to best allocate their saving. This is where money as an asset appears—at the very end of the process, not the beginning as in neoclassical theory.

The money households use to purchase financial assets will be channeled back to firms, another example of the reflux principle. As Keynes (1936) reminds us in his *Economic Journal* articles published after the *General Theory*, there is very little difference between consumption and financial saving, from the point of view of firms.

With these revenues, firms will reimburse their loans to the banks and money is destroyed. At the end of the monetary circuit, the final increase in money supply will be identical to the increased saving of households in their bank accounts. Once firms have reimbursed their loans, they will seek to renew their loans once again in order to continue production. Keynes's multiplier price depends on the ability of firms to renew their loans.

Policy Implications

The differences between neoclassical and post-Keynesian approaches to money and credit are not simply theoretical, but carry important implications in terms of monetary policy. From a neoclassical perspective, an increase in the money supply leads to a decrease in the rate of interest. Given the neutrality of money, this leads only to an increase in prices with no affect on the real economy in the long run. The economy grows through shocks to the supply side of the economy, such as technological shocks that shift the production function.

For circuit and post-Keynesians economists, however, the importance of a policy of low interest rates cannot be underestimated. Growth is demand-led; firms will adapt their production to changes in the level of demand. Say's law does not operate in contemporary economies of production. Low interest rates will keep firms creditworthy and banks optimistic (reducing the possibility of a credit crunch), thereby encouraging investment and strong economic growth (Rochon and Vernengo 1999).

Conclusion

Post-Keynesian/circuit theorists base their approach to monetary economies on history and institutions; they favor a description of the "real world." For neoclassical economists, the supply of money is imposed on the system without any reference to the needs of trade. For circuit theorists, money is credit-driven and demand-determined, to use Moore's (1988) now famous expression. Money (composed of bank deposits) is never scarce, and the rate of interest is not the price of money.

Bibliography

Bernanke, B., and M. Gertler. 1995. "Inside the Black Box: The Credit Channel of Monetary Policy Transmission." *Journal of Economic Perspectives* 9, no. 4 (Fall): 27–48.

Dow, S. 1996. "Horizontalism: A Critique." *Cambridge Journal of Economics* 20: 497–508.

Hahn, F. 1965. "On Some Problems of Proving the Existence of an Equilibrium in a Monetary Economy." In *The Theory of Interest Rates*, ed. F. Hahn and F.P.R. Brechling. London: Macmillan.

Howells, G.A. 1997. "The Demand for Money: A Rejoinder." *Journal of Post Keynesian Economics* 19, no. 3 (Spring): 429–435.

Kaldor, N. 1955. "The Lessons of the British Experiment Since the War: Full Employment and the Welfare State." Paper presented at the Centenary Congress of the Société Royale d'Economie Politique de Belgique, Brussels. Reprinted in *Collected Economic Papers. Volume 3. Essays on Economic Policy 1.* London: Duckworth.

———. 1964. "Monetary Policy, Economic Stability and Growth." A Memorandum submitted to the Committee of the Working of the Monetary System (Radcliffe Committee), June 23, 1958. Reprinted in *Collected Economic Papers. Volume 3. Essays on Economic Policy 1.* London: Duckworth.

Kashyap, A., and J. Stein. 1994. "Monetary Policy and Bank Lending." In *Monetary Policy*, ed. N.G. Mankiw. Chicago: Chicago University Press.

Keynes, J.M. 1936. *The General Theory of Employment, Interest and Money.* London: Macmillan.

Minsky, H. 1957a. "Monetary Systems and Accelerator Models." *American Economic Review* 47, no. 6: 859–883.

———. 1957b. "Central Banking and Money Market Changes." *Quarterly Journal of Economics* 71, no. 2: 171–187.

Moore, B. 1988. *Horizontalists and Verticalists: The Macroeconomics of Credit Money.* Cambridge, UK: Cambridge University Press.

Palley, T. 1991. "The Endogenous Money Supply: Consensus and Disagreement." *Journal of Post Keynesian Economics* 13, no. 3 (Spring): 397–403.

———. 1994. "Competing Views of the Money Supply Process: Theory and Evidence." *Metroeconomica* 45, no. 1: 67–88.

Parguez, A., and M. Seccareccia. 1999. "A Credit Theory of Money: The Monetary Circuit Approach." In *What Is Money*, ed. J. Smithin. London: Routledge.

Pollin, R. 1991. "Two Theories of Money Supply Endogeneity: Some Empirical Evidence." *Journal of Post Keynesian Economics* 13, no. 3 (Spring): 366–395.

Rochon, L.-P. 1997. "Keynes's Finance Motive: A Re-Assessment. Credit, Liquidity Preference and the Rate of Interest." *Review of Political Economy* 9, no. 3: 277–293.

———. 1999a. *Credit, Money and Production: An Alternative Post-Keynesian Approach*. Cheldenham, UK: Edward Elgar.

———. 1999b. "The Creation and Circulation of Money: A Circuit Dynamique Approach." *Journal of Economic Issues* 33, no. 1: 1–21.

———. 1999c. "A Neoclassical Interpretation of Minsky's Early Views: Minsky as a 'Special Case.'" Working paper no. 99–01, Kalamazoo College.

———. 1999d. "Horizontalism: Setting the Record Straight." Working paper no. 99–02, Kalamazoo College.

Rochon, L.-P., and M. Vernengo. 1999. *Credit, Effective Demand and the Open Economy: Essays in the Horizontalist Tradition*. Cheldenham, UK: Edward Elgar.

Romer, C., and D. Romer. 1990. "New Evidence on the Monetary Transmission Mechanism." *Brookings Papers on Economic Activity* 1: 149–198.

Rousseas, S. 1960. "Velocity Changes and the Effectiveness of Monetary Policy, 1951–1957." *Review of Economics and Statistics* 42, no. 1: 27–36.

Smithin, J. 1994. *Controversies in Monetary Economics: Ideas, Issues and Policy.* Aldershot, UK: Edward Elgar.

18

Hidden Inflation

An Estimate of the Cost-of-Living Inflation Rate

Jim Devine

Despite seemingly low inflation in recent years and because of official recalculations of the inflation rate that reduce it even further, our measures of "inflation" underestimate the true increases in the cost of living. The official measures of inflation are market-oriented, that is, measuring only the decrease in our money's power to purchase products currently available for sale. This chapter presents an alternative measure of inflation, the cost-of-living (COL) inflation rate, which takes into account nonmarket elements of people's cost of living such as pollution and crime. These elements raise our need for money income to keep our standards of living from falling.

The COL measure suggests that in terms of the issues that working people care about, inflation is actually higher than the officially measured rate: for the period 1951 to 1994, the COL inflation rate averaged 4.9 percent, almost 1 percentage point higher than the official inflation rate (4 percent per year). This means that while it took about six dollars in 1994 to buy the basket of *marketed consumer products* that cost one dollar in 1950, it took more than eight dollars in 1994 to get the same *standard of living* that one dollar bought in 1950. Extrapolating, while official inflation rates fell to about 1 percent per year in 1998, the COL inflation rate still hovered at about 3 or 4 percent in 1998.[1] This rise in the cost of living has significantly undermined the real benefit received from our wages. To understand this assertion, however, we must reexamine the basics.

Preliminaries

Even though most people do not see the disease of inflation as a major problem in the 1990s, it was a major public concern in previous decades as people saw that, with inflation, you needed a raise just to *maintain* real income and make ends meet. In the 1970s, a period of soaring inflation, it was common for a worker to receive a raise, only to find that this pay hike gradually lost all its value as most of the prices in the stores soared. Since the rise in prices (the inflation rate) exceeded the raise in her money wage, her "real wages"—a.k.a. inflation-corrected wages—fell. Usually, real wages are measured as follows:

For a more complete exposition of this chapter's ideas, including its limitations, see James Devine, "Estimates of the 'Cost of Living Inflation Rate' Based on the Genuine Progress Indicator, 1950–1994." An unpublished paper, it is available from me. Thanks to James Konow, Gabe Fuentes, Robert Singleton, Zaki Eusufzai, and Joe Persky for their comments on that longer paper. Of course, all blame for any heresies present below is mine alone.

real wage = (money wage)/CPI

Because the consumer price index (CPI) rose so quickly between 1970 and 1979, average real private-sector weekly earnings fell by 2 percent—even though in money terms wages rose by almost 90 percent.

But what is this CPI? During World War I, the Bureau of Labor Statistics of the U.S. Department of Labor started measuring the consumer price index. This is a measure of the purchasing power of money. You can compute your own simple CPI by calculating how much it costs to buy some "basket" of consumer goods (bread, beans, beer, etc.) at different points in time. By comparing the price of your "basket" for different years, you can see how much average prices have risen (the inflation rate). The U.S. business magazine *Forbes* does this for the very rich, adding up the prices of luxury goods and finding that the "cost of living extremely well" rose by 6 percent between 1997 and 1998 (Lee 1998). (Of course, their money incomes and wealth soared even more. See Tilly, this volume.)

In the 1960s and 1970s, many workers had escalators written into their contracts, protecting their wages from inflation. Though these automatic adjustments have become rare (as union contracts have become much less common outside the government sector), they still exist for U.S. Social Security benefits. These are "indexed," meaning that money payouts automatically rise roughly in step with the CPI. Similarly, the Internal Revenue Service's tax brackets are raised as prices rise, lowering money tax obligations as the value of money income falls.

Debate

From 1996 to 1998, political controversy raged over seemingly technical issues concerning the method of calculation of the CPI.[2] Congress appointed the Boskin Commission to study whether the calculation of the CPI was adequate. In their report, Stanford professor Michael Boskin and his colleagues argued that the CPI should be adjusted downward to reflect changes in the "cost of living." Their argument was that the quality of the basket of consumption goods has risen substantially. For example, the CPI should be adjusted for the availability of higher-quality products or new ones (such as home computers, VCRs, or compact discs) while using prices from low-cost retail outlets, such as Wal-Mart, which have become the "shopping standard," rather than higher-priced department stores that fewer Americans now shop at. These conclusions were based on very little, if any, new research and reflected the bias of the Commission's economists, who were selected by the Republican Congress in the hope that they would find justifications for adjusting the CPI downward.

The Boskin Commission's recalculation has the politically attractive side effect of lowering the official inflation rate by about 0.7 of a percentage point each year (say, from 2.3 percent to 1.6 percent per year). This not only makes the economy's performance look better but helps the federal government balance its budget without passing new laws: a lower measured inflation rate reduces automatic increases in Social Security benefits and automatic cuts in income taxes, lowering government spending and raising tax revenues compared to those using the old formulation of the CPI.

Liberal economists on the other side of the debate argued that the traditional calculation of the CPI was relatively accurate and that Boskin's proposed revisions were unnecessary and driven by political goals rather than by scientific efforts to improve methodology. They were concerned that Social Security beneficiaries would be prevented from getting automatic raises (and taxpayers from getting tax adjustments) high enough to offset the actual inflation rate, which they saw as being best measured by old versions of the CPI.

The Bureau of Labor Statistics has accepted many of Boskin's recommendations, adjusting their estimates of inflation downward. According to *Business Week*, "A significant chunk of the reported downturn in inflation since 1995—perhaps three-quarters of a percentage point—reflects changes in the behavior of statisticians rather than changes in the underlying pace of price hikes" (Koretz 1999).[3] This revision may not be all bad, even from a liberal or labor perspective: with luck, it may prevent the Federal Reserve from provoking a recession to fight or prevent inflation (as it did in 1994).

The problem is that neither side of the debate noticed that, with or without Boskin revisions, the official CPI is not a measure of the "cost of living" that people face. As one BLS official notes, "a more complete cost-of-living index would go beyond [the CPI] to take into account the changes in other governmental or environmental factors that affect consumers' well-being" (Gibson 1998, 3). For example, a cutback in hours at the public library raises the cost of living by pushing people to buy books or lowers their quality of life by preventing them from reading. However, this cutback does not raise the measured CPI.[4] This is *hidden inflation*.

Going further, Robert Kuttner (1996) argues that the CPI leaves out all sorts of aspects of the true cost that people face in order to live, such as the cost of crime, lawsuits, pollution, and family breakdown.[5] A total redefinition of the CPI is needed to include not just marketed products in the basket of consumer goods but also elements affecting the quality of life that are not reflected in market exchanges, such as the quality of the air, the availability of decent public services, and the amount of leisure time.

But such a redefinition implies a gigantic and expensive research project, one that only the government could afford and seems unlikely to engage in. Rather than embarking on this kind of expedition, I follow a hint from Kuttner: he points to the Genuine Progress Indicator (the GPI), calculated by the Redefining Progress think tank, as an example of efforts to measure our economic welfare or "true living standards." The GPI is an alternative measure of national economic "progress" to the real Gross Domestic Product. The GPI adjusts the official national income and product account measures for benefits missed, such as contributions from housework, and costs that should be subtracted, such as that of the using up of nonreproducible natural resources. Table 18.1 breaks down the various components of the GPI. This chapter calculates estimates of the "Cost of Living" (COL) and the "COL inflation rates" using this research.[6]

COL Inflation

While the CPI is calculated by adding up the amounts needed to buy a specific basket of consumer commodities, the COL is measured by the amount of money needed to buy a constant quality of life (a constant amount of use-value) as measured by adjustments suggested by the GPI calculations. Then, a new version of the "real wage" can be calculated:

$$\text{COL-corrected wage} = (\text{money wage})/\text{COL}$$

The basic idea of calculating the COL index is similar to that behind the consumption deflator (CPD) from the National Income and Product Accounts, another official measure of the price level that some macroeconomists see as an alternative to the CPI. The CPD is the average price level implied by calculations of real consumption spending:[7]

Table 18.1

The Genuine Progress Indicator

Genuine Progress Indicator (GPI) =
Personal consumption expenditure, **C** *divided by* the distributional factor **DF**

Plus Extra Current Benefits, **ECB**:
the value of unpaid housework,
the value of volunteer work,
the net benefits of consumer durables,
and services of streets and highways.

Minus Extra Current Costs, **ECC**:
the cost of crime,
the cost of family breakdown
the loss of leisure time
the cost of underemployment,
the cost of commuting,
the cost of household pollution abatement,
the cost of auto accidents,
the cost of water pollution
the cost of air pollution,
and the cost of noise pollution.

Minus Forward-Looking Costs, **FLC**:
the loss of wetlands,
the loss of farmland,
depletion of nonrenewable resources,
long-term environmental damage,
cost of ozone depletion,
and loss of old-growth forests,

Plus Forward-Looking Benefits, **FLB**:
net capital investment
and net foreign lending or borrowing.

Source: Cobb, Halstead, and Rowe (1995).

Note: The "benefit recieved from current consumption" referred to in the text equals C + ECB – ECC, which equals GPI – (C/DF – C) + FLC – FLB. The "net benefits of consumer durables" is the "services" minus the "cost" of consumer durables.

CPD = (money spent on consumer goods) /(the fixed-price sum of those goods)

Adding up the quantities of consumption goods in the denominator using "fixed prices" means using a specific year's prices to correct the sum of money spent on consumer goods for inflation. This is often seen as the benefit to consumers from "real" consumption spending.

One COL estimate, the most conservative one, replaces real consumption in the CPD formula above with a measure of current benefit received:

COL = (money spent on consumer goods)/ (benefit received from current consumption)

where the denominator is a measure of only those parts of the GPI that contribute to an individual's current enjoyment. Like the denominator of the

CPD, the denominator of the COL uses fixed prices, but it changes the official estimates of real consumer purchases by including the impact of extra current benefits and costs missed in the calculation of the CPD.[8] The conservative estimate does not include distributional or future-oriented costs and benefits.

Two types of examples explain the idea of COL inflation. Assume that consumption spending in both money and inflation-corrected terms is constant, so that the CPD is constant and the official inflation rate equals zero. Suppose that the current benefits to consumers missed by the official accounts (extra current benefits) fall: if the amount of unpaid housework, volunteer labor done, leisure time, or the services provided by publicly supplied streets and highways falls, this means that fewer use-values (benefits) are received. Since money spending is constant, there has been a rise in the dollars paid on the market per use-value actually received, that is, a decline in the value of money. As with the public library example above, this is COL inflation.

Second, if the current costs missed by the national income and product accounts (extra current costs) increase, it represents a decline in living standards and a decrease in the value of the money spent. For example, if people are suffering from increased pollution while spending the same amount of money buying consumer goods, their standard of living decreases. Similarly, if individuals suffer from increased costs of commuting (which are necessary to earning income), increased costs of auto accidents and crime, decreased leisure time or family stability, the money that they spend is providing them with fewer benefits than it used to. Finally, spending more money on necessary defensive goods (such as car locks or insurance) does not raise the use-value received. Rather, it implies that the use-values one does receive are more expensive to preserve.

Figure 18.1 shows the effects of using the most conservative estimate of the COL in calculating real wages. Since the COL has increased more than the CPI, real wages calculated using the COL have fallen more steeply in recent decades than those calculated using the CPI. Also, the well-known rise in real wages from 1959 to the early 1970s (the so-called Golden Age) is more moderate when the COL is used to correct for inflation. Recent rises in official real wages also do not show up when the COL is used.

Other COL Estimates

The adjustments to Gross Domestic Product for extra current benefits and costs have often been called for by economists interested in measuring social welfare and do not seem to be very controversial. My "most conservative" COL estimates do not go beyond such considerations. They do not go as far away from the GDP calculations as the GPI does, since the latter includes the effects of increasing inequality and the destruction of future possibilities to live well.

First, though GPI data would allow a different perspective, the COL discussed above ignores distributional issues. As with the CPI and most common-sense conceptions of "inflation," the concept of the cost of living used above is individualistic, referring to an average individual. While widening gaps in the distribution of income encourage the fraying of the social fabric and go against official societal goals, it is hard to assert that changes in distribution imply a higher cost of living for any individual.[9] Those results of rising inequality that raise the cost of living, such as increases in street crime, are already measured as part of extra current costs and thus as part of the COL.

Next, forward-looking costs and benefits, which play a major role in the GPI, play no role in the conservative calculation of the COL above. When

Figure 18.1 **Private Sector Real Wages** (with CPI = COL = 100 in 1982)

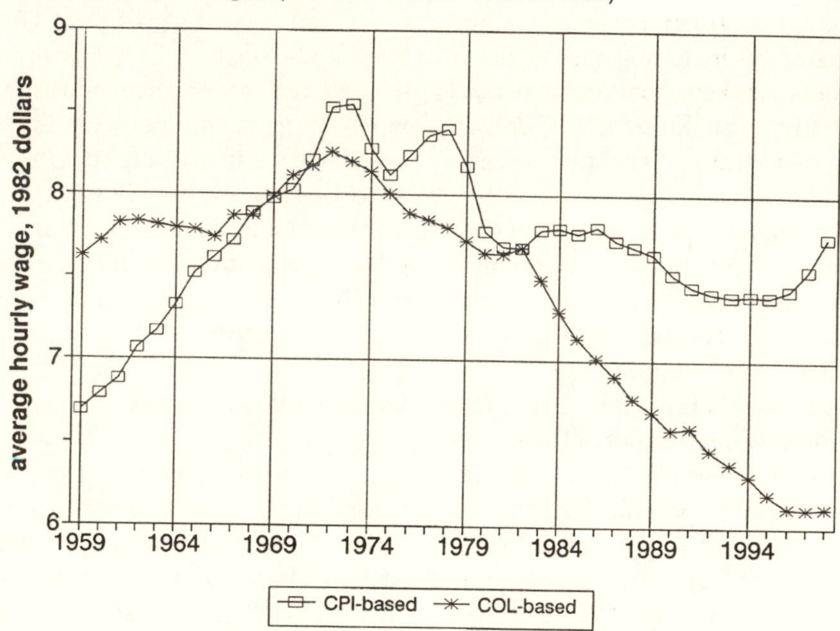

calculating a CPI, aspects of living that refer to future impacts are omitted, since the concern is with current consumption, not with all benefits and costs received for the rest of time (or received by future generations). In other words, the ecologically crucial cost of the destruction of wetlands or the ozone layer has little or no impact on our current cost of living or on the inflation rate as most conceive it. This attitude is very short-sighted, but it is exactly the same attitude as is implicit in CPI calculations.

Though my conservative COL index has higher inflation rates than does the CPI, the gap between the two measures shows little or no upward trend. That is, though the CPI underestimates increases in the cost of living, these estimates are not getting significantly worse over time. On the other hand, less conservative estimates of COL inflation are not only higher but show an upward trend relative to official measures of the inflation rate, reflecting increasing inequality and environmental destruction. Though these more radical estimates of COL inflation do not fit with the common-sense meaning of the word "inflation" (as discussed above), these trends are important.

If we drop the individualistic perspective of both the conservative COL and the CPI to include the effects of distributional shifts, my measures of COL inflation are rising relative to official inflation rates. On average, between 1951 and 1994, bringing in distributional issues added 0.2 percentage points to the conservative COL inflation rate and 1.1 percentage points to the official inflation rate each year. This results from the well-known widening of the gap between the rich and poor, as indicated by the falling share of total income accruing to the poorest fifth of the population. Alternatively, this says that COL inflation has hit the poorest fifth the hardest.

Our ability to maintain low COL and CPI inflation rates simply means that the costs of societal problems are being shoved onto the backs of

Table 18.2

Alternative Measures of the Inflation Rate

Average annual inflation rates calculated using:

	Official Statistics		Cost-of-Living Estimates			
	CPI-U (%)	CPD (%)	"Conservative" estimate (%)	With distributional adjustment (%)	Including forward-looking costs and benefits (%)	Including both distributional and forward-looking factors (%)
decade						
1951–59	1.8	2.2	3.1	2.6	4.1	3.4
1960–69	2.5	2.1	3.6	2.7	4.9	3.5
1970–79	7.1	6.3	7.4	7.9	8.9	9.6
1980–89	5.0	5.2	5.9	6.9	6.5	8.5
1990–94	3.4	3.5	4.0	5.5	5.4	9.8
Overall average	4.1	3.9	4.9	5.1	6.1	6.7
	(1)	(2)	(3)	(4)	(5)	(6)

Notes: (1) the CPI-U is the consumer price index for urban employees, from the BLS; (2) the CPD is the consumption price deflator, from the U.S. Department of Commerce; (3) through (6) the COL measures are calculated using nominal spending on consumption (nC) or on GDP (nGDP), both supplied by the Department of Commerce divided by the appropriate GPI measure:

(3) = nC/(C + ECB – ECC);
(4) = nC/((C/DF) + EBC – ECC);
(5) = nGDP/(C + ECB – ECC + FLB – FLC);
(6) = nGDP/((C/DF) + ECB – ECC + FLB – FLC),

where the symbols are defined in Table 18.1

the poor. (See column [4] of Table 18.2.) In terms of the distributional-conflict theory (cf. Rowthorn 1977), inflation can be reduced if one participant in the conflict—here, the poor—is shoved out. In other words, if the widening distributional gap could have been avoided, there would have been higher COL and CPI inflation rates (or higher unemployment to restrain such inflation). Improving programs (such as the minimum wage, unemployment insurance benefits, or "welfare") that help the poorest earn higher wages, in order to allow constancy of the income distribution, encourages businesses hiring such labor to raise prices. The recent slowing of official inflation rates despite falling unemployment rates is thus linked not only to measurement changes but also to the widening distributional gap.

Both the conservative COL- and CPI-based inflation rates are also falling behind COL rates that include future-oriented costs and benefits, such as the cost of global warming and the loss of old-growth forests and the benefits of net investment. (See column [5] of Table 18.2.) Between 1951 and 1994, including such issues raised the conservative COL estimate by about 1.2 percentage points and the official inflation rate by about 2 percentage points. This indicates that increasingly more of the costs of living on earth is being postponed to the future. We are currently enjoying relatively low inflation, as measured by both the conservative COL estimate and the CPI. However, the long-term costs in terms of the environment or slow growth of potential output (due to inadequate investment) will likely have to be paid in the future, in the form of environmental disaster, slow productivity growth, and the like. My measures suggest that if the nation were paying more of the environmental costs now and/or investing more in the future, both the official and COL inflation rates would be higher.[10]

Policy Issues

It is beyond this short chapter's goal to criticize and reject Boskin-type corrections of the CPI. However, even if those adjustments are needed, my most conservative estimate more than cancels out the Boskin corrections. That is, increases in pollution, commuting time, labor time, and the like more than cancel out the corrections that Boskin advocates. Therefore, as a first guess for calculating inflation rates, we might split the difference, clinging to the CPI as calculated before Boskin-type adjustments.

Should the Federal Reserve make COL inflation (or old measures of the CPI) its central concern? Under a literal interpretation of the seeming current Fed goal of attaining zero inflation, this would cause them to raise interest rates and spark a recession. But this is a wrong interpretation, since monetary policy cannot raise extra current benefits or lower extra current costs. Since the Fed's main constituency (bondholders and bankers) does not care about negative future effects, distributional changes, current external costs, or uncompensated labor, its policy experts understand this point. The job of fixing the extra costs and promoting the extra benefits belongs to other branches of the government. The problems, of course, arise because these other branches are doing inadequate jobs at dealing with these issues.

Where the COL measure is relevant is in indexing. That is, retirees, workers, and taxpayers should have their income protected (via indexing) from rises in the cost of living, not just those reflected by the official CPI. Imposing Boskin-type adjustments on the CPI and thus on indexed incomes implies real cutbacks in benefits received not only because these modifications may be technically wrong, but because they ignore the real meaning of the cost of living and thus overlook hidden inflation. Even though the idea of indexing incomes to prevent loss of real purchasing power seems politically utopian at this point, the Boskin "reforms" are nonetheless attacks on people's standards of living.

Notes

1. Extrapolation was based on the assumption that after 1994, the COL inflation rate moved with both the official inflation rates and a trend line, as it had before 1994.

2. For a taste of the controversy among economists, see Madrick (1997a, b), Gordon and Griliches (1997), and Coy (1997). See also the discussions in the March–April 1997 issue of *Challenge* 40, no. 2; the Winter 1998 issue of the *Journal of Economic Perspectives* 12, no. 1; and Baker (1998a, b).

3. The key reason for the downward trend in inflation is that old CPI numbers have not been reestimated using new methods.

4. This example assumes that we do not benefit from tax cuts that match the decrease in public services. Throughout this paper, I assume that decreases in the tax burden do not cancel out increases in the COL. Given the relative constancy of tax obligations as a percentage of GDP, this is reasonable. But given the increasing regressiveness of the tax system in recent decades, it suggests that the COL has risen faster for the bottom half of the income distribution than is indicated by my numbers.

5. Dean Baker (1998b) argues that the CPI misses the increase in human needs that has accompanied the economy's growth. For example, the fact that we now need telephones, cars, and even the Internet in order to enjoy the economy's benefits fully did not cause the CPI to rise when these innovations became imperative to our lifestyles—even though they hurt the living standards of those unable to afford them.

6. This measure does not deal with the issues that Baker raises (summarized in previous note), but it is a step in the right direction.

7. For simplicity, the formula used follows the old method of calculating deflators.

8. By including the impact of extra current benefits and costs, we are making the same assumption as used in the GPI calculation, which is that these use-values received by people can be quantified and added up.

9. In fact, rising inequality might be seen as a benefit for the very rich, because it means an increase in the supply of personal servants. Further, in practice, they are the ones who determine "societal goals."

10. Alternatively, unemployment would be higher in order to restrain such inflation.

References

Baker, Dean. 1998a. *Getting Prices Right: The Debate over the Consumer Price Index*. Armonk, NY: M.E. Sharpe.

———. 1998b. "The Boskin Commission After One Year." *Challenge* 41, no. 2, (March–April): 6–11.

Cobb, Clifford, Ted Halstead, and Jonathan Rowe. 1995. *The Genuine Progress Indicator: Summary of Data and Methodology*. San Francisco: Redefining Progress.

Coy, Peter. 1997. "It Overstates Inflation! Does Not! Does So!" *Business Week*, June 9, 68–69.

Gibson, Sharon. 1998. *Understanding the Consumer Price Index: Answers to Some Questions*. BLS Web page, http://stats.bls.gov/cip1998g.htm

Gordon, Robert J., and Zvi Griliches. 1997. "Comment on Madrick." *New York Review of Books*. June 26, 64–65.

Koretz, Gene. 1999. "Waving a Statistical Wand," *Business Week*, May 31, 34.

Kuttner, Robert. 1996. "An Index that Confuses Apples with Oranges." *Los Angeles Times*, December 6.

Lee, Samantha J. 1998. "Live Well, Pay Up," *Forbes*, October 12.

Madrick, Jeff. 1997a. "The Cost of Living: A New Myth." *New York Review of Books*, March 6.

———. 1997b. "Reply." *New York Review of Books*. June 26, 65–67.

Rowthorn, Robert E. 1977. "Conflict, Inflation, and Money." *Cambridge Journal of Economics* 1: 215–39.

19

The P-R-I-C-E of Full Employment in Monopoly Capitalism

Elmer P. Chase III

Introduction

Mainstream theories of inflation are misguided, and so are mainstream monetary and fiscal policy prescriptions. Inflation is the result of conflict over income distribution. Mainstream, neoclassical economists believe that unemployment is necessary in order to keep the income distribution unchanged. They call this supposedly "necessary" unemployment rate the "Non-Accelerating Inflation Rate of Unemployment," NAIRU, or the "Natural Rate" of unemployment. This is what Karl Marx analyzed so thoroughly in *Capital* and called the Reserve Army of the Unemployed.

Radical and post-Keynesian economists are strongly opposed to the use of unemployment to control inflation. They propose alternative tax- and market-based anti-inflation/income share mechanisms. These are generalized under the rubric of a "Productivity Regulated Inflation Control Exchange," P-R-I-C-E, mechanism. The P-R-I-C-E is an alternative to the social pathology and massive loss of income associated with maintaining a Reserve Army of the "Naturally" Unemployed. In this chapter a case is presented for combining a P-R-I-C-E mechanism with monetary and fiscal policies to attain real full employment without inflation.

P-R-I-C-E of Full Employment or NAIRU Double Speak

The Phillips Curve depicts an inverse relationship, or trade-off, between inflation and unemployment, while the "Non-Accelerating Inflation Rate of Unemployment," NAIRU, or "Natural Rate," theory depicts an independent, or vertical, relationship at the NAIRU, which is defined as the unemployment rate where the number of the unemployed equals the number of job openings (McConnell and Brue 1996, 339–347). In these mainstream views unemployment is systemic, and certain levels are seen as desirable.

Likewise Radical/Marxist explanations of inflation are available, such as class conflict theories, which describe a clockwise circular pattern in the inflation and unemployment relationship as relative class power shifts over business cycles (Kotz 1987; Chase 1992). Again unemployment is seen as systemic, but hardly desirable.

Shifts in relative power between capital and labor have been used to explain "time variant" rightward (upward) and leftward (downward) shifts in the NAIRU/Natural Rate (Phillips Curve) (R. Gordon 1997; Pollin 1998). The shifts in power also explain why the circular patterns of graphs of the inflation and unemployment relationship, predicted by Radical/Marxist conflict theories, move in a spiral along an ellipse over "long waves," with foci on a ray from the southwest to the northeast (Gordon, Weisskopf, and Bowles 1983; Chase 1992).[1] The P-R-I-C-E mechanism provides alternatives to gyrations in relative class power and the Reserve Army of the Unemployed, which settle power struggles temporarily.

Historical statistics suggest that the price level at the end of the nineteenth century was the same or slightly lower than at its beginning. Capital investments were made; the population and labor force grew; real gross domestic product (GDP) and income grew; the mixture of output changed; the quality of products was enhanced, yet the price level remained unaffected in the long run.

There were brief increases and decreases in the price level over business cycles, but inflation is a persistent rise in the general price level and not brief increases caused by supply disruptions, demand spikes, or differences in the timing of changes in consumption and production. Inflation is a long wave, institutional phenomenon that has commenced during long-wave plateaus in the years immediately before the 1820s, 1870s, 1920s, and the 1970s in the top tier economies. Competition, labor force growth rate changes, increases in unemployment, and institutional changes extinguished inflation and restored accepted income shares and price stability in the nineteenth century (Chase 1992).

The twentieth century brought with it monopoly capitalism and a secular upward trend in the general price level. The spheres of activity in which a "public necessity" required government intervention expanded. The market power of firms to set prices and the political power of firms to shape public policy were concentrated in fewer hands. The exercise of market and political power augmented the Reserve Army of the "Naturally?" Unemployed as the institutional mechanism used to settle conflict over income distribution. Even after the devastation of the long wave's contraction and depression phases, an accepted relative distribution of income remained ephemeral at the beginning of the 1990s long-wave trough (Chase 1992, 26).

Okun (1970) relationship estimates showed that real GDP must grow at a 2.4 percent rate to keep the unemployment rate from rising, and that the rate moves from 2.4 percent at the long-wave trough to 3.5 percent at the plateau. There is an economic recovery for capitalists when real growth rates turn positive, but none for the working class until the rate is 2.4 percent or more. The GDP growth rate averaged 1.9 percent and the unemployment rate averaged 6.2 percent from 1990 through 1996—50 percent below and 34 percent above the respective rates for the 1950s and 1960s. Growth rates above 2.4 percent and a shift in relative power to favor capitalists at the long-wave trough restored unemployment to under 5 percent and inflation to under 2 percent at the millennium's end.

In the 1970s, during the contraction phase of the post–World War II long wave of economic development, inflation accelerated dramatically as the GDP growth rate slowed and conflict over the distribution of income intensified. Henry Wallich and Sidney Weintraub (1971), Arthur Okun (Okun and Perry 1978), and Abba Lerner and David Colander (1980), developed tax-based (TIP) and market-based (MAP) inflation policies (explained in the next section) designed to keep growth rates in nominal incomes per labor hour confined to the growth rate of productivity.

A session at an American Economic Association (AEA) meeting memorialized by three articles (Koford and Miller 1992; Colander 1992; Vickrey 1992) alerted the assembled practitioners of the "dismal science" to the use of TIPs and MAPs as an institutional reform to move the often revised NAIRU to real full employment. The case for the reform was most recently elevated to center stage by the 1993 AEA presidential address of William Vickrey (1993), in which he reiterated his earlier call for a value-added, or markup warrants, MAP. The MAP would control inflation and allow monetary and fiscal policies to be used to move the economy to "Chock-Full Employment," and end the "embezzlement" of inflation and the "vandalism" of unemployment (Vickrey 1992, 341). By my econometric estimate, that "vandalism" is costing the U.S. economy over $1 trillion annually. That is the "deficit" between actual GDP and potential GDP at real full employment.

The P-R-I-C-E of PINK SLIPsters, TIPsters, and MAPsters

NAIRU, TIP, and MAP approaches to controlling inflation and the income distribution were analyzed below (see appendix) within categories of the table titled, "Output, Cost, and Profits of Nonfinancial Corporate Business," which regularly appears in the *Economic Report of the President* (ERP). The categories were manipulated in a manner similar to that used by Bowles and Edwards (1985, 103–363) in their economics textbook to analyze output and incomes. Alternative approaches were then compared.

Sidney Weintraub may accurately be called the father of the TIP proposal (Wallich and Weintraub 1971). He referred to TIP advocates as TIPsters (Gapinski and Rockwood 1979, 239). I used his term and applied the suffix to pink slip, which is what NAIRU entails, and referred to advocates of the NAIRU mechanism as PINK SLIPsters. I also applied the suffix to MAP and referred to its advocates as MAPsters.

Symbols were substituted for the categories of the ERP table utilized. In the equations below: CCA = Capital Consumption Allowance or Depreciation; IBTx = Indirect Business Taxes; CompEmp = Compensation of Employees; PrTxLi = Profit Tax Liability; PrAfTx = Profit After Tax; NetInt = Net Interest; Q = Output or Real Value Added; P = Price with subscripts indicating the category; N = Labor Hours; K = Capital Invested; K_e = Employed Capital; and CU = the Capacity Utilization Rate.

From the categories it followed that:

$$P_q Q = CCA + IBTx + CompEmp + PrTxLi + PrAfTx + NetInt \qquad (1)$$

An incomes version of the GDP from National Income and Product Accounting resulted. The equation indicated that the nominal value added ($P_q Q$), or proceeds of firms, was distributed among various cost and profit categories as "factor" payments or incomes. Most TIPsters and MAPsters divide value added into only two categories, wages and profits, and ignore depreciation and government. The more expansive categories provided above were desirable as will be demonstrated below.

Recognizing that Q = (Q/N) N, the equivalent for Q was substituted into (1) and produced:

$$P_q (Q/N)\, N = CCA + IBTx + CompEmp + PrTxLi + PrAfTx + NetInt \qquad (2)$$

Equation (2) indicated that nominal value added was the product of price, output per labor hour or productivity, and labor hours.

Dividing equation (2) by labor hours (N) and then by productivity (Q/N) isolated output price:

$$P_q = [(CCA/N)/(Q/N)] + [(IBTx/N)/(Q/N)] + [(CompEmp/N)/(Q/N)] + [(PrTxLi/N)/(Q/N)] + [(PrAfTx/N)/(Q/N)] + [(NetInt/N)/(Q/N)] \qquad (3)$$

Equation (3) indicated that output price (P_q) is a function of the ratio of the cost and profit components per labor hour, to productivity or output per labor hour. Increases in costs or profit per labor hour that exceed productivity require price increases to provide the proceeds to make the factor payments.

Simplifying (3) indicated that output price equaled the sum of unit costs and unit profits:

$$P_q = (CCA/Q) + (IBTx/Q) + (CompEmp/Q) + (PrTxLi/Q) + (PrAfTx/Q) + (NetInt/Q) \quad (4)$$

Classical economists recognized that there were reproducible and nonreproducible goods. Demand determines the price of nonreproducible goods such as the paintings of masters long dead. But most goods are reproducible with various time lags. Cost determines the price of reproducible goods. Adam Smith referred to a "natural" price around which market prices would fluctuate, while Karl Marx spoke of socially necessary labor time that determined the underlying values of goods, which were then transformed into costs and prices. The prices of reproducible goods and services are the target of TIPsters and MAPsters, and so they concentrate on costs and productivity.

A standard algebraic transformation to rates of change, approximately accurate for modest changes, holds that the percentage change in the product (quotient) of variables equals the sum (difference) of the percentage change in the variables. Letting the superscript (*) denote the rate of change in a variable, and applying the transformation procedure to equation (2), produced:

$$P_q^* + (Q/N)^* + N^* = (CCA + IBTx + CompEmp + PrTxLi + PrAfTx + NetInt)^* \quad (5)$$

The rate of change in average output price (inflation) implied was:

$$P_q^* = (CCA + IBTx + CompEmp + PrTxLi + PrAfTx + NetInt)^* - N^* - (Q/N)^* \quad (6)$$

The bracketed term to the right of the equal sign, and the rate of change in labor hours (N*), provided a measure of labor cost and other costs per labor hour. (Q/N)* was the rate of change in labor productivity. Therefore it followed that the rate of inflation (P_q^*) increased when the rate of increase in costs and profit per labor hour exceeded the rate of increase in productivity.

Introducing capacity utilization into equation (1) as a proxy for demand showed that price was *inversely* related to demand, and that the profit rate was *directly* related to demand. An equation for the profit rate was produced from equation (1) by rearranging terms to isolate profits after taxes (PrAfTx) to the left of the equal sign, dividing by capital invested (K) to get a profit rate, and separating the K to the right of the equal sign into employed, K_e, and unemployed components: $K = K_e (1/CU)$. The resulting equation was:

$$PrAfTx/K = [(P_q Q - CCA - IBTx - CompEmp - PrTxLi - NetInt)/K_e] \times CU \quad (7)$$

Labor hours (N), output (Q), employed capital (K_e), and capacity utilization (CU) are directly related. Revenues (P_q Q) and labor costs (CompEmp = N x wage rate) decline as Q and N decline with CU and K_e. Other fixed and quasi-fixed costs do not decline with revenues. The profit rate wanes.

Since output price equals unit costs plus unit profit on employed capital times the inverse of capacity utilization, as can be confirmed by multiplying equation (7) by K_e, dividing by Q and CU, and rearranging terms, an imperative exists to raise prices (P_q) to cover rising unit costs, rescue revenues, and restore profit rates. The imperative is strong when labor cost declines are limited by resistance to wage cuts and layoffs when relative power favors labor. In the 1970s the opposite effects of capacity utilization on prices and the profit rate resulted in stagflation, simultaneously accelerating inflation and unemployment.

The PINK SLIPsters' view of inflation is based on the slander that when unemployment is pushed below its "Natural Rate," or NAIRU, or to the left along the Phillips Curve, less productive labor and other inputs are hired. Productivity rates decline. The demand for labor and other inputs increases with output and capacity utilization. Costs rise as the number of jobs exceeds the number of unemployed. With reference to equation (6), the rate of change of the bracketed terms minus the rate of change in labor hours (N*) exceeds the rate of change in productivity (Q/N)*. Inflation (P_q*) accelerates. When "signs of inflation" arise, restrictive monetary and fiscal policies are instituted to increase unemployment and lower capacity utilization to the rates at which inflation does not accelerate, that is, at the NAIRU, or to a more "acceptable" Phillips Curve trade-off of inflation and unemployment.

TIPsters recognize that restrictive monetary and fiscal policies have a direct effect on employment and output, but, at best, only an indirect effect on prices. TIPsters recognize the facts made clear by equations (3) and (6), that prices must increase when costs and profit per labor hour increase by more than productivity. Imposing a tax penalty on offending firms combats the "externality" of inflation from "factor" payments that exceed productivity.

TIPsters recognize that hourly compensation of employees (CompEmp/N) makes up the largest share of unit price. TIPsters simplify their inflation control mechanism by assuming two classes of recipients, labor and capital, and by assuming that their relative income shares are constant or vary little. The result of this simplification is that price becomes a constant markup over the ratio of hourly wages to productivity. With reference to equation (3), a constant markup (m) is substituted for everything except (CompEmp/N)/(Q/N) on the right side of the equation. And the markup (m) replaces everything except CompEmp in brackets on the right side of the rate of price change equation (6). Because of their emphasis on labor costs to the exclusion of other costs, TIPsters are often accused of being unfair to labor. Including all costs and profit eliminates the bias.

Income shares, and therefore markups, are not constant. The data used by Weintraub (1978, 46) to demonstrate near "constancy" produced a markup that ranged from 1.9 to 2.2. The data from the ERP table used in this study indicated that the markup ranged from 1.46 to 1.62 in the years 1948 to 1997. Since a multiplication is involved, even smaller fluctuations than the data showed should not be dismissed. The optimal income distribution, or markup, cannot be clearly determined.

TIPsters also impose an estimated average productivity rate on firms that the TIP would affect. A firm that increased wages by no more than its own productivity rate justified could still be assessed a tax penalty if its productivity rate exceeded the average rate imposed by government TIPsters, while a firm that increased wages by more than its productivity rate but less than the government-imposed estimated rate would escape the tax penalty. The behavioral incentives seem perverse.

The TIPster mechanism is simple. Only the monopoly sector of the economy must be included under its influence—perhaps 1,000 or 2,000 large firms. It is relatively simple and inexpensive to administer. Wage contours throughout the economy would become more stable. The emphasis is shifted from adjusting labor hours to equating changes in costs and profit per labor hour with productivity changes.

The TIPster approach may be considered a

P-R-I-C-E mechanism for controlling inflation and income shares, since firms would be free to raise prices in excess of the assumed productivity increase in exchange for payment of a tax penalty. The payments would offset, or at least discourage, price increases and keep increases in aggregate factor payments in line with increases in real output (Q).

MAPsters seek to move away from the TIPsters' tax penalty mechanism and its coercive connotation. MAPsters would establish a new property right to raise prices, or increase value added (P_qQ). They substitute a market in rights to increase prices, or value added, for the TIPsters' tax mechanism. The rights mechanism is analogous to marketable pollution rights that flexibly control the aggregate of polluting emissions. Congress views property rights and markets more favorably than taxes.

As in the case of pollution control, an aggregate quantity must be specified in advance. In the MAPsters' case the aggregate quantity is nominal value added. Rights equal to the nominal value added of the previous period, plus an additional number to account for expanded value added from presumed productivity increases, are created and distributed to firms on a share of value added basis. Firms that hire more workers (or capital) are issued additional rights, while those that lay off workers (or retire capital) surrender some rights. Firms are then free to buy rights to add output or raise prices beyond levels that their allotment of rights permits, from firms with excess rights to sell. With reference to equation (6), the marketplace in rights would keep the percentage increase in bracketed payments equal to the percentage increases in presumed productivity and labor hours. Nominal value added would equal real value added, and costs and profit payments, so the price level would not rise.

William Vickrey (1992, 1993) expressed the belief that it would be difficult to identify changes in individual prices. The history of price controls and the analysis of administrative problems in implementing a TIP discussed in the referenced Okun and Perry (1978) edited volume supported this viewpoint. "New" variants of price-controlled goods were introduced to evade controls. As a consequence, William Vickrey preferred a market in rights to increase value added (P_qQ) instead of a market in rights to increase prices (P_q), so that prices of "new" products were not an issue. Since rights are issued according to presumed increases in productivity (Q/N) and the presumed productivity of an additional hour of labor (N), a market in rights to raise prices or value added amounts to the same thing.

TIPsters suggested that since marketable value added rights would have a value, a MAP would have to include more firms than a TIP to avoid litigation. They also suggested that the MAPsters lacked an enforcement mechanism that would punish those who raised prices or output without securing the prerequisite rights (Gapinski and Rockwood 1979, 240–243).

The first criticism seemed off the mark. An objective criterion could be used to select those "in" and those "out." The Herfindahl Index, which is calculated as the sum of the squared market shares of individual firms in an industry, has been used by the Justice Department in antitrust cases to measure the concentration and competitiveness of industries. Dominant firms in industries with a Herfindahl Index of market power of 1,000 or more could be included, or criteria used during the price controls of the 1970s could be used for selection. Industries with lower index numbers would likely have enough "competitors" within to diversify away the risk of use of market power to set prices. As for the enforcement criticism, every MAPster is, in the face of lawless firms, a TIPster.

MAPster approaches may also be considered

"Productivity Regulated Inflation Control Exchange," P-R-I-C-E, mechanisms for controlling inflation and income shares, since firms would be free to raise prices and/or output in excess of employment and average productivity increases if they purchased rights in the marketplace from other firms willing to sell them. The rights sold would offset the rights purchased and keep increases in aggregate factor payments equal to average productivity and employment increases.

Equation (6) indicates that if the percentage change in costs and profits does not exceed the percentage change in real value added ([Q/N]* and N*), prices will remain stable. The MAPsters' approach would provide a gage of inflationary or deflationary pressure through the market price of value added rights. The Treasury Department could intervene in the market with rights purchases or sales to adjust the "exchange rate" of rights. Intervention would also seem appropriate when data indicate that output prices have been falling as the result of productivity increases in excess of the presumed average. The growth rate of value added could be managed much as the Fed now operates to affect money supply and interest rates. Equation (7) suggested that by settling the conflict over income shares by means other than contractionary monetary and fiscal policies, P-R-I-C-E mechanisms would encourage higher levels of capacity utilization and employment that would tend to *lower* the price level and *increase* the profit rate.

Conclusion

Whether TIPster, MAPster, or some other type of PRICEster, we are all outlaws in the eyes of the "mainstream" PINK SLIPsters of the economic profession. Whichever P-R-I-C-E mechanism receives consensus support, it should not be based on changes in wages, but rather on all cost and profit categories, and it should not discourage productivity increases from increased efficiency. It should be implemented now as the world makes adjustments necessary for a new long-wave expansion.

Note

1. Long waves, or Kondratieff waves, are economic cycles of fifty-four years that appear in economic time series such as prices and industrial output, often attributed to clustering of innovations and institutional arrangements that support them, and to cycles in global weather patterns (Chase 1992; van Duijn 1983). Post–World War II long-wave phases were: recovery, 1947–1955; expansion, 1956–1964; plateau, 1965–1973; contraction, 1974–1982; depression, 1983–1991; and trough, 1992–2000(?).

References

Bowles, Samuel and Richard Edwards. 1985. *Understanding Capitalism: Competition, Command, and Change in the U.S. Economy*. New York: Harper & Row.

Chase, Elmer P. III. 1992. "The Wasteland Economics of High Unemployment." *Challenge* 35, no. 1: 23–29.

Colander David C. 1992. "A Real Theory of Inflation and Incentive Anti-Inflation Plans." *American Economic Review* 82, no. 2: 335–340.

Gapinski, James H., and Charles E. Rockwood, eds. 1979. *Essays in Post Keynesian Inflation*. Cambridge: Ballinger.

Gordon, David M., Thomas Weisskopf, and Samuel Bowles. 1983. "Long Swings and the Nonreproductive Cycle." *American Economic Review* 73, no. 2: 52–157.

Gordon, Robert J. 1997. "The Time-Varying NAIRU and the Implications for Economic Policy." *Journal of Economic Perspectives* 11, no. 1: 11–32.

Koford, Kenneth J., and Jeffery B. Miller. 1992. "Macroeconomic Market Incentive Plans: History and Theoretical Rationale." *American Economic Review* 82, no. 2: 330–334.

Kotz, David M. 1987. "Radical Theories of Inflation." In *The Imperiled Economy, Book 1: Macroeconomics from a Left Perspective*, ed. Robert D. Cherry, Christine D'Onofrio, Cigdem Kurdas, Thomas R. Miehl, Fred Moseley, and Michele I. Naples, 83–91. New York: Union for Radical Political Economics.

Lerner, Abba, and David Colander. 1980. *MAP: A Market Anti-Inflation Plan*. New York: Harcourt, Brace, Jovanovich.

McConnell, Campbell R., and Stanley L. Brue. 1996. *Economics*. 13th ed. New York: McGraw-Hill.

Okun, Arthur M. 1970. "Potential GNP: Its Measurement and Significance." In *The Political Economy of*

Appendix

Table 19.A

Costs and Profit per Dollar, or Income Shares, and Annual Compund Rates of Inflation Over Post–World War II Growth Cycles

Year	Capital consumption allowance	Indirect business taxes	Compen-sation of employees	Profit	Profit tax liability	Profit after taxes	Net interest	Inflation (%)
1948 to 1953	.079	.098	.633	.183	.096	.087	.007	2.56
1953 to 1959	.088	.098	.648	.159	.082	.076	.009	2.20
1959 to 1966	.086	.101	.640	.158	.069	.088	.014	1.11
1966 to 1973	.086	.102	.658	.129	.058	.072	.025	4.11
1973 to 1978	.094	.097	.666	.114	.052	.062	.025	7.29
1978 to 1984	.107	.094	.664	.097	.038	.059	.038	5.81
1984 to 1988	.102	.096	.658	.103	.034	.069	.041	1.99
1988 to 1994	.100	.100	.664	.098	.032	.066	.038	2.42
1994 to 1997	.095	.102	.652	.128	.037	.091	.023	1.21

Source: Calculated by the author from Table B-15 "Output, Costs, and Profits of Non-financial Corporate Business," *Economic Report of the President*, 1998 and 1999.

Prosperity, 132–145. Washington, DC: The Brookings Institution.

Okun, Arthur, and George L. Perry, eds. 1978. *Curing Chronic Inflation*. Washington, DC: The Brookings Institution.

Pollin, Robert. 1998. "The 'Natural Rate' of Unemployment: It's All About Class Conflict." *Dollars and Sense* 219 (September/October): 12–15.

van Duijn, Jacob J. 1983. *The Long Wave in Economic Life*. Boston: George Allen & Unwin.

Vickrey, William. 1992. "Chock-Full Employment Without Increased Inflation: A Proposal for Marketable Markup Warrants." *American Economic Review* 82, no. 2: 341–345.

———. 1993. "Today's Task for Economists." *Challenge* 36, no. 2: 4–14, and *American Economic Review* 83, no. 1: 1–12.

Wallich, Henry C., and Sidney Weintraub. 1971. "A Tax-Based Incomes Policy." *Journal of Economic Issues* 5: 1–19.

Weintraub, Sidney. 1978. *Capitalism's Inflation and Unemployment Crisis*. Reading, MA: Addison Wesley Co.

20

The Promise of Finance

Banks and Community Development

Carole Biewener

Finance and bank lending have been a feature of many progressive community development initiatives ranging from the Grameen Bank in Bangladesh to the 1977 Community Reinvestment Act in the United States and the French Parti Socialiste's initial plan to "socialize" credit in the early 1980s. However, in these initiatives finance usually has been subordinated to "productive" investment, and access to credit has been predicated upon ensuring adequate profits for moneylenders. As a result, progressive financial policy has often faced the challenge of promoting community development while furthering capitalist class exploitation. This chapter considers these tensions by exploring the class dimensions of various credit policy initiatives. It shows that in some instances if the class aspects and effects of bank lending are taken into account, then communal forms of production may be fostered, thereby furthering community development in a manner that enables nonexploitative class relations. The chapter also argues for developing broader notions of "productive investment" and "rate of return." This would allow important gender, racial, class, and environmental concerns to be incorporated into our understanding of what it means to be "productive" or to have a "return" on an investment.

To develop these points, three aspects of bank lending are addressed: (1) the manner in which moneylending decisions are made, (2) the kinds of expenditures that are financed, and (3) the manner in which loans are repaid. Each offers distinct possibilities for furthering radical social change.

Democratizing Moneylending

Many progressive initiatives have called for the "socialization" or "democratization" of credit by including new constituents in credit allocation decisions, from local government officials and community representatives, to workers, consumers, or environmental planners. In these initiatives banks are seen as providing the arena for establishing some form of collective control over loan allocations. While bankers do not own most of the money they lend out, they do exercise considerable control over who receives this money and for what purposes. Democratization initiatives, therefore, try to foster a "community consciousness" whereby banks operate in some representative manner with "community interests" helping to guide lending decisions. Further, by considering bank capital as a *social* resource, such initiatives also contribute to a socialization of credit by legitimizing the idea of community influence over the use of this form of social wealth.

Banks offer a different arena for collective deliberation concerning the allocation of social wealth as compared to businesses, households, or governments. They therefore enable a different and particular sense of community. For instance, while collectivization of a business may enable workers in that business to have a say in how the labor process is organized and/or to influence how profits are used, this level of "collectivity" is defined in terms of those working in that business or enterprise. It is easy to imagine, therefore, that members of such an "enterprise community" might be interested in maximizing the profits retained within the business by using low-cost component parts produced elsewhere under highly exploitative conditions, by polluting the environment, or by discouraging women from joining their "community" because of higher health-care costs. Thus, as Eric Schragge, a Canadian community development activist, has noted, enterprise-level cooperatives may "mirror the demands of a capitalist economy by looking after their own survival as units in a market place" (1993, iii).

In the case of banks, collective deliberation about how to allocate loans could encompass a broader understanding of who is in the community (such as workers, consumers, retailers, women's rights advocates, and/or environmentalists) and of what constitutes a community (including businesses, households, schools, stores, recreational facilities, and/or roads). For instance, in the Mondragón region of Spain, it appears that a worker-based identity is the primary means for defining who serves on the board of directors for the central savings institution, the Caja Laboral Popular (People's Savings Bank), which serves the more than 150 worker-controlled cooperatives (Gunn and Gunn 1991, 65; Kasmir, 1996, 29). Yet, clearly, a worker-based identity is not the only identity motivating progressive initiatives. For feminists, democratizing credit could have a gender component, with impoverished women, self-employed women, and/or childcare providers also participating as moneylenders. For example, some loan circle funds have been established with the aim of empowering marginalized women by involving them in lending decisions, as in the case of the Grameen Bank in Bangladesh or CIDEL-GP (Centre D'innovation en Développement Économique Local du Grand Plateau), a community development organization in Montreal. For anti-racist activists, democratizing credit may mean including people of diverse ethnicities and races in credit allocation decisions to encourage the development of inner-city neighborhoods, "minority-owned businesses," or, more broadly, communities of color.

Thus, progressive initiatives that focus on banks to foster democratic, community-based practices for allocating social wealth help to broaden our understanding of "community" and, thereby may broaden who participates in credit allocation decisions while also extending the scope of what is considered to be expenditures related to "community development."

In the United States and Canada, emphasis upon local control has proven to be an important means to build alternative community-based organizations, including alternative credit institutions (Gunn and Gunn 1991; Perry 1987; Shragge 1993). All too often, "outside" ownership of assets has enabled the transfer of money out of a community, reducing the amount of financing available locally. Also, some communities have been marginalized by "outside" banks, receiving small amounts of development financing along with limited banking services. In the United States, the 1977 Community Reinvestment Act was passed (and is continually monitored by community activists) to address this practice of redlining, whereby communities of color are systematically denied access to bank services, mortgage loans, and business financing. Another response has been to create new credit institutions—community banks, community development credit unions, and community loan funds—that use local monetary resources for local financing, as well as for garnering external, "outside" money-capital for financing (Squires 1992; Perry 1987).

In and of themselves "local" banks offer no guarantee of progressive lending practices. Indeed, local banks often engage in the most conservative lending practices *and* they often function to draw money out of communities (Gunn and Gunn 1991, 61). With this in mind, the call for "local banks" seems to offer more promise if it is coupled with the democratization of credit, since this allows community representatives to participate in credit allocation decisions. Indeed, a "socially responsible orientation" may enable community development banks or credit unions to attract deposits from institutional savers such as foundations, public agencies, religious organizations, capitalist corporations, and various mutual funds. As Dymski (1996) notes, the South Shore Bank in Chicago is an oft-touted example of such a successful "greenlining" strategy.

In the United States and Canada, progressives concerned with furthering democratic local control in financing have often turned to credit unions in particular: "The co-ops of the financial world, [credit unions] are run by boards of directors elected by depositors, rather than investor-owners, as in a bank" (Gunn and Gunn 1991, 62). As Gunn and Gunn indicate, "the 1980s brought bank and savings-and-loan failures, but dramatic success for credit unions." Since 1980, membership in the United States's 11,900 credit unions has grown from 44 million to 70.4 million, while assets have "exploded to $316 billion from $69 billion" (though still minuscule compared to the $4.4 trillion in assets held by the 10,000 commercial banks) (Gilpin 1997, B1). While most credit unions are oriented toward providing financial services such as consumer loans and mortgages for their members, a "special category of community development credit unions has emerged, aimed at serving communities' local development needs, such as housing or minority-owned businesses" (Gunn and Gunn 1991, 62). By the late 1980s, about one hundred community development credit unions were operating in the United States. Thus, despite the imposing financial imperatives of increasingly globalized and deregulated financial markets, it does appear that in some instances credit unions have been able to channel financing toward local uses and, at times, this has involved community development initiatives. This then brings us to the next issue of what constitutes "community development investments" and, thereby, of what types of initiatives or expenditures are financed.

What Is to Be Financed?

By considering the question of what types of expenditures to finance, some of the limitations of solely focusing on democratizing credit become clear. For without explicitly analyzing the kinds of expenditures to be financed, too often "business development" or "productive investment" are fostered; and this usually means furthering workers' exploitation and marginalizing other gender, environmental, racial, and class aspects of credit.

An important example of this is that of the French Socialist government in the early 1980s with its initial emphasis on "socializing credit" to further radical social change. The French Socialists relied on Keynesian thinking to develop their economic policies (rather than a Marxian class analysis). The "collective will" became identified with investments to expand employment, strengthen the industrial fabric, reconquer the domestic market, and render the French nation more "autonomous" (Biewener 1988, 1990). Credit policies were therefore focused on reorienting bank lending toward financing these particular kinds of investment. The goal became that of simply fostering capitalist growth to achieve full employment levels of output and income; and the economic class consequences, when articulated, were seen as providing job security and higher real income for workers.

The French Socialists' radical Keynesian approach included a concern with new investment spending as a condition for prosperity and growth, but it neglected theorization of the class origins of such prosperity. It included a concern with promoting "productive investments," but it never addressed what it is that makes investment productive. From a Marxian class perspective, it is not machinery that renders capital productive, that ensures "productive" investment. Rather, it is living, human labor. It is workers' performance of surplus labor that produces capitalist profits, wealth, and prosperity. Thus, for Marxists, the French Socialists' "radical" credit policy, which focused on "productive investment," was rapidly reduced to efforts to promote capitalist growth rather than transform the class character of growth.

This tendency to ignore class processes of surplus production, appropriation, and distribution and to define progressive financing primarily in terms of investment is also clearly evident in the United States (Squires 1992; Dymski, Epstein, and Pollin 1993) Alternative credit institutions have usually been justified in terms of financing small-scale businesses in neighborhoods that are "underserved" by the existing commercial banks, with "business" more or less explicitly referring to small-scale capitalists, self-employed producers, or some type of retail outlet (Dymski 1995/96; Bond and Townsend 1996; Squires 1992; Minsky 1993).

Alternatively, if class relations are considered, then the potentially exploitative character of such "business" investment has to be taken into account. Indeed, by including a concern about class relations, a *progressive* understanding of investment might be enabled whereby investments that foster communal class relations are financed (Biewener 1989). There are different class characters to productive investment, depending on what kinds of class relations are fostered. From a Marxian perspective, "investment" is productive in a *capitalist* sense only if the means of production are used to produce commodities that embody surplus labor so that a profit can be realized. In this case the productive investment is capitalist because it enables capitalist exploitation. Alternatively, if money is lent to finance investment in production that involves *noncapitalist* class relations (such as household nonmarket production, cooperatives, or self-employed businesses), then it ceases to function as capital in the process of production. Further, when money is lent to finance investment in cooperative forms of production whereby surplus labor is collectively appropriated by the workers themselves it enables productive investment in a socialist or communal sense. Thus, if "socially responsible" moneylending incorporates such a class-based understanding of "productive investment," this may foster communal production by financing workers' cooperatives or by using access to investment credit as a "bargaining chip" to insist that workers within capitalist enterprises gain greater collective control over the conditions under which their surplus labor is produced, appropriated, and distributed.

In Canada and, to a lesser extent, in the United States there are some examples of initiatives that finance cooperative production. For instance the "Antigonish movement" in Nova Scotia, Canada, has a tradition of creating producer and consumer cooperative associations to counteract "the power of economic interests outside each community" (Perry 1987, 13). In Montreal, CIDEL-GP's loan fund initiative (which is oriented toward financing income-generating projects for poor women) is, in part, motivated by an interest in encouraging cooperative and collectivist types of associations (McMurtry 1993). In the United States, the Santa Cruz Community Credit Union was established in 1977 and set out to distinguish itself by deemphasizing consumer loans and concentrating "a majority of their lending on community development projects, especially locally owned, cooperatively managed businesses. . . . [To this end they] made significant early loans to businesses such as a worker-owned print shop and a Hispanic strawberry production co-op" (Gunn and Gunn 1991, 63).

Thus, while limited in scope, there are some encouraging examples of efforts to finance cooperative forms of production. Such a redefinition of "productive investment" to encompass investment in noncapitalist forms of production opens up myriad radical possibilities for progressive financial policy. First, as discussed above, it allows us to understand that there are differences in the kind of investment made in terms of the class relations these investments may foster. This understanding allows us to recognize that investment in noncapitalist class processes may *also* be productive. Second, by understanding that what is "productive" in a capitalist sense is a very particular and narrow notion of "productive" (productive of surplus-value or of commodities from which profit is derived) then, by considering noncapitalist class processes, we are able to broaden our understanding of "productive" investment and, thereby, redefine productivity in nonsurplus-value terms and even, perhaps, in nonmonetary terms. We could, for instance, measure productivity in terms of a vector of useful outcomes (rather than as a sum of monetary returns), which may include adequate housing, education, nonexploitative forms of production, urban renewal, women's empowerment, ecologically sound production, job expansion, income-generation projects for people of color, or the establishment of "green spaces." This consideration of what renders an investment "productive" brings us to the third aspect of how bank lending may contribute to furthering progressive community development initiatives: that of how a loan is to be repaid and how banks are to account for "profits" or "return."

Repayment and Profit

Some radical traditions have developed a critique of finance inspired by anti-usury sentiments (Amin 1977; Frank 1969; Rodney 1974). In Marxian terms, such anti-usury initiatives aim to promote progressive change by abolishing money as a means for obtaining profits for moneylenders. While this may have radical effects, it leaves open the question of whether or not such initiatives transform exploitative class relations, as this depends on what the money is lent for. Generally, radical anti-usury initiatives focus on two types of strategies: providing cheap financing by reducing the amount of interest paid, or redefining what is accepted or counted as repayment. Let us examine each in turn.

In itself there is nothing radical about reducing or eliminating interest payments. Yet, when tied to financing particular types of expenditures deemed "progressive," such initiatives may be embraced as radical or progressive. Further, by limiting the amount of profit that accrues to moneylenders, presumably more social wealth is available to be spent in other ways. Indeed, interest payments are often posed as drains on the social surplus; and this interest "drain" is often understood as coming at the expense of domestic or community-level productive investments.

However, this simple opposition between interest payments and productive investment is problematic in at least two respects. First, the payment of interest in and of itself does not mean that such money is eventually spent unproductively. What if the financier uses accumulated interest payments to finance new loans for productive investment? In this case, the interest would be spent productively. Thus, the issue of interest payments needs to be recast in terms of who controls the "social surplus" paid out as interest: capitalist financiers, alternative community development credit institutions, or corporate managers and boards of directors? This issue is further complicated when considered within the context of national and/or community development. Here interest payments have often been understood as contributing to an "external drain" by transferring a portion of a community's locally produced social surplus to "outside" or "foreign" financial institutions. Indeed, an extensive literature focusing on "external drain" exists in development studies (Frank 1969; Rodney 1974). In this case, even if interest payments have been used to finance new productive investment, they have often been reinvested in the "home" nation, the "first world," rather than in the community in which they were generated. In this sense then, the labor of the "third world" has financed productive investments in the "first."

Compelling as this argument is, however, the critical aspects of it are, once again, those of who controls the money capital and what is done with it, not whether a financier receives interest payments. Here radicals have argued that locally based financial institutions are more likely to relend any accumulated interest within the communities from which the interest originated, especially if the lending institutions have community representatives who are involved in credit allocation decisions.

The second problematic aspect of criticizing interest payments as "drains" on a social surplus is that all too often the desired alternative is that of "productive investment" without any explicit analysis of "productive investment" in terms of its class or gender or racial effects. This leaves the door open for promoting investments that further capitalist exploitation, gender subordination, racial discrimination, or environmental degradation. Thus, here again we see that it is not enough to argue that bank capital should finance productive rather than unproductive investment. The notion of what "productive" means must be specified so as to enable and legitimize noncapitalist understandings of what constitutes productive investment for a community. Otherwise, in societies imbued with capitalist notions of productive investment, capitalist exploitation will be furthered and alternative notions of community will be stymied.

This brings us to consideration of how the second anti-usury initiative—that of redefining what is accepted as repayment for a loan—might contribute to promoting progressive social change. By transforming how a loan is repaid, measures of value other than that of money would need to be recognized. For instance, as Susan George suggests, a loan may be repaid "in kind" (George 1990). George offers a lengthy list of how such "creative reimbursements" might be made in her discussion of Third World debt. Her list includes: conservation of biodiversity; social conservation/anti-erosion measures; reforestation; development of wells and small-scale irrigation techniques; recording of building techniques, particularly for traditional earthen architecture; development of new biomass sources for energy; collection of traditional knowledge about agriculture, medicine, nutrition, and pharmacy; improvement of local- and village-level food- and water-storage facilities; and compilation of dictionaries and grammars of local languages (1990, 250–251).

Such forms of repayment in kind clearly transform the nature of the "return" on the bank loan and displace profitability in a monetary sense. Instead, a new notion of return or profitability is enabled, one in which the qualitative nature of the use-values generated in "payment" is at least as important as their quantitative worth. Jack Quarter, for instance, emphasizes the importance of fostering credit that is based on social objectives rather than monetary rates of return (1992, 156). Similarly, feminists have argued for redefining economic development in terms of the well-being and creativity of all members of society rather than in terms of per capita gross domestic product. Such a definition not only enables the inclusion of nonmarketed goods and services in evaluating economic productivity, it also shifts the focus away from the products of labor to that of understanding human labor as both "a means and an end of development, of instrumental as well as intrinsic value" (Kabeer 1994, 83). If our notions of development, growth, and productivity are reshaped in this manner, then "activities which contribute to the health and well-being of people would be recognized as productive, whether or not they are carried out within personalized relations of family production, the commercialized relations of market production, or the bureaucratized relations of state production" (1994, 83). This clearly has important consequences for how women's activity is viewed, as women's work to reproduce labor, both biologically and socially, would be recognized as productive and would be valued more highly.

Therefore, while often it may be necessary to promise monetary profits in order to receive a loan, this promise should be understood as deriving from particular cultural, political, and economic conditions. If noncapitalism is conceived, then noncapitalist profitability is also conceivable. Work that helps build such an alternative understanding will thus contribute to enabling progressive financing schemes that validate initiatives other than those that promise high monetary rewards.

Thus, there are a variety of strategies available for using bank financing as a means to further radical social change. Progressives can work to socialize credit by establishing some form of democratic community control over credit allocation decisions. Such community control may foster the use of local resources for financing local community development initiatives and it may enhance a bank's ability to garner outside sources of loanable funds. Further, by enabling a community sense of credit allocation decisions, discussion and debate over what types of expenditures should be financed will be broadened. Community development may then be understood as fostering cooperative relations in industrial enterprises, as well as in and between households, recreational activities, educational institutions, retail outlets, and government agencies. In this manner, new noncapitalist standards for assigning social value will be enabled. We can "invest" in our communities with the promise of an adequate "return" in the form of environmentally sound lifestyles, economically secure neighborhoods, nonexploitative forms of production, and nonpatriarchal social relations. We can build other yardsticks by which to measure "returns" and, thereby, create the conditions for progressive communities.

References

Amin, S. 1977. *Imperialism and Unequal Development.* New York: Monthly Review Press.

Bond, P., and R. Townsend. 1996. "Formal and Informal Financing in a Chicago Ethnic Neighborhood." *Economic Perspectives* (July/August:) 3–27.

Biewener, C. 1988. "Keynesian Economics and Socialist Politics in France: A Marxist Critique." *Review of Radical Political Economics* 20, no. 2/3: 149–55.

———. 1989. "Socialist Politics and Theories of Money and Credit." *Review of Radical Political Economics* 21, no. 3: 58–63.

———. 1990. "Loss of a Socialist Vision in France." *Rethinking Marxism* 3, no. 3/4: 12–26.

Dymski, G. 1995/96. "Business Strategy and Access to Capital in Inner-City Revitalization." *Review of Black Political Economy* 24, no. 2/3: 51–65.

———. 1996. "Financing Strategies and Structures of Impoverishment: The Grameen and South Shore Models." Working paper in economics 96–09, Department of Economics, University of California, Riverside.

Dymski, G., G. Epstein, and R. Pollin, eds. 1993. *Transforming the U.S. Financial System: Equity and Efficiency for the 21st Century*. Armonk, NY: M.E. Sharpe.

Frank, A.G. 1969. *Capitalism and Underdevelopment in Latin America: Historical Studies of Chile and Brazil.* New York: Monthly Review Press.

George, S. 1990. *A Fate Worse than Debt*. New York: Grove Weidenfeld.

Gilpin, K. 1997. "Piggy Banks with Muscles: As Credit Unions Boom, Financial Rivals Cry Foul." *New York Times*, February 26, B1, B21.

Gunn, C., and Gunn, H.D. 1991. *Reclaiming Capital: Democratic Initiatives and Community Development.* Ithaca: Cornell University Press.

Kabeer, N. 1994. *Reversed Realities: Gender Hierarchies in Development Thought*. London: Verso.

Kasmir, S. 1996. *The Myth of Mondragón: Cooperatives, Politics, and Working-Class Life in a Basque Town.* Albany: State University of New York Press.

McMurtry, T. 1993. "The Loan Circle Programme as a Model of Alternative Community Economics." In *Community Economic Development*, ed. E. Schragge, 60–75. Montreal: Black Rose Books.

Minsky, H. 1993. "Community Development Banks: An Idea in Search of Substance." *Challenge* March-April: 33–41.

Perry, S. 1987. *Communities on the Way: Rebuilding Local Economies in the United States and Canada.* Albany: State University of New York Press.

Quarter, J. 1992. *Canada's Social Economy: Co-operatives, Non-profits, and Other Community Enterprises.* Toronto: James Lorimer.

Rodney, W. 1974. *How Europe Underdeveloped Africa.* Washington DC: Howard University Press.

Schragge, E., ed. 1993. *Community Economic Development: In Search of Empowerment and Alternatives.* Montreal: Black Rose Books.

Squires, G.D. 1992. *From Redlining to Reinvestment: Community Responses to Urban Disinvestment.* Philadelphia: Temple University Press.

Section V

The Global Political Economy

21

What Do Undergrads *Really* Need to Know About Trade and Finance?

Matias Vernengo

Introduction

Paul Krugman argues in a recent article that in the last decade of the twentieth century, the essential things to teach students are still the insights of Hume and Ricardo. That is, we need to teach them that trade deficits are self-correcting and that the benefits of trade do not depend on a country having an absolute advantage over its rivals (1996, 124–5).

The idea that trade imbalances are self-correcting is based on Hume's "price-specie-flow mechanism," while the notion that free trade is mutually beneficial to the countries involved relies on Ricardo's "principle of comparative advantage."[1] We will critically discuss both propositions in this chapter and conclude that capital flows might render the balance of payments adjustment unstable (a position held by Keynes), and that there is ample role for trade management if trade depends upon absolute rather than comparative advantage.

The Balance of Payments

As is explained in introductory macroeconomics texts, national trade accounts consist of a balance of payments (BP), a current account (CA) and a capital account (KA) (Baumol and Blinder 1985, 762–763). The CA measures exports and imports of goods—the "trade balance"; and services—tourist expenditures, insurance payments, and so forth. The KA includes "foreign direct investment"—factories, real estate, and so on; and "portfolio investments"—financial investments like stocks and bonds that can generally be sold at short notice. The overall BP is given by the sum of the CA and KA.

In a fixed exchange rate system, an overall BP surplus or deficit may occur. When there is a balance-of-payments surplus the official exchange reserve holdings of the central bank will increase, and they will decrease in the case of a BP deficit. In formal terms,

$$BP = CA + KA = DR \tag{1}$$

where DR stands for the variation in official reserve holdings. For example, if the CA surplus exceeds the KA deficit, there will be an excess demand for the domestic currency. In this case, in order to reduce domestic currency appreciation the central bank will sell domestic currency and accumulate foreign reserves.

The Price-Specie-Flow Mechanism and the Principle of Comparative Advantage

The "price-specie-flow mechanism" was developed by David Hume (1752) not only as an interpretation of the BP adjustment process, but also as an argument against the mercantilist defense of government intervention. According to the price-specie-flow mechanism the BP is self-adjusting. If a country runs a trade deficit, then there will be an outflow of gold (the only "capital" asset) that will lead to deflation in the deficit country and to inflation in the surplus country. As a result of the fall of prices in the deficit country, its exports will become more competitive, thus restoring the trade balance equilibrium. In other words, gold flows will eliminate any trade imbalance. For a complete defense of the free trade doctrine, the idea that the balance of payments is self-adjusting had to be complemented by a proof that free trade is mutually advantageous for the parties involved. This notion was developed as the "principle of comparative advantage" by David Ricardo.[2]

The principle of comparative advantage as stated by Ricardo (1817, 128–155) implies that international trade of two commodities is mutually beneficial for any two countries whose labor productivities for these commodities differs regardless of whether one country is absolutely less productive in both commodities (Baumol and Blinder 1985, ch. 36). In the particular case in which one country has an absolute advantage in the production of both commodities, an adjustment mechanism is necessary to prevent the less competitive country from being outsold in both commodities. This is provided by the "price-specie-flow mechanism," which ensures that price levels in the less productive country will drop sufficiently to offset its absolute productivity disadvantage.

However, one crucial assumption was made by Ricardo to prove the validity of the principle of comparative advantage. This is that the level of employment is fixed. The consequences of abandoning this assumption are analyzed in the following section.

The Theory of Employment and Capital Mobility

Ricardo accepted Say's Law according to which *supply creates its own demand.* Ricardo (1817, 290) argues that

> No man produces, but with the view to consume or sell, and he never sells, but with an intention to purchase some other commodity, which may be immediately useful to him, or which may contribute to future production. By producing, then, he necessarily becomes either consumer of his own goods, or the purchaser and consumer of the goods of other person.

According to this view, the level of output and employment in the economy is determined by the previous conditions of accumulation, that is by the previous conditions on the supply side of the economy. The level of output and employment, in this view, is independent of the conditions of demand.

Once free trade in cloth and wine between England and Portugal is established (the example used by Ricardo), production and employment will not be altered by the new conditions of demand. Thus, all workers previously employed in cloth production in Portugal are transferred to wine production and vice versa in England. It is not relevant that initially the Portuguese people might not demand British products because of their higher prices, since the level of production in England is given by the internal conditions of supply. After the price-specie-flow mechanism is worked out and makes English products attractive to Portuguese consumers by raising prices and wages in Portugal and lowering prices and wages in England, the level of output and employment in both countries is exactly the same as in the no-trade situation.

In contrast, Keynes argued in his *General Theory of Employment, Interest and Money* (1936/1964) that for the proposition saying supply creates its own demand, we shall substitute the proposition that expenditure creates its own income by stimulating production just sufficient to meet the expenditure. In this view, it is demand (spending) that creates its own supply (output). The effects of this proposition, known as the principle of effective demand (PED), for the Ricardian theory of trade are devastating. In particular, it is not possible to show that free trade would be beneficial for the countries involved.

If we take the national income accounts identity, by which the gross domestic product (Y), which measures the value of the output to the economy, is equal to expenditure, we have:

$$Y = C + I + G + X - M \tag{2}$$

where C stands for consumption, I for investment, G for government spending, X for exports, and M for imports. If consumption and imports are a function of income, then the PED tells us that output is determined as a multiple of "autonomous spending," or those expenditures that are independent of the level of income. The well-known formula of the multiplier is given by

$$Y = aZ \tag{3}$$

where Z is autonomous spending, and a is the multiplier.

The main consequence of Keynes's theory of employment for the theory of comparative advantage is that (using the Ricardian example once again) once free trade between Portugal and England is established, the level of employment in each country will depend on the level of autonomous spending. In that case, the effect of the introduction of free trade would be the reduction of the level of employment in the less competitive country (for wine production—England) rather than price deflation.

It must be noted that, in the conventional view, the deflation in the less competitive country is not caused by unemployment since, as we saw, the level of employment is given. Deflation is rather the result of the outflow of gold needed for paying the trade deficit. Clearly this means that, within the conventional view, current account events dominate capital account developments. The outflow of capital is caused by the trade deficit. If the country that is running a trade deficit does not have gold reserves it will need to borrow to finance the negative current account leading to a positive capital account inflow.

The interwar experience of increased capital mobility led Keynes to believe that it was the other way round—that is, capital account events dominate the developments of the current account. In this view, speculative capital flows determine the outcome of the balance of payments. The smooth adjustment mechanism of the price-specie-flow mechanism is substituted by the instability of portfolio capital movements. Capital flows to the country that offers higher remuneration, so that a higher interest rate in England will lead to an inflow of capital from Portugal into England. This capital inflow leads to an appreciation of the pound and, as a result, to a higher trade deficit and greater unemployment in England.

The consequence of a regime of deregulated "free trade" in capital is that global interest rates rise in order to attract capital flows. National monetary authorities lose control of domestic interest rates since they must maintain high interest rates constantly in order to avoid capital flight (Eatwell 1996). Keynes argued: "We cannot hope to control rates of interest at home if movements of capital moneys out of the country are unrestricted" (Keynes 1971–82, vol. 25, 276).

Free mobility of capital flows and the higher rates of interest that they entail have two main consequences. First, the fact that capital flows determine the outcome of the BP implies that trade imbalances might be persistent. A country can maintain a trade, or CA, deficit for long periods by attracting capital flows with rates of interest higher than those of its trading partners. In contrast with the price-specie-flow mechanism, capital flows can lead to persistent trade imbalances.[3]

However, higher interest rates have a negative impact on the level of employment. As we saw, the level of employment is determined by autonomous spending, Z. One of the crucial components of Z is government spending, G. Higher interest rates raise the burden of the government debt and reduce its capacity to spend, reducing total expenditure and hence the level of employment. In fact, after the breakdown of the Bretton Woods system, which led to the liberalization and deregulation of capital flows, levels of interest and of unemployment have been consistently higher all over the world.[4]

Under these conditions comparative advantage might not be the main determinant of trade flows. In fact, if capital is allowed to move freely to the region that offers a higher remuneration, then producers will move to the most productive (or profitable) countries. *Absolute* rather than *comparative* advantage will be the principle determining the trade performance of a country (Brewer 1985).

Myint (1958) pointed out that this was the position taken by Adam Smith in his classic *Wealth of Nations*. Accumulation, in this view, is related to the process of division of labor, which depends, in turn, on the extension of the market. Market demand allows the producer to reap the gains from the division of labor, and division of labor leads to increasing output. This process was dubbed *cumulative causation* by Myrdal (1957), since it can be described as saying that higher demand leads to higher productivity, which leads to higher demand once again.

In sum, if employment is determined by the level of autonomous expenditure, and capital flows dominate the results of the BP, then free trade and free movement of capital flows might lead to higher unemployment and persistent BP disequilibrium. In addition, capital mobility implies that absolute rather than comparative advantage is the main determinant of trade flows.

Consistent with this view, Keynes believed that one should "Let goods be homespun wherever it is reasonably and conveniently possible, and, above all, let finance be primarily national" (Keynes 1971–82, vol. 21, 236). It must be noted, however, that Keynes's theory is considered by many critics as being relevant only in the short run. In this case, if effective demand is relevant only in the short run, then the effects of unemployment on the balance of trade can be ignored in the long run. For that reason, in the following section we discuss the effects of extending the principle of effective demand to the long run.

Growth and the Long-Run Principle of Effective Demand

We have seen in the previous section that free trade might lead to unemployment in a less competitive country, and that speculative capital flows might render the balance-of-payments adjustment process unstable, at least in the short run. However, the principle of effective demand can be extended to the long run, that is, the rate of accumulation in the long run depends upon the rate of growth of autonomous demand.

Kaldor (1970) articulated a simple demand-driven model of accumulation. The development of his ideas dates back to the introduction of his technical progress function at the end of the 1950s, and to his interpretation of the slow rate of growth of Great Britain in the mid-1960s and the so-called Kaldor–Verdoorn Laws (see note 6 to Nell interview in this volume). Notwithstanding the relevance of his previous contributions, it was only after 1970 that he introduced all three elements of his long-term growth model, namely: the supermultiplier, Verdoorn's Law, and the foreign trade multiplier.

Dixon and Thirlwall (1975, 203) have correctly emphasized that "The main thrust of Kaldor's argument is Hicks's view that it is the growth of autonomous demand which governs the long run rate of growth of output." In particular, in the Kaldor model, the long-run rate of growth is assumed to depend fundamentally on the growth of demand for *exports*, which, in a more general context, should be viewed as a proxy for "autonomous demand."[5] In the following we derive the Kaldor export-led growth model as an example of an autonomous demand-driven long-run growth model.

Kaldor derives a "super multiplier," or elasticity of output growth with respect to export (autonomous expenditure) growth g, such that:

$$y = gx \tag{4}$$

where y is the rate of growth of output, and x is the rate of growth of exports.

In this model, following standard convention, the demand for exports is defined as being a function of the rate of growth of foreign income, z, and percentage change in relative prices, $p_d - p_f -$ e, so that:

$$x = h(p_d - p_f - e) + ez \tag{5}$$

where p_d and p_f are percentage changes in domestic and foreign price deflators and nominal exchange rate, e, defined as the domestic price of foreign currency; and $h < 0$ and $e > 0$ are price and income export elasticities.

The rate of growth of domestic (exports) prices, p_d, is then derived by means of the Kaleckian "mark up pricing equation"—see Kalecki (1971) and Goldstein's chapter, this volume. So that, with respect to time, in logarithmic (rates of growth) form we have:

$$p_d = t + w - l \tag{6}$$

where t is the markup, w is the rate of growth of the nominal wage rate, and l is the rate of growth of labor productivity.

In addition, the Kaldorian model assumes, following Verdoorn's Law, that the rate of growth of labor productivity is a function of the rate of growth of output. This can be represented by:

$$l = l_a + fy \tag{7}$$

where l_a is the rate of autonomous productivity growth that is unrelated to output growth (showing that supply considerations are also relevant in this post-Keynesian demand-based theory), and f is the Verdoorn coefficient that links output growth to productivity growth.

Combining equations (4), (5), (6), and (7) and solving for the rate of growth of output, we obtain:

$$y = \frac{g[h(t + w - l_a - p_f - e) + ez]}{1 + ghf} \tag{8}$$

This model is an export-led growth model, and emphasizes the role of the rate of growth of foreign demand, z, in output growth. A common feature with the Keynesian model is the fact that it is the rate of growth of autonomous demand that determines the rate of growth of output, whereas in the Keynesian model the level autonomous spending determines the level of output. In the Keynesian model it was the autonomous component of investment expenditure, and government expenditure, that determined the level of output, in the Kaldorian model it is the rate of growth of exports that determines the rate of growth of output.

The fact that the rate of growth of output depends upon the rate of growth of exports, which in turn depends on the rate of growth of foreign demand, should not be interpreted as implying that the rate of growth is the result of purely subjective decisions of foreign consumers. Kaldor (1981, 603) argues:

> The growth of a country's exports should itself be considered as the outcome of the efforts of its producers to seek out potential markets and to adapt their product structure accordingly. Basically in a growing world economy the growth of exports is mainly to be explained by the income elasticity of foreign countries for a country's products; but it is a matter of the innovative ability and adaptive capacity of its manufacturers whether this income elasticity will tend to be relatively large or small.

The fundamental idea behind the export-led model is that the balance of payments is the fundamental constraint to growth (Prebisch 1959; Taylor 1991). The relevance for trade theory resides in the fact that the Kaldorian model says that growth of output depends on the growth of demand, and the latter sometimes depends on the trade performance of the country. In these circumstances strategic trade policies—export subsidies, for example—are essential for allowing higher rates of growth of domestic output.[6] That is, managed trade is relevant not only for short-run unemployment problems, as in the Keynesian model, but also for long-run accumulation considerations.

Concluding Remarks

We have seen that under certain conditions there is a role for managed trade and finance. We conclude that Krugman's proposition that "all that undergrads need to know about the open economy is comparative advantage and the price-specie-flow mechanism" is incorrect.[7] In the world of Say's Law it might be true that free trade is mutually beneficial for the countries involved. However, that is not true once the principle of effective demand is introduced.

In addition, if capital flows, rather than the current account, dominate the developments of the BP, then there is no reason to believe that the BP is self-adjusting. This implies that the imposition of capital controls is essential for full employment policies to be sustainable. Finally, absolute advantage and cumulative causation imply that the trade performance of a country is also crucial for the rate of accumulation, and that strategic trade policies might have a positive impact on output growth. In other words, it is important for undergrads to understand that under those conditions financial regulation and trade policy are recommended.

Notes

1. The so-called Hecksher–Ohlin model, rather than the Ricardian model, is the dominant explanation of international trade. In the Hecksher–Ohlin model it is the difference in the endowments of factors of production that determines the direction of trade, while in the Ricardian model trade occurs as a result of technological differences between countries. The principle of comparative advantage is, however, an integral part of both models.

2. Strictly speaking, Ricardo accepted the quantity theory of money only in the short run, and denied the validity of the price-specie-flow adjustment mechanism, as is correctly pointed out by Marcuzzo and Rosselli (1986, 147). Yet Ricardo has been interpreted as a precursor of "monetarism" by many authors, as Krugman (1996) implies. The modern day "monetarist" doctrine, analogous to the price-specie-flow mechanism, serves along with the Hecksher-Ohlin model as the second of the two pillars of current conventional wisdom on trade.

3. This resembles the U.S. case, as the United States has had a persistent trade deficit since the early 1980s. However, the United States does not need to maintain higher rates of interest than the rest of the world. The central position of the dollar in world trade, and its role as international currency, implies that foreigners are willing to hold dollars as they are perceived to be of very low risk. Financing the U.S. trade deficit without raising interest rates depends on the willingness of foreigners to hold dollar-denominated assets.

4. The Bretton Woods agreements established the institutional structure of the international monetary system from 1944 to the early 1970s, when fixed exchange rates and strict capital controls were in place.

5. Although the demand for exports depends upon foreign income, in terms of the domestic economy, exports are part of autonomous expenditure. In fact, there is no formal need to restrict autonomous expenditure to exports, as we have seen in the Keynesian multiplier model. Kaldor's assumption is related to the British experience, and might be also relevant for several East Asian countries. In many countries, however, it is the domestic components of autonomous demand that drive the accumulation process. Moreover, global increases in effective demand ultimately depend on worldwide *domestic* market expansion, as all countries cannot be exporters. Pivetti (1992) shows that for the United States, military spending was a crucial variable for the expansion of demand.

6. Stimulating domestic demand is an alternative to increasing exports. In that case, increasing domestic demand by raising wages and supporting labor rights becomes an essential aspect of development. Other policies that foster and protect domestic industries, in addition to subsidies to export industries, would also be part of the solution. For a defense of the introduction of tariffs in the UK, see Cripps and Godley (1978).

7. Interestingly enough Krugman has been one of the main authors in the development of the strategic trade policy literature within the mainstream of the profession.

References

Baumol, William J., and Alan S. Blinder. 1985. *Economics: Principles and Policy*. 3d ed. New York: Harcourt Brace.

Brewer, A. 1985. "Trade with Fixed Real Wages and Mobile Capital." *Journal of International Economics* 18: 177–186.

Cripps, F., and W. Godley. 1978. "Control of Imports as a Means to Full Employment and the Expansion of World Trade." *Cambridge Journal of Economics* 2: 327–324.

Dixon, J., and A. Thirlwall. 1975. "A Model of Regional Growth Rate Differences on Kaldorian Lines." *Oxford Economics Papers* (July).

Eatwell, J. 1996. "International Capital Liberalization: The Record." CEPA/New School for Social Research, working paper no. 1.

Hume, D. 1752. "Of the Balance of Trade." In *International Finance: Selected Readings*, ed. R.N. Cooper. Harmondsworth: Penguin, 1969.

Kaldor, N. 1970. "The Case for Regional Policies." *Scottish Journal of Political Economy* (November).

———. 1981. "The Role of Increasing Returns, Technical Progress and Cumulative Causation in the Theory of International Trade and Economic Growth," *Économie Appliquée* 34, no. 4.

Kalecki, M. 1971. *Selected Essays on the Dynamics of the Capitalist Economy*. Cambridge: Cambridge University Press.

Keynes, J. 1936. *The General Theory of Employment, Interest and Money*. Reprint, New York: Harcourt Brace, 1964.

———. 1971–1982. *The Collected Writings of John Maynard Keynes*. London and Cambridge: Macmillan and Cambridge University Press.

Krugman, P. 1996. "What Do Undergrads Need to Know About Trade?" Reprint in *Pop Internationalism*. Cambridge: MIT Press.

Marcuzzo, M.C., and A. Rosselli. 1986. *Ricardo and the Gold Standard*. New York: St. Martin's Press.

Myint, H. 1958. "The Classical Theory of International Trade and the Underdeveloped Countries." *Economic Journal* 68.

Myrdal, G. 1957. *Economic Theory and Underdeveloped Regions*. London: Duckworth.

Pivetti, M. 1992. "Military Spending as a Burden on Growth: An 'Underconsumptionist' Critique." *Cambridge Journal of Economics* 16: 375–384.

Prebisch, R. 1959. "Commercial Policy in the Underdeveloped Countries." *American Economic Review* (May).

Ricardo, D. 1817. *On the Principles of Political Economy and Taxation*, ed. Piero Sraffa, with the collaboration of Maurice Dobb. Cambridge: Cambridge University Press.

Taylor, L. 1991. *Income Distribution, Inflation and Growth*. Cambridge: MIT Press.

22

The Rate of Profit in the Postwar Mexican Economy, 1950–1993

Abelardo Mariña and Fred Moseley

According to Marxian theory, the performance of capitalist economies depends above all else on the rate of profit. The purpose of this chapter is to derive estimates of the rate of profit and its Marxian determinants in the Mexican economy during the post–World War II period in order to determine the trends in these key variables. The specific questions addressed are: Was there a significant decline in the rate of profit during the period of expansion and prosperity from the 1950s to the 1970s? Has there been a significant increase in the rate of profit since the 1970s? What have been the main causes of these trends, according to Marxian theory? What are the likely future trends of the rate of profit and its Marxian determinants in the years ahead? The answer to this last question will determine to a large extent the possibility of a full and lasting recovery from the deep current economic crisis. Furthermore, our estimates for the Mexican economy will be compared with similar estimates for the U.S. economy, which should provide insights into the similarities and differences in the absolute levels and the trends in these variables between advanced and (large, important) developing countries.

Section 1 of this chapter discusses the conceptual issues involved in the estimation of the rate of profit and its Marxian determinants. Section 2 presents the Marxian analytical framework used in our empirical analysis. Section 3 presents our estimates of the rate of profit and its Marxian determinants in the postwar Mexican economy. Finally, Section 4 summarizes the main conclusions and implications of our analysis.

1. Conceptual Issues

There are several important conceptual issues involved in the estimation of the Marxian variables of constant capital, variable capital, unproductive capital, and surplus-value. How precisely are these Marxian variables defined, and how should they be estimated? This section very briefly presents our interpretation of these conceptual issues. Our interpretation is presented more fully in Moseley (1992, ch. 2).

Money vs. Labor-Time

The issue here is whether the Marxian concepts refer to observable quantities of money-capital or to observable quantities of labor-time. We argue that the Marxian concepts refer to observable quantities of money-capital. Constant capital, variable capital, and surplus-value are components of capital, and therefore the definitions of these components follow from the more general concept of capital. Marx defined the general concept of capital in chapter 4 of Volume 1 of *Capital* as *money* that is invested in order to make *more money*, which Marx expressed symbolically as M - C - M′, where M′ = M + ΔM. The initial money-capital M consists of two components: constant capital invested to purchase the means of production and variable capital invested to purchase labor-power. Surplus-value is the increment of money M that emerges from the circulation of capital. In principle, these concepts correspond to cost and revenue entries in the financial accounts of capitalist firms. Foley (1986) also emphasizes that the Marxian concepts of capital and its components correspond to the money magnitudes in the accounts of capitalist firms.

Noncapitalist Production

We also argue that these Marxian concepts refer only to capitalist production, and do not refer to noncapitalist forms of production, such as government production, household production, and self-employed production. Self-employed production is especially important in developing countries like Mexico, especially in agriculture. However, the income of self-employed producers, like the income of government employees and household employees, is not capital, and hence is not variable capital or surplus-value. The sums of money used to purchase means of production and labor-power in government and household production are not capital because these sums of money are not later recovered, together with an increment of money, through the sale of commodities. Similarly, the income of self-employed producers is not variable capital because these self-employed producers are not wage-laborers; and their income is also not surplus-value because this income is generated by their own labor, not by the labor of others.

Productive Labor and Unproductive Labor[1]

We also argue that the Marxian concepts of constant capital and variable capital refer only to the capital invested in *production activities* (where "production" is defined fairly broadly to include such activities as transportation and storage), and do not include the capital invested in the following two types of activities within capitalist enterprises:

1. *Circulation activities* related to the exchange of commodities and money, including such functions as sales, purchasing, accounting, check processing, advertising, debt/credit relations, insurance, warranties, legal counsel, securities exchange, and so on.
2. *Supervisory activities* related to the control and surveillance of the labor of production workers, including such functions as the transmission of orders, the direct supervision of production workers, the supervision of supervisors and so forth, up to top management, the creation and processing of production and payroll records for individuals and groups of employees, and so on.

Capital must of course be invested in both material and labor to carry out the unproductive functions of circulation and supervision, but according to Marx's theory, this capital nonetheless does not result in the production of value and surplus-value. For this reason, Marx referred to the capital invested in these unproductive functions as "unproductive capital." Since this unproductive capital produces no value, it cannot be recovered out of value it produces. Instead, according to Marx's theory, this unproductive capital is recovered out of the surplus-value produced by productive labor employed in capitalist production.

Marx's concepts of productive capital and unproductive capital are parallel to his more widely discussed concepts of productive labor and unproductive labor. Productive labor is labor employed in capitalist production that produces value and surplus-value. Unproductive labor is labor employed in the unproductive functions of circulation and supervision within capitalist enterprises.[2]

2. Analytical Framework[3]

The rate of profit being analyzed here is the so-called "conventional rate of profit," which is the ratio of the amount of profit (P) to the total stock of capital invested (K).[4] According to Marx's theory, profit (the numerator in the conventional rate of profit) is equal to the difference between the annual flow of surplus-value (S) and the annual flow of unproductive costs (U_f), which consists of the wages of unproductive labor (U_w) and the costs of unproductive materials (U_m):

$$P = S - U_f \tag{1}$$

Similarly, according to Marx's theory, the stock of capital, the denominator in the rate of profit, is divided into two components: constant capital (C) (the capital invested in the means of production) and the stock of capital invested in unproductive functions (U_s)[5]:

$$K = C - U_s \tag{2}$$

However, in our estimates we have not yet been able to distinguish between constant capital and the stock of unproductive capital, so this decomposition is not made thus far in our analysis.[6]

We may then obtain the Marxian equation for the conventional rate of profit:

$$RP = \frac{P}{K} = \frac{S - U_f}{K} \tag{3}$$

Finally, we divide all terms on the right hand side of equation (3) by the annual flow of variable capital (V), the capital invested in labor-power, which is the "source" of surplus-value according to Marx's theory, and we obtain:

$$RP = \frac{S/V - U_f/V}{K/V} = \frac{RS - UV}{CC} \tag{4}$$

From equation (4), we can see that, according to Marx's theory, the conventional rate of profit varies directly with the rate of surplus-value (RS) (the ratio of surplus-value to variable capital) and varies inversely with the composition of capital (CC) (the ratio of the total capital invested to variable capital) and the ratio of the flow of unproductive capital to variable capital (UV). (It should be noted that, rigorously speaking, the composition of capital is the ratio of constant capital only to variable capital and not the ratio of the total stock of capital to variable capital. However, since we are not yet able to distinguish between constant capital and the stock of unproductive capital, we will use the ratio K/V as a rough approximation of the composition of capital.)

3. Analysis of Estimates

This section discusses our estimates of the rate of profit and its Marxian determinants. These estimates are presented in Table 22.1.

Rate of Surplus-Value

Our estimates of the rate of surplus-value break down sharply into two distinct periods: (1) the first twenty-five years until 1976, and (2) the remainder of the period of study until 1993. In the first period, the rate of surplus-value declined 28 percent overall, at an average annual rate of 0.6 percent.

This declining trend is in contrast to a rising rate of surplus-value in the U.S. economy (and in most other advanced countries) during this same period.

Table 22.1

The Rate of Profit and Its Determinants, 1950–1993

Year	Rate of Surplus Value (S/V)	Unprof. Capital/ Var. Capital (U/V)	Composition of Capital (K/V)	Rate of Profit (P/K)
1950	4.9	0.8	10.8	0.37
1951	5.6	0.9	11.6	0.41
1952	5.2	0.9	11.9	0.36
1953	4.9	0.9	12.0	0.33
1954	4.6	0.9	12.0	0.31
1955	5.1	0.9	12.6	0.33
1956	5.2	1.0	13.6	0.31
1957	5.2	1.0	13.8	0.31
1958	4.8	1.0	13.1	0.30
1959	5.0	1.0	13.2	0.30
1960	4.8	1.0	12.3	0.30
1961	4.8	1.1	12.2	0.31
1962	4.7	1.0	11.7	0.32
1963	4.6	1.0	11.6	0.31
1964	4.5	1.0	10.7	0.33
1965	4.4	1.0	10.6	0.32
1966	4.3	1.0	10.1	0.33
1967	4.3	1.0	10.1	0.33
1968*				
1969*				
1970	4.2	1.2	10.6	0.29
1971	4.4	1.2	10.1	0.32
1972	4.2	1.1	9.7	0.32
1973	4.3	1.1	9.5	0.34
1974	4.3	1.1	9.9	0.32
1975	4.0	1.1	9.9	0.29
1976	3.7	1.1	10.0	0.26
1977	4.0	1.1	11.1	0.26
1978	4.2	1.1	11.3	0.27
1979	4.3	1.2	11.3	0.28
1980	4.8	1.3	11.9	0.30
1981	4.5	1.3	11.3	0.29
1982	5.0	1.4	15.0	0.24
1983	6.3	1.5	19.2	0.25
1984	6.8	1.6	19.8	0.26
1985	6.7	1.5	20.7	0.25
1986	6.5	1.6	23.9	0.20
1987	7.4	1.7	24.8	0.23
1988	7.8	1.8	25.1	0.24
1989	8.0	1.9	24.0	0.26
1990	8.3	1.9	23.8	0.27
1991	8.1	1.9	23.8	0.26
1992	7.8	1.9	23.7	0.25
1993	7.6	2.0	24.7	0.23

*Estimates for 1968 and 1969 are missing because there are no national income accounts for the Mexican cross over for these years.

(For the U.S. estimates, see Moseley, this volume.) It is also in contrast to the general conclusion of Marx's theory of a rising rate of surplus-value. According to Marx's theory, the rate of surplus-value should rise mainly as a result of technological change, which increases the productivity of labor faster than the real wage of workers, which in turn reduces necessary labor time and increases surplus labor time (i.e., the process of relative surplus-value). It appears that this process of relative surplus-value was not operating very strongly during the early postwar period in the Mexican economy, and it seems to have slowed down in the 1960s and early 1970s. This may have been due to a combination of: (1) rapid increase of real wages, and (2) slower productivity growth in the wage-goods sector, especially in agriculture.

In the second period after 1976, the rate of surplus-value first increased slowly from 1976 to 1982 and thereafter increased very rapidly (average annual rate of 1.6 percent), so that from 1976 to 1993 the rate of surplus-value more than doubled and in 1993 was approximately 50 percent higher than in 1950. This rapidly rising rate of surplus-value was primarily the result of a drastic reduction of real wages during this period (at least 50 percent). Productivity growth was even slower in the second period than in the first, but, given the decline of real wages, whatever productivity growth that occurred also contributed to the increasing rate of surplus-value.

Another striking feature of these estimates of the rate of surplus-value is their very high absolute level. In comparison to the United States, the rate of surplus-value in Mexico is two to three times higher. This result also seems to be contrary to Marx's general expectation that the rate of surplus-value would be higher in more developed countries (because capitalist development would result in a rising rate of surplus-value).

The explanation of this contrary result might be that Marx's analysis in *Capital* is at a very high level of abstraction and does not take into account many concrete factors, including interactions between different national economies in the global economy. One such concrete feature of this interaction appears to be that advanced technology is imported into developing countries, which reduces the productivity gap between advanced and developing countries. However, the gap in real wages remains more or less the same because of a very large relative surplus population in these developing countries that are still going through the process of "primitive accumulation" (i.e., the expropriation of peasants from the land). The result of this combination is that the rate of surplus-value is higher in developing countries.

The Ratio of Unproductive Capital to Variable Capital

Our estimates of the ratio UV (the flow of unproductive capital to variable capital) also showed different trends in the two periods before and after 1976, although not as different as the rate of surplus-value. In the initial period, this ratio increased slowly (average annual rate, 0.3 percent) and approximately 18 percent overall. In the second period, this ratio increased much more rapidly (average annual rate, 1.7 percent) and 86 percent overall. According to Marxian theory, this increase in the ratio UV had a negative effect on the rate of profit and at least partially offset the positive effect of the increase in the rate of surplus-value on the rate of profit.

Composition of Capital

As discussed above, our estimates of the composition of capital are not rigorously correct because the stock of capital in the numerator is the *total* stock of capital, including the stock of unproductive capital, and not just the stock of constant capital. Nonetheless, our estimates of the "composition of capital" are very interesting and, we think, a decent first approximation of the true composition of capital. We hope eventually to be able to distinguish between the stocks of productive and unproductive capital and to refine our analysis accordingly.

Our estimates of the "composition of capital" also have very different trends in the two periods discussed above. In the first period up until 1976, the composition of capital declined slightly (9 percent overall). By contrast, in the second period, the composition of capital increased very rapidly (average annual rate of 3 percent) and roughly 150 percent overall.

These trends also appear to contradict Marx's expectations that the composition of capital would increase during periods of expansion (such as our first period) and decrease during periods of crisis (such as our second period), due to bankruptcies and the devaluation of capital. These contradictory trends in the postwar Mexican economy appear to be due in large part to trends in the exchange rate of the peso. During the first period, a fixed exchange rate was maintained by the Mexican government, which, due to the higher Mexican rates of inflation, resulted in an overvalued peso and a decline in the relative price of imported goods. During this period, Mexico imported almost all of its machinery and equipment (and still does so today). Therefore, the overvalued peso significantly reduced the constant capital invested in these means of production. We can get some idea of the extent of this reduction of constant capital due to the overvalued peso from the first devaluation of the peso that occurred in 1976. This first devaluation of the peso was about 50 percent. This suggests that in the mid-1970s the prices of the imported means of production in Mexico had been only about half of their real world market levels. If constant capital were somehow calculated instead at the world market prices of these means of production, then the composition of capital would surely have increased significantly during this period, more consistent with Marx's general theory.

Furthermore, there are reasons to believe that our estimates of constant capital may significantly underestimate the increase of the stock of constant capital during this first period. If there is such a downward bias in our estimates of constant capital, then there would be a similar downward bias in the trend of our estimates of the composition of capital, such that corrected estimates would not decrease and would even increase significantly during this period, more consistent with Marx's theory. Preliminary alternative estimates of the composition of capital increased approximately 35 percent, rather than declining 9 percent, as in our estimates.

After the beginning of the crisis in 1976, and especially after 1982, the peso was devalued tremendously (over 10,000 percent!). This extreme devaluation greatly increased the price of imported machinery and equipment, and Mexico continued to import almost all of these capital goods. This combination of dependence on foreign capital goods and extreme devaluation greatly increased the price of capital goods and hence the constant capital necessary to maintain and expand production in the Mexican economy. The further implications of this extremely rapid increase in the composition of capital since 1980 will be examined in the next subsection.

Rate of Profit

Finally, our estimates of the rate of profit declined approximately 30 percent in the first of our two subperiods. This significant decline in the rate of profit would appear to be one of the important causes of the severe crisis in the Mexican economy of the last two decades, as emphasized by previous authors.

This decline in the rate of profit itself appears to have been due almost entirely to a roughly proportional reduction in the rate of surplus-value. During this period, the small negative effect of the slight increase in the ratio UF was offset by a roughly equal positive effect of the small decrease in the composition of capital. Therefore, it appears from these estimates that the rate of profit in the postwar Mexican economy declined, not because of an increase in the composition of capital, as emphasized by Marx, but rather due to a decline in the rate of surplus-value, as emphasized by the "profit squeeze" interpretation of Marx's theory.

However, we mentioned above that there may be an downward bias in our estimates of the stock of capital. If the alternative estimates of the capital stock mentioned above were used to estimate the rate of profit, then the rate of profit would decrease almost twice as much as our estimates during this first period (54 percent compared to 30 percent), and this greater decline in the rate of profit would be due in part to a 35 percent increase in the composition of capital, which is more consistent with Marx's theory.

In the second period (the period of crisis), it is most striking that the rate of profit has not increased. To the contrary, the rate of profit has continued to decline, although at a slower rate (12 percent overall). This is perhaps the most important finding of our study. It is very surprising, given the fact that real wages have been cut in half and the rate of surplus-value has more than doubled during this second period of crisis. It appears that the strong positive effect on the rate of profit of this very significant increase in the rate of surplus-value has been more than offset by the significant increase in the ratio UV and even more so by the significant increase in the composition of capital. The overvalued peso in the first period kept constant capital artificially low, but when the correction occurred in the second period, constant capital adjusted quickly to world market levels and increased very rapidly.

This continued decline in the rate of profit in the Mexican economy over the last two decades appears to be at least part of the explanation of why the Mexican economy has not yet recovered from its current crisis. A recovery from capitalist crises requires, above all else, a recovery of the rate of profit, and this recovery of the rate of profit has not yet occurred in the Mexican economy. In the United States, the rate of profit in the last two decades has not fully recovered, but it has at least increased and recovered about one-third of the prior decline. In Mexico, by contrast, the rate of profit has continued to decline.

4. Conclusion

The main conclusions of this Marxian empirical analysis of the rate of profit in the postwar Mexican economy has shown that: (1) the rate of profit declined significantly until the mid-1970s (at least 30 percent); (2) the rate of profit has not increased significantly since the mid-1970s, in spite of a 50 percent reduction of real wages (indeed, the rate of profit has even declined slightly over this more recent period); and (3) the main reason for this very surprising lack of an increase in the rate of profit is that the composition of capital increased very rapidly during this period, primarily as a result of the sharp devaluation of the peso. Since Mexico imports almost all of its capital goods, the sharp devaluation of the peso greatly increased the cost of capital goods, which in turn increased the composition of capital and depressed the rate of profit. A more rapid increase of unproductive labor has also contributed to the absence of an increase in the rate of profit over this recent period.

This analysis has uncovered an important new variable in Marxian crisis theory—the *exchange rate* of a nation's currency. Marx himself noted in several places the importance of exchange rates to a nation's rate of profit. Yet his general theory of the falling rate of profit was at a much higher level of abstraction and does not include exchange rates. However, it appears that exchange rates can have a significant effect on the trend of the rate of profit of particular countries in particular periods, as in the case of Mexico.

This analysis also suggests that it is unlikely that the rate of profit in Mexico will increase in the foreseeable future. The peso is likely to continue to decline in value relative to the dollar. This continuing devaluation of the peso will continue to increase the price of capital goods, increase the composition of capital, and depress the rate of profit. Wages have already been cut drastically, so further wage cuts, even if they were acceptable (which they are not), are not likely to increase the rate of profit significantly. The only way to get out of this devaluation trap is to stop the devaluation. And that does not appear to be likely any time soon.

Finally, this analysis also reveals another way in which the general strategy of "neoliberalization" (including flexible exchange rates) adopted by the Mexican government over the last decade is internally self-contradictory in a way not widely recognized before: flexible exchange rates result in the devaluation of the peso, which increases the price of imported capital goods and keeps the rate of profit low, which in turn makes a recovery of capital investment and the economy in general highly unlikely. This is another reason why the neoliberal strategy has been a failure and will continue to be a failure.

Therefore, the prospects for the Mexico economy as we move into the twenty-first century is not good. The rate of profit will probably continue to remain low, which in turn will depress business investment and economic growth in general. A small export sector, largely disconnected from the rest of the economy, may continue to prosper, but this will have little or no effect on the lives of the vast majority of Mexicans, who will continue to suffer from inadequate employment and declining living standards to even lower levels. Whether this continuing and deepening crisis will generate significant social movements in opposition to capitalism is the next question, but is beyond the scope of this chapter.

Notes

1. Marx's distinction between productive labor and unproductive labor is controversial and not accepted by all Marxian economists. Criticisms of Marx's concept of unproductive labor are discussed in Moseley (1992, Appendix to chapter 2), along with responses to these criticisms. Marx's distinction is also discussed at somewhat greater length in Fred Moseley's chapter in this volume.

2. The concept of unproductive labor was also used by Marx in the broader sense to include labor employed in noncapitalist production, or "labor employed by revenue." Adam Smith used the concept of unproductive labor to refer only to labor employed in noncapitalist production, not to labor employed in nonproduction activities within capitalist enterprises. In this chapter, the term unproductive labor refers only to the latter category of capitalist employees employed in nonproduction activities.

3. See Moseley (1992, ch. 4) for a more complete presentation of our analytical framework.

4. The "conventional" rate of profit, which is net of unproductive costs and is related to the total stock of capital invested, is different from the Marxian rate of profit, which is gross of unproductive costs and is related to the productive capital only (see Moseley 1992, ch. 3 and 4). Marx's theory of the "falling rate of profit" is in terms of the Marxian rate of profit, but the conventional rate of profit as a more direct determinant of capital accumulation, at a lower level of abstraction. "Profit" is here defined to include all forms of property income, including interest and rent. However, profit, as we define it here, does not include unproductive costs, which is different from Marx's own definition of profit.

5. Here we make the simplifying assumption that the stocks of both variable capital and the wages of unproductive labor are equal to zero. Since capitalists pay workers only after they have worked, this assumption is not far from reality.

6. It should also be noted that both the stock and the flow of constant capital are evaluated in Marx's theory in terms of the current replacement cost of the means of production, not in terms of the actual historical cost of these

means of production. In other words, constant capital is evaluated in terms of the amount of money that would have to be invested during the current period to purchase the existing means of production, not the actual amount of money spent to purchase these means of production in past periods. If the average productivity of labor in the production of the means of production increases or decreases, or if the value of money increases or decreases, then the replacement cost of the means of production will decrease or increase correspondingly, and so will the current value of the stock and flow of constant capital.

References

Foley, Duncan. 1986. *Understanding Capital.* Cambridge: Harvard University Press.

Moseley, Fred. 1992. The Falling Rate of Profit in the Postwar United States Economy. New York: St. Martin's Press.

23

Globalization, Technology, and Skill Formation in Capitalism

Cyrus Bina and Chuck Davis

Introduction

Despite more than a century of controversy, Marx's method and his labor theory of value remain vigorously relevant to the dynamics of capitalism at the threshold of the twenty-first century. Marx's approach is particularly applicable to the interface of labor process, technological change, and capital accumulation in contemporary capitalism.[1] Moreover, technological change and the accumulation of wealth hold no epochal meaning without the critical analysis of the labor process itself.

Our goal is to capitalize on the above linkage, showing that, from the standpoint of *social capital*, technological change in capitalism is none other than cheapening of labor power. And, to this end, it leads to simultaneous value formation and value destruction, particularly through "skilling" and "deskilling" of labor at the various levels of economic activity. Thus, capital accumulation and the transformation of the labor process are tied to the dynamics of global technological change in contemporary capitalism and, as such, provide the basis for a theoretically informed practice for an undivided and progressive labor movement.

We intend to explore the role of technological change and its effects on the labor process from the standpoint of social capital. This reflects the global spread of capitalist social relations and thus hegemony of social capital over wage labor everywhere. Here, capitalism is viewed as a system that unifies the world through the creation and renewal of subordination of labor by capital. The dynamics of this *universal* subordination emerge in terms of the social form of value globally. The *value form* is necessarily social, representing a moment in capitalist social relations. It is also the outcome of the primacy of social capital (whole) over the individual capital (part). Therefore, in the capitalist mode of production, where invariably the law of value operates, the parts have no *real* significance independently of the whole and, thus, appealing to "micro foundations" may have misleading methodological consequences.

We utilize Marx's notion of social capital and frame our analysis of technological change within the macroeconomic perspective; only then do we attempt to conceptualize its effects from the standpoint of individual capital. The starting point of our argument thus relies on a holistic framework that gives priority to the notion of social capital. In other words, we commence with the study of

We wish to express our appreciation to Heather Boushey for her articulate and reflective comments on the various drafts of this paper.

social structure and then bring the complexities of individual action and choice into the dynamics of technological change. Social capital encapsulates the *overall* social relations in capitalism. Social relations refer to the dynamics of capital accumulation and the characteristics of *capital in general*. The contents of these relations are historically specific to capitalism. This is distinct from the concept of *social capital* that has been utilized in other disciplines. (See the work of Putnam 1992, 167; Coleman 1988; Jacoby 1995, xi; and Fukuyama 1995, 16–17.)

Historically, capitalism has emerged as the *tendency* toward the production and accumulation of surplus value, following a multifaceted, varied, and tortuous period of "primitive accumulation." Primitive accumulation is the historical process of divorcing the producer from the means of production. "It appears as 'primitive' because it forms the prehistory of capital, and of the mode of production corresponding to capital" (Marx 1977 [1867], 874–75). The compulsion for increasing the production of surplus value through accumulation via competition requires *expanding* and *intensifying* the control and subordination of labor under capital. Yet there are physical limits to subordination as well as exploitation of labor—namely the length of the working day—that, in turn, point to the inadequacy of capitalist accumulation based upon the production of absolute surplus value.

Through steady change in technology, continuous subversion of existing skills, and formation of new skills, capitalism, as an historically specific mode of production, attempts to overcome the physical and moral limitations of the working day. The expanded reproduction of value is accomplished by transforming the realm of exploitation based upon the production of *absolute* surplus value to capitalist production proper in which the intensification of labor assumes the production of *relative* surplus value. This is an historical *transformation* that has universally changed the course of class struggle in capitalism.

Technological Change and Global Transformation

Historically, controlling the development of science and technology of production through the introduction of machinery has enabled the capitalist mode of production to engage in constant technological revolution and to *enhance* the productivity of labor by reducing the value of labor power per unit of output. This also has led to further intensification and the reassertion of capitalist control over the labor process through the cycles of production and massive waves of technological change (see Freeman 1994). With the introduction and diffusion of technological innovations, social labor productivity rises, that is to say, a given mass of living labor transforms an ever larger quantity of means of production into an output.

As a social relation, for capital to emerge as a unique global entity, it is essential that there be a global social circuit in place in its commodity, money, and productive *forms*, thus enabling it to unify the spheres of circulation and production worldwide. This has been historically accomplished through the stage-by-stage transnationalization of commodity, money, and productive capital, establishing and spreading a complete global social network of capital (Palloix 1977). This has resulted in the rise of colossal and integrated entities known as transnational corporations (TNCs), which now operate throughout the world. To be sure, today's TNCs are the cumulative outcome of the transnationalization of social capital in all its forms. Yet, while their existence is contingent upon the transnationalization of both commodity and money capitals, they have acquired a full-fledged status via transnationalization of productive capital—including the globalization of technology.

Since the process of technological change goes hand in hand with the restructuring of the labor process, in which the latter is no longer confined within the boundaries of nation states, the adequate treatment of technological innovation is simply impossible within the traditional national frameworks, particularly since TNCs are vehicles for the transfer, transmission, and diffusion of technology, and increasingly affect the locus of generation of technological innovation on a global scale (see *Cambridge Journal of Economics,* Special Issue on Technology and Innovation 1995). In an instance, they account for 75 percent of all research and development in OECD countries (Archibugi and Michie 1995, 130). The reader has to bear in mind that the emergence of the TNC is itself a subset of the dynamic forces that brought the world economy into the epoch of globalization. In other words, pointing to the movement of capital, in its manifold configuration, beyond the nation-state is indeed necessary but not sufficient for the arrival of globalization.

The sufficiency of globalization is where the entire social relations of capital—and thus *social capital*—take hold over the entire world; where the social whole completes the *conquest* of the mode of production. Moreover, this *era*, we argue, has been emerging since the early 1970s and developing throughout the 1980s and 1990s (Bina and Davis 1996). The result is the establishment of newly formed social relations with their own technological and institutional power structure, beyond the boundaries of nation-states. Globalization as a *process* has rendered obsolete the international system centered on the conceptual building blocks of nation-state and national economy.

Given the past three decades of upheaval in the world economy, the global character of capital has already transcended the framework of national boundaries. In the context of social capital's competitive attempt at cheapening of labor power, transnational capital has forced unprecedented restructuring of industrial production, shifting the location of basic industries, resulting in "captive imports," runaway shops, and outsourcing. At the present stage of global capitalism, the centerpiece of global accumulation is the unifying control of the emerging transnational labor processes, and the growing universal and unified subordination of labor by capital (Bina and Davis 1996; Bina 1997). This collectively represents the social *character* and *tendency* of global social capital and thus reflects the magnitude of global crisis in contemporary capitalism.

The present transnational labor process is prima facie a point of departure from the past. It is beyond international trade, or the simple transfer of physical capital, financial capital, or technology from location to location. This qualitative change is reflected in recognition of the universal status of labor and capital as basic global macroeconomic categories. As a result, one needs to approach complex and concrete categories, such as transnational trade, transnational capital movement, transnational development, and implementation of new technology, from those basic categories.

For instance, there is a need to examine the relationship between the evolution of capitalism in the advanced capitalist countries (ACCs) and the transformation of the less developed countries (LDCs), *beyond* the boundaries of nation-states. Attention must be directed toward the global conquest of the capitalist mode of production, not to apparent distinctions contrived by national boundaries, or symptomatic distinctions that are often put forth in terms of regional trading blocs, or the so-called center–periphery dichotomy. The geographical expansion of social capital has always been disruptive and at an *uneven* pace. For example, uneven economic development presently reveals itself both *intra*nationally and *inter*nationally among ACCs and LDCs as a result of the expansion and reproduction of social capital transnationally. An advantage of starting with the analysis of capitalist social relations rather than capital as a national, physical, or monetary entity is the recognition of the *internal* (capitalist) transformation of many Third World nations. This is occurring in conjunction with sweeping changes in labor processes within the advanced capitalist countries. The context of this conjunction is the dynamics of the world economy, especially since World War II.

First, a large number of postcolonial states have emerged from the colonial division of labor and "primitive accumulation" since World War II. Import substitution industrialization and its sequel, "export-led growth," have been the economic strategies that by and large prepared these countries to overcome their internal barriers to capitalist development. This resulted in the *internal* propagation of capitalism in many of these countries and thus paved the way for embracing the *external* penetration of transnational capital. A careful examination of post–World War II land-reform programs in the Third World would point to the massive separation of the immediate producer from the means of production globally. This resulted in an enormous supply of potential wage labor for the import substitution and, subsequently, the export-led industries in the LDCs. Here, in their twentieth-century scenario, the land-reform programs of the postwar period have led to the creation of a home market, hand in hand with the world market (Bina and Yaghmaian 1988, 1991; Yaghmaian 1989).

The transnationalization of productive capital, unlike merchant and finance capital, provides stimulus for further development of relative surplus value through direct technological change and, thereby, deepens the control and domination of labor under capital in LDCs. It also completes the global circuit of social capital and thus unifies both the spheres of circulation and production transnationally. Yet, the real subsumption of labor under capital may not obtain the status of a *sui generis* mode of production through the introduction of machinery alone. This historical task also requires the *limitation of the working day*. In other words, in the absence of the limitation of the length of the working day—through working-class struggle and the enactment of appropriate legislation—production based on machinery coexists with the production of absolute surplus value (Marx 1977 [1867], ch. 10). Here, the successive introduction of machinery can be obstructed by *elasticity* of the working day itself. Today, in many LDCs, the statutory limitation of the working day has already been accomplished. However, in these societies the length of the average working day is considerably longer than their ACC counterparts. In other LDCs, especially in the more traditional sectors, the length of the working day has yet to be socially established and politically defined. This is particularly true in those countries in which the employment of child labor is still prevalent.

Second, over time, there has emerged a series of organizational and technological transformations that have revolutionized the labor process in the advanced capitalist countries. The motivation for these changes—which have expanded and intensified the real subsumption of labor under capital—has been the expansion of surplus value production. Historically, capitalist production technologies shifted across the past two centuries first from artisanal to mechanized factory production, then from simple factories to assembly lines, and finally from assembly-line mass production to continuous and batch processes (Goldin and Katz 1996, 252). These transformations have had one purpose—to cheapen labor power, thus reducing the proportion of necessary labor time to unpaid labor time embodied in commodities. This is the underlying motivation of capitalist production whether expressed through the applications of Taylorism or self-directed work teams, the development of Fordism, neo-Fordism, or flexible and lean production systems, or the computerization of production through computer aided design/computer aided manufacture (CAD/CAM), robotics, or automation. Contemporary labor processes indeed exhibit a unified global theme capable of emerging in many divergent technical and organizational variations.

Globalization of capitalism is a phenomenon that is universally contingent upon reducing the value of labor power through revolutions in technology (see Bina and Davis 1996; Bina 1997). The consequence has been the continuous and progressive *cheapening* of labor power *everywhere* and the increasing social control and domination of labor by capital, following the *tendency* for proliferation of the most technologically advanced labor processes. Thus several decades of intense devaluation on a per unit of output basis, and displacement of workers directly affected by technological change in the advanced capitalist countries suddenly find their cumulative application and affect within the countries of the so-called Third World.

A by-product of this improvement in relative surplus value production is a massive surplus population at the global level. By 1995, the world was experiencing the worst employment crisis since the Great Depression of the 1930s. Thirty percent of the global labor force was either unemployed or underemployed, and there was growing labor market inequality (International Labor Organization 1995, 2). Social capital's global dynamic has degraded the standard of living for workers and increased wealth and income inequality. This process of global socialization and competition, in turn, requires all-embracing and unified counteractions by international labor, on par with the scope and magnitude of actions exhibited by social capital itself.

Technology, Skill Formation, and Contingent Labor

Neoclassical economists contend that as technology advances, it correspondingly creates specialized skills that are conducive to its further application. Thus, advances in technology lead to gradual upgrading of education and skills of the labor force within the economy as a whole (Jerome 1934; Woodward 1965; Griliches 1969; Fallon and Layard 1975; Greenwood and Yorukoglu 1997). In contrast, many neo-Marxian economists argue that technological change in capitalism leads to constant deskilling of the labor force, thus resulting in deskilling and the "polarization" of workers' skills (Braverman 1974, ch. 20). Consequently, the subject of skill formation and skill redundancy has long been a point of contention between these two schools of economic thought.

Here, based on Bina's hypothesis of "destructive creation," we maintain that neither of the above positions reflects the true nature of technological change; and they bear no relation to the actual formation and/or redundancy of skills in modern capitalism (Bina 1997; Bina et al. 1998, 1999). Accordingly, an alternative theory of technological change in capitalism is one of schizophrenia, leading to extrinsic skilling and deskilling of the labor force through the magical wand of capital.[2] "Destructive creation," reverses the order and direction of the structural causation of capital from destruction for the sake of creation, á la Schumpeter, to creation for the sake of destruction. Schumpeter's concept of "creative destruction," however, provides us with a significant insight into the dynamics of chaotic production in capitalism.

Schumpeter placed the dynamics of technological change *within* the core of production and reproduction of capital in its organic unity and contradiction. Yet he did not recognize that the pattern of technological change in advanced capitalism is not one of "creative destruction" but, indeed, "destructive creation." In other words, he missed the crucial point that any attempt at creation in capitalism is *simultaneously* destined for destruction. This, for instance, has been historically proven by simultaneous skilling and deskilling of labor (technical, mental, and manual) as a subset of larger effects of technological change, having to do with the continuous restructuring of social capital.

Contrary to the *intrinsic* and, thus, self-contained characteristic of skills prevailing in all precapitalist modes of production, "skill formation" in capitalism depends upon satisfaction of *necessary* and *sufficient* conditions that must be confirmed by the process of capital accumulation.[3] Necessary conditions for skill formation consist of ability, knowledge, and appropriate training in order to perform particular tasks associated with a particular position. This represents the *use value* of skills. On the other hand, the sufficient condition for skill formation in modern capitalism is through the process of capitalist competition and coercive action of capitalist *control* (see Marglin 1974). This sufficient condition translates into the *exchange value* of skills in the marketplace. Competition among the capitalists forces the advancement and adoption of new technology and, accordingly, leads to redundancy of the existing skills (technical, manual, and/or mental) on the part of workers.[4]

At the same time, the advance of technology creates new skills of *its own*, which, in turn, replaces present workers and/or their skills by new ones. Workers may have a choice in the acquisition of their knowledge and training in order to satisfy the necessary conditions that would authenticate the use value of their skills. Yet they have *no* control over sufficient, and *extrinsic*, conditions associated with the newly demanded skills corresponding with changing technology. This control belongs *exclusively* to capital. Here, capitalist control and competitive transformation of technology simply set the stage for the validation (or invalidation) of sufficient conditions for the formation of new skills. In short, interfirm competition, on the one hand, and intrafirm control of capital, on the other hand, define the meaning of both skilling and deskilling of the labor force in modern capitalism.[5] The fundamental consequence is the *tendency* toward universal contingency of labor, a widespread and critical contingency, regardless of basic education and training, at every level of economic activity. Moreover, viewing worldwide capitalist dynamics, in terms of the above framework, has far-reaching effects on the significance of "the reserve army of unemployed [and underemployed]," which indeed must be alarming for economic policymaking and crisis management in the complex, intertwined, and uncertain world of today.

Parallel with the phenomenon of *instant* deskilling, there is also *instant* devaluation of productive and commodity capitals affected by the "destructive creation" of capitalist technology. Such devaluation bears no relationship with the actual depreciation of capital or even "moral" depreciation of capital in the sense of Marx (1977 [1867], 528). It is destruction at inception. For instance, the value of an entire warehouse full of newly arrived computers can be reduced to a tiny fraction by simply a public announcement pertaining to the future arrival of a newer machine whose technological base has already been known prior to the newly arrived commodities. Clearly, this is not the case of destruction of the old based upon Schumpeter's creative destruction. It is rather a universal attempt at destructive creation.

Thus far, we have established how technological change evolves at the level of interaction among individual capitals. However, having argued at the outset that technological change is of macro character, both interfirm competition and intrafirm control have their roots within social capital. The most significant characteristic of social capital is the continuous cheapening of labor power. This emerges constantly through technological change within the entire mode of production globally. In other words, the macroeconomic role of technological change corresponds to a worldwide, continuous skilling and deskilling of the labor force. Here, competition among individual capitals is inherent in competition associated with social capital. By the same token, the nature of technological change at the level of individual capital is inherent in cheapening of labor power across the board. Consequently, *destructive creation* rather than creative destruction explicates the mechanism and pattern of technological change in contemporary capitalism.

Toward Labor's Revitalization

The global evolution of the capital/labor relation has a profound influence upon the nature of universal class struggle. Labor globally has been constantly weakened through the transnationalization of the labor process and the cheapening of labor power throughout the world, especially during the past three decades. While individual capital moves to restore profitability, social capital, as a whole, manifests its universal characteristics through the proliferation of social relations and competition for labor power worldwide. Capitalist competition continuously pits worker against worker, attempting to drive wages, conditions of work, and the quality of life to the lowest level possible—locally, nationally, regionally, and transnationally. In combating the extraction of surplus value, workers often conduct economic and, in many cases, political struggles to regulate and improve the terms and conditions under which they are obliged to dispose of their labor power.

By transcending social capital's competition for labor power, the expression of working-class unity and struggle limits the ability of capital to cheapen the value of labor power. In concrete historical terms, this counters capital's demand for increased social control and domination of the labor process. The transnationalization of capitalist relations, that is, a universal tendency toward *real* subsumption of labor under capital, brings the common interests of workers in many different countries into sharper focus. Workers are commonly affected by the global integration of labor processes and markets. This elevates the *objective* conditions for labor solidarity to a common international level. On an international basis, workers are integrated into an all-embracing new relationship. If workers gain the ability to confront transnational capital with their own international organizations, they can begin to mitigate the deleterious effects of capital's mobility. However, the organizational capacity for the development of working-class consciousness at the national and global levels has yet to be realized.

Today, the continuing globalization of the labor process has provided the material conditions for the unity of workers across the seemingly insurmountable boundaries of nation-states. The fundamental basis of this dynamic process is the global accumulation of capital in the presence of divided global space among nation-states, and the *objective* conditions for working-class unity—based on local struggles that can no longer remain isolated from the global center stage. While there is a growing objective basis for working-class unity worldwide, there are also countertendencies associated with the nature of social capital itself. For instance, global technological change and intensification of the labor process are frequently tied to the creation and proliferation of contingent labor markets, and the imposition of divide and rule strategy by social capital.

In conjunction with the telecommunications revolution, semiconductor technology grants a new outlook to the spatial control of capital over the global labor process. As Shaiken depicts, "Once the machining knowledge is embodied in the numerical control program, it becomes possible to transfer production from a struck plant to shops that are still working, regardless of whether they are across the street or halfway around the world" (1986, 260). The broadened echo of this transformation can be found in *Cutting Edge* (Davis et al. 1997) as well. Capitalism exhibits a universal tendency to play off one group of workers against another—in an accelerating process of competition between and within the active and reserve armies of workers worldwide, thus aiming to suppress the living standards of workers internationally to the lowest level possible. Additionally, there is a remaining residue of traditional appeal to nationalism among workers and unions. For labor movements to succeed rudimentarily along economic and political lines, they must shed their historic roles as being copiously *national* and *nationalistic* in structure and orientation. Hence there is no *automatic* remedy for unification of the workers' struggles at the global level, for the *necessity* of material conditions must meet the *sufficiency* of conscious activities of workers as a *universal* class. This, of course, precludes any predetermined and general conclusions on the future transformation of the global labor movement.

Notes

1. In Marxian tradition, confusion between formation of value and value accounting has led to some protagonists placing the realm of purposeful human activity and the outcome of such an activity on an equal footing, thus ignoring the source of value in the dynamics of accumulation. See, for instance, Steedman (1981a), Steedman (1981b), Mandel and Freeman (1984), and Fine (1986).

2. The analogy of schizophrenia, devised by one of the authors, refers to the periodic debasement (and crisis) of the existing labor process through the intense internal self-negation of capital. Here, the seditious voice of *change* in technology resembles the incoherent brain signal of a schizophrenic patient who is at the mercy of *fractured* perception of internal emotions and external reality.

3. Under the authority of the guild system the acquisition of skills, the nature of apprenticeship and the skill's intrinsic value for members were protected during an individual's lifetime. A cobbler was a cobbler and would remain a cobbler in this system.

4. During the last two decades or so, there has emerged an articulate literature on the dynamics of Marxian competition in capitalism. The reader is referred to some of the contributions, such as Clifton (1977), Shaikh (1980), Weeks (1981, Ch. 6), Semmler (1984), Bina (1985, Ch. 6), Bina (1989), Dumenil and Levy (1987), Glick and Ehrbar (1990), and Botwinick (1993).

5. Marx, neither in *Capital* nor elsewhere, has ever presented a unified skilling and deskilling theory based on his own method of analysis. To be sure, all his arguments in both *Capital* and *Grundrisse* rotate around the question of deskilling in capitalism. This is contrary to his own method, as the creation and/or destruction of skills are all socially constructed processes subject to the internal dynamics of social capital rather than an arbitrary view of skills. Hence, Marx's theory of skills remains an incomplete theory and, as such, has sadly become the object of crude and misleading interpretation by the neo-Marxian scholars since the publication of Braverman (1974).

Bibliography

Archibugi, D., and J. Michie. 1995. "The Globalization of Technology: A New Taxonomy." *Cambridge Journal of Economics* 19, no. 1: 121–140.

Bina, C. 1985. *The Economics of the Oil Crisis*. New York: St. Martin's Press.

———. 1989. "Competition, Control, and Price Formation in the International Energy Industry." *Energy Economics* 11, no. 3: 162–168.

———. 1997. "Globalization: The Epochal Imperatives and Developmental Tendencies." In *Political Economy of Globalization*, ed. D. Gupta, 41–58. Boston: Glewer Academic Press.

Bina, C., and B. Yaghmaian. 1988. "Import Substitution and Export Promotion within the Context of the Internationalization of Capital." *Review of Radical Political Economics* 20, no. 2 & 3: 234–240.

Bina, C., and B. Yaghmaian. 1991. "Postwar Global Accumulation and the Transnationalization of Capital." *Capital and Class* 43: 107–130.

Bina, C., and C. Davis. 1996. "Wage Labor and Global Capital: Global Competition and the Universalization of the Labor Movement." In *Beyond Survival: Wage Labor in the Late Twentieth Century*, ed. C. Bina, L. Clements, and C. Davis, 19–47. Armonk, NY: M.E. Sharpe.

Bina, C., R. Azari, and H. Falatoon. 1998. "Technological Change: Conventional Wisdom and Critical Assessment." *Proceedings of Western Decision Sciences Institute* 27th Annual Meeting, Reno, Nevada, 276–278.

Bina, C., H. Falatoon, and R. Azari. 1999. "Technological Change: Global Competition and Skilling/De-skilling of Labor." *Proceedings of Western Decision Science Institute* 28th Annual Meeting, Puerto Vallarta, Mexico, 321–27.

Botwinick, H. 1993. *Persistent Inequalities: Wage Disparity under Capitalist* Competition. Princeton: Princeton University Press.

Braverman, H. 1974. *Labor and Monopoly Capital*. New York: Monthly Review Press.

Cambridge Journal of Economics. 1995. Special Issue on Technology and Innovation 19, no. 1: 1–243.

Clifton, J.A. 1977. "Competition and the Evolution of the Capitalist Mode of Production." *Cambridge Journal of Economics* 1, no. 2: 137–152.

Coleman, J.S. 1988. "Social Capital in the Creation of Human Capital." *American Journal of Sociology* 94: 95–120.

Davis, J., T.A. Hirschl, and M. Stack. eds. 1997. *Cutting Edge: Technology, Information, Capitalism, and Social Revolution*. New York: Verso.

Dow, S.C. 1997. "Critical Survey: Mainstream Economic Methodology." *Cambridge Journal of Economics* 21, no. 1: 73–93.

Dumenil, G., and D. Levy. 1987. "The Dynamics of Competition: A Restoration of the Classical Analysis." *Cambridge Journal of Economics* 11, no. 2: 133–164.

Fallon, P.R., and P.R.G. Layard. 1975. "Capital-Skill Complementarity, Income Distribution, and Output Accounting." *Journal of Political Economy* 83: 279–301.

Fine, B. 1982. *Theories of the Capitalist Economy*. New York: Holmes & Meier.

———, ed. 1986. *The Value Dimension: Marx versus Ricardo and Sraffa*. New York: Routledge & Kegan Paul.

Freeman, C. 1994. "Critical Survey: The Economics of Technical Change." *Cambridge Journal of Economics* 18, no. 5: 463–514.

Fukuyama, F. 1995. *Trust: The Social Virtues and the Creation of Prosperity*. New York: Free Press.

Glick, M., and H. Ehrbar. 1990. "Long-Run Equilibrium in the Empirical Study of Monopoly and Competition." *Economic Inquiry* 28: 151–162.

Goldin, C., and L.F. Katz. 1996. "Technology, Skill, and the Wage Structure: Insights from the Past." *American Economic Review* 86, no. 2: 252–257.

Greenwood, J., and M. Yorukoglu. 1997. "1974." *Carnegie-Rochester Conference Series on Public Policy* 46: 49–95.

Griliches, Z. 1969. "Capital-Skill Complementarity." *Review of Economics and Statistics* 51: 465–468.

International Labor Organization (ILO). 1995. *Washington Focus*. (Winter).

Jacoby, S.M., ed. 1995. *The Worker of Nations: Industrial Relations in a Global Economy*. New York: Oxford University Press.

Jerome, H. 1934. *Mechanization in Industry*. New York: National Bureau of Economic Research.

Kula, W. 1976 [1962]. *An Economic Theory of the Feudal System*. London: Verso.

Landes, D. 1969. *The Unbound Prometheus: Technological Change and Industrial Development in Western Europe from 1750 to the Present*. Cambridge: Cambridge University Press.

Mandel, E., and A. Freeman. 1984. *Ricardo, Marx, Sraffa: The Langston Memorial Volume*. London: Verso.

Marglin, S.A. 1974. "What Do Bosses Do?: The Origins and Functions of Hierarchy in Capitalist Production." *Review of Radical Political Economics* 6: 60–112.

Marx, K. 1973. *Grundrisse*. New York: Vintage Edition.

———. 1977 [1867]. *Capital*. Vol. 1. New York: Vintage Edition.

Monthly Review. 1976. Special Issue: Technology, the Labor Process, and the Working Class. 28, no. 3: 1–128.

Palloix, C. 1977. "The Self-Expansion of Capital on a World Scale." *Review of Radical Political Economics* 9, no. 2: 1–28.

Putnam, R.D. 1992. *Making Democracy Work: Civic Traditions in Modern Italy*. Princeton: Princeton University Press.

Schumpeter, J.A. 1942. *Capitalism, Socialism and Democracy*. New York; Harper & Row.

Semmler, W. 1984. *Competition, Monopoly, and Differential Profit Rates*. New York: Columbia University Press.

Shaiken, H. 1986. *Work Transformed: Automation and Labor in the Computer Age*. Lexington, MA: Lexington Books.

Shaikh, A. 1980. "Marxian Competition versus Perfect Competition: Further Comments on the So-called Choice of Techniques." *Cambridge Journal of Economics* 4, no. 1: 75–83.

Steedman, I. 1981a. *Marx After Sraffa*. London: Verso.

______, ed. 1981b. *The Value Controversy*. London: Verso.

Weeks, J. 1981. *Capital and Exploitation*. Princeton: Princeton University Press.

Woodward, J. 1965. *Industrial Organization: Theory and Practice*. London: Macmillan.

Yaghmaian, B. 1989. "Development Theories and Development Strategies." *Review of Radical Political Economics* 22, no. 2 and 3.

24

Capitalism and Industrialization in the Third World

Recognizing the Costs and Imagining Alternatives

David F. Ruccio

Introduction: The Irony of Free Market Ideology

The industrialization that has been achieved in the Third World during the postwar period has occurred largely under the aegis of extensive state involvement in the economy. Now, however, the situation has changed: more free markets (and less state involvement) are trumpeted as the appropriate environment for new forms and higher levels of industrialization. What are the prospects for this new industrialization? Can it be successful? Is there space within the global capitalist environment for the Third World—or the Fourth or Fifth Worlds—to industrialize? If not, is there an alternative?

It is, of course, ironic that the idea of free markets—together with privatization, deregulation, and so on—has acquired such prominence at this time. And not only among the usual neoclassical suspects (including the International Monetary Fund, the World Bank, and the economic advisors in the East who, we are led to believe, had been secretly reading Friedrich von Hayek and Milton Friedman under the noses of the central planners). This new, market-oriented development thinking is summarized by Joseph E. Stiglitz and Lyn Squire (1998). The *World Development Report 1997* (World Bank 1997) is devoted to shrinking and transforming the role of the state in development. (But see Ha-Joon Chang and Robert Rowthorn [1995] for a critical review of the main components of the standard neoliberal view of the state.) Many liberal and left-leaning economists have also come forward and, in the form of disciplinary rectitude, disavow the "excesses" and "mistakes" of their political youth and proclaim their allegiance to the eternal verities of the market. As demonstrated below, the ironies of such old orthodoxies and new conversions abound.

Irony 1: Is the United States a Model to Emulate?

The Americanization of world economic thinking has taken place precisely as the economic and social situation in the United States has deteriorated.

An earlier version of this chapter was published in the Italian journal *A Sinistra,* March 1993, and is printed with the publisher's permission. I would like to thank Ric McIntyre for helpful comments and, especially, Dawn Saunders for her encouragement to make the necessary revisions.

Not for everyone, of course: the latest figures show that the richest 1 percent of Americans reaped three-fourths of the gain in average family income from the late 1970s to the early 1990s. By the middle of this decade, the net worth of these same households—all of them millionaires at a minimum—was greater than the bottom 90 percent of Americans put together. The increasingly unequal distribution of income and wealth in the United States, a tendency that began in 1969 and has persisted to the present, has been documented, using different methodologies, in a wide variety of sources. These include studies by the U.S. Census Bureau (Weinberg 1996), Edward N. Wolff (1995, 1996), Paul Krugman (1992), the Center on Budget and Policy Priorities (1997), and United for a Fair Economy and Institute for Policy Studies (1998). The particulars are interesting, but it is the overall theme that truly stands out: the distribution of income and wealth in the United States (however measured) has been worsening for three decades and is by far the most unequal among the industrialized countries.

The United States is also "Number One" among industrial nations along many other unsavory scales: it now claims more than twice the average rate of intentional homicides (at 12.4 per 100,000 people), the highest incidence of poverty, the largest portion of the total population incarcerated, and a disgraceful degree of economic and social infrastructure in disrepair (these include not only bridges and roads but also the traditional two-parent household enshrined on American television). The sight of "urban jungle vehicles" being maneuvered by American yuppies through city streets is reminiscent (albeit without the bulletproof plating) of chauffeur-driven all-terrain vehicles in San Salvador or Djakarta. In this case at least, the least industrialized have revealed to the most industrialized their future.

Irony 2: Markets "Get It Wrong"

Interestingly, the hegemony of neoliberalist development policy has developed at the same time that economic research and theory offer increased support for government intervention: nonmarket linkages are important for economic development; coordination failures play a key role in business cycles. For example, "post-Walrasian" approaches to microeconomic theory demonstrate the existence of significant informational asymmetries and problems with the enforcement of contractual exchanges, meaning that prices will not clear markets, thereby creating the justification for extramarket intervention. (See, e.g., Samuel Bowles and Herbert Gintis 1990, 1993.)

In addition, the "new trade theory" (now almost twenty years old) demonstrates the significance of noncomparative advantage trade: countries do not necessarily specialize and trade in order to take advantage of their (natural or given) differences. They also trade because there are increasing returns to producing a narrow range of goods and services, which makes specialization advantageous per se (see Krugman 1987 and Baldwin 1992 for summaries of this approach). The policy conclusion of the new models of international trade is that government can often improve on free-market outcomes (e.g., by imposing import tariffs and/or offering export subsidies). However, the new trade theorists have been quick to back away from this implication, on political rather than economic grounds. As Krugman (1987, 132) explains, "There is still a case for free trade as good policy, and as a useful target in the practical world of politics, but it can never be asserted as the policy that economic theory tells us is always right." Robert Kuttner (1996) takes Krugman to task for "backpedalling" in favor of market outcomes.

Thus, most products that enter international commerce are created by imperfectly competitive industries. What this means is that the pattern of specialization and trade around the globe is, in a fundamental sense, arbitrary: who produces what is the result of history, "accidents," and past government policies; it is not dictated—as the strictly neoclassical, comparative-advantage theorists would have us believe—by given tastes, resources, and technology.

The so-called new trade theory is buttressed by the "discovery" that the industrialization success of the East Asian countries owes little to free markets and has been mostly the product of active government involvement. According to Wade (1995), the role of the government in the industrialization successes of countries such as Korea, Taiwan, and Japan went far beyond the neoliberal recipe. Alice Amsden (1989) and Ajit Singh (1995) have argued that the state—and not free markets and "getting prices right"—has been a key factor in the industrialization experiences of Korea and India, respectively.

The Limited Options of the South: Trade (and Poverty) or No Trade (and Poverty)

What is *not* ironic is that the export-oriented path of industrialization advocated by free-market economists and policymakers is the only viable path to industrialization left for much of the South. While many industrial countries have been somewhat sheltered from the "spillover" effects of world crises (the 1980s debt crisis in Latin America, the 1990s financial crisis in East Asia), global economic forces have contributed to economic slowdown in much of the North and the decline in the rate of growth of world trade. In the Third World, both global economic problems and the policies that have been implemented to "solve" them have decimated domestic markets. Using current exchange-rates, the International Monetary Fund (IMF) estimates the industrial countries' share of world gross domestic product (GDP) is 73.21 and that of the developing countries is 17.71; using an alternative purchasing-power–parity rates, the shares are 54.44 and 34.38, respectively. The latter approach to measuring inequality between nations has the effect of lessening the appearance of the gap between the incomes of the North and of the South (International Monetary Fund 1993). But the growth of poverty and income inequality within Third World nations has all but eliminated the possibility of relying on domestic mass consumption as the impetus for industrialization. The only remaining market for the growth of manufacturing and other industries lies outside the South.

Thirty-three percent of people in developing countries have annual incomes that place them below the average poverty line for such countries ($370 in 1985). The absurdity, as the World Bank (1990, 29) itself has shown, is that it would require a transfer of only 3 percent of total world consumption to these people to lift them *all* above poverty. An alternative way of looking at the problem is provided in the *Human Development Report 1997* (United Nations Development Programme 1997, 112). According to the UNDP, the price tag for eradicating poverty and providing basic social services in developing countries would be about $80 billion, which is less than 0.5 percent of world income or, even more dramatic, less than the combined net worth of the seven richest men in the world. So near yet so far!

But the freeing up of markets will, if anything, shift assets from the poor to the rich; or, with recent and ongoing privatization efforts, from the state to (some) private hands. As state enterprises are sold to private—domestic and foreign—investors, the state succeeds in eliminating an important source of fiscal deficits and in filling, on a one-time basis, state coffers, while wealthy individuals and corporations acquire assets for much less than it would cost them to build them up over time. According to the International Labour Office (1995), the proceeds from sales of state-owned enterprises in developing countries rose from just over $2 billion in 1988 to almost $20 billion in 1992.

The reorganization of the newly privatized enterprises involves, in many cases, the loss of labor rights (such as tenure in the company, strike and association rights, retirement and health benefits, and the like) and the laying off of employees (often under the rubrics of "early retirement" and "voluntary departures" with severance pay) (Petrazzini 1996). According to a World Bank sample of the sale of state-owned enterprises in Africa (White and Bhatia 1998, 144–47), employment in those enterprises fell 15 percent from the date of privatization (between 1986 and 1995) to early 1996.

Such displaced workers are then "freed" to join the ranks of the reserve army, or (as it is now referred to in development circles) the "informal sector." Employment statistics for such people, precisely by virtue of the "informality" of the sector (including the fact that many units have very few employees and a large number are illegal or not officially recognized), are notoriously unreliable. However, the magnitude of the informal sector is quite clear. For example, according to the International Labour Office (1997), of the 15.7 new jobs created in Latin America between 1990 and 1994, 8.4 out of 10 were in the informal sector. In Asia, the informal sector absorbs 40 to 50 percent of the labor force, rising to 80 percent in countries such as Bangladesh. And in Africa, the urban informal sector employs 61 percent of the urban labor force and is expected to account for 93 percent of all additional jobs in the region in the 1990s. And, since the public sector has been the major formal sector employer of women in many Third World countries, the loss of jobs associated with privatization and the contraction of the state has had a disproportionate effect on women. Given the low incomes that accompany work in this sector, the result is to further shrink that part of the domestic market devoted to mass consumption.

What Lies Ahead? Seeking Development that Develops Hope

What, then, are the prospects for Third World industrialization? The other side of declining real wages and impoverished informal sector incomes is the growth of profits: both those that are retained by the enterprises and those that are distributed to company officials, bribed politicians, and investors in the rejuvenated or newly created stock exchanges. These profits are, of course, a source of demand, but rarely for the products of domestic industry. Instead, they are used either to employ personal servants (to cook, to clean, or to stand guard) or to import equipment and luxury goods from abroad. Wage-earners and those in the informal sector are, in turn, reduced to participating in mass consumption via television commercials—or actually purchasing goods in the cottage industries of the informal sector and food from the countryside. The only market for industrialization that remains is the international one.

Not surprisingly, the prophets of the "new competition" are waiting on the doorstep, with their slide shows illustrating new forms of organization and slick speeches about "flexible specialization" and the importance of CAD/CAM (computer-aided design/computer-aided manufacturing) and CNC (computer numerically controlled). There is no shortage of "experts" to advise enterprises about the best way to break into world markets; and academic treatises on industrial competitiveness are also plentiful (e.g., Best 1990; Lazonick and Mass 1995; Lazonick et al. 1997). Some enterprises will, in fact, become successful exporters on the basis of such approaches—but mostly in countries where industrialization and the technical and social infrastructure have already reached a high degree of sophistication. For the rest, low-cost (low-wage, assembly) production is the only "arbitrary" advantage that can serve as a platform for export-oriented industrialization.

The fact is that, while some industries will be destroyed by import competition and others will never get off the ground, facing competition from low-wage *maquiladoras* and high-tech "growth poles," Third World industrialization will continue to proceed apace. Not long ago, this development took place under the "hothouse" for industry created by protectionist barriers, government ownership, and more state forms of capitalism. Now, the preferred model is that of free markets and more private forms of capitalism. The question here is not whether such strategies can be successful but, instead, what are its effects? And is there a better way?

The economic and social punishment meted out in the name of industrialization has been well documented. There is the devastation of the rain forests and other ecological disasters, women and children toiling in multinational sweatshops, men waiting in the parking lot for the poor in Third World cities. It is increasingly difficult to argue that more industrialization is better than less—at least if it is the same sort of industrialization that has taken place in the past and that continues to be proffered as the only possibility today.

But are there any alternatives? The first step in the direction of formulating a different way of organizing economic and social life is to challenge the limits within which current economic thinking is confined. For example, introducing class into the analysis of industrialization disrupts the limits imposed by forms of economic discourse that move back and forth between structures and human nature, between governments and markets. Elsewhere (Ruccio 1991, 1992), I carry out such a class analysis of external debt and macroeconomic stabilization and adjustment policies in the Third World. The goal is to identify the various ways in which the surplus labor of workers (their total labor minus the necessary labor they receive in the form of products or money for their continued existence) is, first, appropriated by nonworkers (e.g., by capitalists as well as feudal lords, slaveowners, and others) and, then, distributed to still other groups (such as merchants, bankers, the state, and so on) in the wider society. The pattern of such surplus appropriations and distributions—not the relative amount of government intervention and free markets—is what makes up the class structure of any given society (see Wolff and Resnick 1987 and Gibson-Graham 1996 for general introductions to Marxian class analysis).

This approach allows us to "see" the existence of exploitation in both state-led and private-market forms of capitalist industrialization—and, of course, to begin to imagine alternatives to that exploitation. And when class is brought in, it is necessary to carry out the investigation at all social sites: not only in offices and factories but also in other areas of social life, such as the informal sector and households (see Fraad et al. 1994). Only on this basis can we can begin to recognize the (often unpaid) labor of women and, even more important, the radical class restructuring within both the informal sector and households that is currently taking place as a result of the process of Third World industrialization. It is precisely in such sectors that the injuries meted out by capitalist industry are experienced and, at the same time, that innovative, noncapitalist forms of production are being created.

Creative new approaches can challenge the limits within which economic policy is currently confined. For example, George DeMartino (1996) has suggested an emphasis on *competition-reducing* rather than *competitiveness-enhancing* approaches to trade and development. And much of economic and social life can be taken out of competition altogether. Rather than being structured according to the dictates of competition, whether foreign or domestic, areas as diverse as health care, housing finance, and manufacturing production can be reorganized as noncapitalist, either cooperative or community, activities (see Biewener, this volume, for a related approach). Or, on a national level, a tariff structure can be devised to govern the terms of trade between countries on the basis of various criteria of social welfare such as human rights, environmental protection, and the like, as proposed by DeMartino and Cullenberg (1994) and DeMartino (forthcoming).

Simply put, the time has come to break out of the pendulum swing between government intervention and free markets, to recognize the alien power that is created by both state-centered and market-oriented forms of industrialization and to leave them behind. They promise little success and, even when partial successes are achieved, the economic and social costs are too high. Instead of accepting the existing goals of industrialization and development, and the strategies presented by mainstream economists and policymakers to get there, we need to move beyond them, to begin to imagine and to create the conditions for alternative, communal, and collective, forms of production—in agriculture and services, as well as industry.

References

Amsden, A. 1989. *Asia's Next Giant: South Korea and Late Industrialization*. New York: Oxford University Press.

Baldwin, R.E. 1992. "Are Economists' Traditional Trade Policy Views Still Valid?" *Journal of Economic Literature* 30 (June): 804–829.

Best, Michael. 1990. *The New Competition: Institutions of Industrial Restructuring*. Cambridge: Harvard University Press.

Bowles, S., and H. Gintis. 1990. "Contested Exchange: New Microfoundations of the Political Economy of Capitalism." *Politics and Society* 18, no. 2: 165–222.

———. 1993. "The Revenge of *Homo Economicus*: Post-Walrasian Economics and the Revival of Political Economy." *Journal of Economic Perspectives* 7 (Winter): 83–102.

Center on Budget and Policy Priorities. 1997. "Poverty Rate Fails to Decline as Income Growth in 1996 Favors the Affluent." http://www.cbpp.org/povday97.htm, accessed June 6, 1999.

Chang, H.-J., and R. Rowthorn. 1995. "Introduction." In *The Role of the State in Economic Change*, ed. H.-J. Chang and R. Rowthorn, 1–27. Oxford: Clarendon Press.

DeMartino, G. 1996. "Industrial Policies versus Competitiveness Strategies: In Pursuit of Prosperity in the Global Economy." *International Papers in Political Economy* 3, no. 2.

———. Forthcoming. *Global Economy, Global Justice: A Critique of Neoliberalism, and Alternatives for the Year 2025*. New York: Routledge.

DeMartino, G., and S. Cullenberg. 1994. "The Social Index Tariff Structure: An Internationalist Response to Economic Integration." *Review of Radical Political Economics* 26, no 3: 76–85.

Fraad, H., S. Resnick, and R. Wolff. 1994. *Bringing It All Back Home: Class, Gender, and Power in the American Household*. Boulder, CO: Pluto.

Gibson-Graham, J.-K. 1996. *The End of Capitalism (As We Knew It): A Feminist Critique of Political Economy*. Cambridge, MA: Blackwell.

International Labour Office. 1995. *World Labour Report 1995*. Geneva: International Labour Organization.

———. 1997. *World Labour Report 1997–98*. Geneva: International Labour Organization.

International Monetary Fund. 1993. "Revised Weights for the World Economic Outlook." In *World Economic Outlook*, May 1993 Washington, DC: International Monetary Fund.

Krugman, P.R. 1987. "Is Free Trade Passé?" *Journal of Economic Perspectives* 1 (Fall): 131–144.

______. 1992. "The Rich, the Right, and the Facts." *The American Prospect* no. 11 (Fall): 19–31

Kuttner, R. 1996. "Peddling Krugman," *The American Prospect*, no. 28 (September–October): 78–86. http://epn.org/prospect/28/28kutt.html, accessed February 2, 1999.

Lazonick, W. and W. Mass, eds. 1995. *Organizational Capability and Competitive Advantage: Debates, Dynamics, and Policy*. Brookfield, VT: Edward Elgar.

Lazonick, W., R. Dore, and H.W. de Jong. 1997. *The Corporate Triangle: The Structure and Performance of Corporate Systems in a Global Economy*. Oxford: Blackwell.

Petrazzini, B.A. 1996. "The Labor Sector: A Post-Privatization Assessment." In *Bigger Economies, Smaller Governments: Privatization in Latin America*, ed. W. Glade, 347–368. Boulder, CO: Westview Press.

Ruccio, D.F. 1991. "When Failure Becomes Success: Class and the Debate over Stabilization and Adjustment." *World Development* 19: 1315–1334.

———. 1992. "Power and Class: The Contribution of Radical Approaches to Debt and Development." In *Radical Economics*, ed. B.B. Roberts and S.F. Feiner, 199–227. Boston: Kluwer-Nijhoff.

Singh, A. 1995. "The State and Industrialization in India: Successes and Failures and the Lessons for the Future." In *The Role of the State in Economic Change*, eds. H.-J. Chang and R. Rowthorn, 170–186. Oxford: Clarendon Press.

Stiglitz, J.E. and L. Squire. 1998. "International Development: Is It Possible?" *Foreign Policy* (Spring): 138–151.

United for a Fair Economy and Institute for Policy Studies. 1998. "Executive Excess '98: CEO Gains from Massive Downsizing." http://www.stw.org/html/exec_excess_98.html, accessed June 4, 1999.

United Nations Development Programme. 1997. Human Development Report 1997. New York: Oxford University Press.

Wade, R. 1995. "Resolving the State-Market Dilemma in East Asia." In *The Role of the State in Economic Change*, eds. H.J. Chang and R. Rowthorn, 114–136. Oxford: Clarendon Press.

Weinberg, D.N. 1996. *A Brief Look at Postwar U.S. Income Inequality*. Washington, DC: Bureau of the Census, U.S. Department of Commerce.

White, O.C., and A. Bhatia. 1998. *Privatization in Africa. Washington, DC: World Bank.*

Wolff, E.N. 1995. "How the Pie Is Sliced: America's Growing Concentration of Wealth." *The American Prospect*, no. 22 (Summer): 58–64.

———. 1996. *Top Heavy: The Increasing Inequality of Wealth in America and What Can Be Done About It.* New York: New Press.

Wolff, R.D., and S.A. Resnick.1987. *Economics: Marxian Versus Neoclassical*. Baltimore: Johns Hopkins University Press.

World Bank. 1990. *World Development Report 1990*. New York: Oxford University Press.

———. 1997. *World Development Report 1997*. New York: Oxford University Press.

25

Lessons from Economic Transition in Russia and China

David M. Kotz

In December 1991 the Soviet Union disintegrated and its largest constituent republic, Russia, emerged as an independent state. The political leadership of newly independent Russia embarked on an effort to replace its state socialist system, based on state ownership of enterprises and central planning, with a capitalist market system, based on private property and a market system of coordination. The economic strategy that Russia has relied on to implement this transition goes by several names, the most descriptive of which is the neoliberal transition strategy (hereafter NLTS). This strategy, designed by Western neoclassical economists, calls for limited government involvement in the transition process, relying primarily on individual self-interested initiatives to transform the economy. The other countries that emerged from the former Soviet Union, and the former Soviet Bloc countries in Central and Eastern Europe, have also been following the NLTS.

The other giant state socialist country, China, began its own transition to a capitalist market system earlier, in 1978. China's transition strategy, which might be called a state-directed transition strategy (hereafter SDTS), differs significantly from the NLTS. China's SDTS involves, as the name suggests, a very active role for the state in managing the transition.

By 1996 Russia's historic transition had been ongoing for five years while China's transition was eighteen years old. Everyone agrees that economic performance in China during its transition has been dramatically superior to that of Russia—China's economy has grown very rapidly throughout the transition while Russia's has declined precipitously. Despite the markedly different performance, with few exceptions mainstream neoclassical economists have not altered their belief that the NLTS is far superior to China's SDTS.

We will examine the question of why neoclassical economists have clung to the NLTS despite its disappointing results and despite the presence of an apparently successful alternative. In 1996 the World Bank's annual *World Development Report*, entitled that year *From Plan to Market*, was entirely devoted to analyzing the transition experience of Russia, China, and twenty-six other countries. We will use this major study to examine the neoclassical response to the Russia/China comparison. First, however, we will review Russia's and China's transition strategy and experience up through 1996, the year of the World Bank study.

Russia's Transition Experience

The NLTS, sometimes known as "shock therapy," calls for making the transition from state socialism to capitalism very rapidly, within a few years.

This strategy relies on three main policies: liberalization, stabilization, and privatization. Liberalization refers to the removal of state restrictions on price-setting and other market behavior. Stabilization aims to bring the inflation, released by liberalization, under control through reductions in government spending and tight monetary policy. Privatization calls for turning state-owned enterprises into privately owned companies. In addition to these three policies, the NLTS also insists upon the immediate cessation of state allocation of resources and the removal of barriers to free international trade and investment. In essence, the NLTS calls for transforming a state socialist system into a capitalist market system by eliminating state ownership of enterprises and state control over the economy, expecting that individual initiative and market forces will thenceforth take over the roles of initiating and coordinating economic activity that had previously been performed by the state.

Starting in January 1992, the Russian government adhered closely to the NLTS. Central planning had been largely eliminated during the last two years of the Soviet period in 1990–91, and the remaining elements of central allocation of resources were terminated during 1992. Nearly all prices were freed from state control on January 2, 1992. Government spending was sharply reduced, dropping from 47.9 percent of gross domestic product (GDP) in 1991 to only 26.9 percent in the first half of 1995 (International Monetary Fund 1992, 70, and 1995, 5, 21), which is below the percentage in the United States. Monetary policy has been so tight that the money supply (M2) fell from 100 percent of nominal GDP in 1990 to only 16 percent in 1994 (World Bank 1996, 21). Privatization proceeded faster than anyone had expected; by year-end 1994 nonstate enterprises accounted for 78.5 percent of industrial output (*Statisticheskoe obozrenie* 1995, no. 4, 41). Russia also quickly established a regime of relatively free imports, free international capital flows, and free currency exchange.

Table 25.1

Economic Performance in Russia, 1991–1996

Indicator	Percentage Change, 1991–1996
Gross domestic product	–45
Industrial production	–49
Investment[a]	–72
Agricultural output	–34
Average real monthly pay	–52[b]

Sources: Kotz with Weir 1997, 174, 179; OECD 1997, no. 2, pp. 88, 90; *Statisticheskoe obozrenie* 1996, no. 4, p. 24, and 1997, no.4, pp. 9, 24.

[a]Gross capital formation.
[b]Through October 1995.

Since January 1992 Russia has experienced the most severe, prolonged economic decline of any major country in peacetime in this century. Table 25.1 shows that during 1991–96, real GDP and industrial production both fell by nearly one-half, investment by more than 70 percent, and agricultural output by one-third. Average real pay fell by just over one-half by late 1995. While every sector of Russian production has collapsed, the output of fuel, raw materials, and metals has contracted less than the rest of the economy (Kotz with Weir 1997, 175–78). A reversal of this rapid and prolonged decline is not yet in sight as of mid-1999. Russia's economic trajectory is turning its formerly diversified economy into one centered around the extraction and export of raw materials, which does not hold out a promising future for Russia's well-educated, largely urban population.

Russia's state and nonstate institutions have been unable to pay their employees on time, even at the greatly reduced pay scales. Unpaid wages were estimated at 36.5 trillion rubles ($6.8 billion) in September 1996, which represented approximately 64 percent of the nation's total monthly wage bill (*OMRI Daily Digest* 1996). An estimated 55 percent of the population is forced to obtain over half of their food by growing it themselves in their tiny backyard plots (*RFE/RL Newsline* 1999). About 70 percent of transactions are conducted based on barter and other money substitutes.

The human cost of this economic decline has been enormous. Russia's death rate rose from 11.4 per thousand population in 1991 to 15.5 in 1994, before falling to 14.3 in 1996 (*Rossiiskii statisticheskii ezhegodnik* 1994, 43, and *Statisticheskoe obozrenie* 1997, no. 1, 7). The elevated death rate was fueled by sharp increases in deaths due to alcohol-related causes, suicide, murder, circulatory diseases, respiratory diseases, and infectious and parasitic diseases, the causes of which can be traced, directly and indirectly, to elements of the NLTS and the economic decline that followed its introduction (Field, Kotz, and Bukhman 2000). The increased death rate during 1992–96 produced an estimated 2.1 million premature deaths in Russia during that period.

Russia's economy was battered further in August 1998 when the Russian government became unable to make payments on its foreign debt, producing a financial collapse. Russia's currency lost about three-fourths of its value in relation to the dollar, Russia's import-dependent consumers took another hit to their living standard, and many of Russia's major banks were driven into insolvency. For Russians this experience seemed the final proof of the failure of the NLTS.

The NLTS has also been applied since 1992 by most of the other newly independent states (NIS) that emerged from the Soviet Union and, since 1990, in the formerly state socialist countries of Central and Eastern Europe (CEE). Economic performance has varied among these states, but all went through severe economic depressions after introducing a NLTS. While some began to grow several years later, none had even reached its pretransition level of GDP by 1995 (World Bank 1996, 173).

China and the State-Directed Transition Strategy

When China began its transition to a market system in 1978, Western experts sought to persuade the Chinese leadership to pursue a NLTS. However, this advice fell on deaf ears in China. Instead, the Chinese leaders developed a radically different SDTS.

Rather than simply liberalizing prices, China maintained a dual system of prices, under which state enterprises had to provide a certain quantity of output at the lower plan price, with output above that level sold at the market price. Price controls were kept on many retail goods through 1991, thirteen years after the transition began (World Bank 1994, 2, 193).

Direct administrative measures were combined with periodic brief spells of selectively tightened credit to keep inflation under control. Rather than cutting state spending, the state undertook substantial investments in infrastructure to facilitate economic growth. Rather than tight monetary policy, China allowed substantial credit expansion, while directing credit into productive investments by means of government control of bank lending (banks remained state owned and controlled) and direct setting of interest rates. In contrast to the sharp monetary contraction in Russia, in China the money supply (M2) rose from 25 percent of GDP in 1978 to 89 percent in 1994 (World Bank 1996, 21).

Rather than privatizing state enterprises, the state encouraged the formation of new nonstate enterprises by worker collectives, townships and villages, and eventually private individuals. The state continued to pour investment funds into state enterprises, which remained under state control. Central planning was not immediately dismantled, but was retained for the state sector, although it was loosened over time. The new nonstate sector of the economy grew rapidly, producing about 55 percent of GDP by 1995 (World Bank 1996, 15). In agriculture individual families were given free use of a plot of land, but they did not become owners of the land and could not sell or lease it. The land remained public property.

While China has welcomed foreign investment, it has retained significant protection of its domestic market. The Western powers have sought to pressure China into opening its market to imports, but so far this has not been successful.

Although gradualism is an important feature of the Chinese strategy, the differences between the SDTS and the NLTS go well beyond the matter of the speed of transition. Rather than seeking to directly convert the state-owned, planned economy into a private, market-based one, China sought to use its state-owned, planned economy as a base for launching a new nonstate, market-based sector. China's strategy was a "two-sector" one, in contrast to the "one-sector" approach of the NIS and CEE states. While China sought to encourage a growing sector of nonstate enterprises, to do so successfully it retained and improved its state sector.[1]

The economic performance of China since 1978, as measured by macroeconomic indices, has been one of the best in the world. Real GDP grew at an average rate of 9.4 percent per year during 1978–95 (World Bank 1996, 18). GDP did not decline in any year during that period, never falling below a 3 percent per annum rate of increase. Since 1995 economic growth has remained rapid—GDP grew by 8.9 percent in 1997. Agricultural output rose at a 6.2 percent annual rate in the decade after 1978. Such rapid growth tends to create inflationary pressures, but these have been successfully contained without resort to the tight fiscal and monetary policy demanded by the NLTS: the average rate of consumer price inflation in China during 1978–95 was a moderate 8.4 percent per year, compared to Russia's rate of 513 percent per year during 1991–95 (World Bank 1996, 18; Kotz with Weir 1997, 179).

Average living standards have risen rapidly in China since the transition began. While inequality may have increased, the degree of income inequality in China has been much lower than in Russia, indicated by a gini coefficient of 38 for China compared to 48 for Russia in 1992–93 (World Bank 1996, 69).

The rapid growth in China has not been confined to the nonstate sector. During 1978–91 the real output of state enterprises grew at 7.7 percent per year, compared to an overall annual GDP growth rate of 8.6 percent for that period (Naughton 1994, 477, 479).

China's SDTS has not been without serious economic and social problems. Environmental and job safety concerns are mounting. China's growth may not be able to keep up with the millions of peasants who are continuing to leave their villages in search of employment. Crime and corruption have apparently been spreading. However, by the usual macroeconomic indices, China's SDTS must be judged a remarkable success.

The Response of Mainstream Economics to the Russia/China Comparison

Russia in 1991 and China in 1978, despite their similarities as large state socialist countries poised to embark on a market transition, differed from one another in many ways besides their different transition strategies. Nevertheless, the macroeconomic records of the Russian and Chinese transitions are so dramatically opposite to one another that it strongly suggests that the latter was based on a workable strategy while the former was not. Although many of the NIS and CEE countries tried the NLTS—each having its own unique history, institutions, and immediate pretransition circumstances—none escaped a severe economic downturn that left negative net growth after five or more years.

Some Western economists doubted the efficacy of the NLTS from the start. As the evidence of severe transition difficulties in CEE and the NIS mounted, the ranks of the critics grew. However, the critics have been drawn mainly from the margins of mainstream economics, particularly specialists in the Soviet economy and those attuned to institutional and historical problems of economic development.

The critics have pointed to six problems with the NLTS, especially as applied to Russia: (1) building a market system takes many decades and requires an active state role in the process; (2) dismantling the old centralized system of economic coordination before an effective market system can be built leads to economic chaos; (3) sudden liberalization in a formerly tightly controlled economy sets off an inflation that is very difficult to contain; (4) tight fiscal and monetary policies ensure a long depression and also prevent the restructuring and modernization of industry, which require substantial state spending and adequate credit; (5) privatization in a society having no legitimate wealthy class degenerates into theft of state assets with no economic gain for society; (6) a free trade policy in a transition economy exposes domestic producers to superior foreign competition before they are ready to compete.

Mainstream economics has proved largely impervious to the apparently impressive Russia/China contrast, as well as to the arguments of the critics of the NLTS. A good example of the reaction of mainstream economics to the Russia/China contrast is found in the World Bank study cited above, *From Plan to Market* (hereafter *FPTM*), which seeks to provide a comprehensive analysis of the experience of economic transition (World Bank 1996).[2] A look at *FPTM* provides a window into the reaction of mainstream economics to the uncomfortable Russia/China contrast.

FPTM does make one concession to the critics of orthodox neoliberalism. It hedges on the importance of immediate privatization. Perhaps feeling the pressure of the Chinese example, it states that "the need to privatize is not equally urgent in all settings. Slower privatization is viable." However, the report quickly adds that slower privatization is "not necessarily optimal" (p. 50). Perhaps it is being suggested that if China had immediately privatized, its growth rate would have been even higher than 9.4 percent per year.

Despite its documentation of China's remarkably rapid transition growth, and of the severe depression experienced by Russia (and the other NIS and CEE countries), *FPTM* avoids drawing the most obvious conclusion. It does so by (1) downplaying the severity of Russia's economic collapse; (2) attributing the differential Russia/China records to different initial conditions rather than different transition strategies; and (3) suggesting that China's impressive achievements occurred in spite of, rather than because of, its different strategy. These three points will be examined in turn.

Downplaying the Severity of Russia's Economic Collapse

While admitting that large declines in output occurred in NIS and CEE, *FPTM* qualifies this by the remark that "Official data overstate the output decline" (p. 18). The usual culprit of growing unreported economic activity is cited. Yet, in the case of Russia, government statisticians include estimates of unreported activity in the official data. It would be difficult to explain why they would systematically underestimate such activity, thereby making the Russian government look bad.

In the face of five or more years of negative net growth in 26 of the 28 transition countries, *FPTM* refers to "a short-term drop in living standards" in "some of the countries undergoing transition" (p. iii). Economists do not normally consider five years to be "short-term." At another point even short-term problems are forgotten. *FPTM* states that during the transition only "overbuilt sectors" should contract, yet in Russia all sectors have experienced large declines. Surely Russian agriculture, food processing, and textile industries were not overbuilt relative to people's needs. Here we see a victory of prior belief over actual experience.

Some important aspects of Russia's collapse are found in the charts and tables but left unremarked upon in the text. The most egregious omission is the lack of comment on the collapse of investment in Russia, the rest of the NIS, and the CEE countries. While economic progress requires more than just high investment, the latter is a necessary part of any path leading to modernization and rapid growth.

Initial Conditions and the Russia/China Record

FPTM attributes China's impressive growth record, in contrast to the sharp economic declines of other transition economies, mainly to "China's favorable initial conditions" (p. 19). The major differences in initial conditions between Russia and China cited in *FPTM* are that China had a much lower level of per capita income, a much larger share of agriculture in total employment (71 percent vs. 13 percent for Russia), a much more limited social safety net, and a more decentralized economy and political structure. The report concludes that "Differences in initial conditions and structural characteristics therefore explain a good deal of the divergence of transition outcomes" (p. 21). While the differences between China and Russia cited above do suggest that China had the potential to achieve a faster growth rate during transition than did Russia, it is difficult to see how these initial conditions could explain the collapse suffered by Russia. Indeed, in a later section, which addresses the output collapse in CEE and the NIS, the report points to three main factors: demand shifts due to liberalization, the dissolution of CMEA (the Soviet Bloc trade association) and the Soviet Union, and supply disruptions due to the disappearance of central planning "before new market institutions could develop" (pp. 26–27). The first and last of those three factors are aspects of the NLTS—measures that China's strategy avoided—yet the conclusion that the strategy chosen played a key role is not drawn. The possibility that "overzealous stabilization" might have played a harmful role—one that lasted for many years—is discounted on the grounds that the evidence allegedly does not support this claim, although no support for this conclusion is provided (p. 26).

China's Achievements Happened in Spite of, Not Because of, its Strategy

The matter of China's transition experience is posed in *FPTM* in the following way: "Why has China been able to reform in a partial, phased manner and still grow rapidly . . . ?" (p. 19). This is viewed as a "puzzle" (p. 19), since the authors assume that China's strategy is obviously inferior to the NLTS. As was noted above, *FPTM* answers this "puzzle" by attributing China's rapid growth to its favorable initial conditions—basically, being underdeveloped and not so centralized. They state that "Institutional development is . . . crucial for sustaining the momentum of the reform" in China, worrying that China is lagging in this respect in that "China's banks . . . are less market-based than those of CEE" with "many loans . . . still allocated through a central credit plan" (pp. 13–15). They evidently discount the possibility that China's state-owned, state-directed credit system might be contributing to its very high rate of domestic investment, in contrast to the low rate of investment in the CEE countries with their market-based credit systems.

In a similar vein, *FPTM* worries that China has "a state sector that remains a drag on the economy" (p. 23). Why it is a drag on the economy is not explained, probably because it is thought to be obvious that state enterprises are inherently inferior to private enterprises and hence must be a drag on the economy. This "drag on the economy" not only grew nearly as rapidly as total output since 1978, but has provided a stable and reliable source of inputs, and market for outputs, for the new nonstate sector.

FPTM states that the evidence provides "the clear message that sustained and consistent reform pays off" (p. 17). Yet *FPTM* characterizes the most successful reform of all, that of China, as a "piecemeal" approach. Within the framework of the authors of *FPTM*, China's approach is seen as "inconsistent," since it combines plan and market, state and nonstate property, fixed and free prices.

Concluding Comments

It is not difficult to figure out why most mainstream Western economists have continued to support the NLTS, despite the dismal economic results it has yielded in Russia and elsewhere, and despite the presence of an alternative strategy that has worked quite well. The NLTS emerged as an application of the textbook economic theory that has made up the core of mainstream Western economic thought for generations. That theory holds that private property and free markets are the optimal economic institutions. The deduction was made that, if private property and free markets are optimal, then privatizing property and freeing markets from state control is always desirable, and the faster the better.

However, the abstract static equilibrium model, which underlies the textbook claims of the optimality of private property and free markets, cannot have much to say about best mode of transition from one economic system to another. If ever there was a disequilibrium matter, transition is it. Experience seems to be showing that the conclusions most economists have drawn about transition strategy, based on the standard neoclassical equilibrium model, are unwarranted.

The evidence strongly suggests that the NLTS followed in Russia is an unworkable means to convert a state socialist system to a capitalist market system, whereas the SDTS represents a viable transition strategy. A case can be made that a SDTS would have been economically workable in Russia in 1992 had its government been disposed to follow such a path at that time. There is also reason to believe that a SDTS could be successfully introduced in Russia even after all these years of liberalization, privatization, and economic collapse (see Kotz 1998).[3] The economic and political power of the IMF and World Bank, and of the leading capitalist governments that stand behind them, would make it difficult for any country among the NIS and CEE to make such a shift in strategy. However, a large, resource-rich country such as Russia could defy these pressures. The real obstacle to such a shift for Russia lies more in the political power of the Russian new rich, who have benefited from the NLTS despite its disastrous effects on the economy, than in either foreign pressure or domestic economic obstacles to implementing an alternative course of economic development.

Notes

1. Despite retaining a sector of state-owned enterprises, nearly all analysts agree that China's economy is becoming a capitalist system. Its SDTS is producing an economy in which a growing share of the large enterprises are owned by wealthy investors, who derive profits from the work of hired wage workers, and in which market forces play the main coordinating role. Such an economy is capitalist, even if the state continues to play an active role in the economy.

2. The report was prepared by a team of nine principal authors.

3. It is beyond the scope of this essay to consider a third alternative—that of Russia abandoning the NLTS, not to adopt a SDTS for building capitalism, but rather to resume the effort to build democratic socialism that began in the USSR in the Gorbachev era.

References

Field, Mark G., David M. Kotz, and Gene Bukhman. 2000. "Neoliberal Economic Policy, 'State Desertion,' and the Russian Health Crisis," pp. 155–73. In J.W. Kim, J.V. Millen, A. Irwin, and J. Gershwin (eds.), *Dying for Growth: Global Inequality and the Health of the Poor.* Monroe, ME: Common Courage Press.

International Monetary Fund. 1992. *Economic Review: Russian Federation.* Washington, DC: The International Monetary Fund.

———. 1995. *Russian Federation—Statistical Appendix.* IMF Staff Country Report 95/107. Washington, DC: The International Monetary Fund.

Kotz, David M. 1998. "Capitalist Collapse: How Russia Can Recover." *Dollars and Sense,* Nov.–Dec. 10–11, 39.

Kotz, David M., with Fred Weir. 1997. *Revolution from Above: The Demise of the Soviet System.* London and New York: Routledge.

Naughton, Barry. 1994. "What Is Distinctive About China's Economic Transition? State Enterprise Reform and Overall System Transformation." *Journal of Comparative Economics* 18: 470–490.

OECD. 1997. *Short-Term Economic Indicators: Transition Economies.* Paris: Centre for Co-Operation with the Economies in Transition.

OMRI Daily Digest. 1996. Part 1, no. 187, September 26. New York: Open Media Research Institute.

RFE/RL Newsline. 1999. Vol. 3, no. 28, Part 1, February 10. Prague, Czech Republic: Radio Free Europe/Radio Liberty.

Rossiiskii statisticheskii ezhegodnik. 1994. Moscow: Goskomstat rossii.

Statisticheskoe obozrenie. Various years. Moscow: Goskomstat rossii.

World Bank. 1994. *China: Internal Market Development and Regulation.* Washington, DC: The World Bank.

———. 1996. *From Plan to Market.* World Development.

26
The Asian Financial Crisis

What Went Wrong?

Ilene Grabel

The Asian financial crisis erupted in May 1997 in Thailand and quickly spread to Malaysia, Indonesia, the Philippines, South Korea, and eventually Brazil and Russia. The crisis has proven to be far more disruptive and less tractable than the Mexican financial crisis of 1994–95. While Mexico ultimately required $50 billion in financial assistance to weather its crisis, the International Monetary Fund (IMF) ultimately doled out $184 billion through 1998 to stanch the Asian crisis.

This chapter is motivated by the parallels in the conventional wisdom on the causes and consequences of the Asian and Mexican crises. In the Mexican case, mainstream economists in academia and the IMF dismissed the significance of the crisis by advancing what I have elsewhere termed the "Mexican exceptionalism thesis." This thesis entails the claim that the crisis was largely an aberration stemming from Mexico's "peculiarities"—in particular, from economic mismanagement, corruption, and instability that were seen to be endemic to Mexico (Grabel 1996, 1999). This explanation initially seemed plausible, insofar as other emerging economies were avoiding a similar fate. When the Asian crisis struck, these economists again resorted to the exceptionalism thesis—this time citing excessive corruption, unsustainable real estate investment practices, and misguided government policies. But in the face of what now seems to be a recurring pattern, the thesis is far less persuasive. Instead, the emergence of the Asian crisis so soon after Mexico suggests that there may be deep structural problems in the neoliberal strategies that these countries pursue to achieve economic development.

Rejecting the exceptionalism thesis, this chapter argues that these crises resulted from the widespread adoption across Southeast Asia (and in other emerging economies) of a neoliberal policy regime that embraces *financial liberalization*. This entails deregulation of the domestic financial sector and the removal of controls on cross-border capital inflows and outflows. Emerging economies pursued this strategy during the 1980s and 1990s under pressure from domestic and international interest groups, the IMF, and mainstream monetary economists. These advocates promised that financial liberalization would attract foreign private capital and induce sustainable economic growth and rising prosperity. But the advocates did not foresee that liberalization would also create powerful incentives and opportunities for domestic borrowers to rely excessively on loans denominated in foreign currencies. Nor did they foresee that the inflows of *portfolio investment* (i.e., the purchase of stocks and bonds by foreigners) could and would leave emerging economies instantaneously at the first sign of financial instability.

Advancing a post-Keynesian analysis, I argue that financial liberalization encourages a reliance on foreign borrowing and portfolio investment at the same time as it strips governments of the ability to control capital inflows and outflows. As a consequence, liberalization renders emerging economies vulnerable to a self-reinforcing cycle of investor exit, currency depreciation, and financial crisis. I refer to this vulnerability as the problem of "increased risk potential." Moreover, once a crisis emerges, governments find themselves at the mercy of the IMF for financial assistance, and hence subject to IMF dictates. I call this the problem of "constrained policy autonomy." Paradoxically, the IMF's insistence on further liberalization in the wake of crisis exacerbates rather than ameliorates these problems, and induces severe recessions. I therefore reject current IMF efforts to resolve the crisis, and I offer some thoughts about the types of measures that policymakers in emerging economies should consider in order that history not repeat itself.

Boom and Bust in Southeast Asia

Up until the crisis, most Southeast Asian currencies were pegged to the dollar. The peg was critical in two respects. First, the dollar's depreciation after 1985 enhanced the competitiveness of Southeast Asian exports in global markets. Second, the yen's relative appreciation to the dollar encouraged inward Japanese foreign direct investment in the region's real estate and manufacturing plants. At the same time, inward portfolio (financial asset) investment to Southeast Asian (and other emerging) economies increased dramatically because of the opportunities for speculative gains created by financial liberalization (which eased access to domestic stock markets to foreign investors) and because of the region's strong growth prospects. These capital inflows helped fuel speculative activities (and rising asset prices) across the region.

Private lending to and within Southeast Asia also grew dramatically during this time. As a result of financial liberalization, potential borrowers gained access to foreign lenders. U.S. and Japanese banks led the way in providing loans to the region. Critically, these loans were denominated in dollars and yen, respectively, which required the borrower to acquire foreign currency to repay the debt. But in the context of rapid economic growth and rising exports, these loans seemed secure. Moreover, the region's real estate boom inflated collateral values, allowing firms to increase their debt levels relative to their income flows (their "leveraging") considerably.

By mid-1996, the region was ripe for crisis. The Japanese economy had begun to encounter severe problems (including a decline in economic growth and corporate profit rates) that led its firms to reduce foreign direct investment and foreign lending. Partly as a consequence, property values throughout Southeast Asia began to decline, posing severe problems for domestic borrowers and lenders that had put up these assets for collateral for loans. At the same time, the dollar's appreciation after 1995 undermined the region's export competitiveness (because of the dollar peg) and induced debt distress on the part of the now overleveraged private sector. Finally, once investors became bullish on the United States after 1996, portfolio investors turned their attentions away from emerging economies in general (and Southeast Asia, in particular).

The ensuing crisis took investors and IMF officials completely by surprise. Up until the eve of the crisis, IMF reports and business accounts were uniformly bullish about economic prospects in Southeast Asia, Russia, and Brazil. Indeed, through 1996 four of the countries headed for crisis were among the world's top six recipients of private capital flows. Moreover, the crisis occurred *after* the IMF had implemented a new set of safeguards in April of 1996 that were intended to prevent financial instability of the sort that had plagued Mexico. The IMF's Special Information Dissemination Standard created a Dissemination Standards Bulletin Board to inform investors worldwide about economic conditions in a wide range of countries. The IMF hoped that once provided with accurate information, investors would act prudently in allocating funds to emerging-market economies.

When the first signs of trouble emerged in Thailand in May 1997, investor skittishness regarding the region intensified. Anticipating financial instability, investors began to sell Asian currency and stock holdings. This skittishness—or what became known as the "Asian flu"—soon infected Russia and even Brazil. The massive sell-off exacerbated the crisis, putting pressure on currency and stock prices, and fueling predictions that governments would abandon the currency peg and devalue their currencies. Southeast Asian central banks first attempted to stem the investor exit and protect the peg by widening the band of flexibility, expending "official reserves,"[1] restricting speculation against the currency and stocks, and raising interest rates. When these efforts failed, governments abandoned the peg, a move that shook international financial markets and intensified the stampede of foreign investors out of Southeast Asian markets. As governments approached the IMF for assistance, the IMF demanded further neoliberal reforms as a condition for aid.

Rejecting Exceptionalism

In the wake of the Asian crisis, proponents of the "exceptionalism thesis" assert that the crisis resulted from corruption and inappropriate regulation of the region's economies. For example, McKinnon and Pill (1998) argue that overregulation created perverse incentives that encouraged banks and investors to pursue risky strategies, as they knew governments would assist them if they failed.[2] In contrast, other economists such as Goldstein (1998) argue that regulation of certain sectors of the economy (such as banking) was inadequate, lacking the kinds of safeguards and oversight that are typically found across wealthier countries.

To date, mainstream proponents of these arguments have failed to explain how the corrupt ties that bound firms and governments and the inappropriate regulatory regimes throughout Southeast Asia led to crisis only in 1997, while having generated rapid economic growth up until that time. Moreover, they have failed to explain just why foreign investors and lenders (which mainstream theory posits as acting rationally) were willing to commit vast resources to these economies for so long, if indeed corruption and regulatory mismanagement were so widespread. The claim that investors and lenders simply did not know about these problems rings hollow, since the attributes of these economies had long been recognized, and since the ability of investors to obtain accurate information about these economies was enhanced by the IMF's Data Dissemination Standard.

Heterodox economists have provided more compelling explanations of the crisis. For instance, Chang (1998) has shown that in the case of South Korea corruption and mismanagement intensified only after the government committed itself to neoliberal reform. He argues that financial liberalization entailed a dramatic reduction in state regulation and coordination of the economy, and thereby opened the door to risky and corrupt practices. This argument is generally applicable to the region. The financial liberalization implemented throughout the region from the late 1980s onward created incentives and opportunities for domestic banks and investors to pursue activities that created a vulnerability to crisis. Financial liberalization drove up asset values (like stock and real estate prices), and then allowed domestic borrowers to exploit these inflated values to secure additional foreign loans. Hence, a speculative bubble ensued. For a time, this leveraging seemed benign. But when the difficulties of the mid-1990s discussed above emerged, this leveraging proved fatal. When these countries abandoned the dollar peg and allowed their currencies to devalue, borrowers suddenly faced rising repayment costs on existing loans and increasing difficulties securing new loans. Suddenly, even well-respected, seemingly stable financial institutions and industrial enterprises faced insolvency.

Turning to the Russian difficulties in 1998–99, exceptionalism (regarding corruption, tax evasion, and crime) is similarly problematic as a primary explanation of the recent investor exit from that country. Given that these problems have been apparent since the collapse of the Soviet Union, one cannot invoke their discovery now to account for a sudden investor exit from the stock and the government bond market. The same is true in the case of Brazil, a favorite of international investors since the early 1990s, despite the well-known overvaluation of its currency. It seems far more reasonable to attribute the recent exits from Russia and Brazil not to their exceptional features, but to a general emerging market contagion made possible by the ability of investors to flee the country (itself a consequence of financial liberalization implemented as part of the neoliberal regime).

Risk and Policy Autonomy

The post-Keynesian perspective on the crisis offered above alerts us to two important difficulties that financial liberalization introduced to Southeast Asian economies. First, financial liberalization introduced the problem of increased risk potential. The expansion of portfolio investment inflows and foreign borrowing provided governments and the private sector with resources to which they might not have otherwise had access. However, the liquidity of portfolio investment ensured that markets would be destabilized quickly once currencies and stock prices started to come under pressure. A dependence on foreign loans (especially short-term loans) on the part of the private sector in Southeast Asia and foreign bond sales on the part of the public sector in Brazil, Russia, and Mexico also introduced increased risk to these economies. The economies were rendered vulnerable to the costs of currency depreciation and lender/bondholder herding.

The absence of restrictions on international capital flows (called "capital controls") also introduced increased risk into the economies involved in the Asian crisis. When U.S. interest rates rose in February 1995, investors began to exit Mexico during that country's crisis. The same dynamic obtained in the current crisis when economic circumstances changed in the United States and Japan in 1996–97. Insofar as bailouts stipulate that afflicted economies increase their openness to international financial flows, these economies are rendered more vulnerable to the risk of experiencing the cycle of investor and lender flight followed by currency depreciation and financial crisis. Financial openness also introduces the possibility of a cross-border contagion. The likelihood that investors and lenders will see emerging economies in an undifferentiated fashion—the "guilt by association" of the Asian flu (or the "tequila effect," as the spillover from the Mexican crisis was termed)—makes the possibility of cross-border contagion more likely in the case of emerging economies as compared to wealthier economies like the United States.

Constrained policy autonomy intensified the

dilemma for Asian policymakers. Prior to the crisis, countries in Southeast Asia were not compelled to implement neoliberal policies in order to attract private capital flows, and in fact pursued distinctly non-neoliberal strategies while continuing to attract investment. By contrast, countries such as Russia, Brazil, and Mexico had to overcome investor pessimism or disinterest; thus governments' commitment to neoliberal policy was critical to the attraction of private capital flows. For this reason, in countries that require "rehabilitation" in the eyes of investors, the range of macroeconomic and social policies is constrained by the overriding objective of attracting private capital flows.

Clearly, for countries involved in the Asian crisis (and Mexico following its crisis), the crisis has had the effect of reducing policy autonomy. Following the emergence of the crisis in each country, governments and central banks were compelled to implement (or intensify, in the case of Brazil) contractionary macroeconomic policies that would aggravate the consequences of the crisis for the majority of the population, and introduce the possibility of loan defaults, bank distress, and slowdowns in economic activity. In those countries where a bailout followed the crisis (viz., Indonesia, Thailand, the Philippines, South Korea, Russia, and Mexico), all of the bailouts stipulated that governments introduce or intensify neoliberal reform and increase the openness of the economy. This was also the case with the preventative bailout of Brazil.[3] The influence of the IMF and the United States on macroeconomic and social policy in countries that accepted bailouts has been substantially increased.

Two caveats should be noted here. First, the power of the IMF to dictate policy is not absolute. Indeed, Russia resisted important IMF conditions following the crisis. But resistance to the IMF can be very costly for a capital-poor country.[4] Second, crisis not only empowers external actors like the IMF and the United States to push for neoliberal reforms, it also empowers those domestic interest groups that have long pushed for neoliberal reform. Backed by IMF sanctions, domestic neoliberals are sometimes able to take advantage of the crisis to push for reforms that were not politically possible in earlier periods.

Preventing Future Crises

The measures implemented to address the Asian crisis are unlikely to prevent a recurrence. Indeed, the increased external orientation and neoliberal reform occasioned by the crisis renders these economies vulnerable to serious recessions and to a repeat of recent history should private capital flows return (only to exit again). In fact, all of the countries involved in the crisis are now experiencing severe slowdowns in economic activity. In concluding this chapter, I briefly outline some measures for preventing similar crises in emerging economies.

Capital controls are one such measure that deserves serious reconsideration in light of the Asian crisis. Capital controls augment policy autonomy (by restricting investors' ability to flee whenever a government pursues a policy of which they do not approve) and enhance state capacity. More germane to the present discussion, they also reduce macroeconomic instability by dampening capital inflows and outflows. Heterodox economists Crotty and Epstein (1999) have made a particularly forceful case for the necessity and feasibility of such policies in emerging economies.

Although they have fallen from favor in mainstream economic theory, capital controls remain an important component of economic management in some emerging economies today. Measures in place in Chile and Colombia since 1991 (often referred to as the "Chilean model") represent an extremely promising direction for policy. The measures balance the need for capital with the need to protect the economy from instability. In Colombia, foreign investors are free to engage in (less liquid) direct investment, but are precluded from purchasing debt instruments and corporate equity. Consequently, foreign capital is much less able to flee Colombia en masse. In Chile, foreign investors may engage in portfolio investment, but they must keep their cash in the country for at least one year. Investors are therefore much more apt to base their investment decisions on a company's long-term economic prospects than on the opportunity for short-term speculative gain. To the surprise of many mainstream economists, Chile and, to a lesser extent, Colombia, have not only succeeded in securing large portfolio and foreign direct investment inflows from 1991 through the summer of 1998, but have remained largely untouched by the financial volatility that plagued so many emerging economies following the Asian and Mexican crises.[5]

The Chilean model also offers valuable lessons on the matter of discouraging the kinds of private sector borrowing that contributed significantly to the current crisis. The Chilean government tries to discourage borrowers from taking on short-term foreign loans by imposing a kind of "reserve requirement tax" on loans with a maturity of less than one year. Borrowers who take on such loans are required to deposit 30 percent of their loan proceeds in a non–interest bearing account for a number of months. This also reduces the risk potential of foreign borrowing, and thus deserves wide consideration elsewhere.

The Chilean Central Bank in October 1998 reduced the reserve requirement tax from 30 to zero percent (though the authority to restore the tax has been maintained). The decision to reduce the tax was made because the country experienced a reduction in capital inflows following events in Asia. Much has been written—incorrectly—to the effect that this policy change signals the end of the Chilean model. But in fact reduction of the reserve requirement tax by the Chilean Central Bank at the time when the policy is not warranted is desirable—it demonstrates that the policy is being deployed only as needed. This flexibility has been characteristic of Chilean capital controls since their implementation in 1991.

Finally, it would also be advisable for governments in emerging economies to consider designing simple measures, or "ex-ante circuit breakers" that might indicate whether their countries are vulnerable to a crisis triggered by investor exit. Such "circuit breakers" would make apparent when a country faced high levels of risk of investor flight. As a country approached the danger range, policies might be put in place to slow the entry and exit of portfolio investment. There would have to be, say, three thresholds for this indicator—for emerging economies at the lowest, medium, and highest levels of wealth.

One such indicator of a country's vulnerability to the exit of portfolio investors could be the ratio of total accumulated foreign portfolio investment to a measure of domestic investment in manufacturing and machinery (such as the measure called "gross domestic capital formation"). If a large proportion of domestic investment were financed by inward portfolio investment, this would provide an indication of the country's vulnerability to a reversal of those flows and its excessive reliance on a particularly liquid type of international capital flow. As a country approached the danger range, policies restricting new foreign capital inflows would be introduced. These capital inflows would have to "wait at the gate" until domestic capital formation increased by a certain level.

The design of measures to prevent crises in emerging economies is of paramount importance, given the significant costs and the spillover effects of the Asian crisis. Most emerging economies are experiencing fallout from the crisis as they face the exit of foreign investors from their mies are experiencing fallout from the crisis as they face the exit of foreign investors from their economies and as they confront stiff export competition from crisis-afflicted countries. Moreover, exporters in wealthy countries like the United States find that crisis-battered economies are not good markets for their goods, and U.S. producers of consumer goods must compete with inexpensive imports offered by countries seeking to export their way out of collapse.

The Asian and Mexican crises provide more than enough evidence that the world economy ultimately pays a price when financial systems in emerging economies collapse under the weight of pressures created by the wrong economic policies. Neoliberal policies have been given more than a fair chance to succeed. Recent events demonstrate that these policies have failed to promote sustainable economic growth in emerging economies. It is time for heterodox economists to design alternative policy regimes that prevent financial crises, balance the opportunities of openness to international capital flows against its rather severe costs, and create opportunities for governments to pursue strategies that promote equitable economic growth and the reduction of poverty.

Notes

1. Official reserves refer to the portfolio of foreign currencies and gold held by governments. Governments often expend official reserves in order to protect the value of their own currency during periods of turbulence, such as when speculators are dumping their currency in foreign exchange markets. In practice, however, governments of emerging economies are often unable to pursue this strategy successfully because the market power of speculators generally dwarfs that of governments.

2. This is the problem of "moral hazard."

3. Brazil received a "pre-bailout" in May 1999. The IMF provided assistance prior to the emergence of the country's most serious difficulties following criticism that it had waited too long to get involved in Asia. In the event, the preventative bailout did not stave off a crisis or a currency collapse.

4. Indeed, the IMF has since revoked the Russian bailout.

5. There are many reasons why foreign investors remain enthusiastic about Chile despite its capital controls. Chief among these reasons is the country's newly privatized social security program.

References

Chang, Ha-Joon. 1998. "Korea: The Misunderstood Crisis." *World Development* 26, no. 8: 1555–1561.

Crotty, James, and Gerald Epstein. 1999. "A Defense of Capital Controls in Light of the Asian Financial Crisis." *Journal of Economic Issues* 33, no. 2: 427–433.

Goldstein, Morris. 1998. *The Asian Financial Crisis: Causes, Cures and Systemic Implications*. Washington, DC: Institute for International Economics.

Grabel, I. 1996. "Marketing the Third World: The Contradictions of Portfolio Investment in the Global Economy." *World Development* 24, no. 11: 1761–1776.

______. 1999. "Rejecting Exceptionalism: Reinterpreting the Asian Financial Crises." In *Global Instability and World Economic Governance*, ed. Jonathan Michie and John Grieve Smith, 37–67. London: Routledge.

McKinnon, Ronald, and Huw Pill. 1998. "International Overborrowing: A Decomposition of Credit and Currency Risks." *World Development* 26, no. 7: 1267–1282.

27

The Roots of the Asian Financial Crisis

A Story of Export-Led Growth and Liberalized Capital Flows

Stephanie Seguino

Introduction

The outbreak of the Asian financial crisis in 1997 has perplexed many observers, in part because it followed on the heels of one of the most impressive regional growth records the world has witnessed. The heterogenous structures of Asian newly industrializing economies (NIEs) that experienced the financial crisis complicate efforts to disentangle its causes. This chapter evaluates several competing explanations for the crisis and proposes a synthesis of the two primary views. The explanation proposed here focuses on the linkages between liberalized capital flows and the export-led growth strategy adopted by Asian economies.

Background to the Financial Crisis

There has been little dispute that the Asia region has experienced rapid GDP growth over the last three decades. Growth strategies varied with first-tier NIEs (Korea and Taiwan and, to a lesser extent, Singapore) targeting expansion of exports to fuel aggregate demand, generate the foreign exchange to move up the industrial ladder to the production of more sophisticated goods, and achieve economies of scale in capital-intensive industries.

Second-tier NIEs such as Thailand, Malaysia, and Indonesia sought to replicate that export-oriented growth experience, but with fewer government interventions and a financial sector that was broadly liberalized by the early 1990s, a time when foreign direct investment from Japan had begun to dry up. Optimism that the Asian economies would continue to grow at a rapid pace is evidenced by the rush of foreign capital into this region over the last several years. Presumably, the successful track record of these export-oriented economies was sufficient collateral for lenders.

The character of recent capital inflows is significant. A large portion of the financial flows into Thailand and Korea took the form of private bank loans to domestic banks that then on-lent these funds to domestic firms. In contrast, in Indonesia, the bulk of foreign capital flows was funneled directly to domestic firms. Much of the capital inflow was in the form of short-term rather than long-term loans or the more stable form of capital inflow, foreign direct investment. By mid-1996, for example, 70 percent of bank claims on Korea and Thailand had a maturity of one year or less (Taylor 1998). Macroeconomic imbalances apparent in early 1997 did little to stem enthusiasm; even the International Monetary Fund (IMF) continued to grant high approval ratings to the region's economies.

By May 1997, the failure of a major Thai financial house (Finance One) and the country's large current account deficit fueled fears that the government would be forced to devalue the baht, leading to a loss of confidence and a reversal of capital flows. Freed to float in July, the baht depreciated more than 20 percent in one week. A year later, its value had fallen by more than 50 percent, resulting in a sharp increase in the real cost of servicing short-term debt.

Foreign banks and investors quickly lost confidence or believed that other lenders and investors would soon lose confidence in the region's ability to pay off loans or to generate satisfactory returns on investments. The resulting financial stampede amounted to almost $100 billion exiting this region during the latter part of 1997, further depressing domestic currency values.

The roots of the financial panic are, however, complex and differ by country. In some countries, decreased confidence was attributable to concerns over property market gluts (e.g., in Thailand), current account deficits (in Indonesia and Thailand), as well as to bankruptcies of major firms (in Korea and Thailand). But in other cases, such as Taiwan, currency instability has been due to worry over the effects of devaluations in other Asian countries that might hurt Taiwan's exports. The latter phenomenon further contributed to the perception of the panic's infectious nature or "contagion."

South Korea experienced the "contagion" of capital outflows only after a series of Japanese bankruptcies in October. With Japan the largest external lender to Korea, it was feared these banks might recall their loans from the Korean conglomerates, the *chaebol*, which would force more bankruptcies in Korea. With Korean goods now facing competition from Asian neighbors with sharply depreciated currencies, foreign lending declined precipitously. The result was currency and liquidity effects similar to those of other Asian countries that had fallen before it. A year later, the Korean and Indonesian currencies had gone the way of the Thai baht, declining 55 percent and 80 percent in value respectively.

The real economy effects touched off by the financial crisis have been severe. Capital outflows led domestic banks to sharply curtail lending to domestic firms at the same time that the IMF imposed conditionality on bailout packages requiring recipient country banks to maintain strict debt-to-capital ratios. But devaluation makes imported intermediate goods sharply more expensive, *raising* the borrowing requirements of domestic firms. The cash flow shortage could not be met by domestic credit, causing the number of nonperforming loans to rise. This further exacerbated the solvency problems of domestic banks and heightened the loss of confidence of foreign lenders.

Competing Views on the Roots of the Financial Crisis

In this section we focus on the conditions and policies that led to this episode of financial market and real economy instability, which portends long-lasting effects. The numerous explanations of the causes of the crisis in circulation can usefully be distilled into two broad and competing perspectives. These are discussed and assessed below, and a third perspective that is a synthesis of the dominant views is presented.

One broad area of thought on the roots of the crisis, dubbed the *fundamentalist view*, argues that macro fundamentals were wrong in the crisis-hit countries and that state-level macro management errors played a significant and determining role in the crisis. The competing point of view is that *financial instability* was at the heart of the crisis, and this was facilitated by lax regulations on capital mobility. The third perspective I propose is a demand-side explanation that emphasizes the uneasy relationship between an export-led growth strategy and capital account liberalization. I argue that reliance of developing economies on export-led growth contributed to depressed demand in industrialized countries, and resulted in a glut of manufacturing goods on world markets that drove down their prices. Liberalized capital markets overreacted to the emergence of current account deficits, and the effects of the financial crisis has undermined the ability of these economies to adjust.

The Fundamentalist Position

The *fundamentalists* hold that internal problems in Asian economies are the primary factor leading to the crisis. Proponents argue that governments in the region (in particular, repressive governments), under pressure to stimulate economic growth, engaged in corrupt interactions with business (a.k.a. "crony capitalism"), funneling loans to firms that were not creditworthy and projects that were not profitable. The results were bankruptcies and property market speculative booms, followed by high vacancy rates and collapses of firms and banks excessively exposed to real estate ventures. The reaction of financial markets may have been excessive, it is argued, but despite that, the root causes are to be found in macro mismanagement at the national level.

Fundamentalists point to significant real appreciation of currencies, arguing that exchange rate misalignment contributed to balance-of-payments problems. In Thailand and Indonesia, the combination of fixed exchange rates and large, rapid, and unsterilized capital inflows led to inflation, causing large and widening current account deficits. These deficits are seen as a primary cause of the financial crisis. China's devaluation of the yuan in 1994, the declining value of the yen, and the investment boom that led to a surge of imports also contributed to the worsening current account deficits.

In support of the fundamentalist view, there is some evidence that all of these conditions existed, though the extent differs by country. Figure 27.1 plots current account deficits of selected Asian economies for the period 1989–97. Current account deficits were worrisome in size only in Thailand and Malaysia, although in Hong Kong the trend was also problematic. Trends in competitiveness, measured as real effective exchange rates, do not correlate well with current account deficits, however. In Korea, real exchange rates were virtually unchanged since 1991, whereas in Thailand they had appreciated by 10 percent during the same period, and in Indonesia more than 40 percent (IMF 1998). Most countries in the region were, however, experiencing declining rates of export growth, regardless of trends in competitiveness. This composite set of facts suggests that: (1) it is misleading to rest on any single explanation for the domestic sources of the financial crisis; (2) additional causes of the crisis must be sought outside the domestic policymaking realm; and (3) we may question the ability of financial markets to adequately interpret macroeconomic signals.

The Financial Panic View

The *financial panic* view is that the carriers of the Asian flu are to be sought among the large and rapid unregulated capital inflows, not in the real sector. In rebuttal to the *fundamentalists*, those in the financial panic camp and others note that current account deficits were not the result of excessive imports of consumer luxury goods, but rather that these deficits are precisely what is to be expected of developing economies that must import intermediate and capital goods to upgrade their economies. Temporary fluctuations in current account balances result from external shocks to demand and prices of traded goods. Moreover, as a number of observers have noted, in Korea, the

Figure 27.1 **Current Account Deficit as Percentage of GDP**

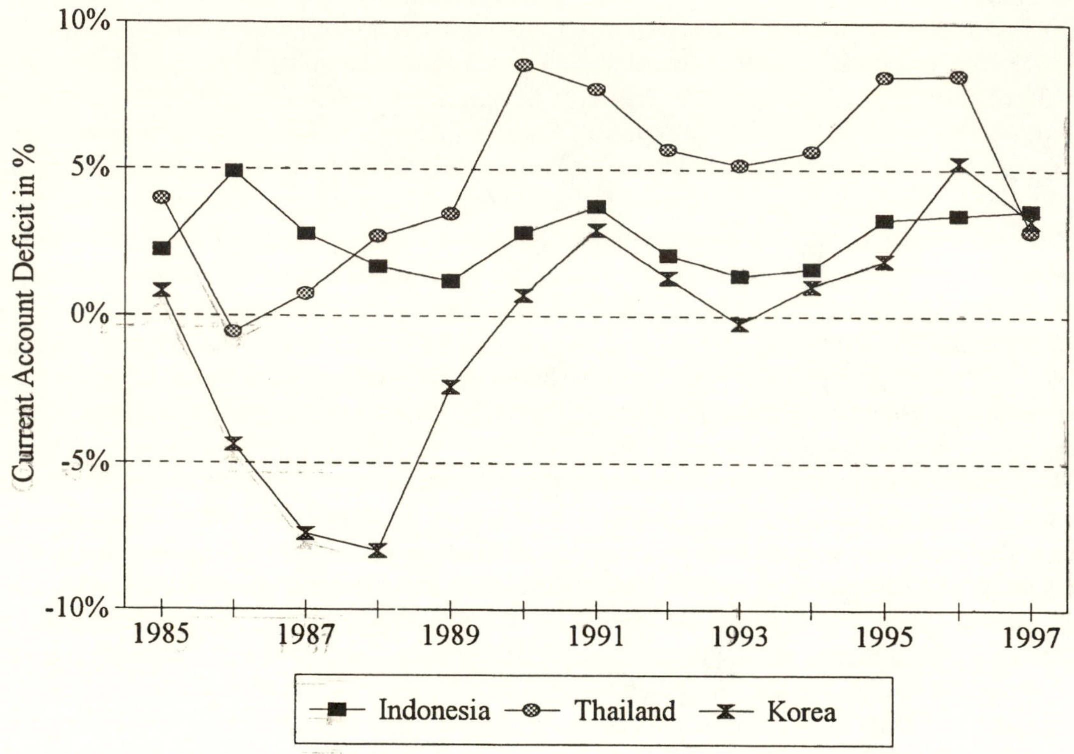

Note: Signs are reversed. A deficit is given a positive value and a surplus a negative value.

current account deficit had evaporated by the time the financial panic hit that country.

Stiglitz (1998) and others argue that property market gluts were not excessive. The vacancy rate in Thailand, for example, was about 15 percent, much lower than the vacancy rate of 20 to 25 percent during the 1980s U.S. savings-and-loan crisis. Nor were inflation rates and government deficits out of control; in fact, several Asian countries had government surpluses.

Further, crony capitalism, some argue, is misunderstood in light of the North Asian model, which differs fundamentally from the U.S. hands-off-markets model. In Asia, household saving rates of around 30 percent of GDP are mediated through the banking system and on-lent to firms (rather than through, say, the corporate bond or equity market). The developmentalist state influences the allocation of bank credit to ensure that funds are funneled to large projects that meet the goals of the state's industrial policy, including technology upgrading. Consultation between business and government has thus enabled firms to move up the industrial ladder and to become players in world markets (Wade and Veneroso 1998). As part of this package, governments regulated firm borrowing, but implemented policies to shield firms from disruption in demand and interest rate shocks, which raise the real cost of borrowing. At the same time, firms have been disciplined by the state's requirements to meet certain performance targets.

Seen from this backdrop, it is not too much government that led to the financial panic, but *too little* government regulation. The influx of huge sums of foreign capital in the 1990s that predated the crisis was attributable not only to propitious external factors but also to financial market liberalization in several Asian countries. Korea, for example, prompted by its desire to be accepted as an OECD member, dropped its widespread regulation of capital inflows that had served it so well for many years. Thailand and Indonesia also liberalized financial market regulations, partly due to external pressure, and this resulted in a proliferation of commercial banks that faced very few regulations (Bello 1997).

Why did private foreign banks and investors continue to pour money into the region, in the face of widely available macro and financial data that would suggest more caution? Either conditions were not so bad after all, or they were bad, and the markets did a poor job of detecting risk. A third possibility, consistent with post-Keyensian theory on the instability of financial markets, is that financial market participants exhibit less than fully rational behavior and, in particular, that financial market outcomes are influenced by the tendency to herd behavior. In the case of Asia, because investors and banks did not want to be left out of a growing region, they may have ignored prudential lending criteria in an effort to develop clientele and gain market share. It is likely they thought that the recriminations to be faced for *not* investing in that high profit region would be greater than for losing money so long as others were also losing money. The result of herd behavior in deregulated financial markets is that waves of optimism are frequently followed by panic, fueling real sector volatility. Korea and Taiwan as well as Japan, however, had escaped this fate up to 1997, in part because their financial sectors were so tightly controlled.

The failure of Asian governments to regulate financial flows, especially short-term lending, was exacerbated by their central banks' inability to act as lender of last resort since much of the debt is owed in foreign currency. Because central banks could lend only as much as they had in foreign reserves, when the herd moved in the opposite direction—taking capital out of the country and causing the domestic currency to depreciate—the banks had no power to reverse the trend in order to protect the financial system.

The Asia crisis highlights a major problem with unregulated flows of capital of the kind observed in Asia in the early 1990s, which is that they are subject to wild swings and herd behavior in *both* directions. Without central bank ability to act as lender of last resort, the panic was self-feeding. This is in part because of Asia's financial system, which differed from country to country but bore some similarities in that firms are highly leveraged. The higher interest rates proposed by the IMF under the terms of Asian "bailout" packages were intended to prevent capital outflow but only made the situation worse since firms faced a significant real increase in financing costs that they could not meet. In this precarious situation, high interest rates, instead of promoting capital inflows, led to more capital outflow. The feedback effects between capital mobility and the real sector are difficult to disentangle. It can be argued, however, that while the panic may have been set off by some underlying macroeconomic weaknesses, the lack of speed bumps on capital outflows prompted repercussions in the real economy that exacerbated problems that were otherwise not severe.

Export-Led Growth and Liberalized Capital Flows

A third explanation of the sources of the crisis combines elements of the previously discussed views and places major emphasis on the limitations of the export-led growth strategy when coupled with liberalized capital flows. Evidence of the problems associated with this strategy showed up in current account deficits that were rising in several of the hardest hit Asian countries. The source of the current account deficits, however, must also be sought in external global demand conditions rather than exclusively within the realm of macro policy. Deficits stemmed in part from a slowdown in export growth rates rather than a profligate citizenry importing excessive quantities of consumer goods. Further, the slowdown in export growth post-1994 can be observed in most Latin American economies as well, suggesting insufficient demand globally to absorb largely low-tech wage goods destined for developed-country workers. (A compatible argument advanced by Erturk [1999] links the crisis to overproduction. This is based on the notion of immiserizing growth, resulting from overreliance on low-tech manufactured goods that have taken on the pricing characteristics of primary commodities.) I argue that the rapidity and severity with which financial capital responds to perceived macro problems started the crisis off, and undercut the ability of these economies to respond accordingly to global demand imbalances.

What provoked the slowdown in export growth in the Asian economies and the resulting current account deficits? To help explore this question, reconsider Figure 27.1 which gives data on current account deficits relative to GDP for selected Asian economies. Thailand's deficit is substantially higher than that of Korea and Indonesia, providing some support for the view that the imbalance in the current account led to the currency crisis, fueled by fear of a devaluation in that country.

Of particular interest, however, is the similarity in the *trends* in the current account deficits in these countries. Asian deficits jumped in response to external events such as U.S. and Japanese recessions in 1991, and the Mexican and Chinese devaluations in 1994, which resulted in competitive pressures on export markets. For example, China's share of the region's clothing exports rose from 37 percent to 60 percent in recent years, posing a particularly severe problem for Indonesian and Thai exports. Further, the declining value of the yen relative to the dollar put competitive pressure on Korea's high-tech exports. A worldwide semiconductor glut forced prices down 80 percent in 1996, and was largely responsible for Korea's current account deficit since semiconductors provide 30 percent of export earnings.

Moreover, Korea was increasingly linked with second-tier NIEs as a high-end supplier, exporting semisophisticated goods to Indonesia, Thailand, and Malaysia, countries in which Korean conglomerates had invested heavily in recent years. Korea and Japan in turn purchase a number of low-end goods and components from second-tier NIEs. By 1990, 50 percent of the total trade of the region was intraregional trade, so that shocks to one economy were transmitted to others. This shows up in Figure 27.2, as GDP growth rates for Korea, Thailand, and Indonesia by the early 1990s have begun to trend together.

There also appears to be a linkage between the unrestrained capital inflows into Asia (and other regions) and the slowdown in developed economy growth. GDP growth rates in the United States and Europe have been at historic lows and therefore were unable to generate sufficient demand to absorb global low- and mid-tech exports. Rising incomes in developing countries have also not been sufficient to overcome the decline in demand from developed economies. Further, greater capital mobility and lower investment rates in industrialized economies have led to weakened worker bargaining power, evidence of which is observed in higher unemployment rates in Europe and low real

Figure 27.2 **Growth Rates of Real GDP**

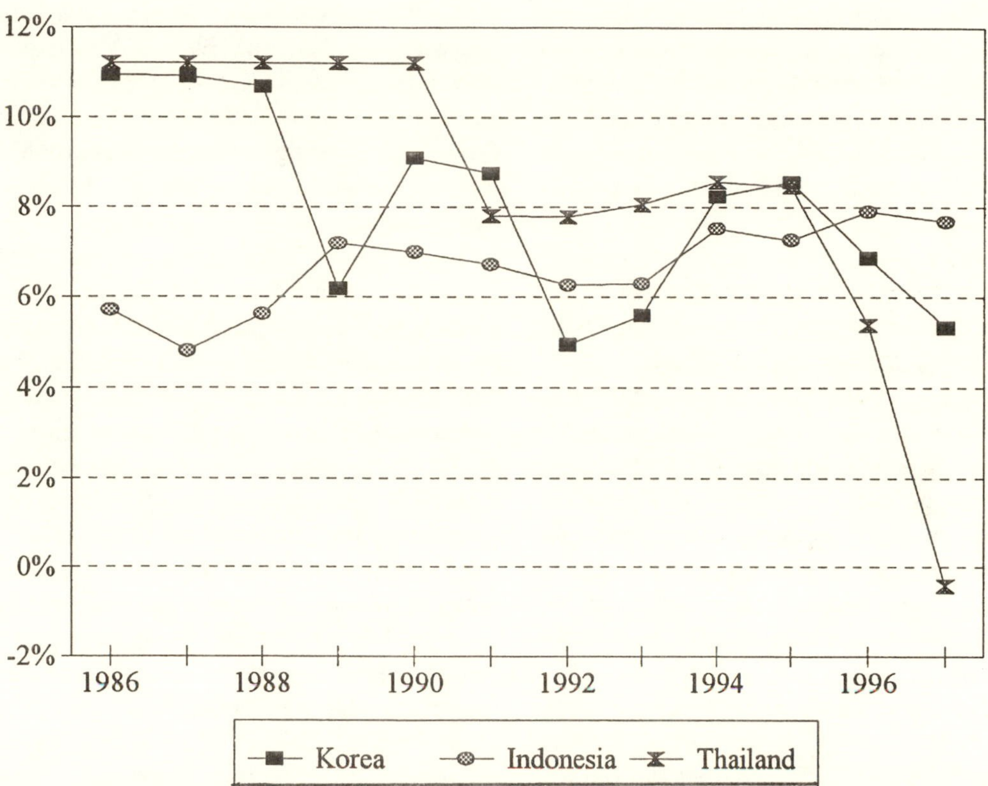

Note: Signs are reversed. A deficit is given a positive value and a surplus a negative value.

wages in the United States, as well as widening income inequality. Since workers' expenditures are weighted toward low- and mid-tech imports from Asian economies, the redistribution of income has dampened demand for exports from that region. The Asian crisis appears to be a warning sign that there has been a shift toward global stagnation due to insufficient demand (Meade 1990).

If declining demand for exports is a factor in the Asian crisis, we would expect to see evidence of a global glut of exports. Such evidence is found in the worldwide oversupply of semiconductors that drove down prices. Further, in the twelve months preceding the Asian financial crisis, the U.S. import price index, excluding petroleum, was falling. In European countries, import price indices had been falling since the early 1990s.

The gender dimension of the crisis highlights the demand-side factor. Thailand's export-led growth was significantly predicated on tourism, with a key emphasis on sex tourism. By 1990, tourism provided 20 percent of all foreign exchange earnings, though it is difficult to obtain exact estimates of the portion of these that come from sex tourism. The real estate boom was in part stimulated by this "export" of services. While some argue that capital inflows were injudiciously invested in the property sector, there is some reason to believe that these were reasonably profitable investments, had demand for sex services continued. But demand did decline, notably among Japanese and Korean male tourists but also among Europeans due to economic stagnation in Europe as well. These trends are likely to have negatively affected Thailand's current account deficits, which, as noted, were, according to some, a precipitating factor in the financial crisis in Thailand.

It may be argued that there is insufficient evidence of a secular trend to the export slowdown in developing economies, and growth rate decline in developed economies, to support the view advanced here. The key issue is that liberalized cross-border capital flows *speed up* market reactions to emerging real or perceived macroeconomic imbalances, leaving countries with little room to adjust and maneuver.

Could alternative state policies have altered the trajectory or depth of the crisis? The experience of Korea in the early 1980s suggests so. Declining export demand due to recession in developed economies, along with land speculation and excess licensing in some industries, led to a rapid buildup of current account deficits. As a result, average debt–equity ratios reached 488 percent in 1980, a similarly high level to that observed in 1997 (Amsden 1989). Rather than imposing short-run austerity measures to manage external shocks, the state borrowed its way out of balance-of-payments difficulties, using its clout to force firms to restructure and upgrade. Only one major *chaebol* went bankrupt during this period, indicating the state's willingness to bail out troubled firms. The result of the state's stabilization program was a surge in export growth in the 1980s and rapid economic growth throughout the decade. The institutional structure that mediated between the Korean state and foreign financial markets was sufficient to avoid herd behavior of financial markets and to delay actions that could have further exacerbated macro imbalances in Korea. That cushion does not exist in the current context of liberalized capital flows and limited government regulation. Yet the IMF continues to cling to liberalization as a solution to the current crisis.

The response to the current Asian crisis in the United States and Europe has been to relax tight monetary policies and to resist the urge to raise interest rates to slow growth, as has been the dominant strategy of the central banks in recent years. Depending on how responsive monetary authorities are to this problem, we may see some increase in aggregate demand that will pull export-oriented economies out of their slump. Another solution to the problem would be to take steps to induce wage hikes in industrialized and developing countries, but it is clear that the institutional support for this solution does not currently exist. Likewise, we cannot be sure that monetary authorities will be sufficiently flexible in their policies to permit a reinvigoration of industrialized economies. With regard to the developing and, in particular, Asian economies, the reins are held by the IMF and that institution has squelched monetary expansion through its high interest rate policy to stem capital outflows. The larger current problem for this region is indeed the IMF's policies.

Effects of the Crisis

The economic contraction that has been set off domestically by IMF policies has reduced sales further, causing cash flow problems to extend to even healthy firms. Bankruptcies are occurring at an alarming rate, with over 50,000 predicted in Korea for this year (*Korea Herald* 1998). Layoffs have resulted in more than a tripling of the unem-

Figure 27.3 **Real Wage and Unemployment Trends in Korea, Pre- and Post-Crisis**

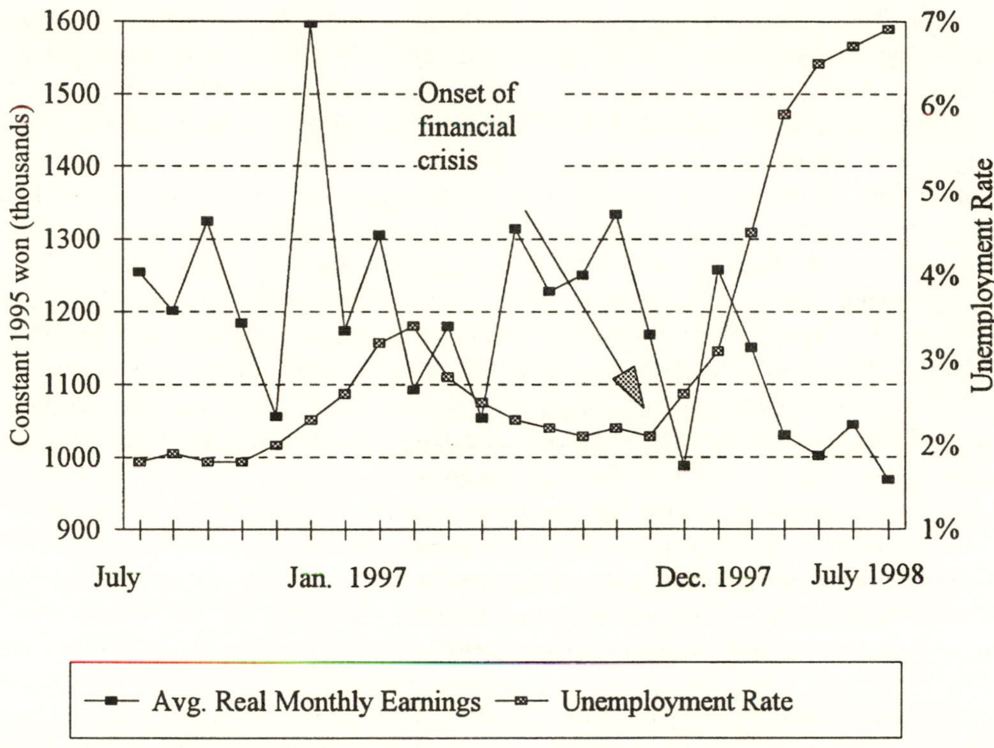

Note: Signs are reversed. A deficit is given a positive value and a surplus a negative value.

ployment rate in Korea since December, from 1.9 percent to 7.0 percent (Figure 27.3). Real wages have fallen more than 22 percent in the last year. Because Korean firms have been significant investors in second-tier NICs, the crisis there spills over to these countries. They, in turn, facing their own difficulties, import less from Korea. The domino effect is obvious.

In the longer term, how are remaining firms to pay off their mountain of debt denominated in dollars, and at interest rates that have topped 30 percent in recent months? The answer for firms with a high debt load and little in the way of retained earnings is that they will be forced to use their cash flow to pay off debt, and will therefore have little left over to invest. Reports from Korea validate this prediction, with firms' profits wiped out by high interest rate costs. The likelihood is for prolonged stagnation and indeed depression in this region. Further, the requirement to pay off foreign debts by exporting is leading to a series of competitive devaluations in the region, with many countries holding their breath over China's decision on whether to devalue or not. Recent news that China has laid off 600,000 textile workers is not encouraging on this front.

The gender effects of this crisis are particularly disturbing. While women have been absorbed rapidly into the labor force to work in export industries, be they producing goods or working as sex workers, they are the first targeted for massive layoffs at all educational levels. The exception is the sex industry in Thailand, where the state has redoubled its efforts to attract tourist dollars. The reassertion of patriarchal norms in times of economic crisis is apparent. One question that remains is whether jobs that had been designated as "female" jobs in the export sector will now become "male" jobs. As yet we do not have precise information on how this crisis is affecting job segregation, although the evidence is that women in white collar jobs are affected particularly seriously by job layoffs relative to men. We also know that the repercussions in terms of divorce, domestic violence, and women's economic insecurity are severe, and that women are faring worse than men. In Korea, for example, the growth of unemployment for females has been seven times higher than for males (Wiltrout 1998).

An additional problem is the effect on labor flows in the region. Labor migration from poorer countries to wealthier ones in search of low-wage work in so-called "dirty" or undesirable jobs had been typical in recent years. Thus the Nepalese had been invited as guest workers to Korea, the Malaysians to Singapore, and the Pakistanis and Indians to Malaysia. Those countries hit by the crisis are now expelling foreign workers, contributing to social disruption and cross-border tensions.

Conclusions

The Asian crisis has produced numerous casualties. As is frequently the case, those with least power get most of the bad news that capitalism's periodic crises generate. This is sobering news. It is sobering because for over a decade multilateral development banks and neoclassical economists have touted the benefits of a free market/free trade regime based on export-oriented manufacturing as the path to raising living standards. Can we be so sanguine today about the continued prospects for this strategy in a world of liberalized capital flows and declining bargaining power of workers in industrialized countries?

Hart-Landsberg and Burkett (in the following chapter) argue that the Asian financial crisis was an indicator that the strategy of export-led growth had reached its logical limits and that the window of opportunity for other countries to pursue a similar path is narrowing. They base this argument on shifts in political-institutional factors that undermined the growth regime as well underlying macro phenomena.

The view advanced here is that as the global economy integrates (a process that is speeded up by liberalized capital markets), global stagnation becomes a possibility if not reality. Insufficient global demand to purchase developing country exports can emerge, and liberalized capital flows inhibit and ultimately deform the ability of governments to intervene to stabilize their economies.

A solution is to take the necessary steps to stabilize otherwise unstable markets, including financial markets, and to reorient economic growth so that it is based more on domestic demand. While a reduced export orientation may slow growth insofar as reduced foreign exchange earnings limit the ability of countries to upgrade technology, there are clearly numerous other means by which to raise productivity. Further, the stability that is induced by greater reliance on domestic demand may have productivity-enhancing effects not accessible in an open export-oriented economy with unstable capital flows. The impetus to underpay women and other disadvantaged groups would weaken, and instead, higher wages would be a stimulus to demand and growth. An additional strategy that is suggested by the previous analysis is to stem the rising income inequality in developed economies in part to bolster demand for developing country exports. The political difficulties of achieving this goal are readily apparent. Although the road to growth with equity and stability is challenging, the Asian crisis teaches us that a change in growth strategies is necessary, both for developed and developing economies.

References

Amsden, Alice. 1989. *Asia's Next Giant: South Korea and Late Industrialization.* Oxford: Oxford University Press.

Bello, Walden. 1997. "Addicted to Capital: The Ten-Year High and Present-Day Withdrawal Trauma of Southeast Asia's Economies." Unpublished manuscript.

Erturk, Korkut. 1999. "A Kaldor Inspired Model of Economic Meltdown in East Asia." Paper presented at the Allied Social Science Association Meetings, January 3–5, 1999, New York, NY.

International Monetary Fund. 1998. *International Financial Statistics*. Washington, DC: International Monetary Fund.

Korea Herald. 1998. "Number of Bankrupt Firms Likely to Reach 50,000." January 22, 1998.

Meade, Walter Russell. 1990. *The Low-Wage Challenge to Global Growth.* Washington, DC: Economic Policy Institute.

Stiglitz, Joseph. 1998. "Sound Finance and Sustainable Development in Asia." Keynote addess to the Asia Development Forum, March 12.

Taylor, Lance. 1998. "Lax Public Sector, Destabilizing Public Sector: Origins of Capital Market Crises." Working paper, New School for Social Research.

Wade, Robert, and Frank Veneroso. 1998. "The Asian Crisis: The High Debt Model vs. the Wall Street–Treasury–IMF Complex." Working paper, Russell Sage Foundation, March.

Wiltrout, Kate. 1998. "South Korean Women Lose Past Gains." *Boston Sunday Globe*, September 20.

28

Mainstream Responses to the East Asian Crisis

A Radical Interpretation

Martin Hart-Landsberg and Paul Burkett

The 1997–98 economic collapse of Thailand, Indonesia, Malaysia, and South Korea came as a shock not only to government and business leaders, but also to development economists. Even after the assault on Asian currencies moved into full swing in mid-1997, the Asian Development Bank's chief economist still predicted that "these economies should be growing again at a fair clip in the second half of 1998 and thereafter" (Gargan 1997, C15). The end of the year, however, found the economies of Thailand, Indonesia, Malaysia, and South Korea in a tailspin, with all relevant economic and social indicators in sharp decline (Woodall 1998, 5).

Prior to the crisis, mainstream discussions of the East Asian economic experience had largely been limited to a debate over the nature of the forces underpinning the region's rapid growth. The International Monetary Fund, the World Bank, and the U.S. government championed the *neoliberal* view that credited East Asia's economic success to fiscal and monetary discipline, a willingness to allow domestic resources to be allocated along the lines of comparative advantage in trade, and—especially in the case of the three Southeast Asian economies of Thailand, Indonesia, and Malaysia (SEA-3)—an openness to foreign direct investment. Alternatively, *structural-institutionalist* economists and some Japanese and other regional government officials emphasized the positive role played by activist state policies in promoting the competitive advantages that neoliberals tended to take as given (Wade 1992; Amsden 1994).

Structural-institutionalists often thought of themselves as operating outside the mainstream of economic development theory, and they were certainly treated that way by most neoliberals. Nonetheless, both perspectives shared a crucial common ground that we believe justifies treating them as alternative mainstream approaches. Both agreed that East Asia's economic successes demonstrated that it was possible for Third World countries to develop within the basic institutions of global capitalism. Indeed, both perspectives embraced the ideology, which has become so familiar in the years following the collapse of the Soviet Union, that "there is no alternative" (TINA) to capitalism.

In this chapter, we argue that the East Asian crisis has thrown both versions of mainstream de-

The authors extend gratitude to Dawn Saunders and to participants in the annual URPE meetings in New York City, January 3–5, 1999, for helpful comments on earlier versions of this chapter.

velopment theory into crisis precisely because it threatens this shared vision. The chant of "there is no alternative" increasingly rings hollow, as it becomes clear that the only alternatives offered *by capitalism* are "discipline" and "stability," terms which, we argue, increasingly carry antisocial, and antihuman developmental implications. In fact, the East Asian crisis threatens to echo the "TINA" notion back onto capitalism as: "*This* is no alternative!"

As we will demonstrate, neoliberal responses to the East Asian crisis contradict their own precrisis accounts of the region's economic "successes" while failing to grapple with the true depth of the problems facing East Asian workers and communities. Moreover, while the structural-institutionalist approach provides a welcome recognition of the necessity of planning for development, its overall usefulness is undermined by the liberalization pressures produced by capitalism itself both domestically and globally. We conclude that alternative, socialist development visions have never been more in tune with the socioeconomic and political needs of workers and communities than they are today.

Neoliberal Responses to the Crisis

Neoliberals usually blame Third World economic problems, especially balance-of-payments deficits and currency depreciations, on overly expansionary macro policies and resulting wage and price inflation. However, the overall stance of fiscal and monetary policy had not been particularly lax in South Korea and the SEA-3. In fact, most neoliberals had previously credited East Asian macro-policy discipline and the resulting macrostability for the region's economic success (Stiglitz 1997, A19). In addition, any focus on "overheating" as a cause of the crisis would have drawn attention to the role played by capital inflows. Since openness to both portfolio capital and foreign direct investment was a key element in neoliberal accounts of East Asian successes, most neoliberals were motivated to refocus their attention elsewhere as the crisis deepened.

Determined to place blame on East Asian policymakers rather than capitalist market dynamics, conservative neoliberals redirected their fire away from policy decisions affecting *aggregate demand* toward those involving resource *allocation*. They argued that the primary cause of the crisis was the state's infringement on market forces, including government control over bank lending decisions, misguided state planning efforts and, perhaps most importantly, corruption (*Economist* 1997; Sanger 1997).

Other more left-wing neoliberals, while sharing the conservative goal of transforming the East Asian countries into open, liberal political economies of the U.S. type, nonetheless had a somewhat different understanding of the crisis. While conservative neoliberals blamed financial problems mainly on government meddling in bank lending decisions, left-wing neoliberals pointed to *inadequate regulation and supervision* of financial institutions in an environment of volatile short-term international capital movements. This position was argued most forcefully by Joseph Stiglitz, the World Bank's chief economist, who observed, "Inadequate oversight, not over-regulation, caused [East Asia's economic] problems. Consequently, our emphasis should not be on deregulation, but on finding the right regulatory regime to reestablish stability and confidence" (1997, A19).

This emphasis on instabilities from inadequately regulated financial markets also led left-wing neoliberals to dispute the effectiveness of the fiscal and monetary austerity policies imposed by the International Monetary Fund. Observing that the previously successful East Asian economies "do not have spendthrift governments, but rather huge private-sector debt problems," left-wing neoliberals suggested that "austerity adds to economic pain without solving the debt problem" (Kahn 1998, C8). Moreover, for left-wing neoliberals corruption figured less as a cause of insufficient financial liberalization than as *a cause and consequence* of inadequate regulation and supervision of financial institutions. Finally, left-wing neoliberals expressed serious concerns about the unfair distributional consequences of the financial bailouts organized by the International Monetary Fund. Paul Krugman, for example, "wonder[ed] whether it would not have been better to let South Korea declare a moratorium on foreign debt repayment while it moved swiftly to cleanse the balance sheets of the banks and conglomerates" (quoted in Passell 1997, C2).

Critique of Neoliberal Responses

There was an air of unreality about conservative reactions to the crisis. Even neoliberals such as Jeffrey Sachs (1997) detected "a touch of the absurd in the unfolding drama, as international money managers harshly castigated the very same Asian governments they were praising just months before."

More specifically, conservative neoliberals failed to explain how the same corruption that brought East Asian growth to a sudden halt had long been been supported economically by export markets, foreign direct investment, and portfolio capital inflows. In reality, authoritarianism had helped to repress labor and other popular movements, thereby lowering (or socializing) the costs of industrial capital accumulation. Repression had also ensured support from powerful external actors such as the United States and Japan, both of whom sought regional political stability and attractive opportunities for their transnational corporations and financial investors (Hart-Landsberg 1993, ch. 5–7; Petras 1998). Although neoliberals did not want to admit it, there had been solid profit interests behind the "admiration for authoritarian countries such as Indonesia" held by "prominent Asian and western business leaders" (Lee 1998, A17).

Authoritarianism also provided a congenial environment for corruption. However, this played a "positive" economic role insofar as it helped keep ruling coalitions together, thereby ensuring, especially in South Korea, that industrial planning decisions were actually carried out (Hart-Landsberg 1993, 165–67). Although such corruption was eventually bound to disrupt growth, it was only *after* East Asian countries partially liberalized their financial systems and opened themselves up to short-term capital flows (at the advice of conservative neoliberal agencies) that financial-sector corruption began to rage out of control to the point of seriously disrupting investment and growth (Bello 1997; Hart-Landsberg 1998).

The only real attempts by conservative neoliberals to address the contradictions between their precrisis and postcrisis accounts involved appeals to changed circumstances. They argued that although state interventionism may have provided a viable path toward industrialization and growth in the past, things were now different. The observation that the success of South Korean investment planning depended on external support associated with the Cold War—support no longer available—was a clear example (Woo-Cumings 1997). However, this kind of response suggested a definite narrowing of development options in the global capitalist economy. After all, if South Korea's authoritarian industrialization depended on special Cold War circumstances, what did this say about the options now available to other Third World countries?

For left-wing neoliberals, the preferred response

to the crisis included measures to strengthen financial-sector regulations and to reduce speculative short-term capital movements. Foreign direct investment and other long-term capital flows, on the other hand, were still to be encouraged. This approach opened up such important issues as the role of capital controls in the relative insulation of China and Taiwan from speculative bubbles and deflation, but failed to carve out a viable path beyond conservative TINA-type thinking. Insofar as the left-wing neoliberals blamed inadequate financial regulations on authoritarianism and corruption, their analysis is subject to the same criticism applied to conservative neoliberals. Left-wing neoliberals also failed to consider whether "sound" prudential regulations might be contradicted by financial-sector competition and the need to maintain "confidence" among speculative domestic and external investors. After all, foreign investors had willingly poured billions of dollars into these imprudently managed financial systems.

Left-wing neoliberals conveniently did not ask why so much foreign capital had been available for short-term investment in the East Asian countries and other "emerging markets"—a question that might have forced them to reconsider their allegiance to capitalist "market forces." The accelerating flows of money capital from the developed countries into domestic and Third World speculation, and the growing weight and even dominance of financial activity in developed country economic activity, had evolved despite an abundance of unmet economic and social needs in the United States and other developed countries. Similarly, the movement of huge sums of money capital into speculative construction and other questionable areas in the East Asian countries, where many workers and communities still lacked access to basic goods and services, just did not jibe with the purported wisdom of market processes, at least from a social as opposed to a purely bottom-line point of view.

The advice of left-wing neoliberals to favor longer-term capital inflows such as foreign direct investment was not without its own dangers. Rapid direct investment inflows had been a major factor enabling East Asia's high-growth economies (especially the SEA-3) to maintain their overvalued exchange rates. These exchange rates had cheapened imports of machinery and other industrial inputs while dampening domestic inflation; but they also increased East Asian vulnerability to speculative attacks. Moreover, it was the drying up of foreign direct investment, largely as a result of competition from lower-wage countries (especially China) and the mobility of regional investment by Japanese, South Korean, and Taiwanese companies, that had forced the SEA-3 countries to open themselves up to heavy short-term capital inflows as a way of financing their growing trade deficits (Hart-Landsberg 1998). These deficits were themselves largely a function not just of rapid growth and "overheating," but of the structures of export-oriented production created by Japanese and other transnational firms in the SEA-3 countries. These structures were highly dependent upon imported machinery, other intermediate goods, and financial resources from Japan and other "higher rung" countries in the region (Hart-Landsberg and Burkett 1998).

While expressing alarm about the upward redistribution of income and wealth under the financial bailout plans organized by the International Monetary Fund, left-wing neoliberals did not extend such concerns to export-led growth itself. They failed to emphasize, for example, how the competitive "successes" of East Asian exporters had been based on a class-biased socialization of the costs of industrialization in the form of low hourly wages, long and intensive work times, high industrial accident rates, and superexploitation of young female workers as well as serious environmental damages and a plundering of natural resources (Bello and Rosenfeld 1990; Seguino 1997; Hart-Landsberg and Burkett 1998).

Structural-Institutionalist Responses to the Crisis

As mentioned earlier, structural-institutionalists (hereafter structuralists), in contrast to neoliberals, emphasized the role of state intervention and industrial policy in East Asia's economic successes—especially South Korea and Taiwan. Not surprisingly, structuralist postcrisis writings have focused on South Korea rather than the SEA-3. The structuralists blamed the South Korean crisis mainly on the overly rapid liberalization of the financial sector, especially of loans denominated in foreign currency. According to Alice Amsden and Yoon-Dae Euh, "It was the government's decision to allow banks and other financial institutions to borrow without interference that created the current crisis" (1997, A23). Robert Wade and Frank Veneroso took a similar position, arguing that, "the rush to capital liberalization in the early to mid 1990s without serious institutional support stands out as the single most irresponsible act in the whole crisis" (1998, 5).

In this view, financial liberalization encouraged overborrowing by South Korean industrial firms at the same time that the weakening of the government's commitment to industrial policy enabled these companies to make questionable use of both foreign and domestic loans. A leading structuralist economist, Ha-joon Chang, argued that the South Korean government's abandonment of "its traditional role of coordinating investments" was the prime factor "allowing excess capacities to emerge in industries like automobiles, shipbuilding, steel, petrochemicals and semiconductors," and that this excess capacity in turn reinforced "the fall in export prices and the accumulation of nonperforming loans" (Chang 1997). Then, once the South Korean currency began to depreciate, the foreign debt burdens of South Korean banks and industrial firms became larger in local currency terms, driving even more companies into default (Amsden and Euh 1997; Chang 1997).

Structuralists shared many common understandings of the crisis with left-wing neoliberals while advocating somewhat different responses. Both perspectives agreed that the crisis was mainly financial, not reflecting adversely on the fundamental strength and "soundness" of the South Korean economy. As a result, both structuralists and left-wing neoliberals favored strengthening financial regulations and measures to reduce short-term capital flows. For structuralists, however, such regulation was not only a means for keeping the banking system and business balance sheets safe and stable, but also a necessary tool of activist industrial policies. This explains why structuralists were much more likely to strongly support *selective* credit controls and *stringent* controls on short-term capital flows.

Structuralists and neoliberals also agreed on the need for upgrading production and investment into higher tech, higher value-added sectors. Significantly, structuralists did not even dissent from the neoliberal call for the gradual removal of trade protection in *preestablished* industries. However, structuralists did part ways with left-wing neoliberals in their *consistent* advocacy of strongly interventionist state policies, including trade protection and export subsidies, as necessary weapons in the industrial upgrading process. Most neoliberals, even the left-wing ones, would have such upgrading develop "naturally" with government support limited to the provision of "public good" facilities (education, basic research, transport, communications) and the establishment of the stable domestic environment required by domestic entrepreneurs and foreign corporations. Structuralists were more sensitive to the potentially adversarial relations between host countries and transnational corporations than were left-wing neoliberals. As a result, the structuralists supported a stronger government negotiating stance vis-à-vis the transnationals to ensure effective transfer and indigenization of productive capabilities (Amsden 1989).

Both structuralists and left-wing neoliberals strongly rejected the International Monetary Fund's austerity policies as the proper medicine for South Korea and the other East Asian countries in crisis, believing that such policies would only accentuate their credit crunches and recessions. Indeed, both groups of economists worried that imposition of fiscal and monetary austerity was likely to generate major political backlashes with uncertain consequences (Chang 1997; Sachs 1997). However, structuralists were more willing than most left-wing neoliberals to sacrifice some "stability" (as defined by the IMF and global financial markets) in exchange for more effective achievement of industrial development goals. Among other things, this meant that structuralists had a much greater willingness to accept higher rates of inflation as a necessary price of development (Wade and Veneroso 1998, 10).

Critique of Structural-Institutionalist Responses

For both structuralists and left-wing neoliberals, development is mainly a matter of making technological and managerial improvements in the system of production. Despite the structuralists' preference for a more activist state engineering of industrialization, they share the neoliberal allegiance to "modernization" on capitalist terms. This helps explain structuralism's general disregard of the liberalization pressures produced by state-capitalist development itself.

Especially as regards South Korea, structuralists tend to treat such "premature" liberalization as a symptom of a lack of strength and will among state managers (Amsden and Euh 1997; Chang 1997). In reality, South Korean trade gains gave the *chaebol* greater independence from a weakening state, allowing them to evade financial controls and use their profits for speculative rather than productive investments. In addition, as South Korean enterprises penetrated the United States and other high-income markets, developed country governments pushed harder to open up South Korean markets—not only in agriculture but increasingly in industrial and financial sectors. This in turn threatened South Korea's activist industrial policies by eroding the fat domestic profit margins previously used to subsidize the export and import-substitution efforts of domestic firms. As the structuralists themselves emphasize—while blaming it on the shadowy intrigues of the "Wall–Street–Treasury–IMF Complex"—the opening of the domestic financial system seriously muddied up the South Korean government's financial controls over domestic business operations and gravely disrupted its sectoral investment planning efforts (Chang 1997; Wade and Veneroso 1998).

The structuralists' focus on *national* industrial policies causes them to ignore the systemic roots of regional and global overproduction with its disruptive effects on export-led growth. They disregard the connection between competitiveness in terms of low unit labor costs on the one hand, and limited domestic wage-based demand on the other. Combined with the limits of developed country markets and growing competition from lower-wage countries (especially China), the regionwide subordination of wage-based demand to the export effort had, by 1996, produced falling export prices and steep declines in export growth rates for South Korea as well as the SEA-3. Finally, the growth of disruptive economic liberalization pressures, and the effective reduction of state-capitalist industrial policy options, have indeed been worsened by the end of the Cold War. Simply put, the United States no longer has an overriding interest in promoting any new industrialization successes (and potential competitors) in East Asia or anywhere else. In all these ways, structuralists have evaded the most important implication of the East Asian crisis, namely, the closing off of development possibilities within capitalism.

Conclusion: East Asia and the Politics of Development Theory

Our survey of mainstream responses to the East Asian crisis reveals not only their theoretical and practical bankruptcy, but also that this bankruptcy is symptomatic of a global capitalist system that is increasingly incapable of accommodating national development efforts even on its own terms of competitiveness and growth. The East Asian crisis is sweeping away contrary illusions about the opportunities for "modernization" within the capitalist framework—illusions whose basis had been largely provided by the special circumstances of the Cold War and by the relatively strict subordination of financial capital to industrial capital in the immediate post–World War II era. With these circumstances no longer present, "successful" national capitalist growth now—even more than before—hinges on a country's ability to keep unit labor costs internationally competitive, that is, to keep working-class living conditions below international standards for labor of comparable productivity. This systemic bias not only makes any development "success" inherently self-limiting, but also creates a powerful tendency toward global overproduction and further downward pressures on worker and community conditions on a global scale.

East Asian workers and communities are fighting back against attempts by domestic and global capital to downwardly redistribute the costs of the crisis. Strikes and protests against IMF-sponsored wage cuts, mass layoffs, privatizations, and cuts in food subsidies and other social expenditures have been heating up throughout the region. As a result, "East Asia has become the focal-point of the international class struggle," and "a new 'Asian model' may emerge—a model of working-class resistance to capitalist globalization" (McNally 1998, 13).

Even prior to the crisis, struggles by young women electronics and garment workers for basic workplace and collective bargaining rights in Malaysia and Thailand, Korean workers' struggles for employment and income security, and the growing militancy of Indonesian workers and students (ousting the brutal Suharto), all confronted authoritarian governments that were forcibly defending capitalist property rights at the expense of human and social needs. The East Asian crisis has intensified this tension between "the worker's right to live" and capitalist social relations (Jeong and Shin 1998, 14–15). Indeed, as the crisis spread and deepened in 1997–98, structuralist economists joined neoliberals in expressing fears that popular unrest might threaten the region's long-run security and prosperity (Kristof 1997a; Chang 1997; *Economist* 1998). Neither mainstream school considered worker–community resistance to IMF austerity as pointing a way out of the crisis to a more human, democratic, and sustainable form of development. For both schools, development choices were best left to elite technocrats and market competition, while the best that could be hoped for from democratic institutions was the effective *management* of popular unrest.[1]

This makes it all the more essential that we in the West find ways to encourage, support, and learn from the debates and struggles currently taking place in East Asia. Only through critical engagement with popular anticapitalist struggles can we begin to envision and fight for worker–community-centered economic systems that do not hold human development hostage to capitalist exploitation and competition, whether market- or state-led. We must also investigate and help realize the hidden potentials that worker–community struggles hold for democratic forms of development not constrained by capitalism's market forces and elite-technocratic planning.

Note

1. For example, Chang's (1997) structuralist account of the South Korean crisis emphasized the need to manage the "massive political resistance" to the "sharp rise in unemployment" and "fiscal retrenchment" under IMF stabilization policies. Chang suggested that "the new government of Kim Dae Jung, with its more consensual approach to politics and stronger ties to the small firms and trade unions that are going to be hurt most in the process, may be in a better position to pull the country through a period of deflation and job losses and toward robust growth." This suggestion paralleled the neoliberal argument that formally democratic governments—if properly "disciplined" by international financial markets—could legitimize IMF-type austerity more effectively than could more openly dictatorial regimes (Kristof 1997b).

References

Amsden, Alice H. 1989. *Asia's Next Giant: South Korea and Late Industrialization*. New York: Oxford University Press.

______. 1994. "Why Isn't the Whole World Experimenting with the East Asian Model to Develop? Review of *The East Asian Miracle*." *World Development* 22, no. 4 (April): 627–633.

Amsden, Alice H., and Yoon-Dae Euh. 1997. "Behind Korea's Plunge." *New York Times*, November 27, A23.

Bello, Walden. 1997. "Addicted to Capital: The Ten Year High and Present Day Withdrawal Trauma of Southeast Asia's Economies." *Focus-on-Trade* (Focus on the Global South, Bangkok, Thailand), no. 20 (November).

Bello, Walden, and Stephanie Rosenfeld. 1990. *Dragons in Distress: Asia's Miracle Economies in Crisis*. San Francisco: Institute for Food and Development Policy.

Chang, Ha-joon. 1997. "Perspective on Korea: A Crisis from Underregulation." *Los Angeles Times*, On-Line Edition, December 31.

Economist. 1997. "The Asian Miracle: Is It Over?" March 1, 23–25.

______. 1998. "East Asia's New Faultlines." March 14, 16–17.

Gargan, Edward A. 1997. "Currency Assault Unnerves Asians." *New York Times*, July 29, C1, C15.

Hart-Landsberg, Martin. 1993. *The Rush to Development: Economic Change and Political Struggle in South Korea*. New York: Monthly Review Press.

______. 1998. "The Asian Crisis: Causes and Consequences." *Against the Current* no. 73 (March/April): 26–29.

Hart-Landsberg, Martin, and Paul Burkett. 1998. "Contradictions of Capitalist Industrialization in East Asia: A Critique of 'Flying Geese' Theories of Development." *Economic Geography* 74, no. 2 (April): 87–110.

Jeong, Seongjin, and Jo-Young Shin. 1998. "Debates on the Current Economic Crisis within the Korean Left." Paper presented at the Summer Conference of the Union for Radical Political Economics, Bantam, CT, August 22–25.

Kahn, Joseph. 1998. "IMF Concedes its Conditions for Thailand Were Too Austere." *New York Times*, February 11, C8.

Kristof, Nicholas D. 1997a. "Battered Economies in Asia Raise Fears of Unrest." *New York Times*, November 30, A1, A6.

______. 1997b. "Asian Democracy Has Two Masters." *New York Times*, December 21, Section 4, 4.

Lee, Martin. 1998. "Testing Asian Values." *New York Times*, January 18, A17.

McNally, David. 1998. "Globalization on Trial: Crisis and Class Struggle in East Asia." *Monthly Review* 50, no. 4 (September): 1–14.

Passell, Peter. 1997. "South Korea Is Facing Some Difficult Economic Choices." *New York Times*, December 18, C2.

Petras, James. 1998. "The Asian Crisis," *Z Magazine* 11, no. 1 (January): 10–11.

Sachs, Jeffrey D. 1997. "The Wrong Medicine for Asia." *New York Times*, On-Line Edition, November 3.

Sanger, David E. 1997. "The Stock of 'Asian Values' Drops." *New York Times*, November 23, Section 4, 4.

Seguino, Stephanie. 1997. "Gender Wage Inequality and Export-Led Growth in South Korea." *Journal of Development Studies* 34, no. 2 (December): 102–132.

Stiglitz, Joseph. 1997. "How to Fix the Asian Economies." *New York Times*, October 31, A19.

Wade, Robert. 1992. "East Asia's Economic Success:

Conflicting Perspectives, Partial Insights, Shaky Evidence." *World Politics* 44, no. 2 (January): 270–320.

Wade, Robert, and Frank Veneroso. 1998. "The Asian Crisis: The High Debt Model vs. The Wall Street–Treasury–IMF Complex," The Russell Sage Foundation Web site, http://epn.org/sage/imf24.html, March 2.

Woo-Cumings, Meredith. 1997. "How Industrial Policy Caused South Korea's Collapse." *Wall Street Journal*, Interactive Edition, December 8.

Woodall, Pam. 1998. "Frozen Miracle: A Survey of East Asian Economies." *The Economist*, March 7, 1–18.

Section VI

Exploring Policy Questions

Theory and Applications

29

The Rise and Fall of the U.S. Welfare State

Anwar M. Shaikh and E. Ahmet Tonak

Introduction

The growth of welfare states is one of the hallmarks of modern capitalist democracies. European welfare states began with pension and social insurance programs in the late nineteenth and early twentieth centuries, and then grew into comprehensive systems of social support between the 1930s and the 1950s. By contrast, the U.S. state only began its excursions into social insurance and public assistance during the Great Depression of the 1930s, and was typically much less comprehensive in the postwar period (Skocpol 1987). Nonetheless, in the postwar period the welfare role of the state grew rapidly throughout the advanced capitalist world, as evidenced by significant rates of increase in state expenditure and taxation, particularly for social expenditures. But in thinking about the financing of the welfare state, it is misleading to focus on the rise in social expenditures alone, because taxes rose equally sharply (OECD 1985, 16–17). Thus when considering the impact on worker incomes, it is more appropriate to look at the net social wage: social benefit expenditures received by workers minus taxes paid by them. When this is positive, it represents a net addition to workers' wages, a net transfer from the state to workers; but when it is negative, it represents a net tax on workers, which is a net transfer in the other direction.

One of our principal findings is that over the postwar period from 1952 to 1997, the net social wage as a percentage of employee compensation is very modest indeed: it seldom fluctuates beyond ±4 percent, and its average is a mere 0.6 percent (Figure 29. 3, p. 253). In effect, social wage flows largely recirculate income among wage and salary earners as a whole. And even here, the redistributive effect within the working population appears quite limited in most countries (OECD 1985, ch. 7, section B, 203).

Year-to-year movements of the net social wage are strongly affected by the level of unemployment, since this affects government expenditures on welfare, unemployment insurance, and so on, and the taxes paid by workers. And unemployment in turn depends on the long waves of accelerated growth and slowdown that are characteristic of capitalist economies. Thus when in the United States the long boom of 1947–1968 gave way to a subsequent long phase of slowdown and stagnation from 1969 to 1989, the resulting rise in structural unemployment in the latter phase triggered automatic rises in government spending and simultaneous declines in tax revenues. Combined with the increased defense spending in this period, the average government budget deficit rose almost sixfold as a percentage of GDP.

The Right was able to take advantage of the structural fiscal disequilibrium and mushrooming government debt of this period by focusing an attack on the welfare state. Public assistance and unemployment benefits were sharply restricted, and unions were systematically undermined. Union membership declined rapidly during this period, real wages fell, worker concessions and givebacks became commonplace, and the number of people in low-wage jobs rose sharply (Rosenberg 1987). On the other hand, military spending was maintained even as social spending was slashed, and corporate taxes were lowered.

These policies had their desired effect. The Reagan–Bush era ushered in a dramatic rise in profits beginning in 1982. The subsequent neoliberal Clinton era from 1992 to the present has proved equally profit-friendly, though as we shall see, the attack on labor was moderated once favorable conditions for a new round of the accumulation of capital had been restored (Albelda 1999, 15; Mishel et al. 1999).

Measuring the Social Wage

At the most abstract level, the net national product may be thought of as being divided into a portion that goes to labor, and a remainder, the surplus product, which is appropriated by capital. But at a more concrete level of analysis, it becomes essential to examine the role of the state in modifying this division of the net product. Capitalist accumulation depends on the level of profits, while the standard of living of workers depends on their access to consumption, healthcare, education, and so forth. The modern welfare state intervenes by extracting taxes from both sides while simultaneously redirecting expenditures back toward them.

Our primary focus is on the extent to which the state's involvement in taxation and expenditures serves to redistribute a portion of the nation's surplus product to, or from, the working class. In keeping with our focus on class, we define the category of "working population" as consisting of those members of the population not having ownership of capital as a principal income source. Our task is to assess the impact of government activities on the income and consumption of this population by properly accounting for both the expenditures directed toward them and the taxes deducted out of their income stream.

In accounting for after-tax income, it is important to note that there are two traditional methods. The first, which concerns the *observed incidence* of taxes, is to calculate the income workers actually obtain after the deduction of all taxes flowing out of gross wages. This is the measure with which we are concerned. But in economic analysis, it is also common to try and estimate the income that workers *might hypothetically* obtain in the absence of some particular taxes. This latter measure of *tax-shifting incidence* is adopted by Miller (1988, 1989), for instance, and many others. Both are relevant, but they ask rather different questions (Shaikh and Tonak 1987, 193, note 8). Were we to extend our study to the second methodology, our conclusions on the paucity of the net social wage would be strengthened, because the resulting (counterfactual) measure of the net social wage would be considerably more negative, and quite similar to those reported in Miller.[1]

On the side of government labor benefits, we count all social welfare expenditures (health, education, welfare, housing, transportation, parks and recreation, transfer payments to workers, etc.), but exclude other government spending (transfer payments to businesses, expenditures for general administration, defense, etc.).[2] This is in sharp contrast to conventional methodology, which tends to treat all government expenditure as a direct social benefit, so that an increase in military spending is viewed as essentially equivalent to an increase in social welfare expenditures.

On the side of taxes we count all those that are levied directly on the working population (income taxes, Social Security taxes, property and other taxes), but exclude those levied on businesses (sales taxes, profit taxes, etc.).[3] As noted previously, our primary concern is with the observed incidence of taxes, not with a comparison between their existing levels and the hypothetical alternative benchmark. This latter, counterfactual "tax-shifting" question is important in its own right. But it is a different question than the one we seek to address here.

A further issue arises because one set of social expenditures (E_1) and taxes (T_1) is entirely associated with workers, while another set (E_2, T_2) encompass both workers and nonworkers. To address this, we assume that workers receive a portion of the latter set in proportion to the share of labor income in personal income (LS). The net difference between overall social expenditures received by labor and taxes paid by labor is the net social wage (NSW). Finally, we compare this net social wage to total employee compensation (EC), which is the total cost to capitalists of hiring workers (Tonak 1984).[4] This is the gross wage of workers, and is made up of wages, salaries, employers contributions for social insurance, and other labor income.

$$\begin{aligned} NSW &= NSW_1 + NSW_2 \\ &= (E_1 - T_1) + (E_2 - T_2)*LS \\ &= \text{the net social wage.} \end{aligned}$$

E_1 = government expenditures on labor training and services, housing and community services, income support, Social Security, and welfare (except the small items called military disability and military retirement, which we treat as a cost of war);

E_2 = government expenditures on education, health, and hospitals, recreational and cultural activities, energy, natural resources, passenger transportation, and postal service;

T_1 = total (employee and employer) Social Security taxes;

T_2 = personal income taxes, motor vehicle licenses, personal property taxes (primarily on homes), and other taxes and nontaxes (a very small category, which includes passport fees, fines, etc.);

LS = the labor share = the share of wages and salaries in total personal income.

The preceding derivation allows us to see that changes in the measure of the labor share affect only a part of measure of the net social wage.[5] Table 29.1 provides a detailed derivation of the net social wage, and depicts the typical magnitudes involved, for 1964. All further detail is provided in the data appendix, for 1952–1997. It is worth remarking that, as in Table 29.1, NSW_1 is positive, and NSW_2 is negative (and is therefore a net labor tax) throughout the postwar period. In effect, direct income support for labor always exceeds direct (Social Security) taxes deducted for this, while general expenditures on health, education, and so forth, always fall short of the general taxes on income and property (see the Appendix). Over the whole period, the portion of the net labor tax that arises from the latter virtually cancels out the labor benefit represented by the former.

Figure 29.1 demonstrates that, as in all advanced countries, U.S. total labor benefits and total labor taxes rise hand-in-hand over the postwar period. This underscores the importance of looking at both sides of the balance in addressing the social wage issue.

Figure 29.2 looks at the same two measures expressed relative to total employee compensation. Three things are evident here. First, although both the benefit ratio and tax ratio rise over time, the former initially rises more rapidly than the latter during the boom period 1952–1969, as real ben-

Table 29.1

The Estimation of Social Wage(1964) (in billions of dollars)

Expenditures	**Total**	**Labor**
Expenditure Group I Total: Entirely Allocated to Labor = E_1	***34.08***	***34.08***
Income support, Social Security, and welfare (excluding military[1]	29.88	29.88
Housing and community services	3.50	3.50
Labor and training services	0.70	0.70
Expenditure Group Partially Allocated to Labor = $E_2 \times LS$		***36.07***
Expenditure Group II Total = E_2	***50.02***	
Education	28.20	28.20
Health and hospitals	5.10	3.57
Recreational and cultural activities	1.20	0.84
Energy	1.40	0.98
Natural resources	2.10	1.47
Postal service	1.10	0.77
Passenger transportation = transportation x GCONS	10.92	7.64
Transportation	15.60	
Gas consumption of passenger cars = GCONS[2]	0.70	
$E_1 + E_2 \times LS$ ***= Total benefits and income received by labor***		***70.15***
Taxes		
Tax Group Paid Entirely by Labor = T_1	***30.08***	***30.08***
Contributions for social insurance	30.08	30.08
Tax Group II Labor Total: Partially Allocated to Labor = $T_2 \times LS$		***43.57***
Tax Group II Total = T_2	60.43	
Total income taxes = federal + state and local income taxes	49.83	35.93
Federal income taxes	45.83	33.04
State & local income taxes	4.00	2.88
Other taxes and nontaxes[3]	1.10	0.79
Motor vehicle and licenses	1.10	0.79
Personal property taxes	8.40	6.06
Other personal property taxes	0.70	0.50
Tax on owner-occupied nonfarm housing	7.50	5.41
Tax on owner-occupied farm housing	0.20	0.14
$T_1 + (T_2 \times LS)$ ***= Total taxes paid by labor***		***73.65***
$NSW_1 = E_1 - T_1$		***4.01***
$NSW_2 = (E_2 - T_2) \times LS$		***–7.50***
Net total social wage = $NSW_1 + NSW_2$		***–3.49***

Source: National Income and Product Accounts of the U.S. statistical tables.

[1] This excludes military "retirement" and "disability."

[2] These shares are calculated using information from various volumes of *U.S. Statistical Abstracts* (e.g., Table 1107 in 1979).

[3] This is the sum of federal nontaxes, state and local other taxes and nontaxes.

Figure 29.1 **Labor Benefits and Taxes** (in billions of $)

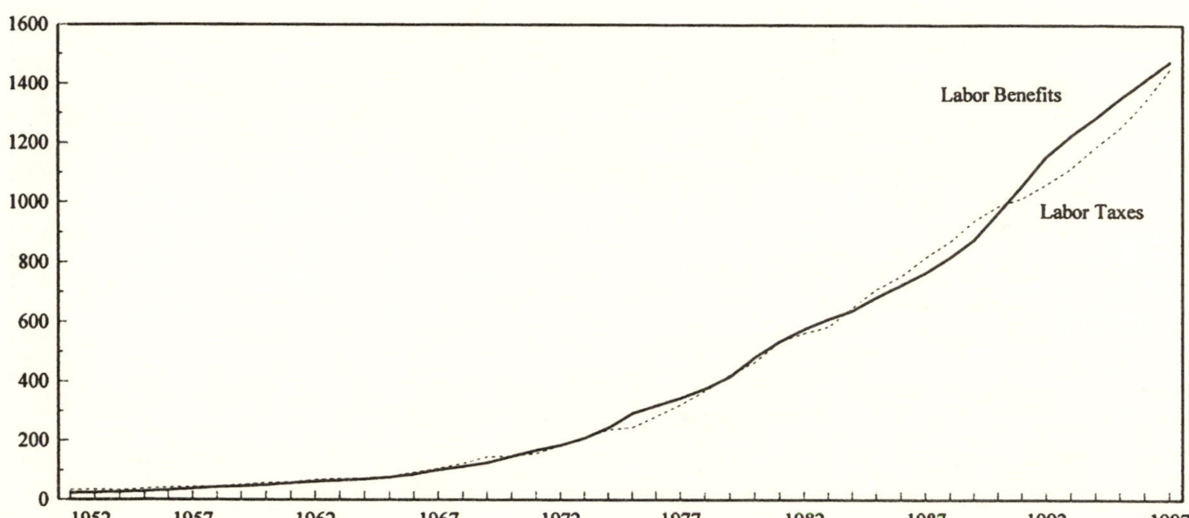

efits are raised and coverage extended. However, as the boom runs out in the late sixties, from 1969 to 1975, the unemployment rate more than doubles (from 3.6 percent to 8.5 percent), poverty deepens, and the consequent rise in payments for unemployment and welfare causes the benefit ratio to accelerate and the tax ratio to decelerate—thus automatically expanding both the net social wage and the overall government deficit.

After 1975 the unemployment rate drops somewhat, and with it, the benefit ratio. But even though unemployment and poverty remain high relative to the averages in the boom phase, it is in this period that the counterattack by capital and the state begins. Under Reagan and Bush in particular, this assault succeeds in dismantling the social safety net and undermines workers' organizations. The already low unionization rate in the United States drops sharply, restricted eligibility requirements for welfare prevent any increase in the numbers of people being aided, total real benefits actually decrease, and the purchasing power of the average benefit declines substantially (Amott 1987, 51). Thus when the unemployment rate rises sharply in the early part of the Reagan–Bush era, the benefit ratio barely fluctuates, and even falls below the tax ratio for the first time in 14 years.

The sharp rise in real profits in the Reagan–Bush era eventually restores growth and lowers unemployment—albeit at reduced real wages and worsened working conditions for most workers. The rise of the benefit ratio and the more modest fall in the tax ratio at the end of this period is merely the familiar reflex of the rise in the unemployment rate.[6] It is interesting to note, however, that in the subsequent Clinton era the tax ratio rises as unemployment falls, as one would expect, but the benefit ratio remains stable instead of falling. This would seem to indicate that the noncyclical base of the benefit ratio was raised under Clinton.

Figure 29.2 also shows that the Reagan–Bush era restores the negative net social wage of the early half of the postwar period, except in periods of peak unemployment. Once again, the exception, albeit a modest one, comes in the Clinton era, where the benefit ratio does not fall when un-

Figure 29.2 **Labor Benefit and Tax Ratios and the Unemployment Rate**

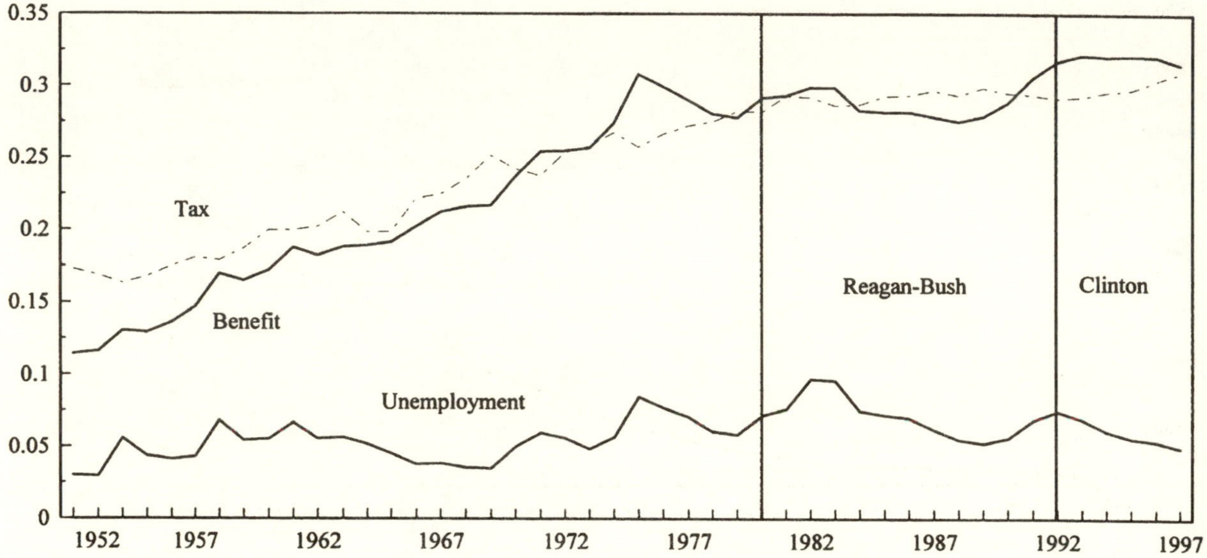

employment falls, so that the net social wage remains positive. But of course the tax ratio is rising (as increased employment pushes people back into higher tax brackets), and by 1997 the two ratios are virtually the same.

Figure 29.3 combines the preceding benefit and tax ratios into the net social wage ratio, which is the net social wage as a fraction of employee compensation. The three phases identified earlier are immediately evident. In the boom period from 1952 to 1969 the net social wage ratio is negative, although the security afforded by stable growth allows workers to improve their relative strength and gradually reduce the extent of their subsidy to capital. The second phase from 1969 to 1975 marks the onset of the economic crisis in which the sharp rise in unemployment and poverty drags the benefit ratio upward and raises the net social wage ratio. However, in the Reagan era the counterattack by capital and the state initiates a dramatic secular decline in the base levels of the net social wage, and this swamps any built-in rise in the face of the highest unemployment rates since the Great Depression. It is only then, starting from this new level, that the next increase in unemployment under Bush (1988–1992) gives rise to an automatic-stabilizer rise in the net social wage. As the unemployment rate declines in the Clinton years, the net social wage ratio follows suit, but not to as great an extent. As we noted earlier, this is because the base benefit ratio seems to have been raised in this period. Finally, it is interesting to note that over the whole period from 1952 to 1997, the average net social wage ratio is 0.6 percent—virtually zero!

Figure 29.4 looks at the impact of the net social wage in terms of the average real wage per worker (real employee compensation per full-time equivalent worker). From this point of view, the true real wage is the sum of the net social wage and the observed (apparent) wage, both in constant-dollar terms. Several things are striking. In keeping with the relatively small size of the net social wage ratio, the true wage is seldom

Figure 29.3 **Net Social Wage Ratio** (net social wage/employee compensation)

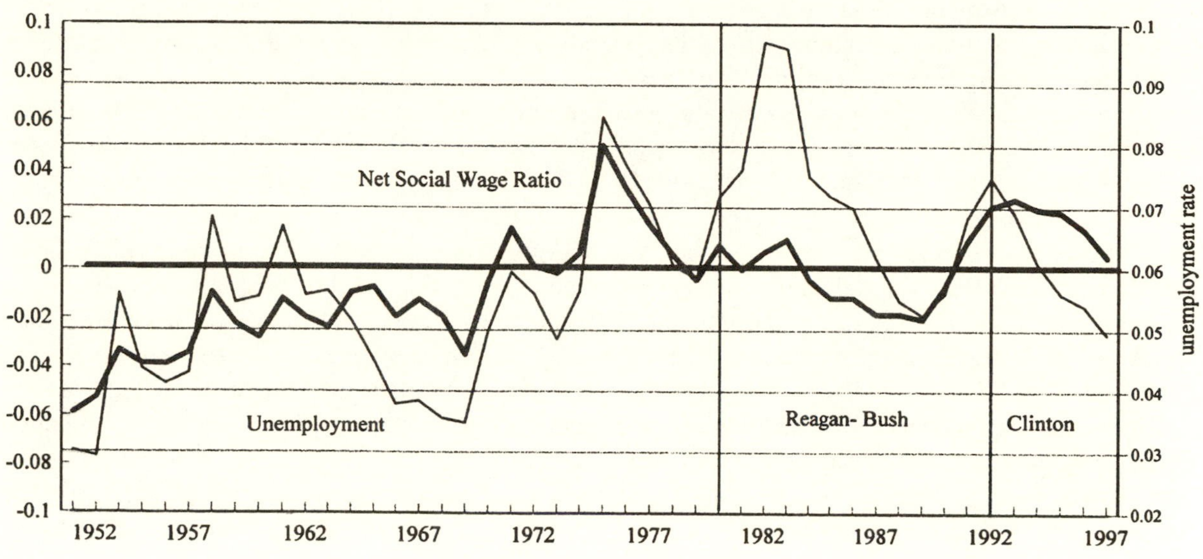

Figure 29.4 **Apparent and True Real Wage** (per full-time equivalent worker, 1982 dollars)

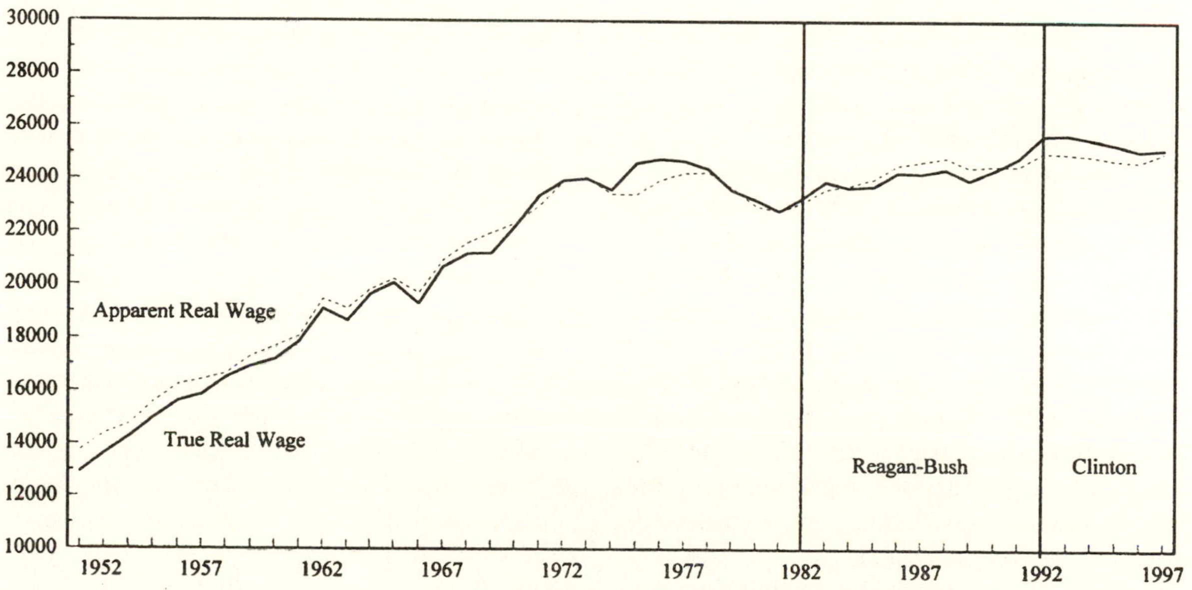

very different from the apparent one. Indeed, the former is frequently below the latter, particularly in the boom phase from 1952 to 1969, although this deficiency narrows over time. As the boom gives way to stagnation and decline after 1969, both measures of the real wage decelerate, and in the late 1970s to the early 1980s they even fall. Although they rise modestly for a while thereafter, they once again stagnate in the Clinton era. Overall, their post-1969 average rate of growth remains much lower than that in the pre-1969 boom phase. The legacy of the concerted attack on labor benefits and supports is clearly evident in all of this.

Figure 29.4 reminds us of the fact that in spite of the great development of the welfare state, the actual basis of the average standard of living of workers remains the real wage they are able to garner from their employers. Its steady rise in the boom phase, and its stagnation and decline in the subsequent crisis phase, forcibly remind us of the important role that class struggle, and the size of the reserve army of labor, continue to play in this age-old saga.

Finally, Figure 29.5 looks at the net social wage in relation to the total government budget deficit; both scaled by expressing them as a fraction of employee compensation. Note that a government deficit (an excess of expenditures over receipts) is plotted here as a positive number, to make it consistent with the sign convention used for the social wage. Thus a negative budget deficit is a budget surplus, that is, a net tax receipt, while a negative net social wage is a net tax payment. It is quite striking to then observe that until the Reagan–Bush era, the two variables behave in very similar ways. In the boom phase from 1952 to 1969, the net tax on labor (the negative social wage) accounts for a substantial part of overall total government surpluses. On the other hand, in the crisis phase from 1969 to 1980, the net benefit to labor (positive net social wage) is the substantial cause of the reduced budget surpluses and subsequent deficits. It is Reagan and Bush who break this nexus by simultaneously expanding the relative budget deficit and also slashing the net social wage. Since the net social wage is negative for most of this period, it cannot be said to have any part in the corresponding budget deficits. On the contrary, precisely because it is negative, we can say that during this interval the net tax imposed on labor made the deficit smaller than it would have been otherwise. It was the greatly expanded defense expenditures that account for the increased total government deficit in this period. In fact, the net tax on labor actually covers almost 16 percent of defense expenditures between 1987 and 1989.[7] Clinton, by phasing out budget deficits and also the net social wage, effectively restores the historic relation between the two.

Summary and Conclusions

The postwar history of advanced capitalist countries is marked by a tremendous extension in the role of the state. In particular, the great expansion in government spending on social programs has given rise to the notion of the modern capitalist state as a welfare state. But while this may be true, it does not follow that the welfare state is a net provider of goods and services, as some have tended to claim. On the contrary, when one accounts for the parallel rise in taxation that is an equally characteristic feature of the modern state, then something surprising emerges. By and large, it is the taxes of the working population that essentially pay for the corresponding state expenditures on health, education, Social Security, unemployment, public assistance, housing, and a host of other social programs. Over the whole postwar period, which is effectively the last half of the twentieth century, the average net balance between

Figure 29.5 **Net Social Wage and Deficit Relative to Employee Compensation**

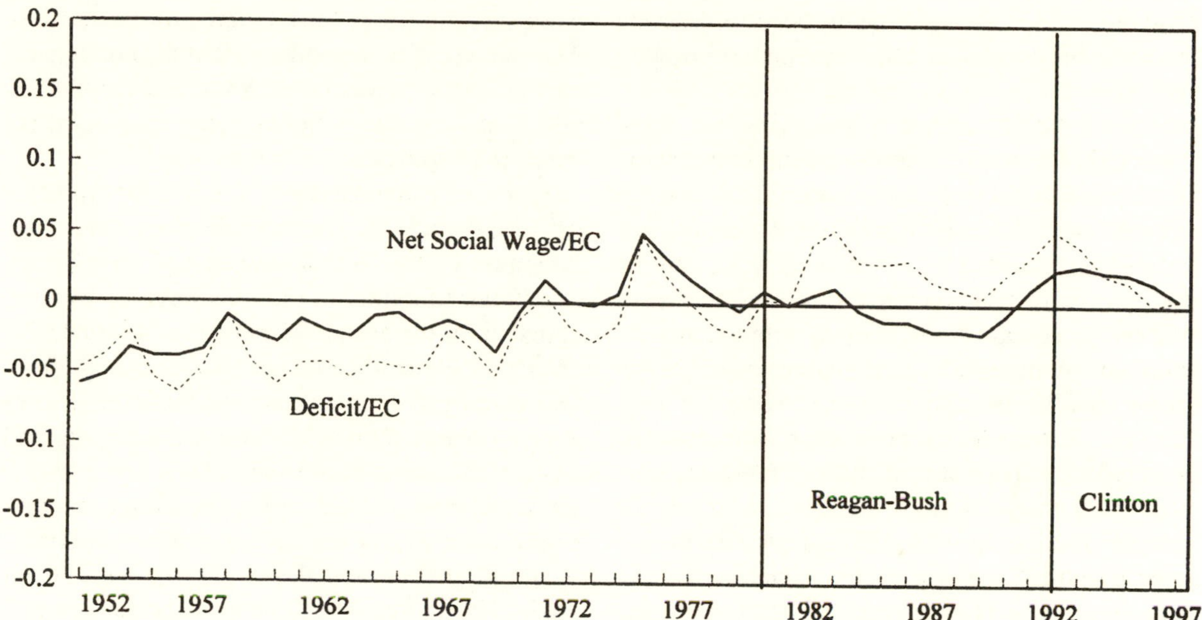

taxes directly paid of employee compensation and the social expenditures directly received by the corresponding population *is a mere 0.6 percent of total employee compensation*. It is, in other words, effectively zero.

We call the concept that we deploy to make this comparison the net social wage. It is the difference between social benefit expenditures (health, education, welfare, housing, transportation, parks and recreation, transfer payments to workers, etc.) and taxes levied directly on the working population (the labor share of income taxes, Social Security taxes, property and other taxes, etc.).

We find that the net social wage fluctuates within fairly narrow boundaries, largely between ±4 percent of employee compensation (Figure 29.3), and over the whole period from 1952 to 1997 its average is essentially zero. But from year to year, its variations are substantially driven by variations in the rate of unemployment. This is because a rise in the relative number of unemployed people induces increased relative state expenditures on income maintenance and unemployment compensation, while the corresponding drop in the relative number of employed people reduces relative tax receipts (Figure 29.3). This very same mechanism increases the relative budget deficit when the unemployment rate rises. For this reason, fluctuations in the net social wage also tend to be highly correlated with the budget deficit (Figure 29.5).

But there is more to the matter than the issue of cyclical fluctuations. The level and trend of the net social wage are also of great importance. And here, it is striking that during the long boom of 1952–1969, the net social wage was actually negative—that is, there was a net tax imposed on labor during this period. But because it was a boom period with low unemployment and steadily rising real wages, benefits per worker rose more rapidly than did taxes, and over time the benefits received by labor became more and more consistent with their taxes.

All this began to unravel when the long boom ended. By the early 1970s the unemployment rate began to rise sharply, and it continued to trend upward until 1983. This period of economic privation was attended by increasingly sharp attacks on the welfare state, on unions, and on other institutions that supported the working population. Real employee compensation per worker began to fall in the mid-1970s, and its growth remained anemic afterward. And as the welfare state was dismantled, real benefits per worker were slashed, absolutely and relative to taxes, particularly in the Reagan–Bush era of 1980–1992. Thus even though unemployment reached record highs in that period, the net social wage actually fell, and even became negative. Workers were living at a reduced standard of living and yet paying a net tax—in the very period touted as one of "tax-cutting" for the benefit of working people. The rhetoric and reality of the times could not have been more discrepant. It is a particular irony that the net tax on labor helped substantially offset the greatly expanded defense expenditures of this period.

A critical result of this attack on labor, and its associated support for capital, is that it served to restore the conditions of accumulation: profitability began to rise sharply after 1982, and has continued up ever since. The ensuing rise in the U.S. rate of accumulation eventually began to offset the continued displacement of labor from "downsizing," and by the 1980s the trend of unemployment reversed itself (Figure 29.2).

Clinton's neoliberal regime has benefited greatly from these events (one might say it survived only because of them) and has shown little inclination to change the structures in place. As unemployment fell in the 1990s, the net social wage fell in typical correspondence with it. But since it seems not to have fallen quite to the same extent, there is some evidence that the noncyclical base of benefits was raised somewhat in Clinton era. In any case, by 1997 the net social wage had essentially come back down to zero.

Our study demonstrates that the net transfers effected by the U.S. welfare state have a very limited impact on the standard of living of workers. It is striking to note that the real wage of workers adjusted for the net social wage is not very different from the unadjusted real wage, that is, from real employee compensation per worker (Figure 29.4). Thus in spite of the welfare state, the real basis of the standard of living of workers remains the wage they are able to win from their employers. Its steady rise over the boom phase, followed by its stagnation and decline in the subsequent crisis phase, forcibly remind us that class struggle and the reserve army of labor continue to play a central role—as ever—in its determination.

Notes

1. On the side of social expenditures, if we were to count veteran's benefits and services and military retirements and disability (both of which we exclude as costs of war), and on the side of taxes shift 50 percent of business taxes (corporate income taxes and indirect business taxes) to the labor account, our resulting estimates of the net social wage would fall between Miller's estimates of the SSA and O'Connor methodologies (Miller 1989, 85, Table 3).

2. The excluded expenditures consist of two kinds: (1) central executive, legislative and judicial activities, international affairs, space, national defense, civilian safety, veteran benefits, and agriculture, which are the general expenses of reproducing and maintaining the system itself (what Marx calls the *faux frais* of capitalist society [Marx 1977, 446]); and (2) those such as economic development, regulation and services, net interest, and others and unallocables, which represent expenditures directed mainly toward small businesses, related administrative activities, and interest payments to the highest income brackets. All of this group is therefore excluded from labor income and consumption.

3. The excluded taxes also consist of two kinds: direct

and indirect business taxes, and estate and gift taxes. Since the former set is levied on business, and the latter almost exclusively on those with substantial nonlabor income and wealth, both are excluded from the labor account.

4. Within Marxian terminology this is the same as (nominal) variable capital if we abstract from the distinction between productive and unproductive labor. At a more concrete level, variable capital is the total employee compensation of productive labor alone. Strictly speaking, we should remove the incomes of corporate officers and managers from employee compensation, and add in a wage equivalent for self-employed people. But since these two corrections appear to be offsetting, we ignore them in the present study.

5. As indicated in note 4, detailed estimates of the labor share that exclude corporate officers and other management salaries, and that add in the wage equivalent of most self-employed persons, would not significantly change the labor share. A variation in the labor share, in turn, would only affect NSW_2.

6. When the unemployment rate rises, employee compensation falls and total benefits rise (since there are more people receiving them). Thus the benefit ratio, the ratio of benefits to employee compensation, rises. On the side of taxes, if all people paid the same tax rate, total taxes would go down, but the tax ratio would remain unchanged. But in point of fact, a reduction of employee compensation moves people into lower tax brackets, and so the tax ratio actually falls (modestly) when the unemployment rate rises. These patterns are evident in Figure 29.2.

7. Data on the combined budget deficit and labor subsidy can be derived from the appendix. Data on defense expenditures are available from various years of BEA, *Survey of Current Business.*

Bibliography

Albelda, Randy. 1999. "What Welfare Reform Has Wrought." *Dollars and Sense*, January–February.

Amott, T.L. 1987. "Welfare Reform. A Workhouse Without Walls." *The Imperiled Economy*, Book 2. New York: URPE.

Marx, K. 1977. *Capital*, Volume 1. New York: Random House.

Miller, J. 1986. "The Fiscal Crisis of the State Reconsidered: Two Views of the State and the Accumulation of Capital in the Postwar Economy." *Review of Radical Political Economics* 18, no. 1/2.

______. 1988. *A Negative Net Social Wage and the Reproduction Crisis of the 1980's*. Conference on International Perspectives on Profitability and Accumulation, New York City.

______. 1989. "Social Wage or Social Profit? The Net Social Wage and the Welfare State." *Review of Radical Political Economics* 21, no. 3.

Mishel, Lawrence, Jared Bernstein, and John Schmitt. 1999. *The State of Working America 1998–1999*. Ithaca, NY: Cornell University Press.

OECD (Organization of Economic Cooperation and Development). 1985. "The Role of the Public Sector: Causes and Consequences of the Growth of Government." *OECD Economic Studies*, Special Issue 4, no. 1. Paris.

Rosenberg, S. 1987. "Restructuring the Labor Force: The Role of Government Policies." *The Imperiled Economy*, Book 2. New York: URPE.

Skocpol, T. 1987. "America's Incomplete Welfare State. The Limits of New Deal Reforms and the Origins of the Present Crisis." In *Stagnation and Renewal: The Rise and Fall of Social Policy Regimes*, ed. M. Rein, G. Esping-Andersen, and L. Rainwater. Armonk, NY: M.E. Sharpe.

Shaikh, Anwar, and E. Ahmet Tonak. 1987. "The Welfare State and the Myth of the Social Wage." *The Imperiled Economy*, Book 1. New York: URPE.

Tonak, E. Ahmet. 1984. *A Conceptualization of State Revenues and Expenditures: The U.S., 1952–1980.* Unpublished Ph.D. dissertation, The New School for Social Research.

———. 1987. "The U.S. Welfare State and the Working Class: 1952–1980." *Review of Radical Political Economics* 19, no. 1.

Appendix: Estimation of Net Social Wage*

	1952	1953	1954
DERIVATION OF LABOR SHARES			
Labor Share=LS=EC/TPI	0.711	0.718	0.708
Employee Compensation=EC=Apparent Wage	196.35	210.42	209.37
Total Personal Income=TPI	275.98	292.90	295.73
EXPENDITURES			
Total Benefits and Income Received by Labor=E1+(E2 x LS)	22.46	24.48	27.28
Expenditure Group I Total: Entirely Allocated to Labor=E1	9.69	10.73	12.80
Income Support, Social Security and Welfare (exluding Military)	7.69	8.83	10.90
Housing and Community Services	1.70	1.70	1.60
Labor and Training Services	0.30	0.20	0.30
Expenditure Group II Total=E2 x LS	12.78	13.75	14.49
Group II Total=E2	17.96	19.14	20.46
Education	8.90	9.90	11.20
Health and Hospitals	2.30	2.40	2.40
Recreational and Cultural Activities	0.30	0.40	0.40
Energy	0.40	0.30	0.30
Natural Resources	1.20	1.30	1.10
Postal Service	0.90	0.70	0.50
Passenger Transportation=Transportation*GCONS	3.96	4.14	4.56
Transporation	6.60	6.90	7.60
Gas Consumption of Passenger Cars=GCONS	0.60	0.60	0.60
TAXES			
Total Taxes Paid by Labor=T1+(T2 x LS)	34.00	35.54	34.24
Tax Group I Labor Total: Paid Entirely by Labor=T1	9.33	9.55	10.63
Contributions for Social Insurance	9.33	9.55	10.63
Tax Group II Labor Total: Partially Allocated to Labor=T2 x LS	24.67	25.99	23.61
Tax Group II Total=T2	34.68	36.18	33.35
Total Income Taxes=Federal+State&Local Income Taxes	31.13	32.28	29.15
Federal Income Taxes	30.13	31.28	28.05
State & Local Income Taxes	1.00	1.00	1.10
Other Taxes and Non-taxes	0.55	0.60	0.70
Motor Vehicle and Licenses	0.50	0.50	0.50
Personal Property Taxes = Other + Nonfarm & Farm Owner Occupied	2.50	2.80	3.00
Other Personal Property Taxes	0.30	0.30	0.30
Tax on Owner Occupied Non-farm Housing	2.10	2.40	2.60
Tax on Owner Occupied Farm Housing	0.10	0.10	0.10
NSW1=E1-T1	0.36	1.18	2.17
NSW2=(E2-T2) x LS	-11.89	-12.24	-9.13
NET TOTAL SOCIAL WAGE=NSW1+NSW2	-11.53	-11.06	-6.95
DATA FOR FIGURES			
Unemployment Rate	0.030	0.029	0.056
Labor Tax Ratio = Labor Taxes/EC	0.17	0.17	0.16
Labor Benefit Ratio = Labor Benefits/EC	0.11	0.12	0.13
Net Social Wage Ratio = Net Social Wage/EC	-0.06	-0.05	-0.033
Apparent Real Wage per FEE= EC/(CPI*FEE) (in 1982-$)	13748	14365	14729
True Real Wage per FEE = (EC + Net Social Wage)/(CPI*FEE) (in 1982-$)	12941	13610	14239
CPI	26.58	26.78	26.87
Full-Time Equivalent Employees (FEE; thousands)	53741	54690	52909
Total Government Surplus or Deficit/EC (with changed sign)	-0.05	-0.04	-0.02
Total Government Surplus or Deficit (Federal, State and Local)	9.32	7.92	4.28

1955	1956	1957	1958	1959	1960	1961	1962	1963	1964
0.712	0.719	0.717	0.701	0.713	0.719	0.711	0.749	0.720	0.721
225.92	244.74	257.76	259.76	281.24	296.66	305.56	342.42	345.52	370.99
317.28	340.55	359.65	370.33	394.35	412.53	429.95	456.95	480.05	514.48
29.20	33.29	37.83	44.03	46.35	50.98	57.35	62.44	65.09	70.15
13.35	15.40	18.26	22.60	23.53	25.26	29.35	31.15	32.29	34.08
11.65	13.10	15.76	19.80	20.63	22.26	25.95	27.25	28.69	29.88
1.40	2.00	2.20	2.50	2.50	2.60	2.90	3.30	3.00	3.50
0.30	0.30	0.30	0.30	0.40	0.40	0.50	0.60	0.60	0.70
15.85	17.89	19.57	21.44	22.82	25.72	28.00	31.29	32.80	36.07
22.26	24.90	27.30	30.56	32.00	35.77	39.40	41.76	45.57	50.02
12.60	13.80	15.00	16.80	17.50	19.40	21.30	22.90	25.40	28.20
2.50	2.80	3.10	3.30	3.60	3.80	4.10	4.30	4.70	5.10
0.50	0.50	0.60	0.70	0.80	0.90	1.00	1.00	1.10	1.20
0.20	0.40	0.50	0.70	0.70	0.80	1.10	1.00	0.90	1.40
1.00	1.20	1.40	1.50	1.50	1.50	1.70	1.80	2.00	2.10
0.60	0.80	0.70	0.90	0.70	0.90	1.10	1.10	0.90	1.10
4.86	5.40	6.00	6.66	7.20	8.47	9.10	9.66	10.57	10.92
8.10	9.00	10.00	11.10	12.00	12.10	13.00	13.80	15.10	15.60
0.60	0.60	0.60	0.60	0.60	0.70	0.70	0.70	0.70	0.70
37.93	42.82	46.62	46.52	52.63	59.26	61.08	69.27	73.38	73.65
12.03	13.50	15.50	15.93	18.78	21.90	22.90	25.38	28.53	30.08
12.03	13.50	15.50	15.93	18.78	21.90	22.90	25.38	28.53	30.08
25.90	29.32	31.12	30.60	33.86	37.36	38.18	43.89	44.86	43.57
36.38	40.80	43.43	43.62	47.48	51.95	53.73	58.58	62.33	60.43
31.70	35.43	37.63	37.23	40.58	44.25	45.43	49.58	52.43	49.83
30.40	33.83	35.93	35.43	38.38	41.75	42.63	46.38	49.03	45.83
1.30	1.60	1.70	1.80	2.20	2.50	2.80	3.20	3.40	4.00
0.68	0.78	0.80	0.80	0.60	0.70	0.80	1.00	1.00	1.10
0.60	0.70	0.70	0.80	0.90	1.00	1.00	1.00	1.10	1.10
3.40	3.90	4.30	4.80	5.40	6.00	6.50	7.00	7.80	8.40
0.30	0.30	0.30	0.30	0.50	0.60	0.60	0.60	0.70	0.70
3.00	3.50	3.90	4.40	4.70	5.20	5.70	6.20	6.90	7.50
0.10	0.10	0.10	0.10	0.20	0.20	0.20	0.20	0.20	0.20
1.33	1.90	2.76	6.67	4.75	3.36	6.45	5.77	3.77	4.01
-10.05	-11.43	-11.56	-9.16	-11.04	-11.64	-10.18	-12.60	-12.06	-7.50
-8.72	-9.53	-8.80	-2.49	-6.28	-8.28	-3.73	-6.83	-8.29	-3.49
0.044	0.041	0.043	0.068	0.055	0.055	0.067	0.056	0.056	0.052
0.17	0.17	0.18	0.18	0.19	0.20	0.20	0.20	0.21	0.20
0.13	0.14	0.15	0.17	0.16	0.17	0.19	0.18	0.19	0.19
-0.039	-0.039	-0.034	-0.010	-0.022	-0.028	-0.012	-0.020	-0.024	-0.009
15569	16233	16412	16645	17309	17674	18064	19475	19119	19829
14968	15601	15852	16485	16923	17181	17844	19086	18660	19642
26.81	27.19	28.12	28.88	29.17	29.59	29.88	30.25	30.64	31.04
54126	55445	55857	54047	55708	56724	56604	58125	58979	60271
-0.05	-0.06	-0.05	-0.01	-0.04	-0.06	-0.04	-0.04	-0.05	-0.04
12.25	15.77	11.90	2.05	12.20	17.30	13.27	14.50	18.38	15.55

	1965	1966	1967
DERIVATION OF LABOR SHARES			
Labor Share=LS=EC/TPI	0.718	0.698	0.731
Employee Compensation=EC=Apparent Wage	399.82	422.95	475.52
Total Personal Income=TPI	556.73	605.75	650.73
EXPENDITURES			
Total Benefits and Income Received by Labor=E1+(E2 x LS)	76.54	85.60	100.96
Expenditure Group I Total: Entirely Allocated to Labor=E1	37.31	42.09	50.43
Income Support, Social Security and Welfare (exluding Military)	32.71	36.99	44.43
Housing and Community Services	3.70	4.00	4.40
Labor and Training Services	0.90	1.10	1.60
Expenditure Group II Total=E2 x LS	39.23	43.51	50.53
Group II Total=E2	54.62	62.31	69.15
Education	31.30	36.60	41.30
Health and Hospitals	5.50	6.00	6.50
Recreational and Cultural Activities	1.20	1.30	1.50
Energy	1.40	1.30	1.70
Natural Resources	2.40	2.80	3.00
Postal Service	1.20	1.50	1.50
Passenger Transportation=Transportation*GCONS	11.62	12.81	13.65
Transporation	16.60	18.30	19.50
Gas Consumption of Passenger Cars=GCONS	0.70	0.70	0.70
TAXES			
Total Taxes Paid by Labor=T1+(T2 x LS)	79.48	93.78	106.88
Tax Group I Labor Total: Paid Entirely by Labor=T1	31.60	40.58	45.55
Contributions for Social Insurance	31,60	40.58	45.55
Tax Group II Labor Total: Partially Allocated to Labor=T2 x LS	47.88	53.20	61.33
Tax Group II Total=T2	66.68	76.20	83.93
Total Income Taxes=Federal+State&Local Income Taxes	55.28	63.80	70.23
Federal Income Taxes	50.88	58.40	64.13
State & Local Income Taxes	4.40	5.40	6.10
Other Taxes and Non-taxes	1.10	1.20	1.50
Motor Vehicle and Licenses	1.20	1.40	1.40
Personal Property Taxes = Other + Nonfarm & Farm Owner Occupied	9.10	9.80	10.80
Other Personal Property Taxes	0.70	0.70	0.70
Tax on Owner Occupied Non-farm Housing	8.20	8.90	9.90
Tax on Owner Occupied Farm Housing	0.20	0.20	0.20
NSW1=E1-T1	5.71	1.52	4.88
NSW2=(E2-T2) x LS	-8.66	-9.70	-10.80
NET TOTAL SOCIAL WAGE=NSW1+NSW2	-2.95	-8.18	-5.92
DATA FOR FIGURES			
Unemployment Rate	0.045	0.038	0.038
Labor Tax Ratio = Labor Taxes/EC	0.20	0.22	0.22
Labor Benefit Ratio = Labor Benefits/EC	0.19	0.20	0.21
Net Social Wage Ratio = Net Social Wage/EC	-0.007	-0.019	-0.012
Apparent Real Wage per FEE= EC/(CPI*FEE) (in 1982-$)	20226	19692	20950
True Real Wage per FEE = (EC + Net Social Wage)/(CPI*FEE) (in 1982-$)	20077	19311	20689
CPI	31.55	32.50	33.38
Full-Time Equivalent Employees (FEE; thousands)	62654	66086	68007
Total Government Surplus or Deficit/EC (with changed sign)	-0.05	-0.05	-0.02
Total Government Surplus or Deficit (Federal, State and Local)	18.45	19.90	8.95

1968	1969	1970	1971	1972	1973	1974	1975	1976	1977
0.734	0.742	0.738	0.733	0.735	0.734	0.734	0.721	0.727	0.732
524.72	578.26	618.12	660.05	726.79	813.08	892.42	951.27	1061.54	1182.86
714.55	779.28	837.10	900.20	988.85	1107.55	1215.93	1319.00	1459.38	1616.10
113.29	125.29	146.44	167.66	185.07	208.57	244.38	292.84	317.85	343.32
58.63	64.56	77.56	92.55	103.76	119.43	142.68	177.82	194.85	209.85
51.83	57.76	70.06	83.45	93.56	108.33	129.88	163.32	178.46	192.45
5.20	5.10	5.70	6.60	7.40	8.40	10.10	11.50	12.70	13.20
1.60	1.70	1.80	2.50	2.80	2.70	2.70	3.00	3.70	4.20
54.66	60.73	68.88	75.11	81.30	89.14	101.70	115.02	122.99	133.47
74.44	81.84	93.28	102.44	110.62	121.42	138.57	159.48	169.09	182.35
45.20	50.00	56.60	62.70	68.50	75.50	84.20	96.10	104.80	112.40
7.30	8.40	9.80	10.80	12.00	13.40	15.10	16.90	17.50	19.10
1.80	2.20	2.40	2.70	2.80	3.20	4.00	4.80	5.10	5.30
1.60	1.80	2.00	2.00	2.20	2.20	3.40	4.30	5.30	6.90
2.50	2.50	3.00	3.20	3.50	3.50	4.20	4.90	5.00	5.40
1.20	1.40	2.40	2.70	2.30	2.90	3.10	4.90	3.60	4.20
14.84	15.54	17.08	18.34	19.32	20.72	24.57	27.58	27.79	29.05
21.20	22.20	24.40	26.20	27.60	29.60	35.10	39.40	39.70	41.50
0.70	0.70	0.70	0.70	0.70	0.70	0.70	0.70	0.70	0.70
123.37	145.45	149.65	156.71	184.18	209.85	238.48	245.01	282.77	321.92
50.45	57.78	62.00	69.60	79.55	97.88	111.65	121.05	137.75	155.38
50.45	57.78	62.00	69.60	79.55	97.88	111.65	121.05	137.75	155.38
72.92	87.67	87.65	87.11	104.63	111.97	126.83	123.96	145.02	166.55
99.30	118.15	118.70	118.80	142.35	152.53	172.80	171.88	199.38	227.55
83.98	100.88	99.40	97.70	119.50	128.00	146.40	142.88	167.15	192.15
76.18	91.08	88.50	85.30	102.30	109.10	126.00	120.38	140.85	161.75
7.80	9.80	10.90	12.40	17.20	18.90	20.40	22.50	26.30	30.40
1.53	1.78	1.90	2.10	2.45	2.53	2.90	3.40	4.03	4.50
1.60	1.90	2.10	2.20	2.40	2.60	2.70	2.80	3.10	3.30
12.20	13.60	15.30	16.80	18.00	19.40	20.80	22.80	25.10	27.60
0.80	0.80	0.80	0.90	0.90	0.90	0.90	0.90	0.90	0.90
11.20	12.60	14.30	15.70	16.90	18.30	19.60	21.60	23.90	26.40
0.20	0.20	0.20	0.20	0.20	0.20	0.30	0.30	0.30	0.30
8.18	6.78	15.56	22.95	24.21	21.56	31.03	56.77	57.10	54.48
-18.26	-26.94	-18.77	-12.00	-23.32	-22.84	-25.12	-8.94	-22.03	-33.08
-10.08	-20.16	-3.21	10.95	0.89	-1.28	5.91	47.83	35.08	21.39
0.036	0.035	0.050	0.060	0.056	0.049	0.056	0.085	0.077	0.071
0.24	0.25	0.24	0.24	0.25	0.26	0.27	0.26	0.27	0.27
0.22	0.22	0.24	0.25	0.25	0.26	0.27	0.31	0.30	0.29
-0.019	-0.035	-0.005	0.017	0.001	-0.002	0.007	0.050	0.033	0.018
21584	21973	22337	23008	23913	24064	23451	23439	23985	24259
21169	21207	22221	23389	23943	24026	23607	24618	24778	24698
34.79	36.68	38.84	40.48	41.81	44.43	49.32	53.83	56.93	60.62
69875	71740	71245	70865	72695	76058	77163	75401	77737	80440
-0.03	-0.05	-0.01	0.01	-0.02	-0.03	-0.02	0.05	0.02	0.00
17.22	29.85	6.68	-3.63	11.63	22.22	13.55	-46.28	-21.28	-1.52

	1978	1979	1980
DERIVATION OF LABOR SHARES			
Labor Share=LS=EC/TPI	0.733	0.731	0.721
Employee Compensation=EC=Apparent Wage	1338.46	1503.25	1653.89
Total Personal Income=TPI	1825.90	2055.85	2292.98
EXPENDITURES			
Total Benefits and Income Received by Labor=E1+(E2 x LS)	375.57	417.60	482.38
Expenditure Group I Total: Entirely Allocated to Labor=E1	228.72	256.10	304.83
Income Support, Social Security and Welfare (exluding Military)	207.12	231.40	275.83
Housing and Community Services	15.90	18.50	22.10
Labor and Training Services	5.70	6.20	6.90
Expenditure Group II Total=E2 x LS	146.86	161.50	177.55
Group II Total=E2	200.34	220.87	246.16
Education	121.10	133.80	147.60
Health and Hospitals	21.00	22.40	25.80
Recreational and Cultural Activities	6.00	6.50	7.10
Energy	10.20	9.60	9.80
Natural Resources	6.00	7.30	8.20
Postal Service	3.70	4.10	5.80
Passenger Transportation=Transportation*GCONS	32.34	37.17	41.86
Transporation	46.20	53.10	59.80
Gas Consumption of Passenger Cars=GCONS	0.70	0.70	0.70
TAXES			
Total Taxes Paid by Labor=T1+(T2 x LS)	367.85	424.12	466.18
Tax Group I Labor Total: Paid Entirely by Labor=T1	177.03	204.23	225.00
Contributions for Social Insurance	177.03	204.23	225.00
Tax Group II Labor Total: Partially Allocated to Labor=T2 x LS	190.83	219.89	241.18
Tax Group II Total=T2	260.33	300.73	334.38
Total Income Taxes=Federal+State&Local Income Taxes	223.43	262.23	292.08
Federal Income Taxes	188.43	224.03	249.48
State & Local Income Taxes	35.00	38.20	42.60
Other Taxes and Non-taxes	5.00	5.50	6.30
Motor Vehicle and Licenses	3.60	3.70	4.00
Personal Property Taxes = Other + Nonfarm & Farm Owner Occupied	28.30	29.30	32.00
Other Personal Property Taxes	1.00	1.10	1.20
Tax on Owner Occupied Non-farm Housing	27.00	27.90	30.50
Tax on Owner Occupied Farm Housing	0.30	0.30	0.30
NSW1=E1-T1	51.69	51.87	79.83
NSW2=(E2-T2) x LS	-43.97	-58.39	-63.63
NET TOTAL SOCIAL WAGE=NSW1+NSW2	7.72	-6.52	16.20
DATA FOR FIGURES			
Unemployment Rate	0.061	0.059	0.072
Labor Tax Ratio = Labor Taxes/EC	0.27	0.28	0.28
Labor Benefit Ratio = Labor Benefits/EC	0.28	0.28	0.29
Net Social Wage Ratio = Net Social Wage/EC	0.006	-0.004	0.010
Apparent Real Wage per FEE= EC/(CPI*FEE) (in 1982-$)	24264	23714	23007
True Real Wage per FEE = (EC + Net Social Wage)/(CPI*FEE) (in 1982-$)	24404	23611	23232
CPI	65.24	72.58	82.38
Full-Time Equivalent Employees (FEE; thousands)	84551	87335	87260
Total Government Surplus or Deficit/EC (with changed sign)	-0.02	-0.02	0.00
Total Government Surplus or Deficit (Federal, State and Local)	20.95	33.85	-6.62

1981	1982	1983	1984	1985	1986	1987	1988	1989	1990
0.712	0.708	0.706	0.703	0.705	0.707	0.711	0.712	0.701	0.699
1827.80	1927.60	2044.22	2257.01	2425.01	2572.45	2757.72	2973.90	3151.65	3352.75
2568.50	2724.10	2894.40	3211.40	3440.85	3639.55	3877.80	4178.85	4496.40	4796.23
535.44	576.37	610.20	638.57	683.04	724.88	767.70	817.91	877.60	966.21
344.29	378.61	402.41	415.79	444.08	470.17	495.16	527.56	571.40	633.98
314.09	348.61	373.61	385.09	409.78	433.67	455.06	485.96	528.00	587.98
23.50	24.00	22.90	25.00	28.20	30.20	33.80	35.10	36.70	39.10
6.70	6.00	5.90	5.70	6.10	6.30	6.30	6.50	6.70	6.90
191.15	197.76	207.79	222.78	238.96	254.70	272.54	290.35	306.19	332.24
268.61	279.48	294.21	316.99	339.06	360.36	383.23	407.99	436.84	475.28
159.40	169.50	179.80	194.90	212.00	229.10	244.20	262.60	285.50	308.30
27.20	27.40	27.90	30.00	32.00	33.70	36.40	39.80	42.50	46.60
7.60	7.90	8.20	9.30	9.80	10.70	11.20	12.10	13.20	14.70
15.10	13.10	10.10	10.20	8.30	6.80	5.60	4.40	3.60	4.60
9.20	9.40	11.00	10.80	11.80	11.90	12.40	13.10	14.20	14.70
5.10	5.00	5.90	6.70	6.50	6.00	7.70	6.90	7.00	9.10
45.01	47.18	51.31	55.09	58.66	62.16	65.73	69.09	70.84	77.28
64.30	67.40	73.30	78.70	83.80	88.80	93.90	98.70	101.20	110.40
0.70	0.70	0.70	0.70	0.70	0.70	0.70	0.70	0.70	0.70
535.72	562.87	585.24	648.00	710.66	754.73	818.25	871.77	941.20	988.95
261.63	280.63	301.93	345.53	375.95	402.00	423.33	462.80	491.20	518.50
261.63	280.63	301.93	345.53	375.95	402.00	423.33	462.80	491.20	518.50
274.10	282.25	283.32	302.47	334.71	352.73	394.92	408.97	450.00	470.45
385.18	398.88	401.15	430.38	474.93	499.05	555.33	574.68	642.00	673.00
337.98	346.95	345.08	369.38	408.78	428.10	480.13	495.48	554.63	579.00
290.08	295.05	286.78	301.88	336.68	350.70	394.13	405.58	453.23	472.70
47.90	51.90	58.30	67.50	72.10	77.40	86.00	89.90	101.40	106.30
7.50	8.43	9.48	10.80	12.15	13.45	14.50	15.70	17.28	19.00
4.20	4.60	4.90	5.30	5.90	6.30	6.80	7.10	7.60	7.90
35.50	38.90	41.70	44.90	48.10	51.20	53.90	56.40	62.50	67.10
1.30	1.40	1.50	1.60	1.90	2.00	2.30	2.40	2.70	2.90
33.90	37.20	39.80	42.90	45.80	48.70	51.10	53.40	59.20	63.60
0.30	0.30	0.40	0.40	0.40	0.50	0.50	0.60	0.60	0.60
82.66	97.99	100.49	70.26	68.13	68.17	71.84	64.76	80.20	115.47
-82.95	-84.49	-75.53	-79.69	-95.75	-98.03	-122.39	-118.62	-143.80	-138.21
-0.29	13.50	24.96	-9.43	-27.62	-29.85	-50.55	-53.86	-63.60	-22.74
0.076	0.097	0.096	0.075	0.072	0.070	0.062	0.055	0.053	0.056
0.29	0.29	0.29	0.29	0.29	0.29	0.30	0.29	0.30	0.29
0.29	0.30	0.30	0.28	0.28	0.28	0.28	0.28	0.28	0.29
-0.000	0.007	0.012	-0.004	-0.011	-0.012	-0.018	-0.018	-0.020	-0.007
22825	23143	23637	23791	24035	24561	24681	24847	24470	24544
22822	23305	23926	23691	23761	24275	24229	24397	23976	24377
90.93	96.53	99.58	103.93	107.60	109.69	113.72	118.35	124.03	130.75
88062	86281	86844	91279	93769	95485	98256	101131	103848	104476
0.00	0.04	0.05	0.03	0.03	0.03	0.02	0.01	0.01	0.02
-2.37	-83.40	-109.52	-69.13	-71.93	-82.60	-45.10	-35.35	-18.30	-74.50

DERIVATION OF LABOR SHARES
Labor Share=LS=EC/TPI
Employee Compensation=EC=Apparent Wage
Total Personal Income=TPI
EXPENDITURES
Total Benefits and Income Received by Labor=E1+(E2 x LS)
Expenditure Group I Total: Entirely Allocated to Labor=E1
Income Support, Social Security and Welfare (exluding Military)
Housing and Community Services
Labor and Training Services
Expenditure Group II Total=E2 x LS
Group II Total=E2
Education
Health and Hospitals
Recreational and Cultural Activities
Energy
Natural Resources
Postal Service
Passenger Transportation=Transportation*GCONS
Transporation
Gas Consumption of Passenger Cars=GCONS
TAXES
Total Taxes Paid by Labor=T1+(T2 x LS)
Tax Group I Labor Total: Paid Entirely by Labor=T1
Contributions for Social Insurance
Tax Group II Labor Total: Partially Allocated to Labor=T2 x LS
Tax Group II Total=T2
Total Income Taxes=Federal+State&Local Income Taxes
Federal Income Taxes
State & Local Income Taxes
Other Taxes and Non-taxes
Motor Vehicle and Licenses
Personal Property Taxes = Other + Nonfarm & Farm Owner Occupied
Other Personal Property Taxes
Tax on Owner Occupied Non-farm Housing
Tax on Owner Occupied Farm Housing
NSW1=E1-T1
NSW2=(E2-T2) x LS
NET TOTAL SOCIAL WAGE=NSW1+NSW2
DATA FOR FIGURES
Unemployment Rate
Labor Tax Ratio = Labor Taxes/EC
Labor Benefit Ratio = Labor Benefits/EC
Net Social Wage Ratio = Net Social Wage/EC
Apparent Real Wage per FEE= EC/(CPI*FEE) (in 1982-$)
True Real Wage per FEE = (EC + Net Social Wage)/(CPI*FEE) (in 1982-$)
CPI
Full-Time Equivalent Employees (FEE; thousands)
Total Government Surplus or Deficit/EC (with changed sign)
Total Government Surplus or Deficit (Federal, State and Local)

* Source: National Income and Product Accounts of the U.S., Statistical Tables (all figures in billions of dollars except real wages per FEE)

1991	1992	1993	1994	1995	1996	1997
0.696	0.694	0.696	0.697	0.693	0.686	0.691
3457.91	3644.94	3814.87	4012.00	4208.87	4409.05	4687.23
4965.65	5255.65	5481.05	5757.93	6072.08	6425.20	6784.03
1056.96	1155.46	1226.40	1285.13	1350.98	1413.09	1476.31
711.29	793.87	849.74	891.62	943.66	996.82	1035.77
663.79	743.57	798.94	838.82	885.26	936.32	973.57
40.30	42.20	42.40	44.50	50.00	52.10	53.70
7.20	8.10	8.40	8.30	8.40	8.40	8.50
345.68	361.59	376.66	393.51	407.32	416.27	440.54
496.40	521.38	541.17	564.76	587.64	606.62	637.61
324.70	336.80	349.80	365.90	387.60	405.60	427.50
48.30	48.80	48.80	50.20	48.50	47.60	49.00
15.20	15.90	16.40	16.90	18.60	19.00	20.10
3.50	9.20	10.50	6.30	6.10	2.50	1.30
15.70	17.10	18.50	19.90	21.50	22.80	22.20
8.50	7.90	7.50	9.80	7.20	6.50	8.80
80.50	85.68	89.67	95.76	98.14	102.62	108.71
115.00	122.40	128.10	136.80	140.20	146.60	155.30
0.70	0.70	0.70	0.70	0.70	0.70	0.70
1015.88	1062.34	1117.13	1186.74	1252.69	1340.89	1451.57
543.50	571.43	596.03	630.50	658.90	687.98	726.95
543.50	571.43	596.03	630.50	658.90	687.98	726.95
472.38	490.91	521.10	556.24	593.79	652.91	724.62
678.35	707.85	748.70	798.30	856.65	951.48	1048.78
574.78	596.23	632.33	676.50	729.40	818.80	910.10
464.38	478.13	508.13	545.30	589.00	666.90	745.80
110.40	118.10	124.20	131.20	140.40	151.90	164.30
22.98	26.23	27.58	29.40	31.95	34.58	37.18
8.30	8.80	8.90	9.50	9.90	10.00	10.60
72.30	76.60	79.90	82.90	85.40	88.10	90.90
3.10	3.30	3.40	3.60	3.80	4.00	4.10
68.60	72.70	75.80	78.50	80.70	83.20	85.90
0.60	0.60	0.70	0.80	0.90	0.90	0.90
167.79	222.45	253.72	261.12	284.76	308.85	308.82
-126.70	-129.32	-144.44	-162.73	-186.46	-236.64	-284.08
41.08	93.12	109.27	98.39	98.30	72.20	24.74
0.069	0.075	0.069	0.061	0.056	0.054	0.049
0.29	0.29	0.29	0.30	0.30	0.30	0.31
0.31	0.32	0.32	0.32	0.32	0.32	0.31
0.012	0.026	0.029	0.025	0.023	0.016	0.005
24532	25050	25004	24932	24762	24698	25041
24823	25690	25721	25543	25341	25103	25174
136.27	140.41	144.56	148.34	152.48	156.97	160.63
103441	103631	105541	108478	111468	113729	116532
0.03	0.05	0.04	0.02	0.02	0.00	0.01
-120.18	-194.60	-163.23	-89.85	-71.38	-5.08	78.97

30

Five Easy Pieces on the Economics of Tax Justice

Max B. Sawicky

Introduction

Of the myriad problems and issues in taxation, five are highlighted in this chapter.[1] The purpose is to motivate a new view of how tax reform could best serve economic equality.

Two of the pieces discuss uses of taxation that promote equality: creating a progressive distribution of the tax burden, and financing redistributive public expenditure. These goals—tax fairness and an equalizing deployment of public resources—provide a backdrop for three debates. The first is the efficacy of traditional tax reform. The second is the nature of consumption taxation. And the third is the premise that consumption taxes would result in a larger public sector and greater progress toward economic equality.

The argument may be summarized as follows: taxing the rich is unlikely to finance a significant expansion of the public sector, and ample revenues are vital because public expenditure has a more powerful impact on equality than progressive taxation does. The fairness of income as a tax base is commonly overstated, and the nature of consumption taxation is often misunderstood. A consumption-based tax system has features that might bolster support for greater revenue collections, a larger public sector, and advances toward equality.

Soaking the Rich

Many assume a vast, untapped source of tax revenues in the custody of upper-income persons. Conservative objections to such a view usually harp on the incentive problems in taxing recipients of relatively high incomes. Logically prior to incentive issues, however, is the more mundane question of just how much income is available for taxation, relative to how much is sought. Whether the targeted source of tax revenue is sufficient depends on the orders of magnitude in question.

In 1996, federal personal income tax revenues were $687 billion and corporate tax revenues $195 billion. The federal budget was $1,698 billion, or 22 percent of GDP (NIPA basis) (*Economic Report of the President* (*ERP*) 1998, Table B-83). For the U.S. public sector (Federal, state, and local) to enter the lower ranks of the European social democracies, it would need at least another 7 percent of GDP, or about $530 billion by 1996 standards.

Corporate profits net of tax were $448 billion (*ERP* 1998, Table B-28), so even under a 100 percent corporate income tax the United States could not finance a modestly social democratic state. If we imagined a whopping 50 percent increase of $100 billion in corporate taxes, we would still have a shortfall of $430 billion. (This increase would reduce dividend payments subject to the personal income tax, so the $100 billion overstates the net proceeds of the increase; the shortfall would exceed $430 billion.)

What about taxing rich individuals and unincorporated business firms under the personal income tax? We need to decide who is "rich," and how much they can be squeezed. Let's set an income threshold defining the poorest of the rich. Suppose we say "rich" is a family with annual income of $200,000 or more. As rich people go, this should be called the "poor side of town." On the other hand, only a million and half families fell into this category, so in relative terms it is a very exclusive group.

In 1996, total income[2] for this group was $807 billion, of which $228 billion was paid in federal income taxes, leaving $579 billion (Cruciano 1999). Putting aside the fact that by taking $100 billion more in corporate taxes, we reduce taxable dividends received by individuals, we need almost three-quarters of the untaxed income of these rich to finance a lean social-democracy.

There is clearly room for increased taxation of the rich, but the likely fruits of such an endeavor are vastly disproportionate to ambitious plans for public sector expansion. The figures above, incidentally, assume no negative incentive effects at all, such as conversion of taxable income into capital gains, timing of transactions to further reduce tax liability, or actual reductions in work effort and investment (Slemrod 1997).

Far more numerous than the "absolute rich" are the "relative rich," meaning those who are merely better off than most others. How should we define this group?

The top two personal income tax brackets, with rates of 36 and 39.6 percent, encompass fewer than 2 percent of taxpayers. Presently the 36 percent bracket begins at $151,750 in taxable income for married couples filing joint returns. Note that "taxable income" means what is left of adjusted gross income (AGI) after deductions are subtracted. So the gross income associated with the bottom of the top bracket is not far from our definition of the rich, which started at $200,000. We clearly need to reach deeper into the income distribution.

Let's consider instead the top quintile of taxpayers. In terms of adjusted gross income, in 1996 this group began below $75,000 a year (Cruciano 1999). That such a level of income reflects much in the way of privilege would surprise and confound most people, but the fact remains that, in relative terms, it is a high-income group. An income in the top 20 percent cannot reasonably be described as "middle class," though that is exactly how most people would regard it. The political implications of focusing tax increases on households of this type are daunting.

The extent of income alone may not seem like a barrier to revenue collection. Wealth could be taxed. But any tax on wealth is really a tax on the income generated by the assets subject to tax. So the limits to income taxation are also limits to wealth taxation.

The rate of tax on wealth reflects a much higher effective tax rate on income. For instance, if capital yields a return of 8 percent, a 10 percent tax on wealth would be equivalent to a capital income tax of 125 percent ($^{10}/_{8}$). It should be clear that high political hurdles separate the wish from the deed in this case. Moreover, every such confiscatory act of taxation reduces the base available to taxation in succeeding periods. The likelihood of capital flight obviously compounds the difficulty.

Finally, if the government simply expropriated assets of the rich, to whom would it sell them to finance current expenditures? Foreigners? It might be supposed that the government could simply maintain ownership of the assets and finance its expenditures from the returns to ownership. But in this case we are back to taxing income—at 100 percent—rather than using the proceeds from the asset sale.

These considerations fuel the suspicion that public sector growth will depend on enthusiastic support for general tax increases among the nonrich.

Fiscal Justice and the Size of Government

Broadly speaking, economic well-being is not narrowly a matter of after-tax money income, but of the entirety of the individual's consumption, including public services. An interest in economic justice, in terms of the pursuit of equality, must take the health of the public sector into account. At the risk of some awkwardness, a measure of economic well-being that takes government spending into account might be called "post-fisc" income.

For the most part, public goods are provided to persons without charge. Exceptions include highway tolls and public university tuition, though these are often subsidized. Some programs provide what are known as transfer payments that are earmarked for individuals. Access to other types of goods is not individualized; the goods are made accessible to all.

Transfers are provided on a means-tested basis, or in a contributory system. Public assistance or "welfare" is an example of a means-tested transfer. Social Security eligibility is based on contributions. Both sorts of benefits have an equalizing effect on individual economic well-being. Services to which all have access are similarly equalizing. This is fuel for the premise that a larger public sector promotes equality.[3] Some public spending is devoted to business subsidies, but this sort of "corporate welfare" is a small share of the federal budget.[4]

For equality, a problematic area is military spending. To some extent, military spending provides real benefits—national security—to the population at large. These benefits, such as they are, do not come without baggage: the efficiency or level of military outlays, not to mention the uses of force they have made possible, have always been controversial. Even if such outlays were without purpose, however, a significant portion of them is devoted to labor compensation.

The other contrasting area is net interest payments. Federal debt, like all financial assets, is held disproportionately by high-income persons. The government's outlays for net interest go to these same persons. As such, this would be considered a regressive type of public expenditure. Taken together, military spending and net interest payments constituted about 17 percent of total U.S. public spending in 1997 (*ERP* 1998).

The growth of the U.S. federal government after 1950 was accompanied by a shift in the composition of revenues. There was a steady ebb in the share of revenues from corporate income taxes and excises. In the 1980s, there was a shift toward payroll taxes. On balance, federal revenue trended toward less progressivity as it grew and then leveled off.

Growth in the state–local sector owes something to greater use of the income tax, but also to increased fees and charges (U.S. Bureau of the Census 1996). These two revenue sources stand at opposite ends of the scale, in terms of progressivity. On the whole, there has been no increase in the progressivity of taxes to which to attribute the unambiguous growth of the U.S. public sector.

The U.S. public sector is markedly smaller than most of its counterparts among industrialized nations. These other nations make extensive use of consumption taxes compared to the United States (Steuerle 1992). Figure 30.1 compares the nations' revenue systems as a share of GDP, on the one hand, to taxes on personal and corporate income

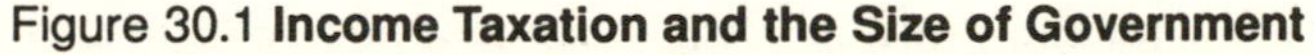

Figure 30.1 **Income Taxation and the Size of Government**

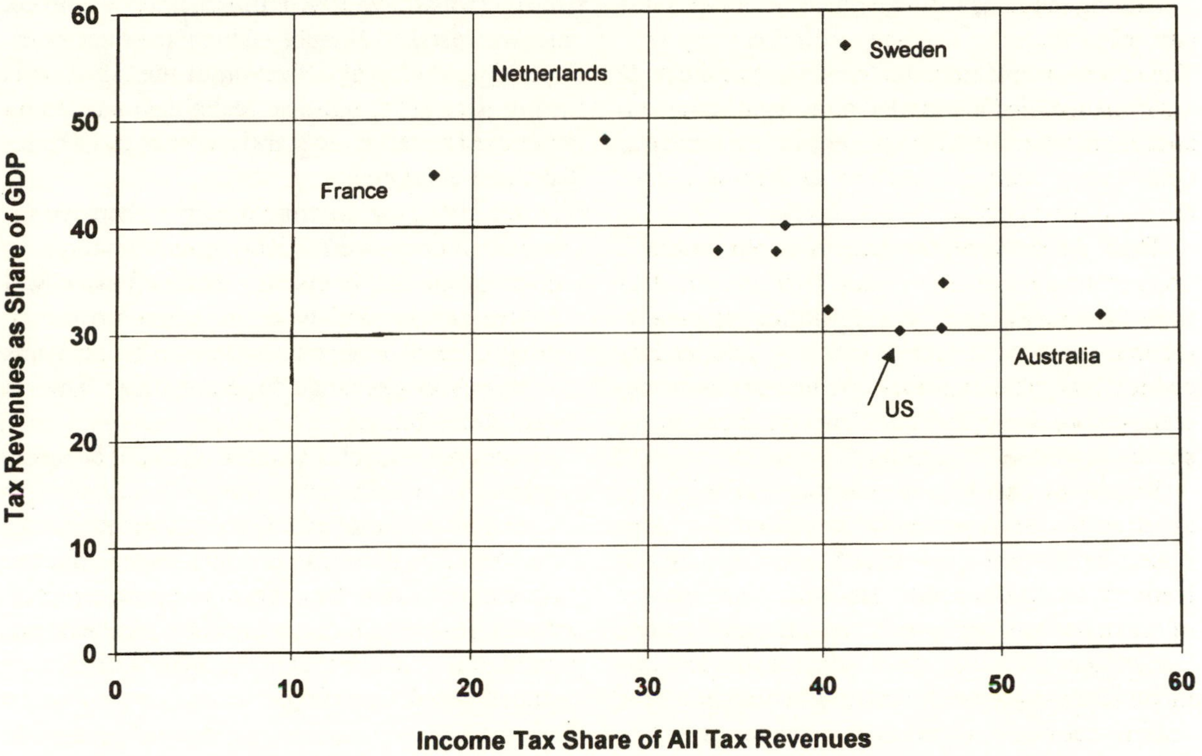

as a share of total tax revenues. With the exception of Sweden, the relationship between the size of revenue systems and the reliance on income taxation is remarkably consistent: less use of income taxes is associated with larger revenue systems. If more revenue makes possible bigger government, and bigger government is better government from the standpoint of equality, an important question is whether a relatively regressive or less progressive tax structure facilitates a larger public sector.

The data in Figure 30.1 are meant to be suggestive, not definitive. Nor is it desirable to overstate the importance of mere tax policy in fundamental differences among nations. Without doubt, a bundle of other factors make for both large public sectors and consumption-oriented tax systems.

Traditional Tax Reform

A popular strategy for advancing public sector expansion is to assert that the rich do not pay their fair share of taxes. By demanding "fair shares" for the rich, some advocates hope to persuade voters to support higher public spending, evidently on the grounds that costs to the average person will be minimal.

What could "fair share" mean? Presently the rich pay a higher average rate of income taxes than the nonrich, but it is always possible to push the rate up. The most direct way is to raise the marginal tax rates applied to high incomes.

Among the rich, as for any income group, some pay more than the average and others pay less. The latter are able to make greater use of the wide assortment of deductions and other legal tax-avoidance methods available in the existing income tax. One way or another, portions of income escape the statutory tax base.

Thus, a second route to higher revenue collections from the rich is to scale back their deductions. By this means, the definition of taxable income approaches that of income as defined by economists. The statutory income tax base becomes more comprehensive. This is the traditional strategy of tax reform in the United States.

We could rightly criticize the availability of assorted tax preferences (also known as "loopholes" or "corporate welfare," or with more objectivity, as "tax expenditures") that enable some of the rich to pay below-average rates, and in some cases lower rates than those with a good deal less income. In this sense, "fair share" could mean the scaling-back or elimination of deductions.

Insofar as deductions benefit the rich, the proceeds from their elimination are limited along the lines of the discussion in the first section. Although the benefits of many "loopholes" are distributed disproportionately to upper-income taxpayers, they are spread among many persons who are not rich by any definition. Proposals to eliminate such preferences altogether typically raise a hue and cry among those who receive or look forward to the same benefits. A good example is the deduction for mortgage interest, which makes home ownership more broadly affordable. Reducing the availability of the preference to high-income persons is less offensive to the average person, but it can make for a more complicated tax system.

Significant progress in reducing deductions was made in the 1986 reform (Aaron and Galper 1988), but the political deal that made the reform possible obviated any possibility of public sector expansion (Musgrave 1990). Enlargement of the tax base was used to finance reduction in tax rates. Expanding the legal definition of the tax base is much easier in the political realm than increasing tax rates. The latter are starkly visible and explicitly affect everyone.

After 1986, the doctrine of comprehensive income taxation was effectively used by liberals to fend off proposals for tax cuts. This defensive wall was breached in 1997 when the Clinton administration accepted major cuts in taxes on capital gains and estates in exchange for Republican support for Clinton's budget.

In summary, income taxation may not be a prerequisite for public sector growth. Under present circumstances, we do not observe politically popular tax reforms that raise revenue levels, enhance progressivity, and finance ever-greater public spending. Although other factors are clearly important, it is possible that our present tax structure restrains public spending.

Some Progressive Consumption Taxes

An alternative to the framework of comprehensive income taxation is a consumption-based tax system. "Consumption tax" usually connotes a sales tax or a value-added tax, neither of which have distributional implications in keeping with a commitment to equality.

A neglected aspect of consumption taxation stems from its most fundamental underlying assumption: if the tax base is consumption, consumers must bear the tax burden. The genesis of this assumption is wound up with the conventional sorts of consumption taxes noted above—sales taxes, excises, or value-added taxes. The simple story is that a tax applied to sales and paid by business firms in their capacity as sellers simply raises the prices of all taxed goods and services. The consumer pays the higher price and bears the burden.[5]

In the conventional story, the monetary authorities "accommodate" the consumption tax by allowing the price level to rise, or failing to prevent it from doing so (Musgrave and Musgrave 1980). Properly speaking, however, for a tax to be borne by consumers, the price level must continuously track the tax rate: a rise in one must be associated with a rise in the other. In the absence of this clearly unrealistic condition, a consumption tax is a very different animal (Hufbauer 1996).

If the monetary authorities or other factors prevent a general price increase, the seller who pays the tax must still recover her costs of production. She must somehow shift the tax burden "backward" to factors of production—labor and capital. Rather than taxing consumption, we seem to face a tax on production or factor income. The distribution of a tax on wages and profits is quite different from a tax on consumption; it is much less regressive. In fact, a proportional tax on income need not be regressive at all.[6]

There is empirical evidence for the proposition that even value-added taxes are not borne entirely by consumers (Grech 1993). Former officials of the Federal Reserve System have cast doubt on the notion that monetary policy would necessarily respond to consumption tax reform (Bull and Lindsay 1996).

If consumption taxes are paid by persons, rather than by business firms, we could expect less pressure on monetary authorities to accommodate such taxes with an easier monetary policy. More important, institutions such as the Federal Reserve, or powerful international economic forces, could easily erase any impact of consumption taxes on a nation's price level. If the tax rate and price level have no systematic relationship, then the incidence of a consumption tax is thrown into question. Insofar as price pressures prompted by a tax reform are restrained by monetary policy, the burden of a consumption tax is far less regressive.[7]

There are other types of consumption taxes. The two leading examples are the flat tax and what is called the "cash flow income tax." To a great extent, both are paid by persons, rather than solely by business firms.

The Flat Tax

Under the flat tax, the consumption tax base is split between workers and business firms (Hall and Rabushka 1995). Workers pay taxes on their wages and pension benefits. The business tax base is the difference between profits and capital expenditures, plus any expenditure on employee fringe benefits other than pension contributions. In terms of national income accounting, the sum of these components is the same as the difference between national income and net investment, or consumption.

Much is made of the single rate under the flat tax, and indeed this explains much of its controversial distributional effect (Gale, Houser, and Scholz 1996). But in the design of taxation, the definition of the tax base is at least as important as the rates. The flat tax need not be flat. Workers could be taxed under multiple, graduated rates, as under the personal income tax. The tax rate on business firms could be higher than the rate on workers. A tax on inheritances could supplement the tax.[8] Distributional problems with the flat tax are not intrinsic to its design, once we get past the single rate.

The Cash-Flow Income Tax

The cash-flow income tax paid by individuals looks like the existing personal income tax, with the crucial addition of a deduction for net saving (see Aaron and Galper 1985; Bradford 1986; and Seidman 1997). There can be exemptions, a standard deduction, itemized deductions, and graduated rates. Moreover, the taxpayer's estate could be included in the tax base in the year of her demise. To be consistent, on the business side the corporate income tax would be replaced with a value-added tax. Here again, the flexible nature of the personal tax makes possible a progressive distribution of the tax burden (Alliance USA 1997).

What's To Like in Consumption Taxes

Why consider consumption taxes, even if we could imagine one with a progressive distribution of the tax burden? An interest in equality suggests a value in bigger, better government. A tax that is no worse in terms of distributional effects and more productive of revenue makes possible a larger, more redistributive public sector.

A basic fact to overcome is that income exceeds consumption by the extent of net investment. Because the maximum potential consumption tax base must be smaller than its income tax counterpart, the prospect that a consumption-based tax system (CBTS) could achieve greater revenue than an income-based system must diminish.

What matters for revenue, however, is not simply the economic base, but the tax base defined in law. Any broad structural reform could occasion a house cleaning that clears the decks of many deductions and broadens the statutory tax base. A consumption-based reform has some added potential benefits.

Easing the Burden, I: Simplicity

If simplicity improves under an alternative system, public opinion might be more congenial to an enlarged revenue system. The ease of paying, administering, and enforcing a tax depend on the complexity of determining tax liability. In this respect, a CBTS has advantages over an income tax.

A major task in tax preparation for business firms is the determination of depreciation. Depreciation is an economic concept—the reduction in value of an asset over time. It requires complicated rules of measurement for tax purposes. Under consumption taxation, depreciation need not be measured. The taxpayer takes an immediate deduction for the cash price of the capital purchase, known as "free depreciation" or "expensing," and that is the end of the story.

The treatment of depreciation under a consumption tax could increase the cash flow of many business firms. This is an outcome that business managers and owners find desirable, since cash flow becomes available for the expansion of the firm's operations, potentially increasing its value. Conversion to a CBTS might encourage elite political support for a larger public sector.

A second compliance burden is the complex treatment of capital gains. This is much simplified under consumption taxation: the taxpayer takes a deduction when she purchases a financial asset, and pays tax on the full proceeds of any sale of an asset. An asset management account could keep track of all transactions and provide the taxpayer with the one number she needs to report on the tax form: net saving (Aaron and Galper 1985).

A third burden lies in the rules governing estates and gifts, under the Estate and Gift Tax, and in the Alternative Minimum Tax faced by high-income persons and corporations. Under a consumption tax reform, these taxes could be abolished.

Simplification could entail higher taxes for some. Clearly such taxpayers would prefer reduced simplicity when it affords them tax savings. On the other hand, a simpler tax system is more transparent and commands greater public respect. Such respect is important because tax collections depend on voluntary compliance. A simpler system is also easier to administer and enforce.

Easing the Burden, II: Efficiency

A second aspect of the tax burden is the inevitable distortion of common economic activities. Any real-world tax system will have important distortions. It must be acknowledged that income tax reform can reduce distortions, in keeping with the traditional income tax strategy discussed above.

One distortion that a consumption tax can forego is the bias of income taxation against saving. This bias is inherent to an income tax as long as the returns to savings—in other words, income from capital—are defined as income.

To see the savings bias in an income tax, consider the choice of consuming today versus consuming later under alternative tax systems. Assume the individual sets his consumption in light of expected returns to saving. A higher rate of return makes future consumption "cheaper," since a given amount can be financed with less saving. An income tax reduces the rate of return to saving, since the returns are taxed annually. This is understood as a relative price effect. It makes future consumption somewhat more expensive, relative to present consumption. By contrast, a consumption tax applies the same percentage rate to consumption, regardless of when it takes place. It does not affect the rate of return to saving.

Other distortions to which an income tax is susceptible stem from inflation and the double-taxation of dividends paid by corporations in the United States. A consumption-based system of the cash-flow type described above eliminates these difficulties more easily than is possible within the income tax framework. Explication is beyond the scope of this article, but see Aaron and Galper (1985).

A Final Word

The outcome of any tax reform depends not only on the tax structure in view, but on the political environment. If politics ever takes a new direction toward accentuated concern for equality, an ascendant labor movement might be able to pressure antagonistic business interests to join in a concord. A question is the extent to which corporate opposition to bigger government stems from the nature of taxation, or from government itself. Insofar as an alternative tax structure would mute business opposition to public sector expansion, a consumption-based tax reform could prove to be the right tool for financing such growth.

Notes

1. A comprehensive survey of taxation is beyond the scope of this paper. Some excellent introductions are Pechman (1987) and Slemrod and Bakija (1997).

2. Adjusted gross income, Figure F, 12, in Cruciano (1999).

3. For different views, see Shaikh and Tonak (1987) and this volume, or Le Grand (1982).

4. The libertarian Cato Institute finds $65 billion in corporate welfare on the expenditure side of the budget (*Cato Handbook for Congress* 1999). Their tally excludes tax expenditures.

5. Standard treatments usually gloss over supply effects from a general consumption tax. Insofar as the tax reduces output, its burden falls on factors of production—land, labor, and capital—and on that account is much less regressive than a tax borne wholly by consumers.

6. Even the existing payroll tax, which applies only to money wages and is capped at $68,400, has been found by the Congressional Budget Office to be progressive for the bottom 80 percent of persons.

7. A significant drop in the price level could easily have significant, negative macroeconomic effects that roused the Fed to take action of some sort. If the Fed "reflates" in response to a tax reform, then the nature of the reform reverts to the traditional notion of a consumption tax.

8. Taxation of inheritances or bequests under the flat tax and the cash-flow income tax, respectively, are not gratuitous add-ons. They are consistent with the fundamental structure of each tax. In the case of the flat tax, inheritances (and gifts) plus labor earnings are the sources of the individual's entire lifetime income, since capital income derives from savings out of these sources. A similar point applies to bequests. For details, see Bradford (1986).

Bibliography

Aaron, Henry J., and William G. Gale, eds. 1996. *Economic Effects of Fundamental Tax Reform*. Washington, DC: The Brookings Institution.

Aaron, Henry J., and Harvey Galper. 1985. *Assessing Tax*

Reform. Washington, DC: The Brookings Institution,.

———. 1988. *Uneasy Compromise: Problems of a Hybrid Income-Consumption Tax.* Washington, DC: The Brookings Institution.

Alliance USA. 1995. "The USA Tax System: Description and Explanation of the Unlimited Savings Allowance Income Tax System. Washington, DC, February.

Bradford, David F. 1986. *Untangling the Income Tax.* Committee for Economic Development. Cambridge: Harvard University Press.

Bull, Nicholas, and Lawrence B. Lindsey. 1996. "Monetary Implications of Tax Reforms." *National Tax Journal* 49, no. 3 (September): 359–380.

Cato Handbook for Congress: Policy Recommendations for the 106th Congress. 1999. Washington, DC: Cato Institute.

Cherry, Robert, Christine D'Onofrio, Cigdem Kurdas, Thomas R. Michl, Fred Moseley, Michele I. Naples, eds. 1987. *The Imperiled Economy, Book 1: Macroeconomics from a Left Perspective.* New York: Union for Radical Political Economics.

Cruciano, Therese. 1999. "Individual Income Tax Returns, 1996," Statistics of Income, Internal Revenue Service.

Economic Report of the President, 1998. 1998. Washington, DC: Government Printing Office.

Gale, William G., Scott Houser, and John Karl Scholz. 1996. "Distributional Effects of Fundamental Tax Reform." In Aaron and Gale.

Grech, John. 1993. "VAT and Inflation." *VAT Monitor.* Amsterdam: International Bureau of Fiscal Documentation, March.

Hall, Robert E., and Alvin Rabushka. 1995. *The Flat Tax.* 2d ed. Stanford: The Hoover Institution Press.

Hufbauer, Gary Clyde, with by Carol Gabyzon. 1996. *Fundamental Tax Reform and Border Tax Adjustments.* Washington, DC: Institute for International Economics.

Le Grand, Julian. 1982. *The Strategy of Equality: Redistribution and the Social Services.* London: George Allen and Unwin.

Musgrave, Richard A. 1990. "Strengthening the Progressive Income Tax: The Responsible Answer to America's Budget Problem." Washington, DC: Economic Policy Institute.

Musgrave, Richard A., and Peggy B. Musgrave. 1980. *Public Finance in Theory and Practice.* New York: McGraw-Hill.

Pechman, Joseph A. 1987. *Federal Tax Policy.* Washington, DC: The Brookings Institution.

Seidman, Laurence. 1997. *The USA Tax: A Progressive Consumption Tax.* Cambridge: MIT Press.

Shaikh, Anwar, and Ertugrul Ahmet Tonak. 1987."The Welfare State and the Myth of the Social Wage." In Cherry, et al.

Slemrod, Joel, ed. 1997. *Does Atlas Shrug? The Economic Consequences of Taxing the Rich.* Office of Tax Policy Research, Conference Proceedings, Ann Arbor.

Slemrod, Joel, and Jon Bakija. 1997.*Taxing Ourselves*. Ann Arbor: University of Michigan Press.

Stansel, Dean. 1998. "Corporate Welfare." In *Cato Handbook.*

Steuerle, C. Eugene. 1992. *The Tax Decade: How Taxes Came to Dominate the Public Agenda.* Washington, DC: Urban Institute Press.

U.S. Bureau of the Census, Census of Governments. 1996. *Governmental Finance, 1991.* Washington, DC: Government Printing Office.

31

Why the Emperor Has No Clothes

The Neoclassical Case for Price Regulation

Ron Baiman

Have you ever wondered how unregulated market pricing is justified when a shrinking number of increasingly powerful firms dominate sector after sector of the national and world economies? Are you experiencing painful cognitive dissonance because the reigning economic paradigm continues to be based on perfectly competitive price-taking firms with *no market power*, even as the economic terrain appears to be increasingly following Marx's prediction of ever rising concentration, if not centralization, of capital (Harrison 1994)?

This is much more than an arcane intellectual issue. The central theme of neoclassical economics is the ideological legitimation of market pricing, and this has immediate and direct effects on real people. For example, in recent regulatory decisions in California regarding electric service, market pricing principles displaced traditional regulatory pricing for approximately $28 billion in services. Similarly, telecommunications deregulation has resulted in "rate rebalancing," or the removal of long-distance to local subsidy, again following market pricing principles (Baiman 1995). These and many other examples of completed, or ongoing, "price and entry" deregulation in airlines, busing, trucking, electric power, health, education, social services, culture, and finance, serve as constant reminders of the scope and power of market ideology in our everyday lives (Dymski 1999; Kuttner 1996; Horwitz 1989).

How is this justified? Within the neoclassical orbit there is a "second line of defense" for skeptics who may have difficulty with the diminishing relevancy of perfect competition to the real economy. In particular, under less than perfectly competitive conditions, when even neoclassicals admit that the Pareto efficiency of perfect competition cannot apply, the Ramsey, or "inverse elasticity," pricing theorem appears to demonstrate that marketlike pricing results in a "second best" welfare outcome. The Ramsey pricing theorem appears to show that consumer welfare is maximized when oligopolistic firms with above marginal-cost average-costs (which includes most major firms in most of the important sectors of the economy) recoup their costs through "near marginal cost" *marketlike*, segment- or product-specific pricing (Baumol and Bradford 1970; Crew and Kleindorfer 1979; Baumol, Joskow, and Kahn 1994).

I would like to thank Dawn Saunders for her very thorough and helpful editorial improvements to this chapter. All remaining errors and deficiencies are, of course, my own.

In this less formal but more realistic "partial equilibrium" analysis, aggregate "consumer and producer surplus" replaces Pareto optimality as a measure of social welfare, and welfare tradeoffs between individuals and firms are necessary to achieve meaningful results. Unlike the high theory underlying the "fundamental theorems of welfare economics" (which are primarily ideological constructions), the kind of welfare analysis upon which the Ramsey theorem is based is *actually used* by practitioners in cost–benefit analysis of price (or tariff, tax, wage, income, etc.) changes (Crew and Kleindorfer 1979; (Mansfield 1994, 102). Applied welfare analysis also serves as the basis for pedagogically effective primary indoctrination into free market ideology in mainstream economic textbooks (Mankiw 1998a, 1998b, ch. 7).

This chapter presents an imminent critique of the standard Ramsey pricing theorem, which shows that: (a) Ramsey pricing does *not* demonstrate that *unregulated* oligopolistic pricing is static social welfare maximizing and therefore is *not* a theorem of "second best" most efficient pricing, (b) the Ramsey demonstration that marketlike pricing is optimal for regulated profit-constrained oligopolistic firms is a generally perversely inequitable result of a theoretically contradictory, and counterintuitive, unweighted consumer surplus aggregation assumption; and (c) when this implausible assumption is replaced by a theoretically justifiable and intuitively acceptable *weighting* of individual consumer surplus by income or wealth, a modified Ramsey pricing rule can be derived which demonstrates that generally *progressive social pricing, rather than regressive market pricing, is necessary for short-term social welfare maximization in oligopolistic markets* (see Baiman 2001, for complete formal expositions of the arguments).[1]

This implies that progressive social pricing for increasing returns to scale, or high fixed cost, oligopolistic sectors such as telecommunications, transportation, electricity, and other residential public utilities; health care, education, cultural services, and other human services, which are of vital and increasing importance in developed and developing economies, are *more* rather than *less* efficient by standard microeconomic social welfare measures (Kuttner 1996; Horwitz 1989).

The (Supposed) "Second Best" Market Pricing Implications of Ramsey Pricing

Although it is not based on the unrealistic and inapplicable assumptions of perfect competition, the Ramsey theorem is based on the standard assumptions of applied static partial equilibrium microeconomic analysis. The terms *social welfare*, *aggregate welfare*, and so forth, therefore refer to "static" welfare measured in "utilitarian" terms. Market shares, demand curves, cost curves, products, and consumer preferences are all assumed fixed. Dynamic issues such as technological change, and the proper level, allocation, and control of investment, as well as the distribution of benefits from it, are set aside. So are incentive issues and other externalities, which are central in other critical analyses. Thus some of the most essential features of markets are ignored, even as the approach is applied to real-world policy decisions. This form of analysis is therefore strictly valid only for the short-term allocation of consumer goods and services with insignificant externalities. However, this is an important allocational problem in its own right, which deserves serious consideration by radical as well as neoclassical economists.

The Ramsey, or "inverse elasticity," pricing formula stipulates that social efficiency is maximized when multi-product producers, with below average-cost marginal-costs, and small or compensating cross-price effects, raise prices relatively more above marginal cost for lower-elasticity products than for higher elasticity products. According to the Ramsey formula, social welfare will be maximized if such producers set the prices p_i of their products i so that:[2]

$$\frac{p_i - mc_i}{p_i} = k\frac{1}{E_i}$$
$$c\,(x_1, \ldots, x_n) - p_1x_1 - \ldots p_nx_n = \lambda \qquad (1)$$

where: mc_i is marginal cost, E_i is the (positive) own-price elasticity, and x_i is quantity consumed, for product i, and: $c(x_1, \ldots, x_n)$ are aggregate costs of producing $(x_1, \ldots, x_n)$, λ is a constant loss level constraint, and k is constant across products (Baumol 1977, 516; Atkinson and Stiglitz 1980, 372). This formula can also be readily generalized to single commodities whose markets can be segmented by income-wealth by simply labeling products consumed in different markets as different products.

When elasticities are higher, price increases will cause larger declines in consumer demand. Therefore, when trying to raise profits through price increases producers will seek to limit reductions in demand by targeting higher relative price increases to lower elasticity markets (see equation 2 below). Since this standard profit-maximizing market pricing strategy appears to generally follow the Ramsey "inverse elasticity" pricing rule, *the Ramsey theorem seems to suggest that market-driven pricing is socially optimal even in imperfect oligopolistic markets.*

Moreover, when (1) holds for small price changes, relative changes in quantity demanded dx_i / x_i induced by price increases above marginal cost $dp_i = p_i - mc_i$, can be approximated as follows:

$$\frac{dx_i}{x_i} = \left(\frac{dx_i}{dp_i x_i}\right)dp_i = \left(\frac{E_i}{p_i}\right)dp_i = k \qquad (2)$$

where k is constant across market segments i. Ramsey pricing thus appears to imply that social welfare is maximized when the deviation of prices above marginal costs is such that it causes an equal proportional change in quantity demanded for each market segment away from the x_i quantities that would be demanded if prices were set at marginal costs mc_i. Since this implies that, for small price changes, Ramsey pricing approximately preserves relative marginal cost pricing allocations, it appears to lend "second best" support to the "first best" marginal cost pricing principle for perfectly competitive markets (Crew and Kleindorfer 1979; Baumol and Bradford 1970).

Trouble in Paradise: The Ramsey Pricing Paradox

Lower-elasticity commodities are more likely to be *necessities* and have a larger share of lower income consumers. Conversely, higher-elasticity commodities are more likely to be discretionary *luxury* goods and have a larger share of higher-income consumers. Raising prices more for lower-elasticity, than for higher-elasticity, commodities and market segments will thus generally result in *regressive* pricing, which increases costs more for lower-income consumers than for higher-income consumers. Progressive pricing, like progressive taxes, would do just the opposite. Since the Ramsey theorem supports this kind of generally regressive, marketlike pricing strategy that penalizes lower-income consumers who can least afford extra price increases the most, and higher-income consumers who can most easily afford price increases the least, it is a generally perversely inequitable pricing formula.

Moreover, even if we disregard the equity question of whose welfare is being increased, and whose is being reduced, the notion that Ramsey pricing increases aggregate social welfare appears counterintuitive. This is because regressive pricing, which includes higher price increases for lower-elasticity consumers and lower price increases for higher-elasticity consumers, would appear to *reduce* aggregate consumer surplus more than, for example, progressive price changes that did the opposite. If consumer welfare is identified with consumer surplus, this can be seen in Figure 31.1, which shows that equivalent relative price increases will reduce consumer surplus *more* in a lower-elasticity market than in a higher-elasticity market.

Figure 31.1 and Figure 31.2 (below) are for illustrative purposes only, as they refer to demand curves for two products at similar prices and quantities demanded. Elasticities for demand curves at different quantities and prices will not generally relate to each other in this way. However, since targeting lower-elasticity markets for higher relative price increases will increase producer revenue above what it would be for "progressive" or "flat" pricing, Ramsey pricing will generally result in aggregate consumer surplus, or welfare, loss, regardless of the slopes of the demand curves in the region of the price increases.

Ramsey pricing thus appear to coincide with the standard monopolistic, or oligopolistic (in the short-run—if the long-run impact of pricing on market share is disregarded), "price discrimination" rule stipulating that monopolistic and oligopolistic multi-product producers with above average-cost demand curves, and above marginal-cost average-cost curves, can maximize profit by setting marginal cost equal to marginal revenue for each product. Under a set of assumptions equivalent to those used to derive (1) this implies that:

$$p_i\left(1-\frac{1}{Ei}\right)=mc_i \qquad (3)$$

for every product i (Chiang 1984, 356–9). This confirms the notion that by exploiting the more restricted options, or preferences, of lower-elasticity consumers, producers can increase profit, and since in a static world increased profit can only come at the cost of reduced consumer surplus, it suggests that higher relative prices for lower-elasticity markets will *reduce* rather than increase consumer surplus relative to more progressive pricing strategies. But the Ramsey pricing rule is a simple variant of price discrimination formula, as a simple algebraic manipulation of (3) gives:

$$\frac{p_i-mc_i}{p_i}=\frac{1}{Ei} \qquad (4)$$

or, from (1), "Ramsey pricing" with k = 1. The difference between unconstrained profit maximization and Ramsey pricing therefore is simply that under Ramsey pricing a revenue constraint prevents the firm from raising the *overall average* of its prices to profit-maximizing levels. Otherwise these formulas are exactly the same. The ratios between relative, above marginal cost, price increases for different products in (1) and (4) are *identical*. Standard oligopolistic profit-maximizing pricing strategy thus appears to maximize consumer welfare.

The irony of the Ramsey pricing result has not gone unnoticed by neoclassical economists. In their classic Ramsey pricing article Baumol and Bradford note that:

> This [Ramsey pricing] result is surely not immediately acceptable through intuition. It strikes us as curious, if for no other reason, because it seems to say that ordinary price discrimination might well set relative prices at least roughly in the manner required for maximal social welfare in the presence of a profit constraint. (Baumol and Bradford 1970, 267)

Looked at from this point of view, the Ramsey result appears highly contradictory.

Figure 31.1 **Consumer Surplus Loss from Price Increases for High- and Low-Elasticity Markets**

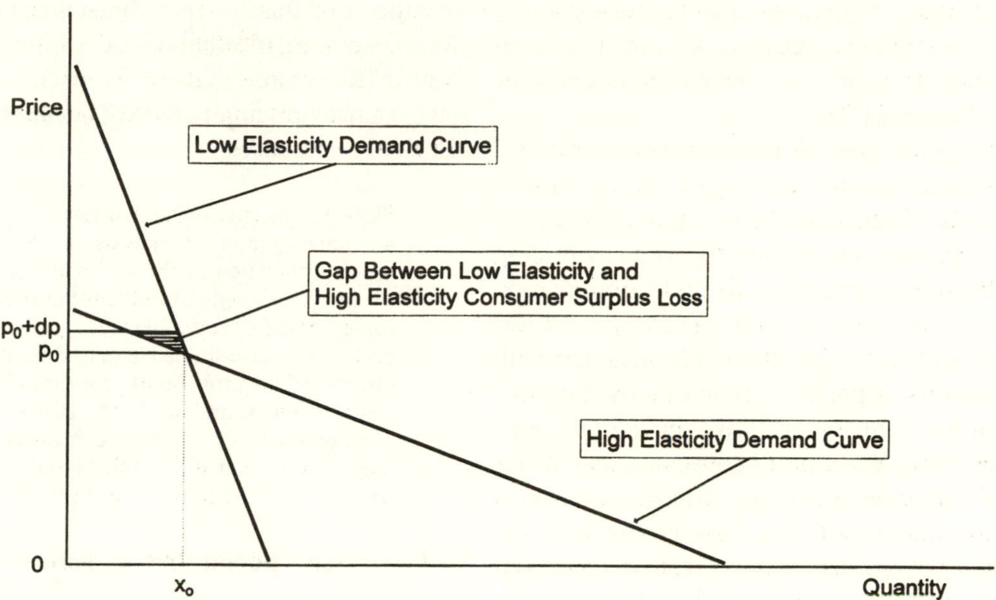

Note: The price elasticity values for these curves will correspond to their (inverted) slopes as they are both being measured at the same base price and quantity values.

Garbage in Garbage out, or "It's the Assumptions, Stupid!"

Closer inspection reveals that the counterintuitive, and generally regressive, Ramsey pricing result is a direct consequence of the theoretically unjustifiable *unweighted* aggregation method used to derive it. Analysis of the different components of the standard Ramsey pricing maximand reveals that the driving factor behind this welfare-maximization-subject-to-a-profit-constraint exercise is constrained profit loss minimization relative to welfare gain across market segments (Baiman 2001). Therefore, when the firm is facing a regulated "rate of return" constraint and the absolute (dollar value) of consumer surplus for different segments is equally weighted, Ramsey pricing will maximize overall consumer surplus because the extra consumer surplus loss for lower-elasticity segments will be more than offset by the reduction in profit loss, or profit gain, which comes from maintaining higher prices in these segments relative to higher-elasticity segments.

In other words, since consumer surplus is aggregated on a dollar-for-dollar basis, it becomes directly comparable to profit, which is aggregated in the same way. Flat aggregation of consumer surplus thus leads to a pricing rule that minimizes profit loss through the gouging of less elastic markets, even though this results in greater consumer surplus loss for the consumers who will generally be most hurt by these price increases. This is possible because, with a flat consumer surplus weighting scheme, the reduction in profit loss in lower-elasticity markets compared to higher-elasticity markets, more than compensates for the increased consumer surplus loss by low-elasticity consumers (see Figure 31.2).

This explains the "Ramsey pricing paradox." When consumer surplus is aggregated on a dollar-for-dollar basis just like profit, the constraint-driven maximization behind the Ramsey pricing result becomes simply profit loss minimization relative to consumer surplus gain, which *regressively* exploits the vulnerability of consumers with fewer options or preferences in exactly the same way that oligopolistic profit maximization does.

When firms face a profit constraint, and the inequitable effect of raising prices most for the most vulnerable and least for the most privileged is *not* taken into account, a perversely regressive market-like pricing strategy, which exploits the most vulnerable and rewards the most secure, becomes "optimal." A "reverse Robin Hood" strategy of robbing the poor to benefit the rich then increases overall consumer surplus. This is because the poor can be easily robbed and their greater loss of (even unweighted) consumer surplus is more than made up for by the increased latitude thereby gained to increase consumer surplus, by keeping prices low, for the rich. This is true in spite of the fact that in the absence of a profit constraint, this kind of "price discrimination" will clearly result in a greater loss of consumer surplus relative to more progressive, or even flat, pricing, as can be seen in Figure 31.1, and as is evident in the derivation of (2).

On the other hand, when profits are unconstrained, the Ramsey theorem, which minimizes dollar profit loss per dollar surplus value gain, no longer applies. In this case unconstrained price discrimination is more likely to simply increase overall profits and *reduce* overall consumer surplus.[3]

Baumol and Bradford reflect further on the similarities between Ramsey pricing and "ordinary price discrimination," but fail to draw out the implications of this for their (mistaken) claim that Ramsey pricing is "second best" welfare efficient.[4] Rather (for reasons that are unclear), they dismiss "the Ramsey pricing paradox" because of "quantitative" differences:

> Since the objective of the [Ramsey pricing and profit-maximizing pricing] analysis can be described as the determination of the optimally discriminatory set of prices needed to obtain the required profit, some degree of resemblance is perhaps to be expected. The case studied here is, thus, in a sense the obverse of the problem of profit maximizing price discrimination, and while the two solutions bear some qualitative resemblance, it can be shown that they may in fact differ substantially in quantity. (Baumol and Bradford 1970, 267)

A Progressive Social Pricing Rule

As has been noted, the traditional Ramsey pricing derivation depends on an equal weighting of consumer surplus across individuals. This allows for aggregation, which is necessary, so that (1) can be interpreted as applying to social welfare.

However, assuming that individual levels of consumer surplus are of equal marginal social benefit violates the common-sense notion that marginal utility from income or wealth generally (on average) declines as income or wealth increases. Unweighted aggregation of individual utilities can only be upheld through a usually unacknowledged and unjustified, theoretically invalid and counterintuitive assumption that consumers derive equal marginal utility from increases in consumer surplus regardless of their income or wealth status.

On the relatively rare occasions (in standard texts) that the inequity of this assumption is pointed out, the standard defense is that Ramsey pricing is an "equity neutral" (post-transfer) Pareto-efficient

Figure 31.2 **Profit Gain from Price Increases for High- and Low-Elasticity Markets**

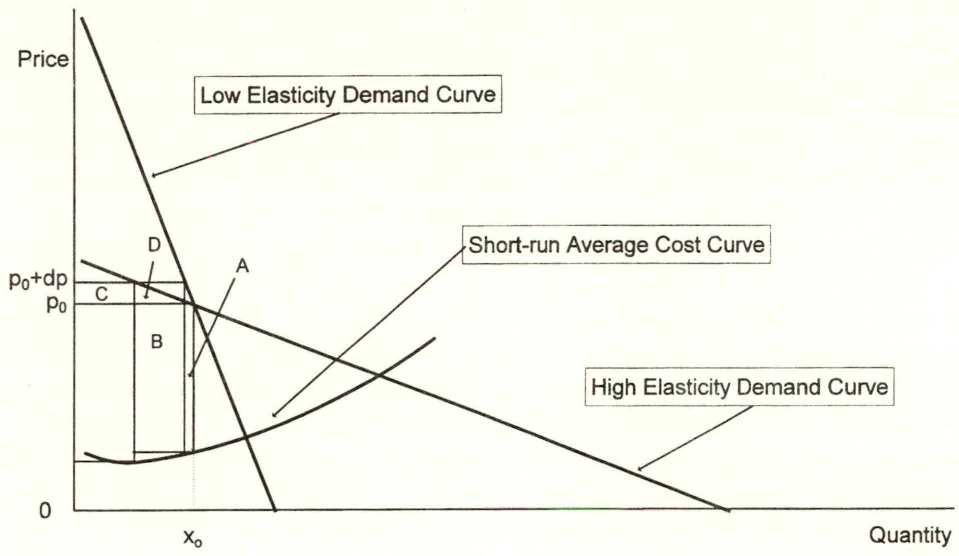

Note: Profit gain for high-elasticity markets equals areas: C – A – B. Profit gain for low-elasticiy markets equals areas C + D – A.

rule in keeping with the "value free" role of economic inquiry (Crew and Kleindorfer 1979, 12; Williamson 1966). The idea here is that if winners (elastic consumers) compensated losers (inelastic consumers) for their losses, the resulting allocation would be Pareto efficient. Of course, such transfers will not occur voluntarily but they are theoretically possible through political programs. Within neoclassical theory equity issues such as income, or wealth redistribution, are thus generally viewed as political issues, which lie outside the bounds of neutral technocratic economic theory.

The Ramsey pricing result, however, shows that, far from being an equity *neutral* assumption, unweighted aggregation leads to *clearly regressive* pricing, which *reduces* static social welfare and long-run social efficiency.

For example, a telephone service price change that resulted in a $100 decline in Donald Trump's telephone bill and $10 increases in the bills of nine low-income customers would *increase* aggregate consumer surplus and thus social welfare according to standard Ramsey pricing methodology. In real economies, with oligopolistic markets and unequal distribution of income and wealth, this kind of neglect of "equity" and exclusive focus on "efficiency" is not possible. (Kuttner 1984). Applying reasonable weights to Trump's gain and to the losses of the low-income consumers shows that aggregate consumer suplus declines or that *efficiency* is *reduced* in this case along with *equity*.

Since interpersonal utility comparison *must* be made in order to aggregate consumer surplus, it would seem eminently more reasonable to openly posit and justify a practical weighting scheme that would take declining average marginal utility of income into account, rather than assuming that social utility is an unweighted sum of individual utilities—directly contradicting the law of diminishing marginal utility.

When this is done, it can be shown that social welfare, or in this context, weighted aggregate consumer surplus, will be maximized when prices for different products or segments obey the following progressive social pricing rule (Baiman 2001):[5]

$$\frac{p_i - mc_i}{p_i} = \frac{1}{Ei}\left(\frac{\lambda - \left(\frac{\mu}{y_i}\right)^{\varepsilon}}{\lambda}\right) \tag{5}$$

where, extending the notation of (1), m is average income-wealth for all consumers of the firm's products; y_i is mean, or median, income-wealth for consumers in market segment i, or for consumers of product i; $1 > (m/y_i)^{\varepsilon} > 0$ is constant across segments or products; and e (greater than or equal to 0 and not equal to 1) is a policy determined estimate of how much less marginal utility households get on average from each additional dollar of consumer surplus as their income/wealth increases (Baiman 2001).[6] Note that (4) reverts back to the standard Ramsey pricing result (1) only if $y_i = m$ or if $e = 0$, proving that the standard regressive formula will obtain only with unweighted consumer surplus aggregation.

Policy Implications

The progressive social pricing principle directly contradicts the mistaken but hegemonic neoclassical view that market pricing is (static) welfare maximizing. This doctrine has legitimated the wave of deregulation of many previously "price and entry" regulated industries (Kuttner 1996; Vietor 1994; Horwitz 1989). For example, in his influential text *The Economics of Regulation*, Alfred Kahn, Cornell University economist and former chair of the Civilian Aviation Board (CAB) and Public Utilities Commissioner for New York State, writes: "The central policy prescription of microeconomics is the question of price and marginal cost. If economic theory is to have any relevance to public utility pricing, that is the point at which the inquiry must begin" (Kahn 1993, 65).

As markets will tend to move prices toward marginal cost, or near-marginal cost, inverse-elasticity pricing, market pricing directly contradicts the progressive social pricing principles for *static* social welfare maximization derived above. In particular, progressive social pricing for many social and physical infrastructure sectors such as telecommunications, transportation, electricity, and other residential public utilities, and, health care, education, cultural services, and other human services, which are of vital and increasing importance in developed and developing economies, are *more* rather than *less* efficient by standard microeconomic measures as they are more likely to increase properly weighted static social welfare.

For example, the intensely discriminatory pricing systems used by the deregulated U.S. airline industry may represent a particularly extreme case of consumer welfare *loss* due to market pricing. Moreover, in this case there can be little doubt of the role that marginal cost and near-marginal cost Ramsey pricing principles played in legitimating airline price deregulation as the policy was supported by the chair of the CAB at that time, Alfred Kahn, author of the quote above (see also Kuttner 1996, 255–270).

In this age of increasing reliance on unregulated market pricing it is important to clarify the basic principles that support or do not support market pricing. The progressive pricing principle demonstrates that it is incumbent upon those who support deregulated market pricing to show that dynamic benefits from market pricing, where these may exist, *will more than compensate for* static welfare losses from the dismantling of regulated progressive social pricing where this has occurred. In this regard it should be noted that as oligopolistic concentration ratios increase in the world economy, market-induced static welfare losses due to price discrimination can only increase. Analysis of the costs and benefits of market versus social pricing should also include the possible loss of long-term dynamic benefits due to lack of planning and regulation (Kuttner 1996).

For example, in U.S. telecommunications, deregulation has led to "rate rebalancing," or reductions in tariffs for higher-income long-distance customers and increases for lower-income local customers. Evidence suggests that most of the large rate reductions in long-distance service in the 1980s and early 1990s were a result of mandated elimination of long-distance to local subsidies. Absent this, long-distance rates declined more slowly than they had before divestiture (Taylor and Taylor 1993; Baiman 1995).

Finally, it should also not be assumed that regulated progressive pricing is incompatible with dynamic market competition. The very successful Canadian "single payer" health care system is an example of a uniform price regulated system, which allows for competition over service quality while eliminating market-driven regressive pricing. It may also be possible to capture *both* static and dynamic pricing efficiency by implementing progressive social pricing systems that regulate *relative* pricing across products (and market segments) for producers who compete to have the lowest possible overall (median or weighted average) price, and the highest possible quality. For a proposed telecommunications regulation scheme of this kind see Baiman 1993.

Notes

1. Strictly speaking, Ramsey pricing will be *regressive* and social pricing *progressive* only if own-price elasticities of demand are inversely correlated with income-wealth. As is explained in the text below, this will often (but not always) be the case. However, the central point of this chapter, that equity must be explicitly taken into consideration in welfare evaluation and pricing, will be unaffected by the progressive or regressive *net* result of its incorporation. In the chapter, in order to simplify the exposition, the inverse correlation is assumed to hold.

2. Another, closely related, sales tax version of the Ramsey pricing "inverse elasticity rule" stipulates that consumer welfare is maximized when sales taxes on different goods obey the "inverse elasticity rule," so that for every good i, when cross-tax effects are negligible: $t_i p_i = k/ E_i$, where t_i is the sales tax on good i, p_i is the price of good i, k is a constant, and E_i is the own-price elasticity of demand of good i (Varian 1992, 412).

3. If the "Ramsey effect," which *increases* consumer surplus for a *fixed* level of profit by reallocating it to high-elasticity segments, more than offsets the "price discrimination" effect, which increases profits by *reducing* consumer surplus, aggregate *unweighted* consumer surplus might increase. In practice, however, percentage profit increases from deregulation are generally large and will therefore most likely swamp "Ramsey effects." Moreover, when consumer surplus is *weighted* before aggregation, the *net* "progressive social pricing rule" will generally work in a progressive direction, eliminating this offset possibility—see text below and Baiman 2001).

4. It is demonstrated in neoclassical microeconomics that under certain idealized (and generally unrealistic) conditions, prices which result from "perfectly competitive" markets maximize consumer welfare. Prices are considered to be "second best" wefare efficient if it can be shown that they result in the "next best" level of overall consumer welfare after that provided by prices resulting from perfect competition.

5. The weighting scheme employed in this formula is a simplified version of a more precise but complex weighting scheme developed in Feldstein 1972a; 1972b. This more complex weighting scheme is also used with a minor modification in Baiman 2001.

6. As ε increases, the rate of decline of marginal utility of income increases, ε = 0 implies no marginal utility reduction for increased income-wealth, whereas ε close to 1 implies a reduction in marginal utility of income, which is directly proportional to income-wealth.

References

Atkinson, A.B., and Joseph E. Stiglitz. 1980. *Lectures on Public Economics.* New York: McGraw-Hill.

Baiman, Ron P. 1993. "Transitional and Long-Term Telecommunications Policy Recommendations for New York State." Unpublished internal staff report for New York State Department of Economic Development.

———. 1995. "Neoclassical Economics and the End of Equitable, Open, and Universal Telecommunications Services in the United States." *Review of Radical Political Economics* 27, no. 3.

———. 2001. "Why Equity Cannot Be Separated from Efficiency: The Welfare Economies of Progressive Social Pricing," *Review for Radical Political Economics* 33, no. 2 (Spring).

Baumol, William J. 1977. *Economic Theory and Operations Analysis*, 4th ed. Englewood Cliffs, NJ: Prentice-Hall.

Baumol, William J., and David Bradford. 1970. "Optimal Departures from Marginal Cost Pricing." *American Economic Review* (June): 809–822.

Baumol, William J., Joskow, Paul L., and Alfred E. Kahn. 1994. The Challenge for Federal and State Regulators: Transition from Regulation to Efficient Competition in Electric Power. December 4. FERC (Federal Energy Regulatory Commission) Docket no. RM 95-8-000.

Chiang, Alpha C. 1984. *Fundamental Methods of Mathematical Economics.* 3d. ed. New York: McGraw-Hill.

Crew, Michael, and Paul R. Kleindorfer. 1979. *Public Utility Economics*. New York: St. Martin's Press.

Dymski, Gary A. 1999. *The Bank Merger Wave: The Economic Causes and Social Consequences of Financial Consolidation*. Armonk, NY: M.E. Sharpe.

Feldstein, Martin S. 1972a. "Distributional Equity and the Optimal Structure of Public Prices." *American Economic Review* 62: 32–36.

———. 1972b. "Equity and Efficiency in Public Sector Pricing: The Optimal Two-Part Tariff." *The Quarterly Journal of Economics* 86, no. 2 (May).

Harrison, Bennett. 1994. *Lean and Mean: The Changing Landscape of Corporate Power in the Age of Flexibility.* New York: Basic Books.

Horwitz, Robert B. 1989. *The Irony of Regulatory Reform.* New York: Oxford University Press.

Kahn, Alfred E. 1993. *The Economics of Regulation.* Cambridge, MA: MIT Press.

Kuttner, Robert. 1984. *The Economic Illusion: False Choices Between Prosperity and Social Justice.* Boston: Houghton Mifflin.

———. 1996. *Everything for Sale.* New York: Alfred Knopf.

Mankiw, N. Gregory. 1998a. *Principles of Microeconomics.* New York: Dryden.

______. 1998b. *Principles of Macroeconomics.* New York: Dryden.

Mansfield, Edwin. 1994. *Microeconomics.* New York: W.W. Norton.

Taylor, William E., and Lester D. Taylor. 1993. "Postdivestiture Long-Distance Competition in the United States." *American Economic Review* (May).

Varian, Hal R. 1992. *Microeconomic Analysis*, 3d ed. New York: W.W. Norton.

Vietor, Richard H.K. 1994. *Contrived Competition.* New York: Belknap/Harvard.

Williamson, O.E. 1966. "Peak Load Pricing and Optimal Capacity Under Indivisibility Constraints." *American Economic Review* 56 (September): 810–827.

32

Broadening the Concept of Pay Equity

Lessons for a Changing Economy

Deborah M. Figart and Heidi I. Hartmann

Introduction

According to neoclassical economists, wage discrimination exists when two individual workers are paid differently although they are equally productive. But orthodox economic models that view market wages as reflecting productivity are contradicted by the role institutions and culture play in wage-setting.

In fact, a major reason for the wage gap between men and women is that men and women do not perform equal work, meaning they do not work in the same job categories for the same employers. In exploring this reality (which has not been evident in standard neoclassical approaches), feminist scholars shift the focus of analysis to discrimination against entire job categories rather than individual workers. They seek confirmation that the female domination (or minority concentration) of a job category, in addition to the productive characteristics of the workers in the job or the jobs requirements, affects its wage level. This form of wage discrimination is empirically demonstrated by a negative correlation between wages and the percentage of women and racial-ethnic minorities in an occupational category (Treiman and Hartmann 1981; England 1992; Sorensen 1994; Lapidus and Figart 1994; Figart 1997). In other words, the higher the percentage female or minorities in a job, the lower the average wage.

Gender typing of jobs in the economy is considerable. In a national labor force that is 46 percent female, six out of ten women still work in female-dominated occupations, according to the Women's Bureau in the U.S. Department of Labor (see www.dol.gov/dol/wb). Many women work in clerical and professional specialty occupations. Kindergarten teachers, dental hygienists, nurses, secretaries, and typists, for example, are all more than 90 percent female. About eight of ten men are employed in male-dominated occupations, especially in craft and managerial positions.

Pay equity or comparable worth is a policy designed to reduce the gender-based wage gap, the difference in average or median pay between women and men. In the United States, the wage gap measured 40 percent in 1963, when the Congress passed the Equal Pay Act mandating that men and women receive equal pay for equal work, and 40 percent in 1980. The gap narrowed by 11 percentage points to 29 percent from 1980 to 1990.

The Institute for Women's Policy Research estimates that over half of the narrowing in the 1980s was due to a decline in men's real wages. And the gap has hardly budged in the 1990s.

Pay equity advocates argue that once jobs become identified as women's work, they pay less. The same dynamic can apply to minority-concentrated occupations, especially in local labor markets. Economic institutions reflect ideas of gender-appropriate work and pay. For example, concepts such as skill are historically constructed, socially contingent, and strongly gendered (see Phillips and Taylor 1986; Horrell, Rubery, and Burchell 1989; Steinberg 1990; Wajcman 1991). How personnel administrators view different jobs, which is in turn based on their perception of how others perceive them, becomes embedded in the pay policies at the firm. The market is an aggregation of these socially constructed institutions (Bridges and Nelson 1989; Steinberg and Haignere 1991; England 1992). Therefore, the pay equity movement challenges the belief in benevolent market forces found in traditional economic doctrine.

Pay equity policies seek to raise the wages of jobs held predominantly by women (or jobs with a high concentration of minorities) until they equal the wages of comparable jobs held predominantly by men (or whites). Pay equity policy generally requires that the content of jobs be evaluated in terms of such compensable factors as skill, effort, responsibility, and working conditions, and that jobs of equal value be paid equally. In large firms, the alignment of relative pay rates of diverse jobs is typically done with job evaluation, a widely used technique to compare jobs within an organization based on uniform compensable criteria (skill, effort, etc.). If a study shows that there is gender or racial bias in an organization's compensation system, an adjustment plan is then developed to raise the wages of underpaid jobs. This strategy confronts forms of discrimination not addressed by older policies such as equal pay for equal work or affirmative action.

In this chapter, we review how comparable worth came to prominence at a particular historical juncture between women's increased participation in the public sphere and overall economic restructuring. We show that some of the underlying conditions responsible for putting pay equity on the policy and employment agenda have waned. We argue that there are connections between the attenuation of pay equity activity in the United States and changes in the global political economy. While the basic contours of the market-based economic system remain unchanged, the rules of the game that seemed to apply during the postwar period (1945 to 1973) are in flux (see Gordon, Edwards, and Reich 1982). These changes have led to a weakening of the struggle to raise women's wages. Finally, we discuss new strategies for the future of pay equity and offer suggestions for how the movement can adapt to changing times. We argue that the stage is now set for a resurgence of political activity around working conditions and wages and particularly women's earnings.

The Pay Equity Movement

An active pay equity movement in the United States is arguably twenty-five years old. Several events crystallized this movement and the legitimacy of pay equity or comparable worth as a public policy. In 1974, the first generally recognized pay equity study was undertaken in the state of Washington. In 1979, the first national conference on the issue was convened by a coalition calling itself the National Committee on Pay Equity (NCPE). This coalition is still active today. Two years later, a landmark court case, *County of Washington v. Gunther*, ruled that failing to pay comparable worth constituted a form of sex-based discrimination under Title VII of the Civil Rights Act of 1964. (Later lawsuits were largely unsuccessful.) Also in 1981, a pathbreaking report requested several years earlier by the Equal Employment Opportunity Commission (EEOC), *Women, Work and Wages: Equal Pay for Work of Equal Value* (Treiman and Hartmann 1981), found strong evidence of gender-based wage discrimination and was used as a resource by comparable worth advocates. Finally, in that same year, the public sector strike over pay equity in San Jose, California, gained national prominence.

In the 1980s, the pay equity movement seemed to hold substantial promise for working women. The pace of the movement accelerated as activists around the country demanded pay equity for women's jobs. Most of the activity occurred in the public sector, in state and local governments. By the end of the 1980s, every state except Alaska, Arkansas, Delaware, Georgia, and Idaho had at least investigated gender differentials in their civil service pay scales. Over 50 municipalities, 25 counties, 60 school districts, and nearly 200 public colleges and universities were the focus of campaigns to raise wages in low-paid female-dominated occupations (NCPE 1989). Many called comparable worth a major civil rights issue for the 1980s, a phrase originally coined by then-EEOC director Eleanor Holmes Norton. Such progress was connected to the development (since the 1970s) of the following three trends in the gendered political economy:

The Feminization of the Labor Force

Employment composition in the United States has shifted from manufacturing to services. In the forty years from 1955 to 1995, the share of employment by service and retail industries doubled from 25 to 50 percent while the share of manufacturing jobs declined from one-third to one-sixth (Albelda and Tilly 1998, 44). This transposition of manufacturing and services, according to many experts, is accompanied by lower average wages, less generous benefit systems, a decline of jobs with good career ladders, and less job security. The increased business demand for clerical labor, the increased consumer demand for services, and the increased supply of women interested in working outside the home led to a steady rise in the labor force participation rate of women. More and more families are dependent for their income upon single mothers and wives working for pay in the labor market. Among the prominent economic trends in the postwar era has been the growth in the labor force participation rates of married women with children, especially young children.

Feminist Advocacy in Politics

With the election and appointment of feminist politicians at the state level, state legislatures and administrative agencies were also critical in moving pay equity onto the political agenda. Among public sector initiatives, where most of the visible action took place, State Commissions on the Status of Women often took steps to introduce the reform. Women's groups played a critical role in states such as Massachusetts, West Virginia, and Wisconsin, where strong working women's organizations like 9 to 5, coalitions of broad-based feminist organizations like the Wisconsin's Women's Network, or chapters of the National Organization for Women made women's economic equity a priority. In Canada, activists made pay equity a major priority as early as the mid-1970s. Presently, Canadian legislation at the federal level provides pay equity protections to public sector workers, and Ontario law protects public and private employees.

Public Sector Unionization

Pay equity's achievements owe a great deal to the determination of organized labor (see Portman,

Grune, and Johnson 1984; Gabin 1989; Hallock 1993; Kahn and Figart 1998). The pay equity movement was aided greatly by the expansion of public sector unionism in the 1960s and 1970s. Virtually all of the public sector pay equity activity has occurred at unionized workplaces (NCPE 1996; Hartmann, Sorensen, and Aaronson 1996). Since litigation is an expensive strategy, most class action lawsuits were filed by unions on behalf of workers. Collective bargaining has been key to pay equity implementation in the private sector as well. Indeed, the first major private sector strike over the issue of pay equity led to wage adjustments for clerical and technical workers at Yale University in 1984–85 (Gilpin et al. 1987). Women's increased representation among union members, from 19 percent in 1962 to 39 percent in 1997, was a major impetus for union involvement.

The movement to remedy the undervaluation of female-dominated occupations achieved concrete gains for U.S. working women in the 1980s. Women's wages increased as much as 15 to 20 percent in the state civil services that implemented pay equity wage adjustments. The gender-based wage gap also declined for these workers. These monetary gains for working women have been documented by scholars such as Sorensen (1994), Hartmann and Aaronson (1994), and disseminated through regular newsletters and research briefings by advocacy groups such as the National Committee on Pay Equity.

Many see pay equity as a strategy to enhance the wages primarily of white collar and professional women. But studies of the impact of pay equity remedies that have been implemented (as well as studies of hypothetical economywide implementation) show that the lowest-earning women are among those receiving the largest wage increases due to pay equity. Figart and Lapidus (1995) have estimated that comparable worth wage increases could significantly reduce the percentage of women among the working poor. A new study by the AFL-CIO and the Institute for Women's Policy Research finds that with pay equity, family incomes would rise and poverty rates would fall for the three family types studied: married working women, working single mothers, and self-supporting single women (Hartmann, Allen, and Owens 1999).

Unfortunately, the pay equity movement never really gained momentum in the private sector in the United States, nor did many public jurisdictions besides state civil services take up the remedy. Unsuccessful court cases and the lack of interest by the federal executive branch under Presidents Reagan and Bush slowed reform efforts.

The Backlash in the 1980s and 1990s

Some of the same forces propelling the pay equity movement forward were also undermining its progress. For example, the transition to a service-based economy resulted in the feminization of the labor force, that is, an increased reliance upon women workers in female-dominated jobs. While these jobs were viewed as marginal within the postwar economy, they have become the basis for profitability in the postindustrial economy since the 1970s (Tilly 1997). As female-dominated jobs became the wheels on which the service sector advanced, low wages were the engine. The undervaluation of these jobs became increasingly evident to women. Employers have resisted implementing the type of high-wage/high-productivity system of labor relations in these new service jobs that once characterized male-dominated manufacturing industries. By seeking to raise the value of female-dominated occupations in the economy, pay equity challenged the crux of contemporary accumulation strategies. Not surprisingly, the concept was strongly resisted by conservative think-tanks and political lobbyists (Mutari and Figart 1997).

At the same time that women were increasing their labor force participation and attachment, deindustrialization often divided workers and placed women's wages on the back burner for much of organized labor. The expansion of the service sector was coupled with the weakening of the U.S. manufacturing base, leading to widespread unemployment among industrial workers, especially in the 1980s. Union leaders in specific locals were often torn between the interests of female members in remedying discrimination and male members in saving breadwinner jobs. While unions with large female constituencies continued to press for pay equity, the rest of the labor movement was fighting other battles (see Figart and Kahn 1997, ch. 4). In the 1980s and 1990s, unionism itself was under attack. With fewer resources to resist intransigent employers, many compromises were accepted at the bargaining table, including pay equity wage negotiations.

Meanwhile, conservative political forces built their ranks through a concerted attack on reproductive freedom at both the national and state levels. A defensive posture emerged within the women's movement, preoccupied with maintaining reproductive rights rather than an agenda addressing women's job-related concerns; thus the emphasis in the women's movement shifted away from bread-and-butter issues like pay equity (Burk and Hartmann 1996). Even within the Democratic Party, feminist politicians lost the relatively small amount of clout they had started to amass in the 1970s. The Democratic Leadership Council and other conservative forces within the Democratic Party in the late 1980s sought to distance the party from so-called special interests. Particularly during the Clinton administration, women's political support for the party was maintained by gestures of resistance to encroachments on reproductive freedom.

Delegitimation of the role of government undermined the ability of pay equity activists to translate public sector reforms to the private sector. Conservatives argued that an active government disrupts the benign, efficient, wealth-creating, and freedom-protecting market. Government workers were increasingly viewed as a drain of resources from the private economy. The image of the state as a model employer was no longer credible. Drawing on evidence from Canada, Isabella Bakker (1991) argues that decentralization of the state's functions through privatization and other flexible employment policies reduced the effective coverage of pay equity reform.

Securing a Living Wage for Women Workers

For two decades, pay equity has attempted to extend the concept of a breadwinner wage to female-dominated occupations just as the family wage for men was disappearing, undermined by economic restructuring. Unfortunately, this conjuncture has generated resistance to pay equity among potential allies (Figart and Kahn 1997). It is still a low priority on many progressive agendas. Progressive strategies need to be reformulated to embrace gender and race analysis; progressives need to understand that such a strategy strengthens their movement rather than dividing it. Further, economic issues need to be central to revitalizing a feminist movement in the United States. Continuing economic and demographic trends are favorable for a redirection of progressive movements: the relative share of people of color in the U.S. population will continue to grow, as will the labor force participation of women and the extent to which families rely on women's earnings for their survival. The robust economic recovery in the 1990s and particularly the high profits to businesses and corporations set the stage for a strong movement to redirect some of these profits toward labor, working women, and the spread of family-friendly policies such as subsidized child care and paid family leave.

The pay equity movement needs to address new economic concerns. The long decline in men's real wages in industrialized countries and the increased inequality of wages and income among all workers, including women, point to the weakness of focusing exclusively on the average wage gap between women and men (Humphries and Rubery 1992; Armstrong 1996). With the substantial increase in income inequality and the growth in the numbers of the working poor, public policies described below, structured to complement pay equity reform, can improve women's absolute standard of living as well as their relative economic position.

Raising the Minimum Wage

The 90-cent increase in the minimum wage to $5.15 per hour in 1996–97 still amounts to substantially less than the official poverty threshold for a family of three supported by a single breadwinner working full-time, year-round at that wage. Roughly six out of ten minimum-wage workers are women, and 40 percent of these are the sole support for their families (Mishel, Bernstein, and Rasell 1995). The minimum wage also serves as a key rate for several industries and occupations such as food service and retail sales workers. When the minimum wage is increased, firms try to maintain their internal wage structure by providing additional increments that raise the pay of some workers above the new minimum. Figart and Lapidus (1995) estimate that 65 percent of workers affected by this practice are women. A minimum wage boost, like pay equity remedies, has a large effect on the poorest workers.

Welfare Reform, Women of Color, EEO, and Pay Equity

Changes in welfare regulations, although punitive in spirit, also provide an opening for public discussion of women's wages. Women who enter the labor market as a result of Temporary Assistance to Needy Families (TANF) are likely to be employed in low-paid predominantly female jobs within sales, administrative support, and other service occupations. In fact, many TANF recipients are not new labor force entrants. Research by the Institute for Women's Policy Research has shown about 40 percent of women who received Aid to Families with Dependent Children (AFDC) worked roughly half-time over a two-year period (Spalter-Roth, Hartmann, and Andrews 1992). The problem is that the poverty level among women employed in entry-level jobs is high; such jobs cannot substitute for public assistance.

Many women leaving welfare and many of the working poor are people of color, including new immigrants from Mexico, Latin America, and Asia, who are often relegated to the most disadvantaged places in the labor market. Stronger enforcement of existing antidiscrimination and equal opportunity laws is especially needed. Federal funds for enforcement, cut during the Reagan–Bush era, have still not been restored. And, pay equity remedies, where they have been implemented, have rarely addressed the racial composition of jobs. However, a more comprehensive pay equity policy that targets minority-concentrated as well as female-dominated occupations could potentially target jobs at the bottom of the wage hierarchy. Lapidus and Figart (1998) estimate that among those currently earning less than the federal poverty threshold for a family of three, nearly 50 percent of women of color and 40 percent of white women would be lifted out of poverty with such a broad pay equity policy.

Unions and Pay Equity

Labor unions have played a pivotal role in leveling the playing field for low-wage workers and increasing the rights of the disadvantaged and discriminated against. Union support was critical to the passage of the 1964 Civil Rights Act and, as noted above, unions have played a leading role in fostering pay equity activism among public sector workers. Unions also help lead the effort to raise minimum wages and pass living wage ordinances. Research shows that unions help workers at the bottom most, and particularly help women (of all races) and minority men (Spalter-Roth, Hartmann and Collins 1994). Unfortunately, at the same time that women have been increasing their union representation, the proportion of all workers represented by labor unions has been falling. This decline in unionism has contributed to rising income inequality. New leadership in many unions and in the AFL-CIO is once again putting a priority on organizing new members, especially among the working poor and women and especially in the new service economy jobs. New immigrants are being organized in hotels and restaurants, and women in child care, home health services, hospitals, and universities are also winning union recognition.

The Living Wage Movement

Over thirty municipalities have considered legislation requiring companies receiving corporate welfare (including tax rebates and government contracts, etc.) to pay workers a living wage well above the federal minimum. Such initiatives have already been adopted by Baltimore, Boston, Detroit, Jersey City, Los Angeles, Milwaukee, Minneapolis, New Haven, New York City, Oakland, Portland (Oregon), San Jose, Santa Clara County, St. Paul, and sixteen additional jurisdictions. These efforts extend the breadwinner wage to workers who have previously been left out. Pay equity both complements and provides a compelling argument for these campaigns across the nation.

Approaching Pay Equity Through Legislation

Stronger federal legislation prohibiting wage discrimination based upon work of equal value could also help. One important bill under consideration in the past two congressional sessions is the Fair Pay Act (FPA). The FPA would outlaw discrimination in pay for female-dominated jobs that are equal in skill, effort, responsibility, and working conditions, even if the actual work is dissimilar to comparable male-dominated jobs. (The same prohibition would apply to jobs dominated by persons of color.) Just as importantly, the FPA would require employers to release summary statistics by gender, race, ethnicity, and job category, so workers would know how their own pay scale compares to other jobs in the company. The bill would also protect workers from being fired for discussing salary with coworkers, and allow workers to band together to bring class-action lawsuits for discrimination in pay. This far-reaching measure would require pay equity implementation in the United States much like Ontario's law does, except that rather than requiring all employers to implement pay equity proactively (as in Ontario) it simply requires employers to respond to worker complaints. Another proposed bill under consideration, the Paycheck Fairness Act, would strengthen equal employment opportunity enforcement in the United States. It would provide full compensatory and punitive damages as remedies for equal pay violations, treating gender-based wage discrimination like discrimination based upon race or ethnicity. Like the Fair Pay Act, it would prohibit employers from firing employees for sharing wage and salary information with each other. While much weaker than the fair pay act (there is no comparable worth provision), this bill would help focus employers' attention on inequitable pay. Both bills would provide enforcement through the Equal Employment Opportunity Commission (EEOC).

The National Committee on Pay Equity and the Working Women's Department at the AFL-CIO have also initiated a state-by-state campaign to introduce and pass state legislation, modeled on the proposed federal Fair Pay Act, to require that employers institute pay equity remedies wherever workers' claims of unfair pay are proven.

Conclusion

Pay equity policies, along with living wage ordinances, increased unionization, antipoverty initiatives antidiscrimination measures, and minimum wage laws are important ways of humanizing labor markets. Rather than viewing workers as mere sellers of a commodity, these labor market policies start from the premise that fair and equitable wages and working conditions are a means to achieving economic and social justice.

References

Albelda, Randy, and Chris Tilly. 1998. "Glass Ceilings and Bottomless Pits: Women's Work, Women's Poverty." *Working USA* (January/February): 42–55.

Armstrong, Pat. 1996. "The Feminization of the Labour Force: Harmonizing Down in a Global Economy." In *Rethinking Restructuring: Gender and Change in Canada*, ed. Isabella Bakker, 29–54. Toronto: University of Toronto Press.

Bakker, Isabella. 1991. "Pay Equity and Economic Restructuring: The Polarization of Policy?" In *Just Wages: A Feminist Assessment of Pay Equity*, ed. Judy Fudge and Patricia McDermott, 254–280. Toronto: University of Toronto Press.

Bridges, William P., and Robert L. Nelson. 1989. "Markets in Hierarchies: Organizational and Market Influences on Gender Inequality in a State Pay System." *American Journal of Sociology* 95, no. 3 (November): 616–658.

Burk, Martha, and Heidi Hartmann. 1996. "Beyond the Gender Gap." *The Nation*, June 10, 18–21.

England, Paula. 1992. *Comparable Worth: Theories and Evidence*. New York: Aldine de Gruyter.

Figart, Deborah M. 1997. "Gender as More Than a Dummy Variable: Feminist Approaches to Discrimination." *Review of Social Economy* 55, no. 1 (Spring): 1–32.

Figart, Deborah H., and Peggy Kahn. 1997. *Contesting the Market: Pay Equity and the Politics of Economic Restructuring*. Detroit: Wayne State University Press.

Figart, Deborah H., and June Lapidus. 1995. "A Gender Analysis of Labor Market Policies for the Working Poor in the U.S." *Feminist Economics* 1, no. 3 (Fall): 60–81.

Gabin, Nancy F. 1989. "The Issue of the Eighties: Comparable Worth and the Labor Movement." *Indiana Academy of the Social Sciences Proceedings 1988* 23 (February): 51–58.

Gilpin, Toni, Gary Isaac, Dan Letwin, and Jack McKivigan. 1987. *On Strike for Respect: The Yale Strike of 1984–85*. Chicago: Charles H. Kerr.

Gordon, David M., Richard Edwards, and Michael Reich. 1982. *Segmented Work, Divided Workers: The Historical Transformation of Labor in the United States*. Cambridge: Cambridge University Press.

Hallock, Margaret. 1993. "Unions and the Gender Wage Gap." In *Women and Unions: Forging a Partnership*, ed. Dorothy Sue Cobble, 27–42. Ithaca: ILR Press.

Hartmann, Heidi, and Stephanie Aaronson. 1994. "Pay Equity and Women's Wage Increases: Success in the States, A Model for the Nation." *Duke Journal of Gender Law and Policy* no. 1: 69–87.

Hartmann, Heidi, Katherine Allen, and Christine Owens. 1999. *Equal Pay for Working Families: National and State Data on the Pay Gap and its Costs*. Washington, DC: AFL-CIO and IWPR.

Hartmann, Heidi, Elaine Sorensen, and Stephanie Aaronson. 1996. *Pay Equity Remedies in State Governments: Assessing Their Economic Effects*. Washington, DC: Institute for Women's Policy Research.

Horrell, Sara, Jill Rubery, and Brendan Burchell. 1989. "Unequal Jobs or Unequal Pay?" *Industrial Relations Journal* 20, no. 3 (Autumn): 176–191.

Humphries, Jane, and Jill Rubery. 1992. "The Legacy for Women's Employment: Integration, Differentiation and Polarisation." In *The Economic Legacy 1979–1992*, ed. Jonathan Michie, 236–255. London: Academic Press.

Kahn, Peggy, and Deborah M. Figart. 1998. "Reviving Pay Equity: New Strategies for Attacking the Wage Gap," *Working USA* 2, no. 2 (July-August): 8–17.

Lapidus, June, and Deborah M. Figart. 1994. "Comparable Worth as an Anti-Poverty Strategy: Evidence from the March 1992 CPS." *Review of Radical Political Economics* 26, no. 3 (September): 1–10.

———. 1998. "Remedying 'Unfair Acts': Pay Equity by Race and Gender." *Feminist Economics* 4, no. 3 (Fall): 7–28.

Mishel, Lawrence, Jared Bernstein, and Edith Rasell. 1995. *Who Wins with a Higher Minimum Wage*. Washington, DC: Economic Policy Institute.

Mutari, Ellen, and Deborah M. Figart. 1997. "Markets, Flexibility, and Family: Evaluating the Gendered Discourse Against Pay Equity." *Journal of Economic Issues* 31, no. 3 (September): 687–705.

National Committee on Pay Equity (NCPE). 1989. *Pay Equity in the Public Sector, 1979–1989*. Washington, DC: NCPE.

______. 1996. *The Intersection Between Pay Equity and Workplace Representation*. Washington, DC: National Committee on Pay Equity.

Phillips, Anne, and Barbara Taylor. 1986. "Sex and Skill." In *Waged Work: A Reader*, ed. *Feminist Review*, 54–66. London: Virago.

Portman, Lisa, Joy Ann Grune, and Eve Johnson. 1984. "The Role of Labor." In *Comparable Worth and Wage Discrimination: Technical Possibilities and Political Realities*, ed. Helen Remick, 219–237. Philadelphia: Temple University Press.

Sorensen, Elaine. 1994. *Comparable Worth: Is It a Worthy Policy?* Princeton: Princeton University Press.

Spalter-Roth, Roberta, Heidi I. Hartmann, and Linda Andrews. 1992. *Combining Work and Welfare: An Alternative Poverty Strategy*. Washington, DC: Institute for Women's Policy Research.

Spalter-Roth, Roberta, Heidi Hartmann, and Nancy Collins. 1994. *What Do Unions Do for Women?* Washington, DC: Institute for Women's Policy Research.

Steinberg, Ronnie J. 1990. "Social Construction of Skill: Gender, Power, and Comparable Worth." *Work and Occupations* 17, no. 4 (November): 449–482.

Steinberg, Ronnie J., and Lois Haignere. 1991. "Separate but Equivalent: Equal Pay for Work of Comparable Worth." In *Beyond Methodology: Feminist Scholarship as Lived Research*, eds. Mary Margaret Fonow and Judith A. Cook, 154–170. Bloomington: Indiana University Press.

Tilly, Chris. 1997. "Arresting the Decline of Good Jobs in the USA?" *Industrial Relations Journal* 28, no. 4: 269–274.

Treiman, Donald J., and Heidi I. Hartmann, eds. 1981. *Women, Work, and Wages: Equal Pay for Jobs of Equal Value*. Washington, DC: National Academy Press.

Wajcman, Judy. 1991. "Patriarchy, Technology, and Conceptions of Skill." *Work and Occupations* 18, no. 1 (February): 29–45.

33

The Earned Income Tax Credit

What It Does and Doesn't Do

Robert Cherry and Gertrude Schaffner Goldberg

The repeal of the federal entitlement to public assistance for women and children focuses attention on alternative antipoverty measures. One such program is the Earned Income Tax Credit (EITC), which spends more federal dollars than Temporary Aid to Needy Families (TANF) and provides benefits to nearly three times as many households.[1] Both liberals and conservatives view the EITC as a political success: in 1990 and 1993, when large budgetary deficits discouraged any increases in social spending and public assistance was under siege, Congress significantly expanded the EITC, virtually without debate.

This chapter will describe how the EITC works and whom it benefits. It will show that the EITC cannot be a substitute for other important antipoverty programs. To name just two of a number of reasons: the EITC is available only to individuals who are employed at some time during the year, and the EITC for individuals without dependent children is so small that it is meaningless as an antipoverty program. Other government income transfer programs, targeted job creation, minimum wage legislation, and public assistance are necessary to alleviate poverty for those whom the EITC does not help. Thus, this article concludes with a comprehensive set of policy recommendations—including complementary antipoverty policies and changes in the EITC.

How the EITC Works

The EITC is a refundable tax credit. Persons who work in the paid labor market and earn below a certain threshold are automatically eligible to receive this credit when they file their income taxes. The credit is paid out in the form of a "tax rebate," which can be larger than tax liabilities—what is known as a "refundable tax credit." Thus, very poor families who do not pay federal income taxes receive a "credit" or benefit from the government. Families with children are eligible for a much larger credit than are childless adults. In the 1990s, about 6 percent of Americans filed for the EITC (author's calculations from the *Current Population Survey*).

The structure of the EITC has the following characteristics: a phase-in range for which a credit is paid as a proportion of adjusted gross income (AGI), which is essentially wage income, up to a maximum amount; a range of income on which the maximum credit is paid; a phase-out range in which the credit is reduced at a specified or phase-out rate; and an income cutoff when the credit is reduced to zero. Table 33.1 illustrates these program characteristics for families with one child and with two or more children. In the phase-in range, the EITC functions as a wage subsidy, raising hourly income by 40 percent for families with

Table 33.1

Characteristics of the EITC Program, 1998

Household type	Phase-in Rate(%)	Phase-in Ends	Maximum payment	Phase-out Begins	Phase-out Rate(%)	Terminate eligibility
One child	34.00	$6,679	$2,271	$12,260	15.98	$26,473
Two children	40.00	$9,390	$3,756	$12,260	21.06	$30,095

two or more children (to a maximum credit of $3,756 in 1998) and by 34 percent for one-child families (to a maximum credit of $2,271). For both groups of households, the maximum credit continues until AGI equals $12,260. For each additional dollar of earned income, the EITC declines until a cut-off point where the credit is reduced to zero and eligibility is terminated. There is a small credit for adults over the age of twenty-five who have no dependent children and earn less than $10,000 a year. Nine states offered and EITC for state income taxes adding to the value of the federal benefit in 1998. Since 1986 the federal EITC has been indexed to inflation. By contrast, federal-state welfare programs like AFDC and TANF are not indexed.

The EITC, though means tested, escapes the meanness and stigma usually associated with other public assistance programs. Instead of applying to a public assistance agency, applicants file an extra form with their tax return—there is no "special" application process. This is one of the reasons why the proportion of those eligible who actually claim their benefits is between 80 percent and 86 percent (Scholz 1994), compared to 62 to 72 percent for Aid to Families with Dependent Children (Blank and Ruggles 1993).

Is the EITC an Effective Poverty-Reduction Strategy?

The current system of measuring poverty dates from the 1960s and is based on the presumption that multiplying the cost of an "economy food plan" by three would approximate a minimum threshold for essentials. However, the economy food plan was "for temporary or emergency use when funds are low" and was only 75 to 80 percent of a "low cost food plan" of the Department of Agriculture, which, "if strictly followed," could "provide an acceptable and adequate diet" (Orshansky 1965, 3–4). Over time, this threshold has become less meaningful. A study conducted by the U.S. Bureau of the Census in the late 1980s concluded that in order to be comparable to the original threshold, the poverty level would have to be 50 percent higher than the current official standard (Ruggles 1990, 167). As we provide estimates of the extent to which the EITC reduces poverty, it is important to bear in mind how meager the official standard is.

The EITC has a sizable antipoverty effect: a single mother with two children who works 2,000 hours at the minimum wage of $5.15 an hour has annual earnings of $10,712; with the EITC credit, her total income rises to $14,468. In 1996, there were 4.6 million people in low-income working families who would have been poor without the EITC; 2.4 million of these people were children. Greenstein and Shapiro (1998) point out that this impact was disproportionate for poor children who lived in the South. Indeed, they note that the EITC program lifts more children out of "official" poverty than all other government programs combined. For 1996, the EITC reduced the post-tax and transfer poverty rate of children from 22.3 to 19.1 percent (Liebman 1998)—which may say more about the modest antipoverty effect of other programs than the generosity of the EITC.

Work Incentives and the EITC

The EITC provides a financial incentive to work in the paid labor market. Given its high phase-in rates, the EITC provides substantial work incentives for female householders with low hourly pay. The share of single women with children who worked at some point during the year rose from 72.7 to 82.1 percent between 1984 and 1996. Meyer and Rosenbaum (1998) estimate that during this period the EITC expansions had as large an effect on the increased labor market participation of single mothers as all other factors combined. Dickert, Hauser, and Scholz (1995) projected that the EITC expansion legislated in 1993 would draw approximately 200,000 new workers into the labor market and that 400,000 families would no longer participate either in the food stamp or AFDC program.

For higher-income households, the work incentive effects of the EITC are unclear. Two-thirds of those eligible for EITC benefits are in households with wage income above the official poverty line; indeed over one-third of EITC benefits go to households with incomes over $20,000 (Shaviro 1997). For these households, the phase-out rate reduces the value of additional work effort. To illustrate: for each additional $100 of wage income, the average family with two dependent children would pay an additional $15 to federal income taxes, $8 to social security and unemployment insurance taxes, and $4 to state income taxes. In addition, the family would lose $21 of EITC benefits so that the net income received would be at most $52. If the household lost food stamp or housing benefits the net gains would be still less. After paying for childcare and business-related expenses, a female householder with two dependent children whose wage income rises from $12,000 to $15,000 would gain only $568 in net disposable income (U.S. House of Representatives 1998, Table 7–3). When wage income rises from $15,000 to $20,000, net disposable income rises by only $861.

The work disincentives at higher incomes are, however, not substantiated. For example, a recent study found that the phase-out of the EITC has little or no impact on hours of work (Liebman 1998, 104). Liebman noted that most recipients had little understanding of the link between their work effort and the amount of EITC received. Moreover, since 99.7 percent of all recipients do not receive the credit as part of their weekly earnings, the EITC is viewed as a lump sum that "magically" appears as a tax refund. As a result, few recipients incorporate the phase-out rate into their labor market decisions, thus moderating the potential work disincentive.

The EITC and the Marriage Decision

While EITC benefits are the same, regardless of the marital status of parents, the program nonetheless creates an economic disincentive to marry. Suppose a single mother with two dependent children and an AGI of $12,000 is considering marriage to a childless man with an income of $17,500. If the woman remains single, she qualifies for the maximum EITC benefit of $3,756. If they marry, the couple must file a joint return for their combined income of $30,095, an amount that exceeds the cut-off for EITC benefits. The marriage would cost them the entire EITC credit, a substantial sum for this lower middle-income couple.

If their decision is based solely on economic reasons, the couple might decide to lie to the IRS about their marital status. Indeed, Scholz (1997) reports that 31 percent of overclaimed EITC benefits are by married taxpayers who say they are single. More likely, couples wishing to avoid the marriage penalty may simply choose not to marry. This has led some social conservatives to attack the EITC program as antifamily.

Alternative Antipoverty Policies

Traditional Public Assistance

While the EITC aids many poor households, it is not a substitute for traditional public assistance. The EITC provides no aid to the long-term unemployed or those who are out of the labor market. Moreover, researchers have found that even when EITC benefits were included, part-time or part-year employment generally provided less income than the TANF predecessor, AFDC (Hartmann and Spalter-Roth 1994; Dickert, Hauser, and Scholz 1995). This is important since the Bureau of Labor Statistics categorizes only 35 percent of employed women as full-time, year-round workers.

Temporary Aid to Needy Families, or TANF, provides benefits for a limited time to nonemployed poor parents (usually mothers). However, the benefits this program provides are meager at best, and the rules for its receipt are strict and, in the current political climate, stigmatized. TANF benefits, like AFDC, do not provide enough money to lift a family out of poverty. AFDC benefits were always meager, and their real or inflation-adjusted value had been falling for twenty years. Average benefits were 37 percent lower in 1995 than in 1975 (U.S. House of Representatives, 1998, 414). In 1996, the combined benefits of AFDC and food stamps were below the official U.S. poverty level ($12,320 for a family of three) in all fifty states, and the median state provided benefits equal to only 65 percent of the poverty level. That year, Congress and President Clinton eliminated the AFDC program. Its replacement, TANF, places strict lifetime limits on the number of years any household is eligible for public assistance. Moreover, the new legislation specifically states that TANF is not an entitlement. Within a year of its passage, caseloads fell by 20 percent. Because the jobs that former recipients get often fail to lift them out of poverty, welfare "reform" further impoverishes many who leave the rolls

Minimum Wage Legislation

The majority of poor and near-poor households have no dependent children, and for them, a minimum wage increase is much more helpful than the EITC program. Over the last three decades, business interests have generally been successful in defeating attempts to raise the minimum wage by claiming that it would reduce employment. As a result, the purchasing power of the minimum wage was 20 percent less in 1998 than it was thirty years earlier. Indeed, the combined value of the maximum EITC benefit and year-round full-time earnings at the minimum wage in 1998 was less than the 1968 minimum wage earnings alone. Thus, in many cases, the EITC has not even compensated recipients for wage declines, much less bettered their economic circumstances.

Recent research contradicts the claims of those who maintain that the minimum wage adversely affects employment. For example, Lawrence Katz and Allan Krueger (1992) found no effect on employment in Texas fast-food restaurants after the 1990 minimum wage increase. If fast-food restaurants in a low-wage state do not change their employment decisions in relation to increases in the minimum wage, it is unlikely that other firms whose labor costs are less sensitive to changes in the minimum wage would do so. David Card and Allan Kreuger (1995) summarize other tests that indicate that the 1990–91 minimum wage increase had no adverse effect on employment of low-wage workers. Bernstein and Schmitt (1998) had similar results in their study of the two-stage 1996–97 increase in the minimum wage from $4.25 to $5.15 per hour.

Critics of minimum wage increases like Shaviro (1997) claim that the minimum wage is not a well-targeted antipoverty measure because the vast majority of minimum wage workers are in households with incomes well above the poverty line. In contrast, Bernstein and Schmitt (1998) provide evidence that the minimum wage substantially aids low-income households. When the minimum wage was raised in two stages to $5.15 in 1997, nearly 10 million workers had their wages increased as a direct result. Another 10 million workers, with wages between $5.15 and $6.15 per hour, were also expected to have benefited. Further, Bernstein and Schmitt dispel the view that the typical minimum wage jobholder is a supplemental earner. Instead, they found that 18 percent are single heads contributing their household's entire income. Among other households, the minimum wage worker contributed, on average, 44 percent of the household's income. Most relevant to antipoverty policy, adult female workers comprise 58.2 percent of the 20 million workers directly and indirectly affected by the 1996–97 minimum wage increase.

While the minimum wage is paid by employers, income transfer programs, like the EITC, are funded by the government. Not surprisingly, business groups favor the EITC because it raises employee earnings "without any cost to their employers, easing the pressure to raise wages" (Perez-Peña 1998). As Steve Pressman suggests, "The EITC may reduce the wages that employers offer...since both parties know that wages will be supplemented by the government" (1993, 713). And it may also dampen workers' efforts to raise wages, including the statutory minimum, ultimately affecting the whole lower segment of the wage structure. Finally, the EITC and minimum wage have different impacts on future income. Whereas wage increases contribute toward higher unemployment, old age, and disability insurance benefits, the EITC does not.

Employment Policies

Unlike public assistance, the EITC is worthless to those who are unemployed and of little value to those with very low incomes. This is one reason why full employment must be an important component of any meaningful antipoverty strategy (Collins, Ginsburg, and Goldberg 1994). The link between full employment—which has not been achieved in peacetime—and antipoverty goals had been a prominent part of liberal thinking (Tobin 1965; Freeman 1991). However, since the 1980s full employment has receded as a stated goal of public policy. This is unfortunate since even seemingly low official unemployment rates often mask the employment difficulties faced by disadvantaged workers.

When the national unemployment rates fell to 4.3 percent in 1998, there was a broad consensus that, except for some blemishes, this was a fully employed economy in which anyone who wanted to work could find a job. However, official unemployment rates only measure the share of persons in the labor force (employed or currently seeking work) who are unemployed. Unemployment statistics do not include discouraged workers—individuals who want to work but stop formal job searches so that they do not meet the government's job search criteria. Nor do they take account of the underemployment of individuals who work part-time but desire full-time employment. If we add both groups to the officially unemployed, we can compute an underemployment rate. Jared Bernstein (1997) found that for the twelve-month period ending July 1997, when the national unemployment rate averaged 5.2 percent, the underemployment rate averaged 9.7 percent. He found that while the official black unemployment rate averaged 10.7 percent, the black underemployment rate averaged 17.3 percent. For high school dropouts, the 1997 official unemployment rates for African-American and Latina women 16 to 25 years old were 36.2 and 23.0 percent, respectively; and for high school graduates, 19.7 and 14.1 percent, respectively. This suggests that even after five years of economic expansion, labor markets have not provided enough jobs for many of the very women whose access to public assistance has been severely curtailed. Nor, given the prospects of so many minority men, can marriage solve the poverty problems faced by these women. Cherry (1998) has estimated that the unemployment rate might have been as high as 24 percent for adult black men in 1997 if adjustments were made for labor force withdrawals and reductions in the noninstitutionalized population due to high incarceration rates and census undercount. Thus, a focused employment policy must be an integral part of any antipoverty strategy.

Policy Recommendations

The Earned Income Tax Credit has many advantages as an antipoverty program and a number of drawbacks as well. It has political appeal, is user-friendly, and is without stigma. Further, it is an incentive to employment in low-wage jobs because it makes work pay and may well preserve jobs. On the other hand, the EITC may depress wages or reduce incentives to raise them, thereby dragging down the lower end of the wage spectrum. It uses government money to subsidize low-wage employers, leaves out the poorest of the poor as well as low-wage workers who do not have the "right" family composition, and reduces the rewards of earnings in the phase-out range. Policy should address itself both to improving the EITC and to combining it with complementary employment, wage, and family-support policies.

Jobs for all at livable wages should be the foundation of our antipoverty policy. At the same time, caring for the very young or frail members of one's family is genuine work and should be compensated through some form of income support, either public assistance or family allowances. Public job creation for child and elder care, and construction of affordable low-cost housing, or of mass transportation systems, would be a desirable way to stimulate employment opportunities. And, compared to the EITC, such job creation would mean that policymakers are choosing the types of employment that are publicly subsidized. The minimum wage, moreover, should be automatically adjusted for inflation and annual gains in labor productivity. This would enable minimum wage workers to have a rising living standard without the need for ongoing political action in support of discretionary legislation.

A promising development is the enactment of local "living wage" ordinances. A living wage is usually defined as a wage sufficient for a single, full-time, year-round worker to earn enough for a three-person household to escape poverty, independent of EITC, food stamps, or other government support programs. By 1998, seventeen cities, including Los Angeles and Chicago, had legislated that all firms doing business with city government must pay all their employees the prescribed living wage (Pollin and Luce 1998).

How can the EITC be improved? Benefits to adult workers without dependent children are meager and were almost removed in 1998—a sign that as the program becomes larger and costlier, it will become more vulnerable politically. Instead of cutting benefits to childless workers, eligibility should be extended to workers with annual incomes between $10,000 and $15,000.

Many EITC recipients have little understanding of the relationship between their paid employment and the credits they receive. Recipients in the phase-in range do not realize the value to them of being paid legally rather than working "off the books." Hence the sensible recommendation of the Children's Defense Fund and National Coalition for the Homeless (1998, 6): that government agencies provide "vastly improved information and outreach so that families who are leaving TANF know of their likely eligibility for Medicaid, food stamps, child support help, child care and the Earned Income Tax Credit."

The problem of minimal net gains for workers in the phase-out range could be reduced substantially if the EITC program were universalized by lowering the phase-out rate and guaranteeing a minimum credit to all households with dependent children. One way to do this, without significantly increasing federal expenditures, would be to shift the tax benefits now received through the standard allowance for dependents to the EITC program (Cherry 1999). Universalizing the EITC in this way would also make it more resistant to political attack. If these reforms were implemented, the EITC would become part of a holistic, employment-based antipoverty program, fostering a more equitable and more efficient society.

Note

1. TANF replaced Aid to Families with Dependent Children (AFDC), which was repealed in 1996. The EITC was expected to exceed federal AFDC expenditures by the end of the nineties.

Bibliography

Bernstein, Jared. 1997. "Low-Wage Labor Market Indicators by City and State." Working paper 118. Washington, DC: Economic Policy Institute.

Bernstein, Jared, and John Schmitt. 1998. *Making Work Pay*. Washington, DC: Economic Policy Institute.

Blank, Rebecca, and Ruggles, Patricia. 1993. "When Do Women Use AFDC and Food Stamps: The Dynamics of Eligibility Versus Participation." National Bureau of Economic Research (NBER) Working paper #4429, Boston, August.

Card, David, and Alan Kreuger. 1995. *Myth and Measurement: The New Economics of the Minimum Wage*. Princeton: Princeton University Press.

Cherry, Robert. 1998. "Black Jobs: Missing in Action." *Dollars and Sense* 23, no. 5 (November/December): 24.

———. 1999. "Universalizing the EITC: A Pro-Family Agenda." Paper presented at the Eastern Economic Association Meetings, Boston.

Children's Defense Fund, and the National Coalition for the Homeless. 1998. "Early Findings on Welfare and Well-Being." August 19, Washington, DC.

Collins, Sheila D., Helen Lachs Ginsburg, and Gertrude Schaffner Goldberg. 1994. *Jobs for All: A Plan for the Revitalization of America*. New York: Apex Press.

DeParle, Jason. 1998. "Shrinking Welfare Rolls Leave Record High Share of Minorities." *New York Times*, July 27, p. A1.

Dickert, Stacy, Scott Hauser, and John Scholz. 1995. "The Earned Income Tax Credit Transfer Programs: A Study of Labor Market and Program Participation." In *Tax Policy and the Economy*, vol. 9, ed. John Poterba, 1–50. Cambridge: MIT Press.

Freeman, Richard. 1991. "Employment and Earnings of Disadvantaged Young Men in a Labor Shortage Economy. In *The Urban Underclass*, ed. Christopher Jencks and Paul Peterson, 103–121. Washington, DC: The Brookings Institution.

Garner, Thesia, Kathleen Short, Stephanie Shipp, Charles Nelson, and Geoffrey Paulin. 1998. "Experimental Poverty Measures for the 1990s." *Monthly Labor Review* 121 (March): 39–61.

Goldberg, Gertrude Schaffner, and Sheila D. Collins. 1999. *Washington's New Poor Law: Welfare "Reform" and the Road Not Taken, 1935–1966*. New York: Apex Press.

Greenstein, Robert, and Isaac Shapiro. 1998. *New Research Findings on the Effects of the Earned Income Tax Credit*. Washington, DC: Center on Budget and Policy Priorities.

Hartmann, Heidi, and Roberta Spalter-Roth. 1994. *The Real Employment Opportunities of Women Participating in AFDC*. Washington, DC. Institute for Women's Policy Research.

Katz, Lawrence, and Alan Krueger. 1992. "The Effects of the Minimum Wage on the Fast-Food Industry." *Industrial and Labor Relations Review* 46 (October): 6–21.

Liebman, Jeffrey. 1998. "The Impact of the Earned Income

Tax Credit on Incentives and Income Distribution." In *Tax Policy and the Economy*, vol. 12, ed. James Poterba, 83–119. Cambridge: MIT Press.

Liebman, Jeffrey, and Nadia Eissa. 1996. "Labor Supply Response to the Earned Income Tax Credit." *Quarterly Journal of Economics* 112 (May): 605–637.

Meyer, Bruce, and Dan Rosenbaum. 1998. "Welfare, the Earned Income Tax Credit, and the Labor Supply of Single Mothers." Unpublished manuscript, Northwestern University.

Orshansky, Mollie. 1965. "Counting the Poor: Another Look at the Poverty Profile." *Social Security Bulletin* 28 (January): 3–29.

Perez-Peña, Richard. 1998. "Tax Credit Rise Urged for the Poor in New York." *New York Times*, March 2, B4.

Pressman, Steve. 1993. "Tax Expenditures for Child Exemptions: A Poor Policy to Aid America's Children." *Journal of Economic Issues* 27 (September): 699–719.

Pollin, Robert, and Stephanie Luce. 1998. *The Living Wage: Building a Fair Economy*. New York: New Press.

Rivera, Carla. 1998. "Lessening Reliance on Welfare Reform." *Los Angeles Times*, November 16, B1.

Ruggles, Patricia. 1990. *Drawing the Line: Alternative Poverty Measures and Their Implications for Public Policy*. Washington, DC: Urban Institute Press.

Scholz, John. 1994. "The Earned Income Tax Credit: Participation, Compliance, and Antipoverty Effectiveness." *National Tax Journal* 48: 63–85.

———. 1997. Testimony Before House of Representatives, Committee on Ways and Means, May 8.

Shaviro, Daniel. 1997. "The Minimum Wage, the Earned Income Tax Credit, and Optimal Subsidy Policy." *University of Chicago Law Review* 64 (Spring): 405–481.

Tobin, James. 1965. "On Improving the Status of the Negro." In *The Negro American*, ed. Talcott Parson and Kenneth Clark, 451–473. Boston: Houghton Mifflin.

U.S. House of Representatives, Committee on Ways and Means. 1998. *1998 Green Book: Background Material and Data on Programs within the Jurisdiction of the Committee on Ways and Means*. Washington, DC: U.S. Government Printing Office.

34

Empty Bellies, Empty Promises

Welfare "Reform" in the Nineties

Kimberly Christensen

The Recent Welfare "Reform" Legislation

On August 23, 1996, President Clinton signed HR 3437, the "Personal Responsibility and Work Opportunity Act of 1996" (PRWOA). This bipartisan welfare "reform" bill abolished Aid to Families with Dependent Children (AFDC), ending sixty years of federal income guarantees to the nation's poorest children. In place of AFDC, HR 3437 substituted block grants to the states known as TANF (Temporary Assistance to Needy Families). The level of appropriations for these TANF grants will reduce federal funding to poor families by $55 billion by the year 2002. These savings will primarily come from the denial of benefits to legal immigrants and from reductions in the food stamp program. The bill also imposes severe restrictions on how states may use TANF monies.

Among other provisions, states *must* require all TANF recipients, except those with dependent children under one year of age, to participate in community service work after two months and to be working for pay after two years. Although attending high school or working for a GED degree fulfills this work requirement, attending college no longer does. HR 3437 places a lifetime cap of five years on aid, regardless of economic or family circumstances.

In addition, states are prohibited from using TANF monies to support unmarried mothers under eighteen years old unless they are living with a parent or adult guardian. This provision may seem innocuous until one considers that a significant number of these teens are abused or even impregnated by their biological fathers, stepfathers, or other adult guardians (Reed 1991; Woodman 1995). All TANF recipients must cooperate with child support enforcement authorities. Again, this provision may seem reasonable until one considers that according to a 1997 study, over 20 percent of AFDC recipients had been physically abused within the past year and over two-thirds have been abused at some point in their adult lives (Allard et al. 1997). States that fail to meet these and other requirements can be "sanctioned" with a loss of up to 21 percent of their TANF grants.

Myths vs. Facts

The PRWOA is based on a series of misconceptions, half-truths, and outright falsehoods about the nature of welfare recipients, the nature of our economy, and the likely impact of welfare "reform" on children. For example, contrary to popular belief, AFDC always comprised a trivial percentage of state and federal spending. In 1995, AFDC represented less than 1 percent of the federal budget and three-to-four percent of the average state budget (*Poverty and Race* 1995). Totally eliminating AFDC would have made no discernable difference in the tax bill of the average American taxpayer. Furthermore, workfare programs, a central plank in most states' TANF plans, generally cost *more* to administer than AFDC (Finder 1998).

PRWOA supporters also claimed that AFDC was responsible for the growth in single motherhood, particularly teen motherhood in minority communities, in the past generation. Abolishing AFDC would supposedly reduce this phenomenon and restore the nuclear family in poor communities. Again, the facts say otherwise. The average woman on AFDC was white and had two children, the same as the average American woman not on AFDC (Abramovitz 1996). In 1996, less than 8 percent of AFDC recipients were teens, with most of those being eighteen or nineteen years of age (Albelda and Folbre 1996). Finally, if AFDC receipt were the cause of unwed pregnancy, one would expect those states with the highest AFDC benefit levels to have more unwed births. Exactly the contrary is true; in 1996, those states with the *highest* benefit levels had the *lowest* rates of unwed birth and vice versa (Abramovitz 1996).

Proponents of welfare "reform" repeatedly asserted that the PRWOA would break the "cycle of dependency" among recipients when, in fact, no such "cycle" exists. Over 40 percent of AFDC recipients leave the rolls within one year and nearly 70 percent leave within two years (Spalter-Roth et al. 1995). Furthermore, over 40 percent of recipients worked (often "under-the-table" as housecleaners, babysitters, etc.) to make ends meet while receiving AFDC (Spalter-Roth et al. 1995). Those who do find full-time jobs (and the vast majority do not find full-time, full-year work) are overwhelmingly concentrated in minimum-wage work, which pays approximately $10,500 annually and often offers no health insurance, transportation, and other work-related expenses. Once the costs of childcare are deducted, most former AFDC families are no better off than they were on the typical AFDC grant of $366 a month (de Parle 1999). And finally, the daughters of AFDC recipients were no more likely to receive AFDC than other women of their income level (Abramovitz 1996). The problem is not welfare; it is poverty and a shortage of education, childcare, and decent-paying jobs for women.

Why Was the PRWOA Adopted?

The PRWOA was based on incorrect assumptions about the situation of poor women and children in this country. Its punitive provisions will harm women's physical safety and children's health and well-being. Why, then, was there so much popular support for welfare "reform" in a country that claims to value women and children?

At least two factors account for the popularity of welfare "reform": economic insecurity and anxiety about family life and sexuality. First, despite rising average incomes, the American people are feeling economically insecure—and are looking for a simple solution to their economic woes. But real solutions will not be so easy to find. The past several decades have witnessed a transformation from a post–World War II economy characterized by a stable domestic manufacturing sector and steady employment for a large percentage of the (at least white) working and middle classes to an as-yet-undefined "postmodern" economy characterized by global capital flight, downsizing, and layoffs—even for the more highly educated and skilled. More families are sending more people into the workforce to make ends meet, resulting in less time for family life and leisure. But this increasing workload has not brought the expected rewards (Schor 1992). For a large proportion of

Americans, these changes have brought increased family tensions and more stress, but not the sought-after economic security.

The real reason for this increasing economic insecurity is not welfare moms. The causes include the increasing globalization of finance and investment capital (and the resulting loss of American manufacturing jobs), lackluster productivity growth, and spectacular increases in income and wealth inequality in the United States. For example, in 1996, the pay of the average American CEO was 209 times the pay of the average American factory worker. In 1996, the average CEO's compensation rose by 39 percent, while that of the average worker rose by just 3 percent, barely enough to cover inflation (Reingold 1997). These problems are exacerbated by government policies that have done little to counter this rising inequality and job security, and in some cases (e.g., NAFTA) have worsened the problems.

To truly address our unemployment, underemployment, wage inequities, and maldistribution of income would require creative new policies and courageous leadership, commodities in short supply in Washington these days. Possibilities to be explored include increasing worker control, participation, and ownership in the workplace; restructuring capital–labor relations through progressive labor law reform; and imposing controls over capital flight such as requiring prior notification of plant closings and compensation to those laid off. It would require basic changes in our campaign finance system, as the current system virtually guarantees a corporate stranglehold on elections and policy options. And it would require massive ethical changes in how we view our fellow Americans—the scope and responsibilities of community.

Unfortunately, such changes are unlikely in the near future. When fundamental change is unlikely and problems cannot be adequately addressed, opportunistic politicians can often reduce the attention paid to their own inadequate policies by scapegoating. Welfare "reform" is a case in point, scapegoating some of the least powerful and least wealthy among us for the failures of the most powerful and the wealthy. In doing so, politicians often draw upon (and reinforce) racist stereotypes of women of color (presumed incorrectly to be the vast majority of welfare recipients) as lazy and immoral. Such scapegoating may make good electoral sense, but it does nothing to solve the real problems. And, in this case, scapegoating will cause—and is already causing—massive suffering among poor children and their mothers.

But jobs are not the only thing Americans are insecure about these days. In the past two generations, we have experienced massive changes in our family structures, sexual mores, and child-rearing norms. Over 50 percent of all marriages with children present now end in divorce. Although, contrary to popular myth, teenage child-bearing has not exploded, the out-of-wedlock birthrate has increased dramatically among women of all colors and income levels. Currently, 29 percent of all U.S. births are to unmarried mothers (Woodman 1995). The average age of first sexual experience has declined significantly, so that now over 50 percent of both males and females graduating from high school are sexually active (Woodman 1995). A significant number of unmarried heterosexual couples are living together—and do not face significant social ostracism. And although very significant homophobia remains, there is greater acceptance of lesbian/gay relationships (including serious discussion of legalizing lesbian/gay marriage), and we are in the midst of a virtual "lesbian baby boom" (Weston 1997).

Many of these changes are profoundly liberating and humane. Ironically, many have been brought about by the very "free enterprise" capitalist system that conservative welfare "reformers" so admire. For instance, increased labor mobility has torn apart extended families and traditional communities, and women's increasing economic independence has allowed for more single motherhood by choice. But although they may be positive for those involved, these changes are profoundly unsettling and challenging to many, particularly those committed to traditional religious beliefs about sexuality and family.

It is absurd to think that our minimal federal income supports to fatherless poor children are responsible for these changes in our families and communities, changes that are occurring to a greater or lesser extent in virtually every industrialized country in the world (Folbre 1994). But that is what welfare "reformers" would have us believe. What we need is respect and tolerance for different family, sexual, and reproductive choices; and we need government policies, such as childcare, flextime, and family medical leave, that accommodate the new realities of family life. What we are getting instead is scapegoating of those women who are unable to make it on their own.

The Real Impact of the PRWOA

Supporters of the PRWOA predicted that former AFDC recipients, under pressure from the TANF time limits, would move smoothly from welfare receipt to full-time employment, increasing their families' well-being and the economic prospects for their children. Given the lack of adequate job training, childcare, and other provisions in the bill, it is not surprising that the reality has not been nearly as rosy as the predictions.

Unemployment and Continued or Worsening Poverty Among Former Recipients

Studies of welfare leavers from various states report that between 40 and 70 percent of former recipients did not have a job at the time of the surveys. Of those who were employed, average earnings ranged from $10,000 to $14,000 annually (Brookings Institution 1999). (Note that, in 1998, the poverty line for a family of three was $13,133.) Similarly, a study conducted by New York City's Human Resources Administration found that although 85 percent of those who left welfare were able to find some sort of paid work between their leaving welfare and the time of the interview (roughly five to seven months later), only 23 percent had incomes above the poverty level. In other words, the "average" former recipient who "successfully" left welfare suffers from unemployment on a regular basis, and, even when employed, still lives in abject poverty (Sherman et al. 1998).

Increased Cost to States and Localities

The PRWOA will significantly increase the cost of poor support for states and localities, particularly when labor markets slacken. State and local programs are supported largely by property and sales taxes, two of the most regressive forms of taxation. Workfare requirements further increase the local cost of administering the "reformed" welfare system. (See, e.g., the New York City Independent Budget Office's report, "The Fiscal Impact of the New Federal Welfare Law on New York City.")

Lower Wages for the Working Poor

The PRWOA is already increasing the supply of unskilled and low-skilled women workers. This increasing supply generates downward pressure on wages, particularly in those sectors that employ large numbers of low-skilled women workers (Burtless 1998; McCrate 1997). For example, Mishel and Schmitt have estimated that, nationally, the wages of the 31 million low-wage workers (those who currently make $8/hr. or less) would have to fall by approximately 11.9 percent to absorb the increase in labor supply predicted from the PRWOA. In states with relatively larger welfare populations, they predict that wages would have to fall further: 17.8 percent in California and 17.1 percent in New York (Mishel and Schmitt 1995). McCrate (1997) points out that all such estimates of wage reductions are inherently unreliable. First, a substantial portion of women who received AFDC also worked "under the table" to provide for their families (e.g., 42.9 percent in a two-year period, according to a study conducted by the Institute for Women's Policy Research [Spalter-Roth et al. 1995]). Thus, the labor supply increase of welfare "reform" may be less than predicted. Second, much of the research on the labor supply effect of welfare "reform" is based upon interstate comparisons of AFDC benefit levels with unskilled women's wages. Such comparisons are problematic because they are unable to disentangle the effects of AFDC on wages from the effects of political pressure on both AFDC benefit levels and low wages. Nevertheless, McCrate's analysis still predicts substantial downward pressure on wages from welfare "reform" (McCrate 1997). Thus, the working poor, who represent the model to which welfare mothers are supposed to aspire, will end up paying the lion's share of the cost of welfare "reform" via lower wages.

Undermining Unions' Bargaining Power

The work requirements of the PRWOA are already undermining the bargaining power of unions, particularly unions representing municipal and other public employees (Hanlon 1999). Workfare gives city and local governments a massive financial incentive to fire unionized workers, or to lose them through attrition, and to replace them with TANF-subsidized workers, paid minimum wage or less. Greenhouse, Perez-Peña, and others have documented the direct replacement of unionized, municipal New York City workers with workfare workers receiving less-than-minimum wages; court cases concerning this issue are pending (Greenhouse 1998, 1997; Perez-Peña 1996). This trend will undoubtedly continue, exacerbating the wage-lowering effects of welfare "reform."

Increases in Homelessness and Child Poverty

Over time, significant numbers of TANF mothers with sick children and/or without reliable childcare arrangements will be unable to meet their workfare requirements, and will lose their benefits. This number will increase further as those with minimal job skills, abusive boyfriends, and/or sick children reach their TANF time limits. This denial of benefits will necessarily increase the number of homeless, desperate women on the streets, and increase the number of poorly housed and malnourished children (Janofsky 1996). Clinton's own Department of Health and Human Services has estimated that an additional 2 million children will be pushed below the official poverty line due to the effects of the PRWOA (Edelman 1997). Even before welfare "reform," the United States had a child poverty rate of nearly 25 percent, the highest in the industrialized world. Without doubt, this increase in homelessness and desperation will increase foster placements of children (placements that cost many times the cost of AFDC or TANF), and will likely lead to more drug dealing, prostitution (and HIV infection), and other petty crimes, as desperate mothers turn to the underground economy to support their children.

Increases in Abuse of Women and Children

As their TANF "time limits" run out, the PRWOA will force many women to remain in relationships where they and/or their children are being physically or sexually abused, as they will have no alternate means of support. Simply put, the PRWOA will increase the number of battered women and abused children (Allard et al. 1997; Raphael 1996).

Impact on the Economies of Low-Income Communities

Welfare "reform" will eventually have significant impact on the economies of many low-income communities where disproportionate numbers of people were on AFDC. As more people run into their TANF time limits, food stores and other small businesses in these areas will lose customers, and many will be forced to close. In some low-income areas, this ripple or "multiplier" effect could be devastating (Sexton 1996).

The Welfare Reform We Really Need

Are there alternatives to the PRWOA approach to welfare reform? Can we address the problems of the former AFDC system without penalizing poor women and children? What changes would help women and children to move off of welfare into economic security instead of into desperation? Any humane alternative to the PRWOA would include at least the following:

1. ***Provisions for Victims of Domestic Violence.*** As previously stated, over 20 percent of welfare recipients had been physically abused within the year prior to their being interviewed, and over two-thirds have been abused sometime in their adult lives (Allard et al. 1997). This rate of abuse is significantly higher than that of other American women; approximately 20 percent of wives are physically abused sometime in the course of their marriages (Pagelow 1981). Women who fear for their own or their children's safety cannot be expected to engage in job search activities. Any program to increase women's economic self-sufficiency must be accompanied by serious attempts to increase women's self-sufficiency in other areas. True welfare reform requires substantially increased government support for battered women's shelters and victim-assistance programs, training for police departments in the handling of domestic violence cases, and legislation stipulating mandatory counseling as well as jail time for batterers.
2. ***Childcare.*** The lack of adequate and affordable daycare is a major obstacle to the entry of former AFDC mothers into the full-time labor force. For instance, a 1998 study by New York's Human Resources Administration found that "New York lacks child care for 61 percent of the children whose mothers are supposed to participate in workfare this year" (Swarns 1998, B8).

   Although childcare is a particular problem for women on welfare, it is a need shared by most American families. True welfare reform would make quality childcare available to all Americans, on a sliding scale basis. Until sufficient childcare is available at reasonable cost, we cannot expect mothers to leave their children unattended to work for pay, or to place them in substandard or dangerous private daycare settings.
3. ***Health Care.*** As with childcare, financial coverage for medical care is a concern shared by most Americans, although felt most acutely by those in need. Various proposals to use tobacco taxes or other monies to fund medical care for poor children represent a step in the right direction. A long-run solution to this problem will require some version of national health insurance for our nation's children (Joffe 1999).
4. ***Job Training.*** Real job training would help women to find and keep private sector jobs

that pay living wages. This should include training for positions in the skilled blue-collar trades and other "nontraditional" fields for women. Street-sweeping and other "training" currently offered by most workfare placements does not constitute job training (Finder 1998).

5. ***Educational Benefits.*** Marilyn Gittell has shown that completion of a four-year college degree is the best single predictor of whether a women will be able to stay off of welfare (Gittell 1994). The PRWOA provision that disallows college as an alternative to paid work not only penalizes those women trying to improve their lot, but is financially self-defeating in the long run.
6. ***Pay Equity.*** Enforcing the pay equity laws currently on the books would reduce the wage gap between men and women by approximately one-half (Blau 1998–1999; AFL-CIO 1999). Given the gender composition of the poor (especially the child-rearing poor), strategies for reducing gender pay inequality would also have a significant impact on poverty in general, and children's poverty in particular (Kahn and Figart 1998; Figart and Lapidus 1997). Comparable worth attempts to apply the principle of "equal pay for equal work" to a job market that is profoundly segregated by gender, by mandating equal pay for jobs of equal value to the corporation or institution (Sorensen 1989, 1994). Comparable worth laws, passed in some states and localities, could further shrink the gender wage gap and further reduce women's and children's poverty (Figart and Lapidus 1997).
7. ***Minimum Wage.*** It is unconscionable that an adult can work full-time, year-round, and still be unable to lift herself and her children out of poverty. The minimum wage should be raised to a "living wage" level (i.e., sufficient to lift a family above the poverty line) and indexed to the cost-of-living, like Social Security and other programs that disproportionately benefit the middle class. In thirty-five cities across the country, companies that receive tax abatements must now pay their workers a "living" wage of $7 to $10/hour (Brocht 1999). Similar legislation should be passed—and enforced—on a national level. Recent research demonstrates that not only would such a policy cause minimal, if any, unemployment, but it would have significant antipoverty effects as well (Card and Krueger 1994, 1995).
8. ***Public Employment.*** If necessary, the federal government should organize public employment programs modeled on the WPA (Works Progress Administration of the 1930s), again at wages sufficient to support a family (Rose 1994). Such public employment could meet our immense needs for childcare, eldercare, and the revitalization of our crumbling infrastructure. Unlike the WPA, however, equal opportunity by race and gender is a precondition for such a program to have significant impact upon women's and children's poverty (Rose 1995).
9. ***Housing.*** By allowing home-owners to deduct virtually all of the interest on their home mortgages from their federal income taxes, the government gives a massive de facto subsidy to middle-class home-owners. In 1995, the federal government suffered $51 billion in lost tax revenues due to the mortgage tax deduction, nearly twice the amount spent on all low-income housing programs and rental subsidies (Brouwer 1998). True welfare reform would include programs to increase and upgrade the housing stock for *low*-income families too, including financing for tenant ownership, scattered site public housing, and

so forth. Many of these programs would not require government financing; rather, legislation reforming banking and related industries could encourage such changes. Enforcing and strengthening the CRA (Community Reinvestment Act) and increasing legal and technical assistance to community-based organizations rehabilitating and managing low-income housing represent two productive approaches (Biewener 1999; Campen 1998; Glick 1997).

10. ***Disability Support.*** Prior to the passage of the PRWOA, the SSI program (Supplemental Security Income) supported approximately 1 million disabled children with payments averaging $427 per month, which allowed their parent(s) to remain home to care for them (Purnick 1996). Such support recognizes the reality that placing such children in daycare settings is often impossible, and such placements as do occur may present serious dangers to the children. In addition to eliminating AFDC, Section 212 of the PRWOA also "tightened" eligibility for SSI (Purnick 1996). In 1997 alone, the Social Security Administration, working under these new PRWOA guidelines, terminated benefits for over 95,000 chronically ill and disabled children who had previously been receiving benefits. Over 80 percent of these children had severe mental or emotional problems, such as mental retardation, severe hyperactivity, or mental illness. The benefits for significant numbers of children with severe chronic asthma and other respiratory illnesses were also terminated (Children's Defense Fund 1997). We must realize that some children are simply too disabled or ill to be placed safely in commercial childcare settings. Rather than terminating their benefits, the Social Security Administration must support their parents so that such children can be safely cared for at home without forcing their families into dire poverty.

Conclusion

Our current welfare policies are not only cruel, they are shortsighted. Children who grow up poor are twice as likely to suffer major, long-term physical and mental health problems. They are more than twice as likely to drop out before finishing high school, dramatically decreasing their own chances of ever becoming economically self-sufficient (Albelda and Folbre 1996). "Investing" in our nation's children—in their health, education, and happiness—will pay for itself many times over.

If we truly value our nation's children—and those who care for them—we must remake welfare "reform" to allow them to live with dignity, self-respect, and hope. Punitive scapegoating of welfare mothers will neither solve America's economic problems nor ease anxieties about the changes in family life. It will only serve to harm a new generation of poor children—with deleterious long-term consequences for us all.

Bibliography

Abramovitz, Mimi. 1996. *Under Attack, Fighting Back: Women and Welfare in the United States*. New York: Monthly Review Press.

Abramovitz, Mimi, and Fred Newdom. 1994. "Decoding Welfare Reform." *City Limits*. April.

AFL-CIO. 1999. "Equal Pay for Working Families: National and State Data." Washington, DC: AFL-CIO.

Albelda, Randy. 1995. "The Welfare Reform Debate You Wish Would Happen." *Feminist Economics* 1, no. 2 (Summer).

Albelda, Randy, and Nancy Folbre. 1996. *The War on the Poor: A Defense Manual*. Center for Popular Economics. New York: New Press.

Allard, Mary Ann, Randy Albelda, Mary Ellen Colten, and Carol Cosenza. 1997. "In Harm's Way? Domestic Violence, AFDC Receipt, and Welfare Reform in Massachusetts." Boston: McCormack

Institute and Center for Survey Research, University of Massachusetts.

Bergmann, Barbara, and Heidi Hartmann. 1995. "A Welfare Reform Based on Help for Working Parents." *Feminist Economics* 1, no. 2 (Summer).

Biewener, Carole. 1999. "The Promise of Finance: Banks and Community Development." In *Political Economy and Contemporary Capitalism: Radical Perspectives on Economic Theory and Policy*, ed. Ron Baiman, Heather Boushey, and Dawn Saunders Armonk, NY: M.E. Sharpe.

Blau, Francine. 1998–1999. Institute for Research on Poverty, University of Wisconsin-Madison. "Women's Economic Well-Being 1970–1995: Indicators and Trends" *Focus* 20, no. 1 (Winter).

Brocht, Chauna. 1999. "Living Wage Ordinances." *New York Times*, May 20.

Brookings Institution. February 1999. "The State of Caseloads in America's Cities: 1999." Washington DC: Brookings Institutition Center on Urban and Metropolitan Policy.

Brouwer, Steve. 1998. *Sharing the Pie: A Citizen's Guide to Wealth and Power in the America*. New York: Henry Holt.

Burtless, Gary. 1998. Institute for Research on Poverty, University of Wisconsin-Madison. "Can the Labor Market Absorb Three Million Welfare Recipients?" Focus (Summer–Fall).

Campen, James. 1998. "Neighborhoods, Banks, and Capital Flows: The Transformation of the U.S. Financial System and the Community Reinvestment Movement." *Review of Radical Political Economics* 30, no. 4 (December).

Card, David, and Alan Krueger. 1994. "Minimum Wages and Employment: A Case Study of the Fast-Food Industry in New Jersey and Pennsylvania." *American Economic Review* 84, no. 4.

______. 1995. *Myth and Measurement: The New Economics of the Minimum Wage*. Princeton: Princeton University Press.

Children's Defense Fund. 1997. "High Rates of Termination for Children with Disabilities." Washington DC: Children's Defense Fund, August 15.

Children's Defense Fund and National Coalition for the Homeless. 1998. "Welfare to What? Early Findings on Family Hardship and Well-Being." Washington DC: Children's Defense Fund, December.

Christensen, Kimberly, Ruth Brandwein, and Eva Kittay. 1996. "Welfare Is a Women's Issue: A Teach-In Packet." Women's Committee of One Hundred.

deParle, Jason. 1999. "Bold Effort Leaves Much Unchanged for the Poor." *New York Times* (December 30), A-1/A-20.

Edelman, Peter. 1997. "The Worst Thing Bill Clinton Has Done." *Atlantic Monthly*, March.

Farber, Peggy. 1999. "Day Care: Adventures in Babysitting." *City Limits*, May.

Feminist Economics. 1995. "Explorations: The Welfare Debate You Wish Would Happen" 1, no. 2 (Summer).

Figart, Deborah, and June Lapidus. 1997. "Reversing the Great U-Turn: Pay Equity, Poverty, and Inequality" In *Gender and Political Economy: Incorporating Diversity into Theory and Policy*, ed. Ellen Mutari, Heather Boushey, and William Fraher. Armonk, NY: M.E. Sharpe.

Finder, Alan. 1998. "Evidence Is Scanty That Workfare Leads to Full-Time Jobs." *New York Times*, April 12.

Folbre, Nancy. 1994. *Who Pays for the Kids? Gender and the Structures of Constrain*t. London and New York: Routledge.

——. 1995. *The New Field Guide to the U.S. Economy*. Center for Popular Economics. New York: New Press.

Gittell, Marilyn. 1994. "Reform Requires a College Degree." *Newsday*, March 7.

Glick, Brian, with Matthew Rossman. 1997. "Neighborhood Legal Services as House Counsel to Community-Based Efforts to Achieve Economic Justice: The East Brooklyn Experience." *New York University Review of Law and Social Change* 23, no. 1.

Gordon, Linda. 1994. *Pitied But Not Entitled: Single Mothers and the History of Welfare*. Cambridge: Harvard University Press.

———. 1995. "Thoughts on the Help for Working Parents Plan." *Feminist Economics* 1, no. 2 (Summer).

Greenhouse, Steven. 1997. "Workfare Is Replacing Union Jobs, Lawsuit Says." *New York Times*, May 25.

———. 1998. "Many Participants in Workfare Take the Place of City Workers." *New York Times*, April 13.

Hanlon, Martin. 1999. "Running on Two Tracks: The Public and Private Provision of Human Services." *New Labor Forum* (Spring/Summer).

Hartmann, Heidi. 1981. "The Family as the Locus of Gender, Class, and Political Struggle: The Example of Housework." *Signs: A Journal of Women in Culture and Society* 6, no. 3 (Spring).

Institute for Women's Policy Research. 1996. "The Wage Gap: Women's and Men's Earnings" Briefing paper. Washington, DC.

Janofsky, Michael. 1996. "Mayors Fear Welfare Cuts May Increase Homelessness." *New York Times*, July 30.

Joffee, Jerome. 1999. "The US Health Care System: A Reproduction Crisis." In *Political Economy and Contemporary Capitalism: Radical Perspectives on Economic Theory and Policy*, ed. Ron Baiman, Heather Boushey, and Dawn Saunders. Armonk, NY: M.E. Sharpe.

Kahn, Peggy, and Deborah Figart. 1998. "Reviving Pay Equity: New Strategies for Attacking the Wage Gap." *Working USA* (July–August).

McCrate, Elaine. 1997. "Welfare and Women's Earnings." *Politics and Society* 25, no. 4 (December).

Mink, Gwendolyn. 1995. "Wage Work, Family Work, and Welfare Politics." *Feminist Economics* 1, no. 2 (Summer).

Mishel, Lawrence, Jared Bernstein, and John Schmitt for the Economic Policy Institute. 1997. *The State of Working America 1996–1997*. Armonk, NY: M.E. Sharpe.

Mishel, Lawrence, and John Schmitt. 1995. "Cutting Wages by Cutting Welfare: The Impact of Reform on the Low-Wage Labor Market." Briefing paper. Washington, DC: Economic Policy Institute.

New York City Human Resources Administration. 1998. "Leaving Welfare: Findings from a Survey of Former NYC Welfare Recipients." HRA working paper, September.

New York City Independent Budget Office. 1996. "The Fiscal Impact of the New Federal Welfare Law on New York City." October 31.

Newman, Katherine. 1995. "What Inner-City Jobs for Welfare Moms?" *New York Times*, May 20.

Newman, Katherine, and Chauncey Lennon. 1995. *Finding Work in the Inner City: How Hard is It Now? How Hard Will It Be for AFDC Recipients?* New York: Columbia University Press.

Nichols, Laura, and Barbara Gault. 1999. "The Effects of Welfare Reform on Housing Stability and Homelessness." *Welfare Reform Network News*. Washington DC: Institute for Women's Policy Research, March.

Pagelow, Mildred Daly. 1981. "Factors Affecting Women's Decisions to Leave Violent Relationships." *Journal of Family Issues* 2, no. 4 (December).

Perez-Peña, Richard. 1996. "Transit Pact Is Approved by Workers: Workfare May Replace Subway Cleaning Jobs." *New York Times*, October 23.

Poverty and Race. 1995. 4, no. 4, July/August.

Purnick, Joyce. 1996. "Throwing Out the Disabled, or the Fraud?" *New York Times*, August 8.

Raphael, Jody. 1996. "Prisoners of Abuse: Domestic Violence and Welfare Receipt." Chicago: Taylor Institute, April.

Reed, Philip. 1991. "AIDS in New York's Minority Communities." Lecture delivered at the State University of New York-Purchase in October.

Reingold, Jennifer. 1997. "Executive Pay: Special Report." *Business Week*, April 21.

Rose, Nancy E. 1994. *Put to Work: Relief Programs in the Great Depression*. New York: Monthly Review Press.

———.1995. *Workfare or Fair Work: Women, Welfare, and Government Work Programs*. New Brunswick, NJ: Rutgers University Press.

Schor, Juliet. 1992. *The Overworked American: The Unexpected Decline of Leisure*. New York: Basic Books.

Sexton, Joe. 1996. "The Trickle-Up Economy: Poor Blocks Fear Disaster if Welfare Is Cut." *New York Times*, February 8.

Sherman, Arloc, Cheryl Amey, Barbara Duffield, Nancy Ebb, and Deborah Weinstein. 1998. "Welfare to What: Early Findings on Family Hardship and Well-Being." Washington, DC: Children's Defense Fund.

Social Justice: A Journal of Crime, Conflict, and World Order. 1994. Special Issue on "Women and Welfare Reform." 21, no. 4 (Spring).

Sorensen, Elaine. 1989. "The Wage Effects of Occupational Sex Composition: A Review and New Findings." In *Comparable Worth: Analyses and Evidence*, ed. M. Anne Hill and Mark Killingsworth. Ithaca, NY: ILR Press.

———. 1994. *Comparable Worth: Is It a Worthy Policy?* Princeton: Princeton University Press.

Spalter-Roth, Roberta, Beverly Burr, Heidi Hartmann, and Lois Shaw. 1995. "Few Welfare Moms Fits the Stereotypes" Research-in-brief. Washington, DC: Institute for Women's Policy Research.

Swarns, Rachel. 1998. "Mothers Poised for Workfare Face Acute Lack of Day Care." *New York Times*, April 14.

Weston, Kath. 1997. *Families We Choose: Lesbians, Gays, Kinship Between Men, Between Women*. New York: Columbia University Press.

Woodman, Sue. 1995. "How Teen Pregnancy as Become a Political Football." *Ms.*, January/February. 90–91.

35

The U.S. Health Care System

A Reproduction Crisis

Jerome Joffe

Introduction

A powerful force shaping the U.S. health care system is the mode of expenditure control. The current regime (instituted in the 1970s) emerged from contradictory developments in the preceding period and unleashed a wave of consolidation and privatization among purchasers of care, managed care insurers, and the providers of care. These new market relationships have in turn generated a new crisis of reproduction of the health care system: a new cost control regime can be discerned as various fractions of capital (corporate employers, managed care insurers, and increasingly corporatized and consolidated health care providers), and the state (seeking to reduce social expenditures), compete for market share and market power in health care provision and finance.

While the crisis has surfaced within the intermediary system of purchase and payment, its dynamic is also evident in the production and consumption of health care as it impacts on both providers and patients. The crisis imperils financial viability of the insurance intermediaries and their relationship with corporate and government purchasers. It also threatens to further increase the ranks of the uninsured. The tendency toward breakdown in the cost control system emerges from the contradictory effects of the price competitive regime that had been set in motion to resolve the previous crisis.

This chapter describes and analyzes the consolidation and restructuring that emerged from the price competitive environment and the elements of conflict and growing instability it produced, and concludes with a strategic focus on progressive action to resolve the crisis.

The Dynamics of Health Care Restructuring

Institutional and Structural Change

The historical transformation of the health care system, from atomistic physician practices and social service–oriented hospitals, toward a more integrated production system, has been under way since the end of World War II. This trend was accelerated from the mid-1970s by large infusions of private capital and the imposition of price and service constraints by private and government insurance units.

The health care industry restructuring begun at this time was a response by private corporate purchasers (payers), as well as Medicare, to the slowdown of the rate of growth of the economy and a decline in profits (Nayeri 1995). Employers changed their cost control strategy from compelling their labor force to limit their demand for services through deductibles and copayments, to reducing the number of workers eligible for health benefits and contracting with insurers organized as health maintenance organizations (HMOs). This shift transferred incentives for restrictions on utilization of services from employee-patients to providers of care.

HMOs and Managed Care

HMOs were intended to curtail expenditures by reducing the number of units of service per patient, through management protocols and the monitoring of service use. This included the use of detailed disease-specific practice guidelines and approval requirements for specialist referral, hospitalization, and specific diagnostic and surgical procedures. To provide a financial incentive to physicians to limit services, prepayment for an enrolled population (capitation) was substituted for a fee for each unit of patient service. Over time, capitation would be extended to hospitals and other health care delivery units.

Managed care involved a new relationship between insurers and providers. Mainly by contract and to a lesser degree by direct employment, the insurance function and the delivery function were combined. But this occurred in a regime of intense price competitive markets throughout the health care system, generating consolidation and concentration, initially in local markets, then in regional and even national markets.

The competitive dynamic is shaped by employer groups, insurance units, and providers, including hospitals, physicians, nursing homes, drug manufacturers, pharmaceutical distributors, and equipment supply firms, all interrelated through the markets that tie the components of the health care system together and activate the flow of funds constituting health care expenditures. Employers purchase health care through competing insurance units, which in turn purchase the services of competing providers or alliances of providers.

Market Concentration

To gain market share and price leverage, organizations have consolidated. Both insurers and providers attempt to extend contractual arrangements across local markets, the former with regional employers, the latter to improve negotiating prospects with the regionally extended HMO or to bypass the HMO by contracting directly with large multi-location employers. Employers with a single establishment but with a labor force residing over a sizable geographic area would also prefer contracting with a single managed care agency or provider network.

Health care organizations expand through horizontal and vertical integration, as do firms in other industries. Horizontal integration involves common ownership or joint activity by the same types of delivery unit, for example, a multi-hospital system or a nursing home chain. The advantages of horizontal integration include economies of scale and reduction of competition.[1]

Vertical integration involves tying together different stages of patient care, such as ambulatory care units, hospitals, nursing homes, and even an HMO into one corporate unit. Vertically integrated delivery systems are becoming more prevalent, including the expansion of drug and hospital equipment manufacturers to protect existing markets, penetrate new areas for accumulation, increase market share, and achieve scale economies.

Increased concentration without increased centralization is exhibited in health care as it is in other sectors of the economy. The average size of the production unit may continue to decline, as with the shrinkage of excess hospital inpatient capacity, but concentration will occur through mergers, strategic alliances, or networking (Wolper 1995). Alliances and networks are organized by separately owned organizations for common ventures, such as the formation of a unified medical staff to eliminate clinical duplication, and for the collective negotiation with buyers of services or sellers of inputs.

Consolidation allows new partners to spread fixed costs, an antidote to the excessive inpatient capacity (and long-term debt) held over from overexpansion prior to 1970. Such cost constraints may be moderated by expanding market share and achieving economies of scale, and by downsizing staff and substituting lower-cost workers for high-paid staffers.

The Dynamics of Private Capitalization

In an environment of stringent reimbursement, hospitals need additional capital. New information technologies are required to more economically provide diagnostic and treatment services, to expand marketing services, to underwrite risk, and to develop a sophisticated management information system to monitor staff performance and control costs.

Voluntary hospitals, including major teaching institutions, have reversed their traditional opposition to investor-owned provider units and other sources of private capital, as many face reduced occupancy rates, falling profit margins, and mounting deficits. Survival becomes feasible through mergers, strategic alliances, and joint ventures to establish profit-making outpatient programs and eliminate less profitable services while reducing excess inpatient capacity. Investor-owned provider services such as home health firms and private nursing home chains fill the gap created by this restructuring, and by the shorter hospital stays mandated by cost-control programs.

In addition, for-profit hospitals have been absorbing private nonprofits, including financially viable city hospitals, from privatizing local governments. This results in the loss of services that operated at a deficit, such as trauma care, AIDS care, neonatal intensive care, and burn care. Such costly services have traditionally been cross-subsidized by less costly care in nonprofit institutions.

The restructuring of hospital output results in large part from utilization management imposed on hospitals by financial intermediaries (insurers) with the threat of nonreimbursement. More than half of all hospital surgeries are now performed on an outpatient basis, such as provided by HealthSouth Corporation, a chain of 1,700 outpatient surgery and rehabilitation centers (*Business Week* 1997). Moreover, as Medicaid seeks to economize on long-term care by stimulating development of home care, adult day care, and assisted living as options to nursing home care, nursing homes are incorporating these modalities of care into their product array.

Hotels and real estate corporations financed by banks and real estate investment trusts are also active in the creation of assisted living facilities, marketing their services not only to the impaired affluent elderly, but to state Medicaid programs for the medically indigent.

The growth of for-profit enterprise is thus being significantly shaped by its linkage with not-for-profit facilities. Though only about 15 percent of hospitals are profit-based, the participation of private capital in voluntary hospitals imposes competitive constraints on the voluntary sector as they restructure their service array to concentrate on high margin output.

Contradictions Among Fractions of Capital

The health care system is characterized by not only competing but antagonistic segments of capital.

Despite the size and apparent dominance in the health care market of insurance companies such as Aetna, Cigna, and Prudential, large employer payers have combined to develop countervailing power against increasingly concentrated regional HMO oligopolies. Minneapolis–St. Paul is probably the most managed care–dominated area. To offset this market power, companies such as 3M, Dayton Hudson, General Mills, Cargil, and Honeywell organized the Business Health Action Group to partially bypass the HMO and deal directly with doctors and hospitals.

Besides contracting directly with a provider network, large employers attempt to block growing HMO market power by offering their employees multiple HMO choices and by manipulating incentives to favor lower-priced HMOs. In addition, by using HMOs for administrative services only, and by self-insuring and using their own reserves to pay employee medical bills, large employers limit HMO accumulation potential, gaining investment income and eroding the insurance function in the HMO market (Gabel et al., 1997). Self-insured firms (over 50 percent of all large firms) can contract directly with providers who do not need to finance an insurance component. Contradictions arise from the payment system because capital is fragmented into competitive units as both health care buyers and sellers, some seeking to restrain, others to increase, expenditures.

Contradictions Between Public and Private Sector Cost Control

Payment reductions by Medicare and Medicaid strongly motivate doctors and hospitals to increase charges to the private sector. As the public programs stringently limit their payment rate and balance billing,[2] physicians, hospitals, and other providers attempt to regain income by raising charges to commercially insured patients and gain increased capitation for HMO enrollees. Ironically, as corporate political power leads to Medicare and Medicaid payment reductions or a slowdown in its rate of growth, providers pressure private sector HMOs for higher payments, with the latter then attempting to raise prices to employer payers.

Erosion of Cost Control

Initial savings in insurance costs resulted from (a) the one-time savings caused by the shift from fee-for-service indemnity plans to managed-care plans and (b) the strategy of the managed-care organizations to hold the price line so as to capture market share (Anders and Winslow 1997; Fisher 1998). Employer costs had also been restrained by a steady decrease in the fraction of workers with coverage and by the shifting of premium costs to employees, and for those workers not in HMOs, by increased deductibles and copayments. But after premium reductions in 1994 and small increases in 1995 and 1996 in the private market, prices rose substantially in 1997, although less so in 1998 because of employer resistance (Hammonds 1998).

The competitive diffusion of medical technology also contributes to the pressures on the payment system. Moreover, expenditures are bloated by duplicative marketing, administrative and other transaction costs from a multitude of competitive payers and intermediaries (these costs are estimated at 10 percent of all health care expenditure).

Strong public hostility to constraints imposed by HMOs on patient choice of physician and the continuous intense rivalry for market share have led to relaxation of the constraints and to payments to physicians outside the network over which control can be exercised. This has increased HMO costs and reduced profitability. National insurers such as Kaiser Permanente, Aetna, and large regional insurers such as Oxford Health Plans suffered significant losses in 1997, with the latter two also experiencing notable declines in equity value (Fisher 1998). In 1997, more than half of U.S. HMOs reported losses, giving the industry its first aggregate yearly loss, of $768 million (*Deloitte and Touche* 1998). Any further expansion of the HMO market would require enrolling those with poorer health, who require increasingly costly services, and who are accustomed to selecting their own doctors and specialists, and by enrolling the employees of smaller firms, which entails higher administrative costs and greater actuarial uncertainty.

Changing Status of Physicians

The physician's independent role has been only partially attenuated in hospitals. Although being subject to managed care by HMO and hospital oversight in their practice, physician staff representatives are increasingly being appointed to governing boards of hospitals to gain their acquiescence to cost cutting and service revamping. Various forms of physician–hospital integration involving risk bearing and medical practice management are increasing. Hospitals require physicians for access to patients and often join forces with them to present a united front in marketing to HMOs, as well as to capitalize joint ventures such as free-standing ambulatory care centers and imaging centers.

While there has been a slight increase in the proportion of physicians employed by HMOs, the staff model involving salaried physicians is being rapidly displaced by other modes of HMO physician affiliation. It is, in fact, advantageous for HMOs to allow physicians to absorb the costs and risks of the means of production (the medical practices) while the HMOs maintain control over the product (medical services) through their control over physicians' access to enrolled patients. It is therefore not surprising that from 1989 to 1995 staff model HMOs have experienced a decline in enrollment of 73 percent to less than a million enrollees (U.S. Bureau of the Census 1996).

Growth of Group Practices

Growth in the number of salaried physicians is, however, occurring in group practices (currently close to 35 percent of all employed physicians). New forms of physician stratification are being developed as some of the group practice physicians become partners, their salaried status then being occupied by newly minted physicians.

About 60 percent of office-based physicians practice in groups. By the mid-1990s there were over 600 group practices with more than 50 physicians. Large practices can better negotiate with HMOs and have enabled 28 percent of all groups to develop their own clinical laboratories. Some hospitals, and to a greater degree, physician practice management corporations (PPMs), are buying physician practices to leverage contractual relationships with both HMOs and large employers. Physicians may realize high capital value from such sales and continue to practice as employees of their own professional corporations, tied through long-term service contracts with the PPM. The doctors retain sovereignty over medical policy and physician personnel matters. For example, Phycor, a leading PPM corporation, has built a far-flung network of over 35,000 physicians with contracts covering 3.2 million people by acquiring approximately 100 large multi-specialty practices. Phycor receives some 15 to 20 percent of practice income, but the doctors collaborate in running the clinic through a governing board on which they and PPN partners have an equal number of seats.

With the doctors themselves managing care, they are more willing to accommodate to the pressures of the marketplace. A hierarchy of physicians monitors the practice and sets criteria. Peer-imposed discipline is more acceptable, and the penalty for noncompliance could be expulsion from the group and loss of patients and hospital staff privileges.

Response of Physicians to Managed Care

Notions of HMOs and physicians in inevitably bitter zero-sum conflict are an exaggeration, as new mechanisms of accommodation develop, even if only after bitter market and political battles. The current public antagonism may be partially deflected by making the providers themselves partially responsible for making unpopular decisions and marketing insurance/provider joint ventures in a way that results in a more positive public image (Unland 1998). Physician networks (in conjunction with hospitals) will have a more significant role in planning and implementing care management in the next stage of the evolution of the market-based health care system.

New cohorts of physicians in training are being indoctrinated into the new health care culture. Physicians will try to adapt to the corporate environment by maximizing their autonomy through organization and legislation, but the majority have not challenged, and are not likely to, the legitimacy of the rapidly growing mode of privately capitalized health care, especially as their position in the medical marketplace is being strengthened. While the AMA has loudly criticized gag rules and other practices limiting overtly unethical practices, most physician organizations run seminars in how to get along with the new system rather than overtly and unconditionally opposing it (Amsel 1997).

Progressive physicians and nurses have formed an Ad Hoc Committee to Defend Health Care, calling for a moratorium on for-profit conversions of health care institutions, but they represent a minority within their professions, and the endorsers have no common agreement on what should replace the corporatization trend (Woolhandler and Himmelstein 1997). Direct contracting by large physician group practices with corporate payers, either with or without PPM intermediation, probably would be acceptable to many of them.

Contrary to the notion of physician proletarianization (McKinlay 1985), physicians have been able to organize and capitalize their own corporate bodies. While autonomy in terms of total control over their work process has been reduced in contractual relationships, physicians are able to exercise leverage through their dominance in the division of health care labor, the necessary reliance by larger administrative units on their expertise, and their own corporate organization (Friedson 1993). Proprietors, largely recruited from the upper middle class, are not necessarily antagonistic to corporatization as long as their prerogatives can be maintained.

The Managed Care Industry Reacts to Public Attack

Further moderating conflict between doctors and HMOs, as well as providing evidence of physician political clout, is the passage in many states, often with Republican political leadership, of HMO regulatory legislation. Federal legislation is currently on the table as well. Antigag laws, prohibition of termination of physician contracts without cause, prohibition of exclusionary contracts, and elimination of stringent limits on hospital length of stay for specific procedures all represent removal of barriers to physician autonomy imposed by the initial mechanisms of managed care. Moreover, state regulation of HMOs involves removal of barriers to obtain and provide information as well as eliminating restrictions on freedom to contract. HMO regulation can thus be regarded as *procompetitive* and responds to the interests and ideology of small capital as well as to consumers of health services. Legislated adjustments of HMO practices may moderate opposition to privately capitalized managed care, but comes at a cost to insurers and reduces their market power.

These developments, reflecting the contradictory positions of different fractions of capital in health care and between private capital and the state, create price and institutional instability in the health care system.

Continual Restructuring and Reemergence of a Crisis in Health Care

The reemerging payment crisis in health care poses a serious challenge to the continued growth and stability of insurance intermediaries as the dominant institution for controlling health care costs in the employer finance and purchase system. At the core of the instability of the intermediary system is a series of contradictions between (1) the interests of providers and insurers over the terms on which managed care is organized and how income is distributed; (2) capital-imposed state fiscal policy and the immediate economic interests of various fractions of capital; and (3) the managed care system and political resistance of large sectors of the working and middle classes to the declining access and quality of medical care. As employers learn to deal directly with consolidated providers to reduce administrative costs and profits, insurers face increased financial vulnerability.

Disintermediation within the health care system will involve a substantial increase of direct risk bearing by providers, subjecting them even further to market forces. The continued consolidation of hospitals and physicians (the former into national hospital chains, the latter into integral relationships with physician practice management companies, and both combined into physician-hospital organizations) is solidifying provider bargaining power and enhancing their negotiating leverage. In addition, by assuming greater risk and accepting capitation they are in effect competing with and sharing an increasing portion of the underwriting profit with managed care companies (*Deloitte and Touche* 1997b). As managed care is shifted directly to providers, there will be increased uncertainty over access and quality issues as the latter no longer serve as a buffer between patients and the employer–insurance company nexus.

To further shift costs and risk to the users of the system, copayments and premium sharing are likely to be increased. Large employers will continue to reduce insurance coverage both by limiting the range and depth of specific benefits and by increasing the category of workers totally ineligible for any coverage. The absence of coverage for employees by smaller firms will accelerate. Government extension of coverage to the uninsured, given the current balance of political forces, may be financed by the dilution of benefits for Medicare and Medicaid patients, as was coverage of uninsured children under the Balanced Budget Act of 1997.

Conclusions: Implications for Left Strategy

Any organizing campaign for health care system reform must take account of the dynamics of continual restructuring and its contradictions. It is important to avoid focusing almost exclusively on insurance company–managed care power and corporatized provider organizations as the primary antagonists while the role of employer purchasers (who strongly influence the terms and the channels through which health care is provided) is relegated to a secondary status.

Also, physicians, because of their class location and their strategies to gain influence in a corporatized system, are more likely to resist than to lead radical health care transformation, despite their widespread resentment of insurance company–directed managed care.

Liberal capitalism, with its separation of market and state, "signifies a depoliticization of the class relationship and its anonymizaton of class domination" (Habermass 1975). Incremental health care reform (expanding eligibility for Medicare to younger retirees, including low-income former welfare recipients into Medicaid, placing restrictions on private insurance, etc.) is politically divisive and self-defeating as each labor segment defines and perceives itself to be a separate interest group. Greater solidarity might be expected of workers across a wide range of pay, occupations, and employment status, as all face continued payment pressures and more limited access to quality health care. Workers might thereby perceive the advantages of a *public health system*, which incorporates universal coverage, uniformity of benefits, and funding from progressive taxes, and which shifts the struggle from the marketplace (which inevitably divides users into consumers within their market determined fragments) to the state, where class is more clearly perceived. This would mean capital would no longer control access to (in the form of employer-provided health insurance) or provision of health care (through for-profit managed care or other private insurance intermediaries). Moreover, within such a system, future conflicts over finance and expenditure level can be more clearly seen and fought as class issues.

The organized power of the working class has been instrumental in the struggle for national health care systems in all their diversity, whether in Canada, Great Britain, Germany or in other industrial nations. In some cases, national health care was implemented to offset or mollify the growing power of the working class. In other cases, cross-class alliances developed to build a national health care system (Navarro 1992). In the United States, at its November 1998 national convention, the Labor Party, backed by trade unions a million members strong, identified organizing for a national health program as its leading programmatic issue (McCure 1998). A labor movement that includes health care as part of a broader set of issues of social transformation may be the only social force that is strategically located to lead this political struggle.

Notes

1. Two-thirds of all acute care hospital beds are in multi-hospital systems (Hammonds 1998).
2. Charges to patients above the approved Medicare rates.

Bibliography

Amsel, Larry. 1997. "Corporate Health Care." *Tikkun* 12, no. 3: 19.

Anders, George, and Ron Winslow. 1997. "HMO's Woes Reflect Conflicting Demands of American Public." *Wall Street Journal*, December 22, 1, 8.

Bianco, Anthony. 1997. "Can Dr. Frist Cure This Patient?" *Business Week*, November 17, 74–80.

Bodenheimer, Thomas S., and Kevin Grumbach. 1995. *Understanding Health Policy: A Clinical Approach.* Stamford: Appleton and Lange.

Business Week. 1997. "Behind Oxford's Billing Nightmare." November 17, 98–100.

Deloitte and Touche Health Care Management Update. 1996. "U.S. Hospitals and the Future of Health Care."

———. 1997a. "The Balanced Budget Act of 1997 Public Law 105–33: Medicare and Medicaid Changes."

———. 1997b. "Valuation Insights, Health Care Industry: Creating and Sustaining Value in the Managed Care Industry." Fall.

———. 1998. "HMOs Running in Red. " July 20.

Evans, Robert. 1992. "Canada: The Real Issues" *Journal of Health Politics and Law* 17, no. 4 (Winter): 739–762.

Fisher, Ian. 1998. "HMO Premiums Rising Sharply Stoking Debate on Managed Care." *New York Times*, January 11, 1, 27.

Friedson, Elliot. 1993. "How Dominant Are the Professions?" In *The Changing Medical Profession*, ed. Frederick W. Hafferty and John B. McKinlay, 54–66. New York: Oxford University Press.

Gabel, Jon, Heida Whitmore, Chris Bergsten, and Lily Pan Grimm. 1997. "Growing Diversification in HMOs, 1988–1994." *Medical Care Research and Review* 54, no. 1.

Gray, Bradford H. 1991. *The Profit Motive and Patient Care.* Cambridge: Harvard University Press.

Habermass, Jurgen. 1975. *Legitimation Crisis*. Boston: Beacon Press.

Hammonds, Keith H. 1998. "Where's the Dreaded Spike in Health Costs?" *Business Week* July 20, 35–36.

Hammonds, Keith H., Susan Jackson, and Nicole Harris. 1998. "Health Care Prognosis 1998." *Business Week* January 12, 114–115.

Kongstvedt, Peter R. 1997. *Essentials of Managed Health Care.* Gaithersburg, MD: Aspen.

Kovner, Anthony, with contributors. 1995. *Jonas's Health Care Delivery in the United States.* New York: Springer.

Krupa, Michael. 1996. "Wall Street's Infatuation with the Assisted Living Industry." *Resident Life* August/September, 9–23.

Light, Donald. 1993. "Countervailing Power: Medicine in the United States." In *The Changing Medical Profession*, ed. Frederick W. Hafferty and John B. McKinlay. New York: Oxford University Press.

McCure, Laura. 1998. "Just Health Care: How Do We Get There?" *Labor Party Press* November 1.

McKinlay, John. 1985. "Toward the Proletarianization of Physicians." *International Journal of Health Services* 15, no. 2: 161–195.

Navarro, Vincente. 1992. "Why Some Countries Have National Health Insurance, Others have National Health Services and the United States Has Neither." In *Why the United States Does Not Have a National Health Program*, ed. Vincente Navarro. New York: Baywood.

Nayeri, Kamran. 1995. "Economic Boundaries of Health Care." *Review of Radical Political Economics* 27, no. 4: 56–79.

Pear, Robert. 1997. "Three Big Health Plans Join in Call for National Standards." *New York Times*, September 25, 28.

Unland, James. 1998. "The Range of Insurer/Provider Configurations." *Journal of Health Care Finance* 24, no. 2: 1–35.

U.S. Bureau of the Census. 1996. *Statistical Abstract of the United States.* Washington, DC: Government Printing Office.

Wolper, Lawrence. 1995. *Health Care Administration: Principles, Practices, Structures and Administration.* Gaithersburg, MD: Aspen.

Woolhandler, Steffie, and David Himmelstein. 1997. "For Patients. Not Profits." *The Nation*, December 22, 6–7.

36

The Political Economy of Social Security Reform in the United States

Teresa Ghilarducci

The 1994–96 Social Security Advisory Council released its report in January 1997, almost a year late. The reason for the delay was that for the first time in its fifty-year history, the Council was seriously split between competing proposals designed to secure the health of the system. One set of proposals could fundamentally alter the system's pay-as-you-go (PAYGO) structure by creating private individual accounts. Another proposal would maintain the system by trimming benefits and raising revenue.

The system now pays benefits to 30 million retired workers. Six million younger people receive disability benefits, and another 7 million children and older dependents of beneficiaries receive Social Security income. These benefits are paid for by payroll taxes on current workers. In 1962, 69 percent of Americans over age sixty-five received some Social Security income; in 1994, over 92 percent of those over 65 received Social Security income. Even more revealing of the importance of Social Security is that a full 54 percent of the elderly would be poor without Social Security benefits.

The retirement portion of the system, the old age and survivors insurance (OASI), was established in 1935, the disability insurance (DI), in 1939. Medicare (HI) came much later, in 1960. Therefore, when people are talking about Social Security they are referring to the Old Age, Survivors, and Disability Insurance (OASDI) program. The president appoints an Advisory Council every four years to review the system's finances and effectiveness. The trustees and staff issue an annual financial report. The Advisory Council contains three representatives from business, three from labor, one self-employed representative, and five members from the general public.

Five members of the 1994–96 Council, led by Sylvester Schieber, economist for a pension consulting firm, proposed to replace the PAYGO system with personal saving accounts (PSAs) managed by individuals. The three labor representatives, with two others, backed Council member and former Social Security commissioner Robert Ball's "trim and tuck" plan to raise revenues and trim benefits to keep the system intact. Council chair Professor Edward Gramlich, from the University of Michigan (and now Federal Reserve Bank Board member), along with the representative from the Ford Motor Company, backed a modified privatizing plan. The Council was divided between privatizing and maintaining the system. At the time of this writing, many congressional proposals exist ranging from preserving Social Security and using the federal budget surplus to supplement the Social Security Trust Fund, to proposals that call for full or partial privatization.

Contrary to political and media attention to this issue, Social Security is *not* a system in serious crisis. This chapter examines some of the concerns regarding Social Security finances, as well as the debate regarding full or partial privatization plans. Finally, an alternative view of the current system is presented, arguing that most workers would benefit under a strengthened system without privatization, one that can actually raise savings and prevent financial market collapse in thirty years.

Social Security Finances

The history of Social Security puts the current financial issues in perspective and shows there is no economic crisis, yet the politics of the moment may spur structural changes. The actuaries and staff of the Social Security Administration have always projected how different future levels of fertility, immigration, pay increases, employment, disability, and retirement trends would affect the system's finances. The U.S. Social Security actuaries are unusually conservative. Most nations project out to fifty years; the U.S. Social Security system uses seventy-five years. Three economic and demographic scenarios—dismal, intermediate, and rosy—simulate how different combinations of trends would affect the system. The 1994 Social Security Trustees Report, the annual report that publishes the projections, identified a future funding shortfall—the Social Security Trust Fund would be exhausted by 2029. (The 1998 Trustees Report changed this date to 2032 due to the fast growth in the economy.) Yet, the 1994 report's conclusions were largely unexpected and fueled the privatization proposals.

Unexpected shortfalls have occurred before. In 1983, the shortfall was immediate and a special bipartisan commission—the Greenspan Commission—was formed to solve the problem caused by unexpected high rates of inflation and unemployment. The Greenspan Commission restored half of the financial balance by raising revenues and the other half by cutting benefits. Most of the benefit cuts were achieved by gradually raising the age at which workers could collect full benefits to age sixty-seven. The payroll tax was raised to solve the deficit and create a substantial trust fund for the first time. The Social Security Trust Fund represents, in essence, a mandatory saving mechanism for boomers and younger workers. Now workers partially fund their own retirement by more than they are given credit for. By paying more Social Security tax than required to keep a PAYGO system paying current benefits, workers are saving for retirement.

The Greenspan solution aimed to keep the system solvent for the next seventy-five years. Yet, in 1994, the system showed more shortfall than expected according to the intermediate scenario. (That scenario predicted an extremely low 1.8 percent GDP growth rate—the 1998 intermediate scenario raised the predicted growth rate to 2.0 percent.) The 1998 report shows the system spending the interest on the Trust Fund in 2013 and, in about 2021, the system will have to redeem the Fund's Treasury notes. This means that the system will no longer show a surplus, but will start selling the notes back to taxpayers, causing a demand on government revenues and an obligation on future politicians. The Social Security Trust Fund will act like any pension fund—eventually selling assets to pay benefits. The Trust Fund will be worth approximately $2.87 trillion in Treasury notes in 2018 and it is projected to sell all the notes by about 2032. If tax rates are not increased, or the economy does not reach higher growth, employment, and wage increases, only 75 percent of the benefits after that date could be covered by existing Social Security contribution levels.

Where did the surprise deficit come from? Much of it comes from the assumptions in the intermediate scenario. GDP has never grown at such a low 1.8 percent rate for a sustained amount of time. The 2.0 percent growth rate in the intermediate scenario is lower than the Congressional Budget Office's forecast of 2.2 percent. Wage growth is predicted to grow (after adjusting for inflation) by 1.2 percent a year—slower than productivity. This, of course, lowers the revenue projected from the payroll tax. Notably, if the economy simply continues to grow at its average rate of the last twenty years there would be no shortfall. Another large chunk of the unexpected shortfall comes from wages unexpectedly not growing at the same rate as productivity, an unprecedented gap arising from the erosion of workers' bargaining power in recent years. In other words, half of the problem would not exist if wages grew as fast as the Greenspan Commission predicted.

It is important to know the language of Social Security finances so that the solutions can be easily evaluated. The system's shortfall is expressed in terms of an increase in the payroll tax required to pay current benefit obligations for seventy-five years under middle or moderate economic assumptions. The Social Security shortfall is approximately 2.2 percent. This means the payroll taxes for retirement and disability benefits would have to be increased by 2.17 percent—from 12.4 percent to 14.57 percent. The payroll tax is split equally between employers and workers. Economists generally agree that this hike would not dramatically affect job growth. Therefore, the system's problems, which are not caused by the aging of baby boomers, or the changing ratios of workers to retirees, or people retiring earlier, or people living longer, is not in immediate economic crisis. Raising taxes could be a political problem, but not an economic one. (See Box 36.1 on Social Security Finances, see also Appendix.) It is politics that explains the 1990s Social Security debate, underscored by the extremely divergent interests of labor and the financial sector.

Box 36.1 **Social Security Finances Are Not in Crisis**

If payroll taxes were raised from 12.4% to 14.57%, the system would be solvent for 75 years in 1998.

If we do nothing by 2032, the system could pay 75% of benefits. To restore full benefits, payroll taxes would be 15.7%.

These numbers will change dramatically if work effort, immigration, and economic growth change.

The Social Security deficit is caused by a GDP growth assumption of 2.0% in the next 75 years. The privatizers assume a finance market that will yield a return of 7%—adjusted for inflation—which need a higher GDP of at least 2.5%

Change the growth assumption to 2.5% and there is no deficit

Workers' Stake in Social Security

Less than 20 percent of the U.S. workforce is unionized, but organized labor is the only lobbying group for Social Security–covered workers. (Organized labor is defined as the 13 million members of the unions affiliated with the AFL-CIO and the 1.3 million members of the National Education Association.)

The Social Security system covered only 16 percent of the workforce at its inception in 1935 and has expanded to cover over 90 percent of workers by 1995. Almost all union members are covered by Social Security (except some state and local workers), and 79 percent are covered at work by a pension plan negotiated by the employer and union. In contrast, only 38 percent of nonunion workers have a pension from the employer. Most workers are middle-class and become middle-class retirees, family units with $17,000 to $29,000 (in 1990) of income per year (U.S. Department of Labor 1992; Reno 1993). Middle-class retirees received under 40 percent of their income from Social Security in 1980. However, because of the erosion in pension benefits and coverage, wealth, and wages, Social Security made up 60 percent of retirement income to this group by 1990. Though a common description of the sources of retirement income is a three-legged stool, for the middle class the retirement income security system is a pyramid. Think of the food pyramid: Social Security is the base—the grains, fruits, and veggies; employer pensions make up the middle; and individual wealth and savings are the fats and sugars, making up the small portion at the top (Reno 1993).

Since World War II, workers rely on collectively based, mandatory, and near mandatory ways that current consumption is deferred for retirement income. One aspect of this evolving system is that workers, when negotiating in a group, reveal different preferences for future and current consumption than workers exhibit on their own. Workers choose to save more when the whole group has to save than they do when making individual and voluntary savings decisions. Union employers pay a much larger percentage of total compensation on pensions than nonunion employers. The rate of increase in unionized employers' pension expenses outpaced union wage growth between 1980 and 1990. In the same time period, nonunion employers' pension costs fell as a share of pay while nonunion workers' rate of pay outpaced union wage increases (Employment Cost Index, various years).

Freeman (1981) argues that older workers have more political power in unions and therefore their preferences dominate the trade-offs made in collective bargaining negotiations, thus explaining the rise of pension coverage. Others argue that union employers want pensions to complete implicit contracts (Lazear 1980) that encourage workers to invest in firm-specific skills or settle contracts with least costs (Ghilarducci 1992). Pensions and Social Security could also be "arms agreements" whereby workers agree to hold back consumption and save by changing group norms (Frank and Cook 1995).

Employer-based pensions, many of which are collectively bargained, depend on the Social Security system. A full one-third of company pensions (not union plans typically) are directly integrated with Social Security—meaning an increase in Social Security benefits will lower employers' costs. Benefits in a union pension plan are indirectly integrated with Social Security. The primary union- and company-based pensions are defined benefit pensions that aim to provide a certain amount of monthly benefit for the rest of the retiree's life. Voluntary employer-sponsored pensions are rarely indexed for inflation, whereas Social Security is. The employers bear the risk or reap the gains of unexpected financial loss or gain from the investments of the trust fund backing the pension benefit promises. Social Security is now a defined benefit plan. Social Security privatization would tip the balance toward riskier sources of income.

Social Security is insurance, not a system of separate accounts, and is tilted toward low-income earners, giving them a larger replacement rate than for higher earners. It replaces 80 percent of the preretirement earnings of a low-wage worker and 24 percent for a high-wage worker. The average retirement benefit from Social Security is over $1,000 and is indexed for inflation. (See Box 36.2.)

Current retirees receive much more than they put into the system. And, because the system is maturing, workers born after the 1940s will start receiving a smaller percentage of benefits compared to contributions. If this ratio can be thought of as a rate of return, the return will soon be, on average, 2 percent. But judging the system as one that yields financial returns on money paid in misses the insurance value of the system. The estimated value of the Social Security disability policy is $203,000. A similar dependent and survivor policy for a twenty-seven-year-old average-wage worker with two children is worth $295,000 (Century Foundation 1997). A Social Security benefit is automatically an indexed annuity. On the other hand, private annuities are expensive and annuities indexed to inflation simply do not exist in private markets.

Some argue that the Social Security tax is regressive because high-income workers pay a smaller share of their earnings relative to what low-income workers contribute out of their paycheck. Earnings up to a ceiling of $68,400 (in 1998) are subject to the OASDI tax, which covers only $84.6 percent of all wages compared to the ceiling's historic coverage of 90 percent of wages. However, the rate is not as regressive as it seems. The earned income tax credit pays a credit that covers a significant portion of the Social Security tax for workers who earn less than $25,000 per year (Bluestone and Ghilarducci 1998). In addition, half of Social Security benefits are subject to ordinary income tax for beneficiaries with incomes over $25,000 and $32,000 for couples.

Organized labor perceives the move to privatize Social Security as an erosion of the hard-won victory of leisure at the end of a working life. Unlike the vast majority of the world's workers, American workers can choose to retire; they cannot be forced to retire because of the 1978 Age Discrimination Employment Act. But since the 1950s, male workers have shown they choose to retire and do so when they have sufficient retirement income (Quinn 1977). In 1950, more than 45 percent of men over the age of sixty-five were in the labor force. By 1980, 19 percent of males over sixty-five were working or looking for work. By 1994, that percentage dropped to 16.9 percent (Steurele and Bakija 1995). One of the ways post–World War II prosperity was divided between labor and capital was that workers got leisure at the end of their working lives. One way American employers can get a welcome increase in the supply of labor—which depresses wages—is if older workers do not have adequate pensions and are forced to continue working.

Box 36.2 **Important Myths and Facts About Social Security**

1. Myth: People are living longer and therefore can work longer. FACT: Employers fear a labor shortage and wage increases. The longevity of older men has increased 14% in over 50 years. The percentage who have retired has almost doubled.

2. Myth: People contribute to a individual account. FACT: Social Security is financed by employer and employee premiums to an insurance program.

3. Myth: The Trust Fund has no real assets. FACT: The Trust Fund holds government bonds just like private individuals and pension funds.

4. Myth: People get Social Security because they need it. FACT: Workers who save and have wealth are not penalized under Social Securiy. Eligible workers and dependents, even if they have saved (or inherited) substantial sums, get Social Security because they paid for the premiums and met the criteria. (Social Security does not means test, just as fire insurance does not means test to reimburse for a fire loss.)

Why the Finance Industry Supports the Privatizers' Agenda

The privatizing agenda, represented here by the Schieber plan, would cut workers' 6.2 percent share of the payroll tax to 1.2 percent and require the remaining 5 percent to be invested in Personal Savings Accounts (PSAs). A financial services company, such as a bank, brokerage house, or mutual fund, would manage a worker's account and invest it according to the worker's wishes, whether it be in U.S. Treasuries or junk bonds.

There would be a basic safety net of $360 to $410 per month. *Money* magazine computed benefits under both the Ball and Schieber plans for several kinds of families (Tritch 1996, 119–122). The simulation assumed salaries grew 5 percent a year, workers retired at sixty-two, and the PSAs would earn 8 percent per year. The flat monthly benefit of $413 in 1993 was assumed to increase 5 percent a year. The transition plan is estimated to cost U.S. income tax payers $1.2 trillion, because current benefits would have to be paid while worker contributions are being siphoned off in PSAs. The Schieber plan raises payroll taxes by 1.52 percent between 1998 and 2069. Spouses' benefits are cut from 50 percent of the workers' benefit to 33 percent. (Current benefits are further cut under the Schieber plan by raising the age at which full benefits can be collected to age 69 by 2059 and eliminating retirement before age 65 by 2012, but these were not included in the simulation.)

Money finds that only young workers making large salaries and having no periods of unemployment obtain a substantially larger pension under PSAs than Social Security. Low-wage workers who make poor investments would be the biggest losers. They would have lower wages and likely would invest conservatively—thus earnings would be lower than 8 percent. Administrative costs would further lower the rate of return. Schieber assumes that fees will only be 0.3 percent. However, the average growth fund charges 1.4 percent of the account for administration. If workers want tailored advice the costs could go higher. The PSAs are not indexed to inflation and they may be depleted before a retiree dies.

In addition, the intermediate scenario that puts the system into crisis would also put the stock market in crisis. A low GDP growth rate would cause the privatizers' claim that investing in private financial markets will yield an average return of 7 percent over the next seventy-five years to be wrong. If the economy makes privatizing attractive because of high GDP growth rates, then the current system mimics the rosy scenario and the current PAYGO system works fine (Baker 1997).

The clear winner under privatization is the financial services industry, and they have financed a $2 million campaign to lobby for the change. They stand to gain 130 million new accounts and manage over $40 billion of new money each year (Kostelritz 1995; Calmes 1996, A22; Cutler 1996, 1176–1177; Wayne 1996, A9).

The Chilean Experiment with Privatization

The advocates of privatization use Chile as an example of why the U.S. system should be transformed. In August 1995, the Cato Institute, a conservative research organization in Washington D.C., formed the "Program to Privatize Social Security." Jose Piñera, former Chilean labor secretary under General Augusto Pinochet, is a member of the task force. Eight years after the Chilean coup, the government privatized its Social Security system because, among other reasons, the military government, advised by ideological free market economists from the United States, needed to orchestrate the selling of its state-owned industries. The new Chilean Social Security system went into effect on May 1, 1981, and conveniently bought up the new shares of the privatized corporations. The military, though, kept its own pension system (Ghilarducci 1998).

All Chilean workers who report employment must contribute 10 percent of payroll to an individual pension account. Employers pay nothing (violating International Labor Organization social insurance standards). Workers must pay 3 percent (six times the actual cost) for disability and survivor insurance and 7 percent to health care. On top of these contributions they pay an administrative fee of about 3 percent of payroll (not the account) to these for-profit businesses, Administradoras de Fondos de Pensiones (AFPs), which collect pension income and pay out benefits.

Strict competition, theoretically, keeps these fees low, but the five largest AFPs control 80 percent of the market. Investors in these private businesses are making a 22 percent annual profit rate. Competition has escalated costs. Since 1991, the AFPs' marketing staffs have increased over 300 percent. Over 65 percent of Chilean men and over 78 percent of Chilean women workers have less than $2,500 in their retirement accounts. If the eventual pension is not up to 75 percent of the poverty standard the government has to pay the difference. Argentina, Colombia, Peru, Uruguay, and Mexico either have or will adopt similar plans.

The World Bank and the Inter-American Development Bank promote private, individual advance-funded pensions in order to create strong and deep capital markets (World Bank 1994; Boeker 1995). Neoclassical economics argues that private capital markets are more efficient. But in equilibrium, neither the returns to capital nor the returns to labor can exceed the growth rate of the economy without the other losing. If the capital market consistently outperforms the rest of the economy, it represents a transfer from workers to capital. Under a private personal account a retiree's pension depends on the stock market and not the growth in wage income. Privatized, individual-based pensions could divide the interests of the working class.

Social Security and the Macroeconomic Effect on Savings

Neoliberal economic policies, promoted by the World Bank and a Wall Street–funded campaign for Social Security privatization, erode the security of retirement income and, therefore, the certainty of being able to retire. Part of the neoliberal campaign against Social Security is that the system lowers the savings rate. Since workers have a guaranteed source of retirement income, the argument goes, they are less likely to save for retirement. Since pensions are financed by taxes and not returns on accumulated savings, advocates for diminishing Social Security (Feldstein 1996) argue that lower savings lowers investment and productivity.

Evidence of Social Security's effect on savings could lead to the opposite conclusions. When Social Security passed in 1935, the insurance industry argued that the new system would cause people to stop buying annuities. A year later when friendly senators asked the industry representatives whether the insurance companies wanted legislation to make Social Security voluntary, the industry said no. The insurance industry was thrilled with the new system. People began to plan for retirement and use the industry products when Social Security was established!

In the post–World War II period, pensions emerged as a key union bargaining issue in part because Social Security provided a floor of retirement income and planted the retirement idea. Social Security created a retirement savings motive. The Public Agenda Foundation and the Employee Benefit Research Institute (Farkas 1994) found that 34 percent of people claim they do not save because of low earnings; 37 percent do not save because they underestimate what they need in retirement. The rest are split between those who plan their future and save and those who figure they will work until they die. People did not report they lowered their savings because they thought Social Security would provide enough in retirement. Moreover, consumer debt is at an all-time high when fears over Social Security's solvency is high (Singletary and Crenshaw 1996). Therefore, Social Security can be seen as a key to boosting savings.

In addition, PAYGO schemes can have a stable and calming effect on finance markets, especially compared to the long-term problems posed by advanced-funded systems with uneven demographic bulges. However, one of the arguments for privatizing is wrongly based on the argument that it is a better system when there are unevenly sized cohorts. Privatizers argue that the increase in the number of retirees to workers necessitates abandoning PAYGO. Baby boomers will start retiring in twelve years, and by 2030, 100 workers will support 36 retirees, up from 21 in 1995. But this is misleading: the dependency ratio (workers per young and older nonworking individuals) is not predicted to exceed the ratio in 1965. Privatizing advocates argue that people should save for their own retirement so that smaller generations do not have to support larger retired ones. Instead, they want workers to invest their deferred consumption—rather than put it into current Social Security benefits—and sell assets when they retire. However, just as the baby boomers' demand for financial assets lifted stock and bond prices in the 1980s and 1990s, their sell-off, starting in the year 2020, will lower asset values. (Schieber and Shoven 1994; Bensmen 1994, 53–56).

This de-accumulation will cause the value of assets to fall. The hope for the source of demand to buy the surplus assets in 2020–2035 are the young populations of Mexico, Brazil, China, and India. This works if these nations have private pension systems that invest in foreign assets. This may explain why the World Bank's effort to privatize pension systems spans the globe. Advance-funded plans work in an elaborate system where populations with different age distributions buy and sell each other's investments. The promise that growth will occur because of future buying at higher prices is a feature of Ponzi systems.

More Reasons to Oppose Privatization: Inequality and Cost

Plans to replace or partially replace the current Social Security system with private individual accounts cost money. While Social Security taxes are flowing into private accounts, the current promised benefits still have to be paid. The estimate for new taxes required to pay for the transition range from 3 percent of payroll for the next 35 years to 1.5 percent for the next 72 years (Century Fund 1997). If new taxes aren't raised then the transition would be paid for by benefit cuts—most likely raising the retirement age to seventy.

The other cost of the transition would be an increase in inequality. Most workers are better off under the defined-benefit insurance structure of the current system—even if payroll taxes are raised—for several reasons. Low-income workers would earn lower return on PSAs because they invest more conservatively. In addition, workers who want the guarantee that their savings will not be depleted before they die will buy annuities in the private markets. The problem is that annuity sellers presume that people who expect to live for a long time buy annuities. This causes the annuities offered to be quite low. In other words, the assurance of having a stream of income until you die is very expensive when purchased on the open market, as evidenced by Chile's experiences. In the switch from private accounts to a PAYGO system, workers also lose the security of an indexed annuity and bear all the risks of financial downturns, inflation, living too long, and being disabled.

Raising the retirement age also increases inequality. Millions of Americans, particularly those with physically demanding jobs, are more likely to suffer health problems that will require them to retire earlier than white-collar employees (Bovbjerg 1998). Raising the age at which one can collect full benefits by one year is an effective 7 percent decrease in benefits (Burtless 1998). Lower-income workers in blue-collar jobs will likely experience a disproportionate share of these lower benefits (Bovbjerg 1998).

Conclusion

A political economy approach to Social Security, which explicitly examines who gains and who loses from various reforms, best explains the debate around privatizing the system. Many businesses in the productive or "real" sector have remained on the sidelines of the debate, though some have expressed worries that privatization would cause their pension costs to rise. Financial interests are clear winners. Most workers lose.

References

Baker, Dean. 1997. "Saving Social Security with the Stock Market." Twentieth Century Fund/Economic Policy Institute Report. Washington, DC: Economic Policy Institute.

Bensman, Miriam. 1994. "The Baby Boomer Boomerang." *Institutional Investor* (September): 53–56.

Bluestone, Barry, and Teresa Ghilarducci. 1998. *Making Work Pay*. Annandale-on-Hudson, NY: Jerome Levy Institute at Bard College.

Boeker, P.H. 1995. "Developing Strong Capital Markets: Contrasting Latin American and East Asian Experiences." Washington, DC: Inter-American Development Bank.

Bovbjerg, Barbara (Associate Director-Income Security Issues, Health, Education, and Human Services Division, U.S. General Accounting Office). 1998. Prepared statement before the Senate Committee on Aging, July 16.

Burtless, Gary. 1998. Testimony at the U.S. Senate, Special Committee on Aging, July 16.

Calmes, Jackie. 1996. "Wall Street Quietly Promotes Social Security Overhaul." *Wall Street Journal*. December 3, p. A22.

Century Foundation (formerly Twentieth Century Fund). 1997. New York. http://www.socser.org.

Cutler, Joyce. 1996. "Unions Urged to Withhold Pension Funds from Wall Street, Fight for Social Security." *Labor Relations Week*, November 27, 1176–1177.

Farkas, Stephen. 1994. *Promises to Keep: How Leaders and the Public Respond to Saving and Retirement*. A report from the Public Agenda in collaboration with Employee Benefit Research Institute, Public Agenda. Washington, DC.

Feldstein, Michael. 1996. "The Missing Piece in Policy Analysis: Social Security Reform." Cambridge, MA: National Bureau of Economic Research.

Frank, Robert, and Phil Cook. 1995. *Winner Takes All Society*. New York: Free Press.

Freeman, Richard. 1981. "The Effects of Unionism on Fringe Benefits." *Industrial and Labor Relations Review* 34 (July): 489–509.

Ghilarducci , Teresa. 1992. *Labor's Capital: The Economics and Politics of Private Pensions*. Cambridge: MIT Press.

______. 1998. "Unions' Role in Argentine and Chilean Pension Reform," with Patricia Ledesma. World Development, University of Notre Dame Working Paper to be published summer 2000.

Kostelritz, Julie. 1995. "Touching the Rail." *National Journal*, December 23.

Lazear, Edward. 1980. "Agency, Earnings Profiles, Productivity and Hours Restrictions." *American Economic Review* 71: 606–619 .

Quinn, Joseph. 1977. "Microeconomics Determinants of Early Retirement: A Cross-Sectional View of White Married Males." *Journal of Human Resources* 12, no. 3: 329–346.

Reno, Virginia P. 1993. "The Role of Pensions in Retirement Income." *Pensions in a Changing Economy*. Washington, DC: Employee Benefits Research Institute.

Schieber, Sylvester J., and John B. Shoven. 1994. "The Consequences of Population Aging on Private Pension Fund, Saving and Asset Markets." Prepared for the NBER-JCER joint conference, "The Economics of Aging," September 14–16, Hakone, Japan, NBER. Working paper series no. 4665. Cambridge, MA: National Bureau of Economic Research.

Singletary, Michelle, and Albert B. Crenshaw. 1996. "When Credit Is Due." *Washington Post Weekly Edition*, December 2–8.

Steurele, Eugene, and Jon Bakija. 1995. *Retooling Social Security for the 20th Century*. Washington, DC: Urban Institute Press.

Tritch, Teresa. 1996. "The Privatization of Social Security: Who Wins and Who Loses?" *Money*, April, pp. 119–122.

U.S. Department of Labor. Pension and Welfare Benefits Administration. 1992. *Trends in Pensions*.

Wayne, Leslie. 1996. "Interest Groups Prepare for Huge Fight for Social Security." *New York Times*, December 30, A9.

World Bank. 1994. *Averting the Old Age Crisis*. Oxford: Oxford University Press.

Appendix

Political Economy of Social Security Reform

OPTIONS TO BRING SOCIAL SECURITY INTO LONG-RANGE BALANCE*
(Figures shown are the percentage of the deficit each option will solve)

	%
Current estimate of 75-year deficit—2.2% of payroll.	100
Revenue increases	
Increase the contribution rate 1.1% each, for employees and employers, now.	100
Increase the contribution rate 1% each, for employees and employers, in 2020.	51.0
Eliminate the cap on employer contributions in 2015.	12.2
Invest 40% of the Trust Fund in the stock market by 2014.	12.0
*Extend Social Security to the one-third of state and local employees not now covered (new hires only as was done when federal employees were covered).	10.0
*Tax Social Security benefits for singles with incomes above $25,000 and couples with incomes above $32,000 if joint income tax filers, in the same way government career pensions and private pensions are taxed.	7.0
Benefit Cuts and Improvements	
*Compute benefits over 38 years instead of 35 years as in present law.	12.0
*Correction of the Consumer Price Index by BLS to show a lower inflation.	14.0
*Raise retirement age to 67 by 2011 (now by 2025).	22.0

* The majority of the Social Security Advisory Council approved of these (labor was the main dissenter).

(All sorts of combinations are possible and there are many more options—I have selected the most discussed options. The point of this illustration is to demonstrate that Social Security can be brought into balance for the long run with a small benefit reduction and tax increases and remain within the traditional principles of the program.)

Index

About the Editors and Contributors

Randy Albelda, professor of economics at the University of Massachusetts-Boston, is coauthor of *The War on the Poor.* She has served on the editorial collective of *Dollars & Sense* magazine and has written extensively on the connections among poverty, family structure, and work. She has been active in local, state, and national campaigns on issues of welfare reform, women's equality, job quality, and fair taxes.

Ron Baiman teaches economics at Roosevelt University in Chicago. He is an editor of *Review of Radical Political Economics* and a past member of the steering committee of the Union for Radical Political Economics (URPE). He holds a Ph.D. in economics from the New School for Social Research.

Carole Biewener teaches at Simmons College and is the director of the graduate program in gender/cultural studies. She also edits the "Remarx" section of the journal *Rethinking Marxism.* Her current work addresses community finance in western Massachusetts as part of a project aimed at enabling alternative forms of economic development.

Cyrus Bina is currently teaching at the California State University-San Bernardino. He has been the lead faculty member and founding director of the Center of Unified, Global, and Applied Research (COUGAR) at the University of Redlands and was formerly research associate at CMES, Harvard University. Bina is the author of *The Economics of the Oil Crisis* (1985), coeditor of *Modern Capitalism and Islamic Ideology in Iran* (1992) and *Beyond Survival: Wage Labor in the Late Twentieth Century* (1996), and has written numerous contributions on the subjects of globalization, technology and skill formation, and social capital. He has been an editor of *Review of Radical Political Economics* (1980–1990).

Heather Boushey is currently a post-doctoral fellow at the New York City Housing Authority where she is doing research on welfare reform and the low-wage labor market. She has been on the URPE steering committee for many years and holds a Ph.D. from the New School for Social Research.

Paul Burkett teaches economics at Indiana State University-Terre Haute. His research focuses on the political economy of money, finance, and inflation; East Asian development and crisis; and Marxism and ecology. He is the author of *Marx and Nature: A Red and Green Perspective*, 1999.

Mathieu Carlson obtained his Ph.D. at the New School for Social Research and has taught at the New School, New York University, and Lewis and Clark College. His articles have appeared in *History of Political Economy*, the *Journal of Economic Issues*, the *European Journal of the History of Economic Thought*, and the *History of Economics Journal*.

Elmer P. Chase III, of Elmhurst, PA, has been a URPE Steering Committee member; an associate professor, program head for Organization and Leadership, and economist in academe; a utilities economic policy analyst for a public utility commission; and now occasionally teaches as an adjunct and is "self-employed" as an external degree consultant.

Robert Cherry, a professor of economics at Brooklyn College, is coediting a book for the Russell Sage Foundation on the impact of tight labor markets on black employment problems. He sits on the executive board of Five Borough Institute, a NYC union-allied, public policy organization.

Kimberly Christensen is associate professor of economics/women's studies at SUNY/Purchase College, where she chairs the AIDS Task Force and the Faculty Pedagogy Group. She received the SUNY Chancellor's Award for Distinguished Teaching and the President's Award for Innovative Pedagogy. Her recent publications include a critique of neoclassical approaches to AIDS education, a consideration of white feminists and racism, and writings on welfare "reform."

Chuck Davis is director of private sector programming for the Labor Education Service, University of Minnesota. He has published and educated extensively on industrial relations and political economy. He is former vice president of the University and College Labor Education Association and is a member of Workers' Education Local no. 189, CWA.

George DeMartino is an associate professor at the Graduate School of International Studies, University of Denver. He has worked in the labor movement as an organizer and staff representative. His book, *Global Economy, Global Justice: A Normative Critique of Global Neoliberalism and Egalitarian Policy Alternatives for the Year 2025*, was published in January 2000.

Jim Devine teaches economics at Loyola Marymount University in Los Angeles, California. He researches topics in macroeconomics, economic history, labor economics, and money and banking. He earned his Ph.D. from the University of California at Berkeley, and is a long-standing member of URPE.

William M. Dugger is professor of economics at the University of Tulsa. He is the author of *An Alternative to Economic Retrenchment*, *Corporate Hegemony*, *and Underground Economics*. He is the editor of *Radical Institutionalism and Inequality,* and is the coeditor, with William Waller, of *The Stratified State*. He has served as president of the Association for Social Economics, Association for Institutional Thought, and Association for Evolutionary Economics.

Deborah M. Figart is associate professor of economics at Richard Stockton College. She is coauthor of *Contesting the Market: Pay Equity and the Politics of Economic Restructuring* (1997), coeditor of *Emotional Labor in the Service Economy* (1999), and associate editor of the *Encyclopedia of Political Economy* (1999).

Teresa Ghilarducci is an associate professor of economics at the University of Notre Dame, and directs the university's Higgins Labor Research Center. She is a presidential appointee to the Pension Benefit Guaranty Corporation's Advisory Board and a gubernatorial appointee to the Trustees Board for the Indiana Public Employees Pension Fund.

Gertrude Schaffner Goldberg, a professor of social policy at Adelphi University School of Social Policy, has published a number of articles on social policy and social administration. Among the books she has coauthored are *The Feminization of Poverty: Only in America?* (1990), and *Washington's New Poor Law: A Plan for the Revitalization of America* (forthcoming). Goldberg chairs the National Jobs for All Coalition.

Jonathan P. Goldstein received his Ph.D. in economics from the University of Massachusetts. He has been on the economics faculty of Bowdoin College since 1979. His primary research interests are in the areas of Marxian crisis theory, macroeconomics, and econometrics as applied to issues concerning the business cycle. He recently completed a research project on Russian labor markets in transition and is now studying the impact of Canadian alien workers on the wood harvesting labor market in Maine.

Ilene Grabel is an associate professor at the University of Denver. She has contributed papers to edited volumes and to the *Journal of Economic Issues*, *World Development*, *Cambridge Journal of Economics*, *International Review of Applied Economics*, *Journal of Development Studies*, *Review of Radical Political Economics*, and *International Papers in Political Economy*.

Martin Hart-Landsberg teaches economics at Lewis and Clark College in Portland, Oregon. His research focuses on the political economy of Korea, and East Asian development and crisis. A long-time URPE member, he is the author of *Korea: Division, Reunification, and U.S. Foreign Policy* (1998).

Heidi I. Hartmann is a cofounder of the Institute for Women's Policy Research and is its current director and president. She has held several positions at the National Academy of Sciences and served as a professor and director of women's studies at Rutgers University and on the graduate faculty of the New School for Social Research. At the IWPR she has authored or coauthored reports on family and medical leave, welfare and low-wage work, mother's earnings, pay equity, and contingent work. Hartmann is a recipient of a 1944 MacArthur Fellowship.

Ismael Hossein-Zadeh teaches economics at Drake University. He is the author of *Soviet Non-Capitalist Development.* He has also contributed a number of written works on various issues of political economy both to scholarly journals and to edited volumes.

Jerome Joffe is associate professor of health care administration at St. John's University in New York City. His interests are the political economy of the health care system, including the transformation of the relations of production in medical care, and plan and market as allocative mechanisms.

David M. Kotz is professor of economics at the University of Massachusetts at Amherst. He is the coauthor, with Fred Weir, of *Revolution from Above: The Demise of the Soviet System* (1997). He has written articles for *Dollars & Sense*, *The Nation*, *Z Magazine*, and the *Review of Radical Political Economics*.

Abelardo Mariña-Flores is professor of economics at Universidad Autonoma Metropolitana-Azcapotzalco, Mexico City. He is the author of the books *Input-Output: Basic applications to Economic Structural Analysis* (1993) and (with Victor Flores-Olea) *Critique of Globality. Domination and Liberation in Our Time* (1999). He has published several essays about wages and employment in Mexico.

Julie Matthaei, professor of economics at Wellesley College, has written widely on the economics of gender, race, and sexuality, and has been active for almost thirty years in peace, ecology, feminist, gay liberation, and antiracist movements. She is currently focusing her research on envisioning a path toward a liberatory economy and invites ideas and comments from readers.

Fred Moseley is professor of economics at Mount Holyoke College. He is the author of *The Falling Rate of Profit in the Postwar United States Economy* (1992), *Marx's Method in Capital: A Reexamination* (1993), and most recently "The US Economy in 1999: Goldilocks Meets a Big Bad Bear?" (*Monthly Review*, March 1999).

Ellen Mutari has taught political economy at the New School for Social Research, Rutgers University, and Monmouth University. She is coeditor of *Gender and Political Economy: Incorporating Diversity into Theory and Policy* (1997) and associate editor of the *Encyclopedia of Political Economy* (1999).

Edward J. Nell teaches economics at the New School for Social Research in New York City and is the author or editor of many books and papers. He has also taught at Wesleyan University (CT) and the University of East Anglia (UK) and has been a visiting scholar at universities in Germany, Australia, and Italy. His most recent books are: *The General Theory of Transformational Growth: Keynes After Sraffa* (1998) and *Transformational Growth and the Business Cycle* (1998).

Bruce Pietrykowski is associate professor of economics and assistant dean in the College of Arts, Sciences, and Letters at the University of Michigan-Dearborn. He also directs an undergraduate degree program for workers employed in the auto industry. He earned a Ph.D. in economics from the New School for Social Research. His research has appeared in the *Review of Radical Political Eco-*

nomics, *History of Political Economy*, *Review of Social Economy*, *Economic Geography*, *Rethinking Marxism*, and *Adult Education Quarterly*.

Robert Pollin is a professor of economics and founding codirector of the Political Economy Research Institute (PERI) at the University of Massachusetts-Amherst. His books include *The Living Wage: Building a Fair Economy* (1998). He was on the national steering committee of the Union for Radical Political Economics for nine years.

Louis-Philippe Rochon is the Stephen B. Monroe Assistant Professor of Economics and Banking at Kalamazoo College, Michigan, where he is also the codirector of the Center for Macroeconomic Policy and International Trade. He holds a doctorate from the New School for Social Research. He is the author of numerous articles on credit and money, and of the book *Credit, Money and Production: An Alternative Post-Keynesian Approach*, and coeditor (with Matias Vernengo) of *Credit, Effective Demand and the Open Economy: Essays in the Horizontalist Tradition*, both forthcoming. He is also in the process of writing (with Matias Vernengo) *Economics Without Supply and Demand: A Horizontalist Synthesis*.

David F. Ruccio teaches economics at the University of Notre Dame and is editor of the journal *Rethinking Marxism*. He has published on a wide variety of theoretical and empirical issues concerning economic development, especially in Latin America. He is currently working on a book manuscript titled "Crisis and Transitions: A Critique of the International Economic Order."

Dawn Saunders teaches economics, including labor, gender, and economic history, at the University of Vermont. Her 1994 Ph.D. from the University of Massachusetts (Amherst) explored early twentieth century state welfare programs. Continuing her work on social reproduction issues, she also serves on her local elementary school board in Middlebury, Vermont.

Max B. Sawicky is an economist at the Economic Policy Institute. He resides with his wife and daughter in Silver Spring, Maryland. He is a coauthor of *Risky Business: Private Management of Public Schools,* and has been a contributor to *Newsday*, *Challenge*, *Dissent*, *New Economy*, *Social Policy*, the *Houston Chronicle*, and *In These Times*. He is an at-large national board member of the Americans for Democratic Action and a member of the Labor Party and the New Party.

Stephanie Seguino is assistant professor of economics at the University of Vermont. She worked in developing countries for a number of years. Her recent research has focused on the relationship between growth and income distribution in an effort to understand under what conditions growth with equity may be possible.

Anwar M. Shaikh is a professor in the department of economics at the Graduate Faculty of Political and Social Science of the New School for Social Research. His most recent book (coauthored with E.

Ahmet Tonak) was *The Political Economy of National Accounts: An Alternate Approach to the Measurement of the Wealth of Nations* (1994). He is currently working on the long-term determinants of the exchange rates of OECD countries, the macrodynamics of money and credit, the determinants of the stock market, and a classical explanation of inflation.

Howard J. Sherman is professor emeritus of economics at the University of California-Riverside and is visiting scholar at UCLA in political science. He has published about 80 articles and 16 books, including *Reinventing Marxism* (1995) and *The Business Cycle: Growth and Crisis Under Capitalism* (1991).

Chris Tilly, associate professor of regional economic and social development at the University of Massachusetts-Lowell, is author of *Half a Job: Bad and Good Part-time Jobs in a Changing Labor Market* and coauthor of *Work Under Capitalism*. He serves on the editorial collective of *Dollars & Sense* magazine and has been active in a variety of campaigns on labor and welfare rights.

E. Ahmet Tonak teaches economics at Simon's Rock College of Bard. He has also taught in Turkey at Middle East Technical University, Bogazici University, and Technical University of Istanbul. He cowrote (with A. Shaikh) *Measuring the Wealth of Nations: The Political Economy of National Accounts* (1994, 1996) and coedited (with I. Schick) *Turkey in Transition: New Perspectives* (1987). He has contributed to *RRPE*, *Capital and Class,* and *Monthly Review*.

Matias Vernengo was born in Buenos Aires, Argentina. After studies at the Universidade Federal do Rio de Janeiro, he obtained a scholarship from the Brazilian government to study at the New School for Social Research, where he obtained a Ph.D. in economics in 1999. Currently, he is assistant professor of economics at the Universidade Federal do Rio de Janeiro.